Willful Blindness
A Diligent Pursuit of Justice

Author: James Ramsey
Editor: David Bear
Contribututors: Charles Goldblum, Dr. Joshua
A. Perper, and Dr. Cyril H. Wecht

See page x for brief biographies.

Cover photo - Rooftop of the pedestrian bridge over Strawberry Way on which the murder victim, George Wilhelm, was discovered. Photo credit: David Bear

Contents

Editor's Foreword

"Making a Murderer," the Netflix documentary series that tracked a complicated murder case in Manitowoc County, Wisconsin, has generated considerable public attention across the country. The series harshly questions that county's criminal justice system, highlighting the apparent dysfunction of its police department and courts.

Unfortunately, this case is neither isolated nor without precedent.

Tuesday, February 9, 2016 marked the 40th anniversary of one of Pittsburgh's more sensational murders, the investigation and prosecution of which took many questionable turns.

On the snowy Monday evening of Feb. 9, 1976, just three weeks after the Steelers defeated the Cowboys in Super Bowl X, George Wilhelm, a 42-year-old former armored truck driver, was stabbed 23 times on the rooftop level of the Smithfield/Liberty Parking Garage, Downtown,and thrown over the edge of the structure.

Instead of falling eight stories to the ground, Wilhelm landed one story below, on the roof of the pedestrian bridge that still spans Strawberry Way, connecting the garage to the Duquesne Club and what was then Gimbels Department Store.

Although mortally wounded, Wilhelm lived long enough to make a so-called dying declaration to the police officer who found him. "Clarence — Clarence Miller did this to me."

The police acted quickly. Within several hours and with the help of the victim's family, they had identified the Clarence Miller in question.

Taken into custody the next morning, Miller, 38, a city hall factotum who ran errands for local politicians, quickly fingered Charles "Zeke" Goldblum as Wilhelm's actual killer. A married tax lawyer at a prominent accounting firm and part-time lecturer at the University of Pittsburgh, Goldblum, 26, was also son of the rabbi at Congregation Beth Shalom in Squirrel Hill.

Based on Miller's assertions, police detectives visited Goldblum at his office that afternoon and, after an hour of questioning, took him into custody.

With two suspects behind bars in less than 24 hours after the crime, Wilhelm's murder seemed to be an open-and-shut case. Or was it?

As city homicide detectives investigated the case over the ensuing months, they developed a complex backstory for the murder. It came to involve a fraudulent land deal perpetrated on the victim in 1974, as well as the fire that destroyed the Fifth Avenue Inn, a restaurant owned by Goldblum, just 10 weeks before Wilhelm's murder.

Nineteen months later, Goldblum was tried. The prosecution's case against him was based primarily on the testimony of Miller. Miller's perjured testimony was augmented by a series of police and prosecutorial missteps, including incomplete and faulty analysis of forensic evidence and failure to call crucial witnesses.

But the damage was done. On Aug. 30, 1977, the jury found Goldblum guilty of first-degree murder. Sparing him the death penalty, the judge sentenced him to life imprisonment, plus 15 to 30 years.

On June 9, 1979, nearly two years later, Miller was also convicted of Wilhelm's killing and given the same sentence. In the interim, however, Miller remained a free man on the streets.

Re-arrested upon his conviction, Miller died in prison in 2006, but Goldblum remains incarcerated at State Correctional Institution Mahanoy in Schuylkill County.

Over the nearly four decades since Wilhelm's murder, Goldblum has steadfastly maintained that, although present at the crime scene, he was only a shocked witness to the killing.

Furthermore, citing significant errors by both police and prosecutors, as well as other suspicious developments, Goldblum has subsequently filed various post-conviction petitions, seeking a new trial, to have his sentence commuted, or for clemency. All of his appeals have been denied, primarily for procedural reasons ranging from technicalities about deadlines to skepticism about the issues and evidence his supporters and lawyers provided.

Prisoners frequently claim to be innocent, but many people originally involved with this case have since come to agree with Goldblum, including both the assistant district attorney who prosecuted him and the judge who sentenced him.

After re-evaluating the case years later, the prosecutor, F. Peter Dixon, stated in an affidavit that he had come to believe Goldblum "had nothing to do with the murder of George Wilhelm, other than being a frightened witness to that murder and an accessory after the fact. ... Despite my best efforts in trying these cases, a miscarriage of justice has occurred."

Since 1989, the trial judge, Donald E. Ziegler, has written letters supporting Goldblum's appeals. In a 1998 letter, Judge Ziegler wrote, "Charles Goldblum has now been confined to prison for over 20 years, and my uneasiness with the verdict of the jury has been expressed to the Board of Parole and a former governor on several occasions. It seems to me that the application for clemency should be granted at this time for the following reasons:

1. The length of incarceration
2. The affidavit of the prosecutor
3. The dying declaration of George Wilhelm
4. The questionable credibility of Clarence Miller
5. The written requests by the trial judge
6. The exemplary prison record of Charles Goldblum

Similar conclusions were reached by Dr. Joshua Perper, the forensic pathologist who performed Wilhelm's autopsy; Dr. Cyril Wecht, the coroner at the time Goldblum was tried; and several other noted forensic experts who have examined the evidence.

These efforts and legal support notwithstanding, Goldblum has spent most of his adult life behind bars. Now 67, he is in poor health and walks with a cane.

I first learned of this case in June, 2015, when a friend asked if I wanted to get involved with a book project.

Although raised in the Pittsburgh area and now a longtime resident, I lived elsewhere during the 1970s and missed all of the considerable local notoriety generated by Wilhelm's murder, as well as the numerous twists and turns of the subsequent investigation and prosecutions.

Inclined to believe that police and prosecutors generally work within the law to help juries reach justified verdicts, I was initially skeptical of Goldblum's claims. But as I looked into the case and began sifting through the evolution of evidence and testimony, my assessment changed.

In addition to arguments presented at Goldblum's trial, his post-conviction legal actions both re-examined prosecutorial assertions and revealed new trails of evidence to be followed. Troubling law-enforcement practices and discrepancies between evidence and testimony emerged. Inappropriate criminal investigation practices were discovered. Evidence, including case files, disappeared.

In short, it became obvious something was not right.

Numerous lawyers have been involved in Goldblum's case over the decades, both in his original trial and his long pursuit of redress. But much of the more recent credit for sleuthing out, recognizing and fitting together hidden pieces of the puzzle goes to James Ramsey, a former Pittsburgh police narcotics detective who became involved in Goldblum's case in 2005.

Using his knowledge of police procedures and personnel, Mr. Ramsey has discovered facts and inconsistencies that brought fresh perspective to the case. He is confident Goldblum was convicted unfairly, and he believes he has determined by whom and why.

"Willful Blindness" examines Wilhelm's killing and the prosecutions of Goldblum and Miller through the eyes of several different observers. Each circles through the basic elements of the case, but makes different observations and emphasizing different aspects. Yet while coming from different perspectives, they reach similar conclusions. This multi-dimensional depth provides something like a parallax of proof.

In addition to the personal recollections of Charles Goldblum and investigation reports of Jim Ramsey, other chapters in the book include the sworn testimony of noted forensic pathologist Dr. Cyril Wecht, as well as the transcript of a lengthy interview he gave regarding Goldblum's case. There is also a detailed re-analysis of the entire body of evidence, written by forensic and medico-legal consultant Dr. Joshua Perper, the pathologist who conducted Wilhelm's autopsy.

Like "Making a Murderer," the book documents a judicial process that went awry.

More broadly, it raises questions about a judicial system that refuses to acknowledge its own shortcomings. In Pennsylvania, as in most states, a life sentence means life, with little willingness to re-adjudicate or correct unjust verdicts.

Despite myriad anomalies with its original case, the Commonwealth has consistently denied any prosecutorial wrongdoing, and its courts have rejected all of Goldblum's petitions for justice. He has filed several times for clemency, but the Board of Pardons granted only one full hearing of the case, on May 6, 1999.

More recently, Goldblum requested to be transferred to Israel, which already granted him citizenship based on his claims of innocence. The director of the Board of Pardons also denied that request without explanation.

The reality is that, legal argument or actual guilt notwithstanding, anyone who has received a life-sentence in Pennsylvania is unlikely to ever be released. There are no pardons for life-sentences, and commutations have become rare to the point of extinction.

This was not always the case.

Richard Thornburgh was elected Governor in 1978 pledging to get tough on crime. He changed previous practices and refused to sign more than a handful of the commutation approvals sent to him by the Board of Pardons. Subsequent governors have followed suit.

After the Pennsylvania constitution was amended 20 years later, it has been nearly impossible to get a life sentence commuted. Since 2000, fewer than 20 Pennsylvania lifers have had their sentences commuted; virtually all went directly in hospice care for their final months. This situation, coupled with strict mandatory sentencing regulations, have created a burgeoning population of increasingly geriatric prisoners, who will have to be warehoused for the rest of their lives.

Unfortunately, this is true in many other states.

As a sensational story, the murder of George Wilhelm, its investigation, and the subsequent prosecutions of Charles Goldblum and Clarence Miller were the subject of continuing and extensive news coverage.

The Public Record, the final chapter of *Willful Blindness*, offers a unique historical archive: a small selection of the 117 newspaper articles coverage of the case over the years by The Pittsburgh Press and *The Pittsburgh Post-Gazette.*

Taken together, these articles both provide a record of the case and chronicle the evolution of public perception regarding its many twists and turns. It is informative to follow the evolution of newspaper coverage of this case. Consider the several critical roles this coverage played; in creating public perception of the case; in chronicling the progress and proceedings of the investigation; in following the process of the prosecution and defense; and eventually in shaping jury options of the defendants. While they do not capture all the nuances of the unfolding case, they certainly capture the high points. The full listing of articles can be found on The Public Record page at www.freezeke.com.

That website is a robust resource. As encompassing as *Willful Blindness* is, this volume represents a small fraction of all the documentation and information that has been gathered over the decades in this "Diligent Pursuit of Justice." Readers who would like to delve more deeply into this fascinating and disturbing case will enjoy a visit.

While there, register your verdict whether Charles Goldblum has served more than enough time for any crime that he committed.

David Bear, August 2016

PS. Thanks to Marc Simon for his excellent editing of the manuscript, John Truxal for his perspectives, and Rob Sedler for his electronic expertise. Thanks also to Ernie Orsatti and other Duquesne University School of Law classmates of Zeke Goldblum for their generous and long-standing support of his cause.

Biographies

James Ramsey - After a career as a detective in the Pittsburgh Police narcotics squad, Ramsey became a private investigator. He has been working on the Goldblum case since 2005.

David Bear – A former editor at The Pittsburgh Post-Gazette, Bear is a published author and producer/host of several series heard on public radio stations across the country.

Charles "Zeke" Goldblum – Convicted as a codefendant in the 1976 murder of George Wilhelm, Goldblum is presently serving a term of life plus thirty years in the Pennsylvania prison system.

Dr. Joshua A. Perper – Pittsburgh Medical Examiner at the time of George Wlhelm's murder, Dr. Perper is a noted forensic pathologist. As Chief Medical Examiner of Broward County, Florida, he has conducted many autopsies on famous individuals, including Anna Nicole Smith.

Dr. Cyril H. Wecht – Pittsburgh Coroner at the time of George Wilhelm's murder, Dr. Wecht is a nationally known forensic pathologist who has consulted on numerous high-profile cases, including the assassination of John F. Kennedy.

Case Overview

On the wintry evening of February 9th, 1976, George Wilhelm was brutally stabbed and thrown from the 8th-floor rooftop of the Smithfield/ Liberty public parking garage in downtown Pittsburgh, Pa.

Rather than falling to the ground, Wilhelm landed one story below on the roof of a bridge that connected the garage to the adjacent building.

Although mortally wounded, before he died, Wilhelm was able to tell a police officer who came to his aid the person who had attacked him.

"Clarence - Clarence Miller did this to me."

The following morning, Clarence Miller, 38, was taken into police custody, and, later that afternoon, so was Charles "Zeke" Goldblum, 26, whom Miller had named as the real assailant.

Nineteen months later on August 31, 1977, a jury of his peers convicted Goldblum of first-degree murder. Nearly a year later, Miller was also convicted for his role in Wilhelm's murder. Both men received prison sentences of life plus 15 to 30 years.

While both Miller and Goldblum were involved in a separate conspiracy to commit arson, they were not both responsible for Wilhelm's murder. The arson which occurred two months before the murder, enabled police and prosecutors to convict both men as accomplices in the murder by manipulating evidence and the dishonest use of Miller's testimony against Goldblum. Despite his innocence in the murder, Goldblum has been in Pennsylvania State prisons for nearly 40 years. Miller passed away in prison in 2006.

In 2005, Goldblum's family hired private investigator Jim Ramsey, who has now been involved with this case for over a decade. A retired Pittsburgh police officer and narcotics detective, Ramsey briefly served as a Special Agent with the Drug Enforcement Administration and 4 years as a Special Investigator for the Federal Bureau of Investigation. His experience and intuition have been important elements in figuring out what really happened in this case.

The results of Ramsey's investigation and research strongly indicate that while guilty of bad judgment, arson, and an accessory-

1

after-the-fact to Wilhelm's murder, Goldblum was innocent of the murder for which he has been imprisoned for nearly four decades. He took no part in Wilhelm's killing nor had any motive for attacking him.

This book is the synthesis of reading transcripts, documents, and court decisions, conversations with detectives and officials, as well as interviews with Goldblum and his family. Ramsey has also interviewed many of the detectives and court officials involved with this case, including the trial judge, Donald Ziegler, and the lead prosecutor, F. Peter Dixon.

The analysis in the following pages is based on sound investigative techniques and opinions. Its purpose is not to attack or embarrass anyone, but to provide an objective and thorough review of a police investigation and subsequent prosecution that misinterpreted and manipulated evidence to fit a preconceived theory, ultimately leading to Goldblum's undeserved murder conviction and sentencing.

While criminal cases often involve a strange occurrence or two that warrant further investigation, this case is riddled with them. These anomalies, accompanied by the unexplained disappearance of nearly all the investigative records of this case from different archive locations, raise serious questions.

The disappearance of official records made Ramsey's job more difficult, but his close understanding of police procedures and his acquaintance with the case detectives and prosecutors helped to fill in some of the missing pieces.

These conclusions and opinions are based in extensive investigation and fact gathering. While not incontrovertible, on the face of the facts of the case, they are the most likely and possible.

For example, during his trial Goldblum's jury was not made aware of two essential facts.

First, it was not disclosed that Miller had been diagnosed as a confabulator, resulting from a brain trauma he suffered as a child.

Confabulators have a mental disorder known as confabulatory amnesia or, more simply, confabulation. The condition is defined by a tendency to fill in memory gaps with unconsciously constructed false memories. Due to Miller's brain trauma, his mind created fictional recollections to fill in the memory gaps caused by his injury. Since this process was unconscious and uncontrollable, Miller engaged in what is known as "honest lying," as he portrayed his untruths to be fact. Because confabulators believe their fantasies to be real, they are convincing liars.

Second, Goldblum's defense was not informed that Miller had failed his first polygraph test, conducted on February 13, 1976, four days after the murder, nor did they hear that after a second polygraph test on May 15, Miller admitted to participating in the attack on Wilhelm.By withholding Miller's statement from Goldblum's attorneys, the police and prosecutor deprived the accused an opportunity to cross examine Miller on this important admission. The first failed polygraph test and Miller's confession also strongly suggest that the prosecutors presented testimony that they knew or should have known to be false. At Goldblum's trial, Miller testified that he took no part in the attack. The prosecutors had long known that Miller had admitted to being involved in the attack on Wilhelm, yet they still let him to testify falsely, without bringing it the attention of the court.

Another major contributing factor to Goldblum's murder conviction was the inadequate discussion at his trial of the blood spatter evidence found in Wilhelm's vehicle where he was first attacked. While the jury knew of the blood spatter through the testimony of Detective Ronald Freeman, they were not told of its forensic significance nor shown any actual photos of the spatter pattern.

In a subsequent post-conviction petition, Goldblum asked for a new trial, and several highly respected experts submitted reports on the significance of the distribution and pattern of the blood spatter, based on detailed descriptions offered by the homicide detective at the trial.

The court ruled, however, that the meaning of the blood spatter could not be definitely determined due to a lack of photographic evidence, evidence that should have been captured and preserved by the crime scene detectives. Considering the definitive nature of this evidence according to the forensic experts, including the one who testified for the prosecution at the post-conviction hearing, the court's failure to address this issue properly was an oversight that defies explanation. Goldblum was wrongfully convicted of murder partially due to the failure of the police to properly preserve the evidence in a capital murder case.

While the jury did not know these key facts, the courts did not view them as sufficiently consequential to award Goldblum a new trial.

The case and resulting convictions involve many other questionable occurrences and evidentiary anomalies, but these are the most glaring and cast considerable doubt on the validity of Goldblum's incarceration.

In fairness, it must be noted that many important issues of the case were not presented to the Appellate Courts at one time, but raised piecemeal over the years during subsequent petitions made by Goldblum.

In 1974, George Wilhelm was defrauded of more than $20,000 by Clarence Miller, Thaddeus Dedo, and Fred Orlowsky. Goldblum took no part in this land fraud crime.

In November of 1975, Goldblum had Miller burn his restaurant in a planned arson. Wilhelm took no part in this crime. These two unrelated crimes led to the unplanned February 9, 1976 killing of Wilhelm by Miller.

The prosecution used the land fraud and arson to establish a motive for Goldblum to kill Wilhelm, claiming Miller and Goldblum had conspired to assault Wilhelm in order to silence him.

The facts and evidence do not support this theory.

More troubling, there is evidence that the prosecution never believed these motives. Knowing the motives were false, they presented them as truths anyway.

Objective analysis of Goldblum's supposed motives to assault Wilhelm, ultimately dismantles the prosecution's theory behind the land fraud and arson.

The Pittsburgh detectives and prosecutor involved with the case were aware that Miller was a key player in each of these crimes and that he had clear motive to shift blame for the murder from himself to Goldblum. The facts also strongly suggest that Miller was manipulated by overly aggressive investigators and prosecutors to further their case against Goldblum, who never had any reason or motive to harm Wilhelm.

Independent analysis is presented as far as the facts allow. With so many components, it is best to first consider each crime separately, then determine how they relate to each other and, ultimately, how they came together to play a part in Goldblum's wrongful murder conviction.

When reading the following chapters detailing the land fraud and arson, keep in mind the prosecution's theory of Goldblum's two-part motive to kill Wilhelm:

They contended Goldblum was the mastermind of the land fraud scheme that resulted in Wilhelm being bilked out of some $21,000. Furthermore, they contended Goldblum sought to have Wilhelm silenced through physical violence, using Miller as an accomplice.

They continued by claiming that to repay the land fraud moneys, Goldblum convinced Wilhelm, a solid, harmless, and reputable citizen, to act as the torch in the arson of the restaurant, promising to repay the money after collecting on the restaurant's fire insurance. This alleged criminal connection supposedly provided further motive for Goldblum to silence Wilhelm.

Taken on their face value, these claims paint a damning portrait of Goldblum and provide a solid motive for him to have assaulted Wilhelm.

However, when examined objectively under the light of the relevant facts and evidence, the prosecution's contentions are shown to be unfounded and unbelievable.

Willful Blindness

Why the title?

Willful Blindness is a legal principle that allows knowledge and consequent intent to be proven circumstantially. In most respects, it is a common-sense analysis of human behavior. In Goldblum's case, questionable prosecutorial decisions were made. Then all copies of the police case reports vanished under suspicious circumstances. Reading this account, you will wonder what people were thinking and aware of when they took actions and made decisions.

It is usually hard to discern the thoughts and intentions of others. People have different outlooks and priorities, but regardless of our various points of view, we must make these judgements. We must decide how we think other people would react and make decisions under circumstances about which we may not know all the facts. Against this backdrop, decide what you think most likely happened. Then make a moral judgement and consider how you want people in authority to use their power.

In both Civil and Criminal trials, it is always important to determine how much the parties were aware of and what their intentions were. The more they intend to prove a given result, the more they are held to account.

In Civil cases, if an accused person is found to have been reckless rather than negligent, higher damages will probably be awarded. How much a criminal defendant acted "knowingly" is an important part of determining guilt, degree of guilt, and proper sentencing.

The law must often deal with cases where defendants cannot be shown to have been expressly aware of what was happening around them. The surrounding circumstances must be examined. Juries and courts have decided that defendants acted knowingly if they were aware to a high degree of probability that improper activity was taking place. This has often been referred to as "willful blindness," "deliberate ignorance," or "conscious avoidance."

To act knowingly is not limited to positive or actual knowledge. It also includes that state of mind where one was not actually aware because he or she consciously avoided learning the truth. In more basic terms, those who do not know because they do not want to know, are often considered having acted knowingly. The law does not allow us to intentionally remain ignorant in order to escape responsibility.

The U.S. Supreme Court endorsed use of the term. "Willful blindness is well established in criminal law... a willfully blind defendant is one who takes deliberate actions to avoid confirming a high probability of wrongdoing and can almost be said to have actually known the critical facts."

Willful blindness has two requirements. First, it must be thought to a high degree of probability that person believes a particular fact exists. Second, one must take deliberate actions to avoid learning of that fact. When both requirements are met, courts have decided that the party in question is more than reckless and has engaged in willful blindness. If one had deliberately closed his eyes to what would otherwise be obvious, he is considered to have acted knowingly.

As noted above, much of the evidence of this case is circumstantial. You will have to decide when a sequence of facts is more than mere coincidence. Courts have stated that because secrecy and concealment are often features of conspiracy, prosecutors are allowed to prove their cases with circumstantial evidence.

However, courts have not given prosecutors a blank check.

Circumstantial evidence can also disprove a prosecutor's case. The inferences drawn must have a logical and convincing connection to the facts established.

Do the same thing here.

Do not accept what is written unless a logical, convincing connection is made. Use your common sense and life experiences. Apply circumstantial evidence to the blood spatter photographs that vanished prior to trial. Why was the court unwilling to allow specialists to testify about the direction of the blood spatter on the dashboard of Wilhelm's car when the city's own homicide detectives clearly described it? The answer: they would have to admit that Miller killed Wilhelm based on the forensic evidence and corroborated by their own expert witness, Dr. Toby Wolson. Make conclusions based on your own understanding of human behavior and sense of right and wrong.

For society to function, considerable power must be granted to a select few. Practically speaking there really is no other way. Law enforcement needs the authority to order people to do things and to detain those who break the law. In most cases, the system works fairly well. However, it does not work well when this power is abused. When that happens, it clearly is in society's best interest to hold the responsible parties to account.

As you read the following pages, imagine that you were the first-hand witness. Ask yourself what you would have believed and whether you could have accepted the explanations of police and prosecutors.

Then, decide how comfortable you are with what happened and the decisions that were made. If you would like to register your opinion, visit www.freezeke.com and answer the poll as to whether Charles Goldblum has already served more than enough time for any crime that he committed.

The Land Fraud

While the murder of George Wilhelm was the crime that captured the headlines, the chain of events which brought it about started at least two years before.

In early 1974, Wilhelm was awarded in excess of $40,000 from a workman's compensation settlement that resulted from a back injury he had suffered while driving for an armored car company. Wilhelm dreamed of using this settlement to purchase a parcel of land in North Carolina and mining it for semi-precious stones. That was where the fraud began.

"Big" Fred Orlowsky was the initiator. Having previously lived with and befriended Wilhelm, Orlowsky was aware of his desire to purchase the property in North Carolina. Orlowsky was also acquainted with Clarence Miller and, believing Miller's tales about his high political connections, sought his help to advance the deal.

Miller was a low level factotum in the local Pittsburgh political scene, acting as a runner for judges and Republican politicians, handling minor tasks such as fetching coffee and hanging campaign posters. In part due to his natural tendency to lie as the result of his confabulatory amnesia, Miller constantly exaggerated his connections and level of involvement in local politics.

While initially believing Miller could use his purported connections to purchase public land and push the deal through, Orlowsky soon realized it would not happen. But as Miller testified at trial, the two men decided to "make a buck" by defrauding Wilhelm and selling him falsified land deeds.

Miller led Wilhelm to believe that he could arrange for the purchase of federally owned property through his "connections" in the office of U. S. Senator Richard Schweiker. Taking advantage of his friendship with Wilhelm, Miller then conspired with Thaddeus Dedo and Fred Orlowsky to defraud him.

Wilhelm financed trips to North Carolina to tour the land he thought he would be purchasing. Miller convinced Wilhelm that in order for the deal to go through, he would have to give cash payments to Ken Manella, an aide of Senator Schweiker.

In reality, however, these payments were made to Dedo, who posed as Manella. Wilhelm financed trips to Washington, D.C. and Washington, Pa., where with Miller playing the part of intermediary, he handed the cash payments to Dedo. Orlowsky was also present during these trips. In all, Wilhelm handed over $21,000, expecting to later receive title to the land.

Once the payments were made, Miller, and presumably Dedo, forged deeds to the federally owned property in a most amateur manner, using commercial deed forms from Pennsylvania rather than North Carolina and leaving important sections blank. It was later proven that the typewriter in Dedo's office was used to forge these deeds. On receiving the phony deeds, however, Wilhelm began to suspect he was being swindled.

On October 7, 1974, Wilhelm visited Senator Schweiker's Pittsburgh office on a campaign-related matter. Suspicious of the phony deeds, he asked the secretary (Flora Slocum), about Manella's physical description.

Upon realizing that the real Ken Manella's description did not match the description of the Manella impostor (Dedo), that Wilhelm had met at meetings in Washington, D.C. and Washington, Pa., he proceeded to explain the land deal to Flora Slocum and asked her to call Manella in the D.C. office.

During that conversation, Wilhelm proceeded to explain to the real Ken Manella about the land deal, the deeds, and money being exchanged. The real Ken Manella had no knowledge of previous meetings, deeds being personally conveyed, or money being exchanged.

At that point, Wilhelm confirmed his suspicions that he had been swindled. Wilhelm also realized that the voices did not match. Manella asked that the deeds be tele-typed down to him in Washington, D.C.

Manella received them the same day and then contacted the FBI in Pittsburgh. The following day, October 8, the Pittsburgh FBI contacted Wilhelm and he appeared and was interviewed at their office and filed the complaint.

Subsequently, Miller convinced Wilhelm to withdraw his complaint by telling him if he didn't, the deal would collapse and he would not be able to get the land he wanted. On October 11, 1974, Wilhelm went to the FBI and filed an affidavit claiming the complaint had been a hoax, initiated to embarrass the Senator's office. Although the FBI had opened an investigation, they did not charge

Wilhelm with filing a false report, which normally leads to prosecution.

At Goldblum's trial, to shift blame from himself, Miller testified without corroboration or verification, that Wilhelm knew Goldblum during the time of the land fraud and that Goldblum had masterminded the scheme.

It was Miller's implausible contention, presented as fact by Assistant D.A. Dixon at Goldblum's trial, that having initiated the scheme to defraud Wilhelm, Orlowsky and Miller reached out to Goldblum, who was then a student at Duquesne University School of Law, to be the mastermind of their fraud.

This testimony provided one key to the prosecution's theory that Goldblum was the killer whose motive was to silence Wilhelm over the money in this land fraud.

An objective review of the facts shows how unlikely this was. If the contention that Goldblum was involved in the land fraud is disproved, his motive for murdering Wilhelm and the prosecution's case, begins to fall apart.

The first and most obvious point to disprove is Goldblum's initial involvement in the scheme. Knowing of Wilhelm's financial windfall and his desire to purchase the North Carolina property, Orlowsky sought Miller's help. He asked Miller to exercise his supposed political connections to make the deal go through, despite the government having no plans to sell the land. Knowing he lacked the clout to initiate this process, Miller still decided to take advantage of his friendship with Wilhelm to make some money. Miller enlisted the help of Dedo who had some knowledge of real estate business practices.

If Miller's uncorroborated trial testimony against Goldblum is to be believed, he reached out to Goldblum at this point to act as the mastermind in the fraud. This is extremely implausible, considering that Miller and Goldblum barely knew each other at that point, having met only briefly during the summer of 1973. Furthermore, Goldblum was still a law student with no criminal record, reputation or history. Nor did he have any particular knowledge of or involvement in real estate (as did Thaddeus Dedo). It is completely nonsensical that someone seeking to initiate a fraudulent criminal conspiracy against a close friend would seek the counsel of a casual acquaintance, a full-time student with no background in crime or real estate.

Furthermore, if Miller's statement that Goldblum was involved in the land fraud is true, it is odd that Wilhelm did not mention Goldblum in his affidavit to the FBI. He did name Miller, Dedo (posing as Ken Manella), and Orlowsky, the initiator of the scheme. But he never mentioned the so-called mastermind, Charles Goldblum.

Furthermore, although Wilhelm, Miller, Dedo, and Orlowsky are all named in the FBI's investigation file concerning this fraud, there is no mention of Goldblum.

It should be noted that during the arson investigation, Miller continued to dishonestly implicate Goldblum by manufacturing a relationship between Wilhelm and Goldblum that simply did not exist (This is presented in greater detail in "The Arson" chapter of this book).

At Goldblum's trial, FBI agent Gary Boutwell testified that he verified that a large amount of money was missing from Wilhelm's bank account. He also testified of the documented involvement of Miller, Dedo, and Orlowsky in the fraud, while recognizing that Goldblum's name did not come up at any point in the FBI's investigation. Boutwell further testified that nothing more was done on the case after U.S. Assistant Attorney Richard Thornburgh issued a letter of declination. This letter is, fundamentally, a recognition by the Attorney General that there was likely some misconduct, while declining on behalf of the Department of Justice to prosecute.

What happened at the time of the first investigation bears scrutiny and analysis. Key events in the land fraud and subsequent investigation are:

1. U.S. Senator Richard Schweiker's office told Wilhelm they had no knowledge of his plan to purchase federally owned land and referred him to the FBI.
2. The FBI investigation determined a lot of money had been withdrawn from Wilhelm's bank account. All the money went to Dedo, Miller, and Orlowsky. The file of this investigation mentions Wilhelm, Miller, Orlowsky, and Dedo, but not Goldblum.

Before the meeting, Goldblum explained to Miller that his only option was to come clean, admit the fraud, and fully repay Wilhelm. Since the two knew each other well and had an ongoing relationship, there was simply no other option. Leading up to the meeting, Miller seemed to acquiesce to Goldblum's advice, agreeing to repay the money, and claiming in the face of Goldblum's repeated questioning, that he had the available funds to re-compensate Wilhelm.

During the Sunday meeting, however, Goldblum began to realize that Miller was using his presence in furtherance of the fraud. According to Goldblum, Miller told Wilhelm he would not receive the land, but he continued to deny his own involvement, insisting that the aide to Senator Schweiker had disappeared, and they could not track him down. As Miller made subtle references to Goldblum working to resolve the situation, Goldblum became extremely uncomfortable and spoke little, not wanting to validate Miller's dishonesty.

Ultimately Goldblum realized that he was being used as a prop to forestall Wilhelm's repayment. He got up and left, admonishing Miller for not following his advice. Miller quickly followed, apologizing for the meeting's tense and unproductive nature. He begged Goldblum to return to the same McDonald's the next evening, reassuring him that he would take his advice.

According to Goldblum, the second meeting at McDonald's on Monday night, February 9, began similarly to the first. Miller continued to lie about his role in the fraud, placing the blame on the fictional senatorial aide who disappeared with the money. He continued using Goldblum's name and presence to placate Wilhelm, insisting that as an attorney, he would help resolve the situation.

Still Goldblum stayed with the dual hope of brokering a deal and diffusing the situation, while still keeping Miller out of legal trouble.

Goldblum also feared the potential repercussions, both financial and legal, for himself and his family, if Miller got into legal trouble and told the police about the arson.

Goldblum's motive for staying was not so simple as avoiding potential criminal indictment. Aside from the financial repercussions for his parents if the insurance company did not pay for the burned restaurant, Goldblum believed if he could resolve this situation, he would be able to return to his job, his family, his life, and put his terrible arson decision behind him.

After an increasingly fruitless conversation, Wilhelm decided to move his car from the street to a covered garage. To continue the conversation, Miller went with him. Growing desperate yet still hoping to resolve the situation, Goldblum followed, never suspecting what was about to unfold. They climbed into Wilhelm's blue Plymouth Fury. Wilhelm was behind the wheel, Miller sat on the passenger's side, and Goldblum in the back seat.

As Wilhelm drove up the garage's circular ramps, the conversation with Miller became increasingly heated. When they reached the 8th floor rooftop, Miller finally admitted that he could not repay the $21,000. Wilhelm pulled into an empty space and punched Miller in the face. A violent struggle ensued.

According to Goldblum, quickly after the punch, Miller began to stab Wilhelm inside the vehicle. Wilhelm managed to tumble out the driver's side door and tried to escape by crawling towards the short cement wall at the edge of the garage floor. Miller jumped out of the passenger side and continued the assault, stabbing Wilhelm in the back as he crawled.

Goldblum testified that upon seeing the blood spurting from Wilhelm, he realized this was more than just a fight. He panicked and climbed out of the rear driver's side door, and began backing away from the scene in horror, watching Miller stab Wilhelm as he crawled away.

As Goldblum watched near the exit, Wilhelm pulled himself up on the cement parapet. Miller then upended him over the edge. Rather than falling eight stories to the street below, Wilhelm landed on the ledge of the roof of a walkway one floor below which connected the garage to the Gimbels Department Store and the Duquesne Club across Strawberry Way.

To this day, Goldblum is haunted by feelings of shame, regret, and cowardice for not having intervened on Wilhelm's behalf.

After witnessing Miller flip Wilhelm over the edge, Goldblum stood frozen, looking on in horror. Sensing Goldblum's fear, Miller put his hands out to his sides to show he no longer held a weapon. He said he was not a threat, exhorting Goldblum to calm down. Slowly, Goldblum approached Miller, and they both looked over the wall down at Wilhelm.

At this point, Richard Kurutz, returning to his car after attending night school downtown, exited the elevator. Approximately 90 feet away, Kurutz saw Goldblum and Miller standing at the cement wall, looking over where, unbeknownst to him, Wilhelm lay bleeding on the roof of the covered walkway one floor below.

At Goldblum's trial, Kurutz testified to hearing a *thud* at the same moment he saw the two standing at the ledge. He testified that he believed this noise was the sound of Wilhelm's body hitting the ledge below. The prosecution used Kurutz's testimony as evidence that Goldblum and Miller had conspired and assaulted Wilhelm together.

There is no denying that Kurutz saw Goldblum and Miller together at the ledge. However, Wilhelm had been thrown over the ledge before Kurutz arrived, and his testimony was not as conclusive as the police and prosecutors asserted. The noise Kurutz heard could have been a car door closing or any number of other sounds, and only later did he decide what he heard was Wilhelm's body landing on the ledge below. From where Kurutz stood, the *thud* of a body falling to a ledge on the floor below would not have been very distinct and could easily have been confused with a number of other noises.

It must also be noted that Kurutz testified seeing Goldblum wearing a suit and top coat and not fisherman's coveralls, as Miller testified at Goldblum's trial in an attempt to explain why Goldblum's clothes from that evening had no traces of blood. The coveralls that Miller testified Goldblum was wearing were never found. The police never followed up on this discrepancy. To do so would have further discredited their witness. The Commonwealth was protecting its prosecution.

After being spotted by Kurutz, Goldblum quickly left, walking down the ramp one floor and then using the garage stairs, with Miller following close behind.

In a panic, Goldblum began yelling at Miller and asking why he did this to Wilhelm, while simultaneously pleading with him to leave.

Overcome with fear and adrenaline and unable to think clearly, Goldblum was intimidated by Miller into giving him a ride home and providing him with an alibi. After witnessing the levels of savagery of which Miller was capable, Goldblum feared denying him.

But Wilhelm was not dead, and policemen summoned by a garage worker arrived. When the officers found him lying on the rooftop, they noted that Wilhelm was thrashing around. Fearful that he would fall off, they instructed him to be still. At that point, Wilhelm clearly spoke, "Clarence – Clarence Miller did this to me.

Wilhelm expired within two hours after reaching the hospital.

The forensic evidence and Wilhelm's dying declaration corroborated Goldblum's account of the assault. The police and the DA, to enforce their theory, interpreted Wilhelm's dying declaration to mean that Miller had set him up to be attacked by Goldblum.

This assertion is particularly hard to believe. It does not seem sensible that a man, having been savagely attacked with a blade, dumped off a roof, and bleeding to death, would express a causal relationship in his dying words. It simply makes sense that Wilhelm was saying "Clarence Miller did this to me," as in, "Clarence Miller stabbed me and killed me." Conversely, it is almost ludicrous to contend that Wilhelm meant, "Due to a series of events initiated by Clarence Miller, I am now in this position, though someone else did the actual stabbing."

At Goldblum's trial, two versions of the murder were presented:

1. **The Prosecution's theory**: Miller claimed that Goldblum was the mastermind behind the fraudulent land deal in which Wilhelm was defrauded of $21,000. Wilhelm, furious over the stolen money, began pressuring Goldblum for repayment. Goldblum, in order to satisfy Wilhelm and solve his own financial problems, commissioned Wilhelm to burn down his restaurant, promising to pay him after collecting the fire insurance money. According to Miller, these two crimes were why Goldblum had to silence Wilhelm. At this point, Miller claims Goldblum requested his help to lure Wilhelm to the roof of the Smithfield-Liberty parking garage so that Goldblum could intimidate Wilhelm and scare him into silence. The police believed there was a conspiracy between Miller and Goldblum to attack Wilhelm. They argued that since both men were involved in the conspiracy to lure Wilhelm to the garage roof and assault him, they were accomplices and, therefore, both responsible for murder in the first degree.

2. **Goldblum's contention:** Goldblum claimed that due in part to Miller acting as the torch in the restaurant arson, and to

diffuse the situation between Miller and Wilhelm in order to get back to his more normal role as an attorney, Goldblum attended the Feb. 8 meeting purely to act as a negotiator and mediator between Miller and Wilhelm. During the second meeting to negotiate a solution to the debt owed by Miller to Wilhelm over the fraudulent land deal, a fight between Miller and Wilhelm broke out, leading to the spontaneous and unplanned murder of Wilhelm. Goldblum claims to have initially removed himself from the scene before freezing up, then returning after Miller threw Wilhelm over the wall. Goldblum provided an alibi for Miller out of a fear of Miller's violence, the panic and trauma inspired by witnessing the attack, and the fear that Miller would drag Goldblum down with him, due to his presence at the crime scene. Furthermore, Goldblum felt beholden to protect Miller so that Miller would not inform the police about Goldblum's and his involvement in the arson.

Under scrutiny, the prosecution's theory gives rise to a number of unanswerable questions and begins to fall apart.

Miller testified at Goldblum's trial that this was a planned assault initiated by Goldblum, going so far as to claim that the two of them had previously scouted the roof of the garage as their chosen location for the attack.

If the murder was a planned, calculated assault, why would Goldblum choose a venue as public and well-lit as the roof of a parking garage in the middle of downtown Pittsburgh on a night that stores were open? Why not plan the murder for one floor down where it would be darker? Why not plan it in a secluded place away from downtown altogether?

There are other obvious questions. If Miller was truthful in saying the whole evening was a plot to assault Wilhelm, how did they know to a certainty how he was going to travel to the restaurant? How would they have lured Wilhelm to the roof of the garage if he had taken public transportation? If the assault was planned ahead of time, how were Miller and Goldblum going to get Wilhelm up to the garage roof if he did not drive there in his car?

Assuming they knew to a certainty that Wilhelm would arrive by car, how would they have convinced him to drive to the roof of the particular garage had he not made the decision on his own? More importantly, why meet in a public restaurant where both Miller and Goldblum were known to frequent so near the garage?

The nature of the assault depended on too many unknowable variables to be reasonably considered a calculated, planned event. This is especially true considering that Miller was telling this story to experienced homicide detectives and criminal prosecutors. The Commonwealth took this highly unlikely sequence of events and presented it as fact at trial. A diligent prosecutor and honest detective should have recognized these obvious lies as a ploy by Miller to divert the attention and blame away from himself.

The physical evidence and witness testimony also corroborate Goldblum. Miller's claim that Goldblum was the assailant was accepted by the police despite the following:

1. Miller failed his first polygraph test, which was administered to establish his involvement in Wilhelm's murder.
2. After a second polygraph test administered by the police, Miller made contradicting statements as to how the assault played out and his role in it, claiming that he held Wilhelm down while Goldblum committed the assault. This directly contradicted his trial testimony and demonstrated his unreliability as a witness. Furthermore, the existence of the second polygraph and Miller's admission involving himself went unreported and was never turned over to the defense until a year after Goldblum's conviction, and some 20 months after they were administered.
3. The clothing Miller wore that evening was admittedly bloody, while Goldblum's clothing, which was recovered and examined by the police, showed no trace of Wilhelm's blood.
4. At Goldblum's trial, Miller testified that Goldblum wore fisherman's coveralls during the murder to explain why no blood was found on his clothes. This is contrary to the testimony of Mr. Kurutz, the pedestrian who exited the garage elevator, who described both Miller and Goldblum

to the police, testifying that Goldblum wore a suit and topcoat.

5. Hairs inside of a pair of gloves found near the scene, which were soaked in Wilhelm's blood, were consistent with Miller's, not Goldblum's.

6. The victim's dying declaration named Clarence Miller as the assailant, by first and last name, and him only.

7. The blood spatter evidence on the dashboard of Wilhelm's vehicle also disproved the prosecution's theory. The blood spatters were to the front of Wilhelm, indicating that the assault was performed by somebody in front or to the side of him. Additionally, according to testimony be Detective Freeman, the tails of blood droplets traveled from left to right across the dashboard. Freeman's own testimony regarding the blood spatter strongly indicated that the assailant sat directly to Wilhelm's right, in the front passenger seat of the car.

8. On February 10, when both men were first arrested, Miller had a number of scratches on his forearms and face, in addition to a finger laceration, consistent with defensive wounds resulting from a melee. Goldblum had none.

A good detective and diligent prosecutor should have at least suspected that Miller was lying when he said he was not involved in the murder of George Wilhelm based on this list of contradictory evidence alone.

Unfortunately, the blood spatter analysis of the forensic experts are based on trial testimony describing the distribution and patterns of the blood, rather than photographic analysis. This was not a choice made by the defense, but a decision of necessity. The photos of this blood spatter evidence were never shared with the defense and vanished by the time of Goldblum's trial. Subsequently, the court ruled that the written testimony of forensic experts regarding the blood spatter evidence was inconclusive.

Crime Scene Detective Salvatore Crisanti testified at a deposition and has since given a separate statement, that the blood spatter would have been photographed before it was scraped off the dashboard during the evidence-gathering, as this was standard procedure for all homicides.

Crime Scene Detective Edward Hill stated that he would have photographed any evidence that was in the Wilhelm vehicle.

Detective Sergeant Joseph Modispatcher also stated that he remembered these photographs were available at least a few days before trial.

The lead investigating detective on the murder, Ronald Freeman, also admitted in his deposition that he remembered seeing such photographs, but he could not remember when or where.

It is the duty of the prosecution to properly maintain all evidence leading up to the trial. By misplacing this key piece of physical evidence which, in the light of expert analysis and testimony, would have cast reasonable doubt as to Goldblum's guilt, the Commonwealth committed an irreversible error that interfered with his ability to receive a fair trial.

At a post-conviction hearing for Goldblum, the court eventually ruled that without photographic evidence backing up their analyses, the reports of Dr. Michael Baden, Director of the Forensic Sciences Unit of the New York State Police, Dr. Henry Lee, Director of the Forensics Research Training Center in Connecticut, and John Balshy, a crime scene investigator for the Pennsylvania State Police for 27 years, were all inconclusive and therefore did not constitute grounds for an appeal.

Each of these experts submitted reports finding that Miller, not Goldblum, was Wilhelm's likely assailant. Furthermore, while Dr. Cyril Wecht, a forensic pathologist and Allegheny County Coroner at the time of Goldblum's trial, was allowed to present his findings at the hearing due to his position, his testimony was also ultimately deemed inconclusive due to the lack of photographic evidence. Thus, Goldblum's defense was interfered with and irreparably harmed by the Commonwealth's failure to disclose key exculpatory evidence and to maintain and prevent spoliation of that evidence.

The court based their rejection of the defense experts' blood spatter reports, in large part, on the testimony of the expert called by the prosecution at Goldblum's post-conviction hearing, Dr. Toby Wolson, Criminalist Supervisor in the Forensic Biology Section of the Miami-Dade Police Department Crime Laboratory Bureau.

At the hearing, Wolson testified that without corroborating photographs, all of the testimony related to the meaning of the blood spatter was merely speculative. Intriguingly, when pressed during cross examination, Wolson admitted that if Detective Freeman's description was accurate, then the other experts would be correct in their conclusion that the spatter meant that Miller was most likely the assailant, not Goldblum. Despite this admission, the court ruled that without photographs, all the blood spatter testimony was inconclusive, speculative, and, therefore, inadmissible.

At Goldblum's trial, the Commonwealth stated that no photograph of the blood spatter pattern had been taken, in contradiction to the statements later made by the police investigators involved in the case. Also troubling is the fact that all three copies of the police homicide case file and photos, plus separately maintained files in the Mobile Crime Unit and in the Police Photo Lab have since gone missing. Also, both copies of the Coroner's files were also missing

That the police knew these undisputed facts, were aware of all the inconsistencies, and still accepted Miller's account, is disquieting. For this to happen followed by the disappearance of police records, is deeply disturbing.

Despite the presence or absence of blood spatter photographs or a thorough analysis of the same, one essential and basic fact of the blood evidence directly contradicts Miller's tale of how Wilhelm's murder unfolded.

It was Miller's testimony at trial that Goldblum initiated the assault by striking Wilhelm on the back of the head with a wrench from the floor of the car, although the medical examiner could find no indication of that blow. According to Miller, Wilhelm, after suffering the blow, stumbled out of the car in a panic, at which point Goldblum took the grass shear blade and continued stabbing Wilhelm outside of the car.

This assertion is directly contradicted by the abundance of blood inside the vehicle, some of it misting and cast-off spattering that could only have been produced by a blade or other "critical wound," as testified to at trial by the Allegheny County chief forensic pathologist, Dr. Joshua Perper.

In an attempt to explain this glaring inconsistency, the prosecution offered that perhaps the driver's side window had been open when Goldblum began stabbing Wilhelm, and some of the cast-off went through the window and across the car, before landing on the passenger side dashboard. Disregarding the dubious physics behind this implausible explanation, it is unlikely Wilhelm drove around with his windows open on a cold, snowy night in mid-February. Once again, the physical evidence does not concur with Miller's story.

It is now clear Charles Goldblum had no motive to harm George Wilhelm. Goldblum played no part in the land fraud, and Wilhelm was not the arsonist of Goldblum's restaurant, as Miller testified. It is highly implausible that prosecutors and police could reasonably argue they were not aware that they were presenting perjured testimony. Members of the DA's office at the time have expressly admitted this in connection with the arson.

During his testimony at Goldblum's trial, Miller maintained his innocence. The prosecutors withheld from the defense that Miller took a second and third unreported polygraph test containing contradictory statements regarding the murder and arson and that he suffered a brain injury as a child, which resulted in his diagnosis as a confabulator.

It also seems likely that after Miller's admission on May 15, 1976, the prosecutors were aware of his participation in Wilhelm's murder, and if they objectively examined the facts in his testimony in light of the physical evidence, they would have determined that Miller was fabricating his version of events. Yet somehow the police and prosecutors concluded it was proper to present testimony they did not believe to be true.

In fairness, some courts have allowed prosecutors to take inconsistent positions at separate trials of co-defendants. The State Supreme Court of Pennsylvania made this their ruling in Miller's post-conviction appeal. In these other cases, however, there was a plausible explanation. In this case, however, the forensic and crime scene evidence make the disparity difficult to accept.

The bottom line: both the prosecutors and police most likely presented Miller's testimony knowing it to be untrue.

If they believed Miller participated in the killing and presented his testimony that he did not take part, then they presented perjured testimony. Their motive is clear. It was a key element in building their homicide case against Goldblum. Without Miller's testimony, they would have been unable to establish motive.

In the decades since Goldblum's conviction, the Commonwealth has rationalized extensively, excusing their behavior based on perceived loopholes. This should not happen in any criminal case. It is especially serious in the prosecution of a capital murder.

The Investigation

The police investigation into George Wilhelm's murder began with a simple traffic accident.

Just before 9:30 p.m. on February 9, Pittsburgh Police Officer Thomas Pobicki was working alongside Officer William Holtz and Patrolman John Mammy, who went along for the ride. Responding to a call about an auto accident at 6th Avenue and Smithfield Street in downtown Pittsburgh, the three piled into a cruiser and went out into the cold, snowy, windy February evening, ready to handle a routine situation.

Meanwhile, at the nearby Smithfield-Liberty Garage, Pinkerton guard John Regan, a garage employee who escorted members of the Duquesne Club to their cars on the reserved sixth floor, heard agonizing moans and pleas drifting down from the walkway bridge that connected the garage to the club. Regan, his sense of curiosity piqued and tinged with foreboding, began scouting the area, looking for the source of these cries. Eventually, he discovered Wilhelm, who was lying bloodied on the roof of the walkway. Shaken badly, Regan ran back to his post and summoned the police and an ambulance.

Going through the managing and removal of the wrecked vehicles and the emotions of the drivers, Pobicki, Holtz, and Mammy received the call about a man lying on the walkway between the Smithfield-Liberty Garage and the Duquesne Club, bleeding badly and calling for help. The officers quickly left the accident scene and arrived at the garage and took the elevator to the 8th floor, where they discovered an empty vehicle, its doors open, and a trail of blood through the snow leading to the edge of the roof.

Looking over the edge of the garage, they saw Wilhelm lying on the roof of the covered walkway one floor below, severely injured, and dying, having slipped into unconsciousness after managing to yell out cries for help.

Officer Pobicki then descended to the 7th floor where he was met by Sgt. Bill Reynolds, who had responded separately to the call. A safety fence blocked their access to the roof of the walkway. Sgt. Reynolds fetched a crowbar from the trunk of his car and pried away the safety fence. After both men, braving the elements and the risk of a deadly fall, made their way to Wilhelm's side, Pobicki shuffled around to his head, which Pobicki stabilized, fearing a neck injury, while Sgt. Reynolds held on to the victim's feet.

While Pobicki and Reynolds worked to move Wilhelm from the roof of the walkway, the ambulance sat helplessly at the garage's Smithfield Street entrance, radioing that their vehicle was too tall to fit inside. Luckily, a helpful citizen who happened to be returning to his car after some shopping, volunteered to transport Wilhelm to the ambulance on the street below. Wilhelm was placed into the rear of this helpful stranger's station wagon and driven down.

In the ambulance Wilhelm regained conscious. Pobicki asked who had attacked him. desperate to identify his killer before slipping away, and as Officer Pobicki did his best to keep "Clarence – Clarence Miller did this to me." And then, "I'm gonna die! I'm gonna die!"

In a legal sense, Wilhelm had provided police with one of the most rare, irrefutable, and condemning weapons in a criminal trial: a dying declaration.

A dying declaration requires the express recognition by victims of their imminent death and the identification of the responsible party. It is presumed by the legal system that, in the face of their own death, people would not lie, but would, out of desperate instinct, truthfully identify who brought an end to their life.

These were among Wilhelm's last words, his last desperate and defiant gesture against the man who took his life with the 7-inch blade of a grass shear. Wilhelm, bravely and stubbornly identified his killer before taking his last breath several hours later, lying in the hospital, surrounded by the medical staff unable to bring his body back from the savage trauma which it endured, his family in the hallway clinging to the hope he might survive.

Initially, shortly after 9:30 p.m., Detectives Orlando Diggs and J.W. Carter took the call and went to cover the crime scene and orchestrate the investigation, along with Detective Mike Gorney and Detective Second Grade Ronald Freeman.

Freeman, then one of the most senior men in his seven-man squad, was considered an aggressive, uncompromising, and relentless investigator. As the second-most senior detective on the squad, under only Acting Lieutenant Charles Lenz, Freeman's responsibilities included coordinating the investigation and parsing out the tasks at hand among the more junior detectives.

The medical staff treating Wilhelm initially informed Detective Freeman that although the victim was brutally assaulted and in critical condition, he might not die. When Wilhelm passed away several hours later, the homicide division was called upon to ratchet up their efforts and launch a full scale investigation.

Detective Freeman, then wrapping up an investigation into a double homicide in the Hill District, assigned Detective Diggs and his partner Detective Carter as the primary detectives for the Wilhelm murder case. Both Diggs and Carter were considered to be solid, capable criminal investigators.

Although Diggs and Carter were assigned as the primaries, the homicide investigative squads relied on a system of coordination and hierarchy with the flexibility necessary to deal with the unpredictability of violence in a metropolis. While the less senior investigators were subject to the commands of their superiors, this was not a strictly militaristic command structure. Different sets of partners within the seven-man squads worked simultaneously on multiple cases, with two assigned as primary detectives to certain homicides, prioritizing them, but maintaining the flexibility to assist in other ongoing investigations.

While Acting Lieutenant Charles Lenz was in charge of coordinating investigative efforts from the homicide offices, prioritizing the more important leads from the ongoing investigations, veteran Detective Second Grade Freeman was looked to as a commander in the field. It was expected that each set of detectives maintain the proper sense of autonomy and self-motivation to follow up on leads they felt promising and assist other detectives as needed.

Normally, once detectives are designated as primaries on a certain homicide, they take charge of the investigation and see it through to its conclusion, relying on other squad members primarily for assistance. In this murder case, one that would become highly publicized due to its savagery, the complex nature of the crime, and its underlying story, the friction between Freeman and then Police Assistant Superintendent James Curran led to Freeman pushing himself to the head of the case. He took charge despite Diggs' and Carter's rightful place at the forefront.

After Wilhelm was transported to the hospital, Acting Lt. Charles Lenz dispatched Detectives Diggs and Carter to orchestrate the preservation of the crime scene, to seek out and mark any potential evidence, and ensure that no one interfered with the scene's integrity. Detectives Salvatore Crisanti and Edward Hill from the Mobile Crime Unit then arrived to begin their work, to set about photographing the scene and gathering evidence.

Having taken the necessary steps to block off and preserve the crime scene, Carter and Diggs decided that due to the snowy, nighttime conditions, the efforts of the Mobile Crime Unit to gather evidence would be the most fruitful in the light of day. Between the snow and the darkness, key evidence could be missed or accidentally damaged. A patrol car was placed at the scene, and the homicide team decided to meet at the garage the following morning.

Throughout all of this, Detective Freeman continued to coordinate the final stages of an investigation into a double homicide on which he was the primary investigator before receiving the Wilhelm call. Wilhelm's vehicle was towed to the Public Safety Building and a number of patrol units were left behind to keep the scene secure for further inspections in the morning.

At 10:12 p.m. Detectives Gorney and Freeman, informed of the dying declaration of the victim, were dispatched to identify, locate, and bring in Clarence Miller. Freeman and Gorney reported to the Public Safety Building, from which the Homicide Detectives coordinated their investigative efforts and where they had access to the databases and files essential to following leads and investigating potential suspects.

When they ran the name "Clarence Miller" through the I.D. Section, a database of criminal records for citizens of Allegheny County, the search yielded four separate results for "Clarence Miller" in Pittsburgh with a record. The detectives took the photographs of each Clarence Miller and went to Mercy Hospital and showed them to the Wilhelm family, who were holding vigil outside the surgical ward, still hoping he would pull through.

Although Wilhelm's father did not recognize any of the photographs, his older brother Earl identified one as a good friend of his brother. Earl also recalled that his brother had received a phone call the previous evening around 8:00 p.m. and mentioned he was going to meet "Clarence."

Now, sure of the Clarence Miller they were seeking, the two detectives remained with the family until 12:12 a.m., when George

Wilhelm was pronounced dead. They then accompanied Wilhelm's grief-stricken father and brother to their home and searched through Wilhelm's belongings, looking for the names of acquaintances who could be interviewed for leads that might reveal a motive for his murder.

The following morning, Detectives Diggs, Carter, Gorney, and Freeman, along with Detectives Crisanti and Hill from the Mobile Crime Unit, all reported back to the Smithfield-Liberty Garage to begin the investigation in earnest and make a detailed sweep of the scene for physical evidence.

On the ledge of the garage's 7th level near the walkway roof where Wilhelm was found, the officers discovered a broken pair of dentures which had fallen from Wilhelm's mouth. Just inside the ledge, they found the murder weapon, a 7-inch blade that went from a pointed sharpened edge to a flat, widened metal ridge 6-inches long wrapped in grey tape, all caked with a coagulated red substance.

While Crisanti and Hill meticulously slogged through the process of cataloguing the crime scene, they received a call from the Homicide Unit to report to the parking garage's manager Robert Herle. Herle informed the detectives that a garage employee, Milton Loeher, had been given a pair of bloody gloves found in a nearby alcove by an unidentified man, presumed to be a patron of the garage. The officers noted blood coating the outside of the gloves, some of it saturating through to the inside, before bagging them and returning to the scene of the crime on the 8th floor of the garage.

After photographing and cataloguing evidence on the 7th and 8th floors of the garage, the detectives then moved on to the stairwells, where blood traces told the tale of the perpetrators' escape route. On the fire door leading to the stairwell exiting at the intersection of 9th and Liberty, a smear of blood was noted and photographed. Another spot of blood was found at the top of the handrail, leading down to another blood smear on the handrail leading to the 7th floor. Each blood patch was photographed, scraped and preserved for further analysis. On the right side of the door frame leading to the exit into the street, another small amount of blood was found, photographed, and collected.

This crime had the hallmarks of a murder guaranteed to bring on the spotlight of the press, the interest of the public, and the pressure of City Hall to be resolved. The murder victim was a decent citizen with no criminal past who was well-loved by family and friends. The nature of his death was particularly savage, consisting of 23 stab wounds covering his face, neck, arms, chest, back, and abdomen.

Perhaps most disturbingly, the crime was committed in a high-traffic parking garage in the commercial district of downtown Pittsburgh, on an evening when the stores were open for business.

These factors attracted Assistant Police Superintendent James Curran to the crime scene, a relatively rare occurrence.

According to an article in the February 12, 1976 Pittsburgh Post-Gazette newspaper, when Freeman reported for duty on the morning of February 10, surrounded by the investigative team, he was publicly dressed down by Curran for failing to have staked out Clarence Miller's home overnight once his identity had been determined.

Curran, considered as much politician as policeman, had achieved his position in the Pittsburgh Police Department through his influence in Democratic politics. He was not considered by rank and file police to be a good leader. Freeman, not the sort to react calmly to the uninformed criticisms of his work by a political animal, responded in kind. He made disparaging comments about Curran to other officers at the scene, which the superintendent happened to overhear. As a result, Curran told Freeman he was off the already publicized case, out of the elite Homicide Investigations unit, and transferred to the Auto Squad/Night Turn Felony Squad.

Curran quickly put Freeman's transfer in motion. That evening, activity reports previously authored by "Detective R. Freeman and Detective M. Gorney," were now being prepared by "Detective R. McKay and Detective M. Gorney."

Freeman's banishment didn't last long.

Ambitious with a large ego, Freeman had a reputation as a master of deception and manipulation, which made him an effective detective and a case closer. At the time of Wilhelm's murder, Freeman's personnel file was filled with commendations. They tracked his rapid rise through department ranks, going from police officer to detective third grade in his first four years of service, with another promotion to detective second grade following shortly thereafter.

A homicide detective choosing to remain anonymous in his comments, claimed that early in Freeman's career, his brother, a Catholic priest, had reached out to his Bishop, who in turn asked the Mayor to promote Freeman to Homicide Investigations. Regardless of the source of his promotion, Freeman was on a rapid trajectory into the upper echelons of the Pittsburgh Police Department.

Despite the public spat between Curran and Freeman, and Freeman's subsequent transfer, Freeman was returned to Homicide Investigations two days later and reassigned to the Wilhelm murder. Although his brief banishment had tarnished Freeman's reputation, this increasingly high-profile murder case became the means by which he could undo the damage and get his career back on track. Gradually Freeman pushed himself to the forefront of the case and took over.

At any rate, around 10:00 the morning of the 10th, having received an assignment at the crime scene, Detectives T. Condemi and F. Amity, two members of the homicide squad, transported the murder weapon and the victim's clothing to the Homicide office. Then before heading out to the address of the Clarence Miller identified by Earl Wilhelm, Condemi and Amity appeared before Magistrate Troiano. They presented the victim's dying declaration and the identification by Earl Wilhelm of Clarence Miller as the man George Wilhelm met the evening of February 9. Based on this evidence, Magistrate Troiano issued a warrant for the search of Miller's home at 2451 Glenarm Avenue in the Brookline neighborhood.

Throughout any investigation, each set of detectives is required to submit daily reports, detailing their assigned tasks, the efforts made to complete them, and the results of these efforts. There were no standard forms for these reports, and many of them are colored by the inferences, impressions, and personalities of the detectives submitting them. Yet each report is thorough and detailed, documenting how the detectives spent their time, the content of their interviews and the evidence, leads, or, not uncommonly, dead-ends that the day's work yielded.

The tone of Condemi and Amity's February 10 report on their initial interaction with Clarence Miller began amicably. Having previously established his alibi with Charles "Zeke" Goldblum through leverage and intimidation, Miller entered the interrogation without even bothering to reach out to an attorney, presumably to avoid any appearance of guilt.

The two detectives initially played their cards close to their vests, hoping to elicit an obviously false recounting from Miller that could later be used against him. Although they were armed with Wilhelm's dying declaration and the knowledge that Miller was one of the last people to meet with the victim before his death, the detectives conducted their search of Miller's home and the first half of the interrogation as if they were merely clarifying Miller's relationship with the victim and his whereabouts the previous evening.

The detectives had arrived at the Miller residence around 11:30 a.m., introduced themselves, and informed Miller of their intention to search his home, explaining that he was suspected in the murder of George Wilhelm. They informed Miller that they needed to conduct a search for clothing and interview him to ascertain the nature of his relationship with the victim and his alibi for the previous evening. The detectives noted that Miller was effusive and cooperative, practically tripping over himself to respond to their questions.

The detectives searched the home, but no bloody clothing was found. Their report indicates an oddly formal and amicable scene, as if the detectives were two friends of Miller's who had stopped by to catch up on old times. They maintained this subterfuge until much later in this initial interaction, when they shifted to an aggressive, invasive, and all-knowing style of interrogation.

After completing their search, the detectives pulled Miller aside, explaining that they did not want to upset his family by questioning him in their home and requesting that he come down to the Public Safety Building to issue a statement. Miller, on edge and fearful of appearing guilty, agreed to the suggestion and went with them to the Public Safety Building, not knowing he was facing a hardline interrogation by the detectives.

As that second interrogation began, Miller explained that he met Wilhelm in 1968 during the reelection campaign of Pennsylvania Senator Richard Schweiker. Both were volunteers for the campaign, handling menial tasks such as fetching coffee, making copies, running documents, and hanging campaign posters. He said the two struck up a friendship which they maintained up to the date of Wilhelm's death eight years later.

Miller stated that he awoke the morning of February 9 and hung around his house all day before catching a 7 p.m. bus to downtown Pittsburgh. Once downtown, he claimed to have met with Charles Goldblum around 8:30 in front of Kaufman's department store at 5th Avenue and Smithfield Street. Miller explained that they then met up with Wilhelm at the McDonald's on Wood Street and had coffee together. Then Miller said Wilhelm had to leave to meet an unknown third party.

Furthermore Miller explained that after Wilhelm left, he and Goldblum discussed the prospect of visiting a nearby strip club and adult movie theater, the seedy, infamous "Penthouse Theater." Ultimately they decided not to attend the show, and Goldblum gave Miller a ride home, before going home himself.

Strangely, the use of strip clubs and whorehouses as a bond between the two men became a common tactic through which Miller painted the illusion of a strong friendship with Goldblum; an illusion that would become essential to the detective's theory of Goldblum's guilt.

This was the first time the detectives heard Goldblum's name and the first time the possibility of a second suspect concretely entered the picture.

Miller claimed that upon arriving home at approximately 10 p.m., he was greeted by his wife, two daughters, and his cat, with which he played with for a while, thus explaining the scratches covering his face, wrist, hands, and forearms, in addition to a finger laceration. The detectives accepted Miller's explanation for the scratches at face value, merely noting them in their report, but not pressing the issue.

Still maintaining a mask of indulgent affability, the detectives excused themselves from the interrogation room, to verify the truth of his statement, as they explained to Miller. As Miller barely held himself together in the interrogation room, still unaware of the dying declaration made against him, Detectives Condemi and Amity reached out to two other detectives, Cooper and Longacre, to contact Goldblum.

Cooper and Longacre called Goldblum at his office in the Koppers Building, explained what they wanted, and asked for an interview. Goldblum readily agreed, saying he could account for his and Miller's whereabouts the previous evening. At 2 p.m., Coopers and Longacre arrived at the office of Arthur Young and Associates to take Goldblum's statement.

This first round of interrogation bore an unmistakable similarity to Miller's questioning. The detectives approached Goldblum with some level of suspicion, appropriate to this early stage of the investigation. The detectives already believed Goldblum had been at a meeting with both the murder victim and the man he named as his attacker in his dying declaration.

Worthy detectives walk into such a situation appropriately suspicious and alert, but, simultaneously, they should maintain an objective mindset essential to solid criminal investigations. Unfortunately, the evidence indicates keeping this objectivity and the pursuit of the truth behind the crime would be usurped by the desire to secure a second conviction.

Years later, looking back on these early stages of the investigation, Goldblum laments having not simply followed his conscience and come clean. His motivations for not being truthful to the police, his family, and his friends were a complicated stew of fear and the desire to maintain the life he he had worked hard to build.

At the time, Goldblum was 26 years old, a young tax attorney at a respectable accounting firm, a part-time lecturer at the University of Pittsburgh, a business owner, and a husband trying to start a family despite the many pressures and obligations of his busy lifestyle. He was also, unfortunately and regrettably, a failing restaurateur who, motivated by foolish pride and the desire to preserve his parents' financial integrity, had commissioned the arson of his restaurant to collect the insurance.

Discussing these events decades later, having spent the majority of his adult life in prison, Goldblum is humble and self-critical, both aware of his poor judgments and disappointed with his younger self for having made them.

While not denying his ethical shortcomings and felonious wrongdoings, he points out that in the American justice system, no one should be imprisoned for crimes they did not commit.

During that initial interview with the detectives, Goldblum explained that he had left his office around 5:00 the previous evening and headed to the University of Pittsburgh in Oakland, where he taught an accounting class from 6 to 8 p.m. He then briefly visited his mother, dropping her off at Beth Shalom Synagogue, where his father was the Rabbi. Then he drove back downtown and met Miller at the corner of 7th Avenue and Smithfield Street near a newly established bank. After picking Miller up, Goldblum parked in an alley immediately behind the bank, and the two men went to meet with George Wilhelm.

Unlike Miller's interrogators, Longacre and Cooper, Goldblum's interrogators had no direct evidence linking Goldblum to the murder at this point. Thus, they pressed Goldblum to explain why he had attended the meeting.

Driven by the desperation and fear that had marked his life since the arson of his restaurant two months earlier, Goldblum manufactured the lie that he was meeting with Miller in the hopes of exploiting his supposed political connections to land a position in the DA's office. Goldblum stated that Miller, using his connections with local judges, had worked out an appointment and interview for him. (As it happened, Goldblum did have an interview for a job at the District Attorney's office the morning after the murder and was offered a position, which he said he had to decline because of its low salary.)

The detectives seemed to accept this story as plausible and asked him to recount details of the meeting with Wilhelm.

Goldblum claimed that as the meeting progressed, he began to suspect that Miller and Wilhelm were nothing more than braggarts and hangers-on who lacked any real political connections that could actually help get him an appointment with the DA's office, and so he tried to extricate himself from the conversation. Soon after, Wilhelm explained that he had to go meet someone who owed him money and the three men parted ways. When Wilhelm went to leave, Miller requested that Goldblum give him a ride home, due to the harsh weather.

Unlike Miller, Goldblum made no mention of discussing a jaunt to the nearby Penthouse Theater, but rather said he simply drove Miller home, dropping him off around 9:30 p.m., before returning to his home, arriving at approximately 10 p.m. This was the alibi agreed to by Goldblum after witnessing the horror of Wilhelm's murder, motivated both by the fear of Miller's unpredictable savagery and the selfish desire of protecting himself and his family from the possibility of the restaurant arson coming to light.

After consulting each other, the four detectives were unimpressed with the alibis provided by both suspects. While there were no particularly glaring discrepancies, it was obvious that both men were not being entirely truthful.

Miller had stated the two met in front of Kauffman's, before walking together to McDonald's. Goldblum claimed he had met Miller in front of "a new building with a bank" near the intersection of 7th Avenue and Smithfield Street, and the two drove to a parking spot together before walking to meet Wilhelm. Miller made no mention of the political undertones of the meeting. While Detectives Condemi and Amity did not initially note the nature of the meeting, their report indicates that Miller presented it as three friends meeting for coffee, rather than a meeting with a specific political agenda. The most obvious indication of the two suspects' deceit came in Miller's odd rambling about the alleged discussion of an evening at the Penthouse Theater, before deciding to simply head home.

Perhaps this strange addition was a product of Miller's confabulation, a fantastic detail conjured by his traumatized brain to add an element of believability to a flimsy story. Perhaps Miller believed the detectives would not accuse him of lying about such an embarrassing hobby. Either way, after Detectives Longacre and Cooper reported on their conversation with Goldblum to Detectives Condemi and Amity, the men returned to Miller's interrogation armed with discrepancies, ready to break Miller, and perhaps drag Goldblum down with him.

The rapidity of Miller's acquiescence in the face of the newly confrontational detectives evokes a child confronted by a stern parent. There was no consideration of attempting to manipulate the detectives, doubt them, distract them, or insist on the validity of his original statement. Miller's confabulation, while a prolific source of both believable and unbelievable dishonesty, is also marked by a personality with certain quirks that combine to make him particularly susceptible to old-school, strong-arm interrogation tactics. Miller is noted in police reports and during trial as a man of low natural intelligence with a high street IQ.

Simply put, Miller was a street-smart but unintelligent survivor. He was the type of man who regularly misreads a situation, then panics and then acts out impulsively, both mentally and physically, in a way he feels will yield the best result for him. These core qualities were evident in both his willingness to defraud a friend out of thousands of dollars and the bungling, incompetent, yet successful way in which he pulled off the farce. These qualities also meant that, when confronted with the victim's dying declaration and the inconsistencies between his and Goldblum's statements, Miller immediately broke down and confessed to being involved in the murder. But, displaying his instinct for survival, he immediately began framing Goldblum as the initiator, bully, and mastermind of the crime.

The police report for Miller's second interrogation was starkly different. The detectives were all business, doubting, probing, accusatory, and aggressive. Faced with the discrepancies between his and Goldblum's statements and the stark finality of Wilhelm's dying declaration, Miller broke under the pressure. He took the only path that could possibly lead to self-preservation: blame everything on Goldblum. Thus began the unscrupulous, subjective, and willfully unaware investigative process that led to Goldblum's wrongful conviction for Wilhelm's murder.

Based on the direct evidence of Miller's involvement in the Wilhelm land fraud, Wilhelm's dying declaration, and the physical evidence linking him to the stabbing, the murder prosecution should have landed squarely on Miller's head.

Sensing this after the detectives begin their confrontational approach, Miller began to paint Goldblum as a criminal mastermind, with one foot in the straight world, the other probing and manipulating in a far darker one.

The story is fantastical, yet not impossible. Numerous police reports document leads followed-up with dogged, continued efforts by detectives, ultimately resulting in a dead-end or recognition that the lead was false.

While this should have been the path taken by the "Goldblum as criminal mastermind" lead, it appears the detectives and prosecutors could not pass up the chance for a second conviction of an attorney that would come at little cost to them, yet a steep cost to Goldblum and his family, not to mention basic justice in the American legal system.

After the detectives broke Miller, he gave his first version of Wilhelm's murder and the series of events leading to it on the evening of February 9. In each interview, and even within the same interrogation session, Miller contradicted himself constantly, offered different facts, or manipulated and supplemented past lies to make them more believable and to fit the prosecution's case against Goldblum. Had the detectives taking these statements been concerned only with convicting the man responsible for Wilhelm's murder, these glaring inconsistencies and obvious fabrications would have been revealed, dwelled upon, and then used to dispute nearly all of Miller's claims.

In this initial recounting, Miller started off by claiming that Wilhelm was threatening to create problems for both Miller and Goldblum and their supposed political aspirations by causing what Miller termed a "Watergate scandal over the Senator Heinz campaign," as recorded by the detectives in their February 10, 1976 report on his interrogation. Miller claimed that he and Goldblum were "in politically" and, fearing for their political futures in the face of Wilhelm's meddling, decided that he needed to be intimidated into silence. What possible influence Wilhelm, a disabled truck driver, could possibly have done to influence local politics was apparently not a concern for the detectives once faced with the prospect of a second suspect. The interrogators skated over the ridiculousness of Miller's tale, failing to press for details or explanations.

Miller went on, claiming that Goldblum told him of a "good spot" for Wilhelm's intimidation: the well-lit public parking garage, connected to both a social club and a department store. Miller alleged he and Goldblum had visited the the roof of the Smithfield-Liberty parking garage on the afternoon of Sunday, February 8 to scout it as a potential spot for the assault. According to Miller, after a brief reconnoitering, the two agreed that this would be the place.

At this point, Miller drifted back into the realm of reality, recalling the timeline for his evening of February 9 and admitting that he traveled to the scene with Goldblum.

Like all believable lies, there are sprinklings of truth in Miller's story. This style of lying is consistent with Miller's confabulation diagnosis. While aspects of his tales are ridiculous and unbelievable, manufactured by his brain trauma to supplement memory gaps and inspired by his desire to save himself, elements of truth in his memory lend an air of believability to his fabrications.

As the second interview continued, the timeline remained consistent, with Miller and Goldblum arriving downtown around 9 p.m. to meet with Wilhelm. In the initial version of his story, Miller said Goldblum picked him up at his home. This was not true. Later, Miller changed his story and said they met downtown, on Smithfield Street under Kaufmann's clock.

Goldblum also said they met downtown, but it was near where he parked his car in an alley off 7th Avenue. He was willing to attend the meeting because of the leverage Miller had over him because of the restaurant arson. He wanted to diffuse the tensions between Miller and Wilhelm in order to keep Miller out of legal trouble. Convincing himself he was acting in the role of arbiter and legal counsel, Goldblum begrudgingly attended the meeting. While Goldblum denied none of these damning facts or foolish actions, they do not add up to his guilt for the murder of George Wilhelm.

At this point, however, Miller simply said that he met with Goldblum and Wilhelm at the downtown McDonald's. Once again, no effort was made by the detectives to extract the reason behind the meeting or the substance of what was discussed. According to Miller's first round of lies, the subsequent assault was to silence Wilhelm over a political scandal.

Miller had no explanation for why the meeting took place initially, how Wilhelm was convinced to attend, or what was discussed. That provided an indication of Miller's guilt and lent credence to Goldblum's contention that the three men met over monies defrauded from Wilhelm by Miller. Miller provided no credible details of the political scandal or the substance of the meeting.

His obvious goal was to shift blame and the appearance of guilt from himself onto Goldblum, and the detectives' desire for a second arrest influenced their judgment, removing the lens of scrutiny and insight that normally define a police interrogation. If the detectives were after the truth behind this murder, why would they so readily believe Miller's ridiculous story without corroboration, some semblance of consistency and rationality, or, at least a believable explanation?

Still skirting the edges of reality, Miller described to the officers how the three men made their way to Wilhelm's car, supposedly so that Wilhelm could drive Goldblum to his car parked in the Smithfield/Liberty Garage. Here, Miller begins the process of painting Goldblum as the mastermind initiator in earnest.

As told by Miller and detailed in the February 10 police report, Goldblum instructed Wilhelm to drive to the roof of the parking garage, informing him that he has a regular spot on the top level. Upon reaching the roof of the garage, Wilhelm parked his car and, according to Miller, Goldblum immediately struck Wilhelm on the back of the head with a wrench, which caused him to bail out of the driver's side of the vehicle and fall to the ground.

Miller then alleged that Goldblum leaped from the car and began stabbing Wilhelm with the half grass shear, also stored in Wilhelm's car. Miller recalled the victim calling out to him, asking him for help, but Miller claimed he was too scared to offer assistance. Later in his story, when Miller admits to scrubbing blood from the cuffs of his trousers, the detectives ask him why he was bloodied if he avoided the melee.

Miller, in his attempts to cast guilt onto Goldblum, backtracked and tweaked his re-telling, explaining that he tried to help Wilhelm several times, but was pushed away by Goldblum. This continual revisionist ebb and flow became a consistent pattern in the exchanges between Miller and the detectives.

In Pennsylvania, if two parties enter into a criminal conspiracy to commit a crime, both are guilty of any subsequent or tangential criminal acts that occur as a result of the original conspiracy, regardless of whether or not both parties physically participated. This means that when Miller lied to the detectives and told them that he and Goldblum planned to assault Wilhelm, in the eyes of the law, both men were culpable for the subsequent homicide.

Unaware that he had confessed to first-degree murder, Miller took a break from manufacturing the appearance of Goldblum's guilt and began to exhort his own innocence. He pleaded desperately with the officers, stating repeatedly and emphatically that he did not know that Goldblum intended to kill Wilhelm, and he never would have agreed to set up Wilhelm had he known. The detectives were happy to leave Miller unaware that he inadvertently confessed to murder and used him to secure a second conviction in a highly publicized homicide.

After the detectives managed to calm Miller's pleadings and get the interrogation back on track, they asked how the wrench and grass shear used in the assault came to be at the scene. Miller stated Wilhelm kept both in his car.

While a minor point in the abundance of contradictory physical evidence, it must be asked that if this was a planned assault, as Miller asserted throughout the investigation and Goldblum's trial, then why were the weapons used found at the scene? According to Miller's statements, Goldblum was a violent, calculating criminal who had meticulously planned to brutally assault Wilhelm.

Yet, if the attack had been planned, why didn't either of them bring a weapon to carry out the assault? Additionally, why would anyone choose a well-lit public parking garage connected to both a department store and social club as the venue for a planned assault, especially when both were still open and hosting patrons?

These are simple questions of logic and consistency that the detectives did not ask.

When the detectives got into the issue of the clothing worn that evening by both suspects, Miller continued the deception and absurdity that would define his role as the prosecution's key witness. He lied about the clothing he wore that evening and later convinced his wife to do the same.

He claimed he had worn a blue nylon hooded jacket, a red sport coat, yellow shirt, grey and black checked pants with red stripes and brown shoes. Much later in the investigation, it was proven that Miller wore a different coat that evening and since it was covered in blood, had disposed of it in a city garbage truck.

Pure happenstance led to the uncovering of this lie.

The son of a nearby neighbor testified he was having trouble sleeping that evening and walked to his kitchen where he saw Miller from the window. He was hurrying up the street in bloodied pants, with a balled-up jacket in his hand, which he tossed into a garbage truck. After this fact was revealed at later interrogation, Miller was asked by the police why he disposed of the jacket. By then, confident of his role as the police's favored suspect, Miller admitted that the jacket was bloody, but, harking back to the lame explanation of the blood on his pants, claimed that it only got that way when Miller attempted to come to Wilhelm's aid.

Once again, the detectives swallowed this thin explanation. They had Miller dead to rights but needed him to maintain an appearance of innocence for the jury so they could use him to convict Goldblum.

Miller then described the clothing that Goldblum wore that evening as a dark blue or black top coat, a yellow shirt, and a light suit, all of which were verified through witness testimony as the clothes he wore that evening. All of these clothes were analyzed and found to be without blood, save one small microscopic speck on the cuff of his yellow dress shirt. So while Miller's pant legs were so bloody he felt the need to scrub them and his overcoat so bloody he felt the need to dispose of it, the police chose to believe that Goldblum, with only one microscopic fleck of blood on his shirt-cuff, blood that was never proven to belong to the victim, was the man who had stabbed Wilhelm 23 times.

In a final attempt to shift the blame from himself, Miller claimed that Goldblum specifically requested he bring a pair of his black gloves to the meeting. When the detectives asked for an explanation, Miller simply stated that, "...he wanted to wear them," as is noted in the February 10 police interrogation report. Despite the fact that this assertion made little sense, the detectives did not press the issue for further explanation, taking at face value that before heading to the meeting and for no apparent reason, Goldblum had specifically requested that Miller bring a certain pair of gloves for him to wear. These same gloves were recovered, by chance, near the garage and turned over to the police. The Crime Lab's report later showed that they were soaked with the victim's blood and hair found inside the gloves was consistent with Miller's, but not Goldblum's.

Making a preemptive though nonsensical attempt at explaining away damning physical evidence, Miller admitted to owning the gloves, that they were saturated with Wilhelm's blood and contained hairs consistent with his, yet he expected an impartial observer to believe that Goldblum had requested to wear them.

During the first interrogation, the detectives had noted a scratch on Miller's nose, a laceration on his left index finger, and scratches running up his arms and wrists. When asked how he received these wounds, Miller claimed they were from, "...playing with his cat..." after returning home the evening of the murder.

Again, the detectives accepted this outlandish explanation without further questioning. Furthermore, these suggestive defensive injuries were not photographed by the detectives.

Throughout this entire interview, Miller was visibly nervous. A stuttering, scatterbrained mess, desperately searching for the right words to mollify the detectives and escape the pressure of their interrogation, he told them what he thought they wanted to hear, and ultimately, pushed the blame from himself onto Goldblum.

When the detectives pressed him on the origins of the wounds, Miller began complaining of pains in his chest. The detectives continued, taking advantage of Miller's fragile state and eagerness to cooperate, requesting that Miller give his statement on tape. He agreed, but when the detectives stepped out to get the tape recorder and began setting it up in the interrogation room, he again complained of chest pains, requesting to step out in the hall and have a drink of water. While bending over the fountain, Miller slumped over, passing out in the hall.

All of these physical mannerisms, state of mind and ultimate black-out, were noted in the detective report of this interrogation. They give credence to the claims Miller made in May of 1980, some fours years later, that his intimidation, fear, and blacking-out invalidated his statement.

The detectives called for an ambulance, but before it arrived Miller came-to, insisting he was okay. Seemingly determined to record his statement against Goldblum while his tale was still fresh, they took him back into the interrogation room. However as they were ready to record, Miller once again slipped back into unconsciousness, at which point the detectives got him into an ambulance which transported him to Pittsburgh's Southside Hospital.

At approximately 5:00 p.m., Miller was checked in and taken to a room. He was desperate to reinforce his lies and further ingratiate himself into the detective's good graces. Fearful perhaps of losing his position with the prosecution, Miller demanded that the hospital staff bring the police into his room so he could give them more information. The police did not bother to note much of his babbling. Miller was grabbing at anything he could think of to convince them of Goldblum's guilt. If only the detectives had been as wary of Miller's many other ridiculous claims, the injustice of Goldblum's conviction and decades of incarceration could have been avoided.

Nine months after Goldblum was convicted of Wilhelm's murder, Miller was also tried and convicted of first-degree murder for Wilhelm's death.

On May 9, 1980, Miller filed a petition under the Post-Conviction Hearing Act, and he came clean as to the false and coerced nature of his testimony against Goldblum. In that sworn affidavit, Miller explicitly stated that "...the statements I gave police were not true and not of my own making or free will, but instead, a product of the police interrogator's own design and personal conviction."

Illustrating the investigators' relentlessness in pursuing Goldblum's conviction over honest, objective police work, Miller went on to state that, "...[his] statement was signed under the threat of personal physical injury by police [which] put Petitioner in a mental state of extreme fear."

Furthermore, Miller's recounting of his state of mind during the murder meshes logically with the nature of both the crime scene and the commission of the assault.

In the sworn affidavit of his Post-Conviction Hearing motion, Miller went on to state that, "...the statements that I gave to the police and signed that I saw Charles "Zeke" Goldblum stabb [sic] George Wilhelm are not true, because at that point I blacked out and remember nothing. I wasn't even aware of my own existence, let alone anything that happened about George Wilhelm."

The crime scene was a bloody mess of explosive violence committed in a well-lit public place with a weapon that, by happenstance, was found in the victim's car. These facts do not indicate that either Goldblum or Miller had planned a calculated assault with the goal of intimidating Wilhelm. Rather, they indicate an argument between Miller and Wilhelm spiraling out of control, leading to an impulsive, violent attack during which Miller mentally blacked out.

While some may argue that this was simply a ploy by the compulsively dishonest Miller to seek relief for his conviction, his claims are validated by reality and physical evidence, unlike the steady stream of lies that flowed unrelentingly throughout the investigation and Goldblum's trial.

Miller's testimony at Goldblum's trial, from the murderer's motive to its commission, was refuted by the physical and circumstantial evidence of the crime scene. The contention that Wilhelm had been Goldblum's arsonist was contrary to Wilhelm's passive, law-abiding and decent nature, not to mention his absence from the scene the day of the arson.

District Attorneys involved in the trial have subsequently and openly admitted they did not believe Wilhelm acted as the arsonist. Goldblum's alleged involvement in the land fraud is disputed by his total absence from any of the FBI investigative files or the affidavits submitted by Miller and Wilhelm related to the crime.

Additionally, at Goldblum's trial, Thaddeus Dedo, one of the land fraud conspirators, offered to testify that Goldblum had not been involved in the land fraud. But the prosecution never asked for immunity for Dedo, and absent that, he refused to testify. Dedo's testimony would have been extremely crucial because it would have invalidated the prosecution's central motive for Goldblum to murder Wilhelm, thus, exonerating Goldblum of the crime in the jury's eyes.

Miller's accusation that Goldblum stabbed and killed Wilhelm is completely discredited by the abundance of physical evidence pointing towards Miller and the dying declaration of the victim, expressly identifying him as the killer. Unlike Miller's highly suspect trial testimony, his claims in this document are validated by the evidence and the aggressive nature of the detectives' investigative technique.

The abundance of evidence pointing towards Miller put him in a position of extreme vulnerability. His claim that the interrogation was aggressive and terrifying to the point of physical breakdown was proven true by his hospitalization during the immediate hours after his arrest. His claims of intimidation and manipulation at the hands of the police were proven true by the nature of the trial against Goldblum.

As Goldblum's trial progressed, an increasingly elaborate fiction was constructed, as the prosecution continually forced evidence to fit their theory of Goldblum's guilt, with Miller as the main unifying force. Without Miller's testimony, this elaborate fiction could not have been convincingly constructed, presented to a jury, nor Goldblum convicted.

Detectives Condemi and Amity stayed with Miller throughout his evaluation, treatment and x-rays, before they received a call from his defense attorney Vincent Murovich, for whom Miller did grunt work. Murovich ultimately allowed the police unsupervised, unfettered access to his client.

At 6:38 p.m. on February 11, 1976, after Miller had blacked out and was transported to the hospital, the homicide detectives obtained search warrants for Goldblum's home, car, and office, based entirely on Miller's statements implicating Goldblum in Wilhelm's murder.

At 7:13 p.m., Detectives H. Watson and W. Hennigan began their search of Goldblum's home in Greenfield. They procured the clothing that Goldblum had been wearing the previous night, as testified to consistently by Goldblum, his wife Rosalie, and Miller in separate statements recorded by the police.

The detectives asked Mrs. Goldblum if she knew of or if her husband had mentioned Clarence Miller. Mrs. Goldblum responded that Goldblum was acquainted with Miller through the Clerk of Courts office, where they both worked for the Republican Party. Mrs. Goldblum stated that she saw her husband leave the morning of February 9, but she did not know what time he returned that evening. Just before 8 p.m. having concluded their search of Goldblum's home, the detectives reported back to the Homicide Office and turned the evidence into the Crime Lab.

At 7:30 p.m. Detectives McKay and Gorney traveled to North Braddock to interview Richard Kurutz, who had called into the police following a news report and wanted to give a statement that he had seen two men exit the parking garage around the time of the murder.

Kurutz, who had been attending a class at Triangle Tech, exited the elevator on the 8th floor of the parking garage at approximately 9:25 p.m., when he heard a thumping sound off to his left. He first presumed the noise was ice falling from the garage roof. At that point, he saw two men matching the physical descriptions of Miller and Goldblum looking over the far wall. As Kurutz continued to his car, he noticed Goldblum and Miller walking away and down the ramp.

Although during his testimony at Goldblum's trial Kurutz admitted he could not identify the men by face. His description matched the clothes taken into evidence as those worn by Miller and

Goldblum the night of the murder. Unaware of Wilhelm lying on the walkway roof below, Kurutz said he just got into his car and headed home.

At 8:50 p.m. on the 10th and based on Miller's statements and Goldblum's admission to being at the murder scene and the corroboration of Kurutz as a third party witness, the detectives decided to arrest Goldblum. After a one-hour visit with his family, Goldblum was transferred to the jail and arraigned for the murder of George Wilhelm.

On February 13, Miller was released from the hospital and returned to police custody. At 5 p.m. the same day, his attorney Vincent Murovich arrived at the Public Safety Building and consulted briefly with Miller before the two met with Detectives Condemi and Amity to provide the motive for the murder, according to Miller.

The interrogation began with Miller completely backtracking and disregarding his previous explanation for the motivation behind Wilhelm's murder.

Having consulted with his defense attorney, Miller likely realized how foolish and unbelievable his explanation of a "Watergate scandal over the Senator Heinz campaign" truly was. But he continued his effort to shift the culpability for Wilhelm's murder away from himself and on to Goldblum, taking it in a different direction.

During this interview, as recorded by the report of Detectives Condemi and Amity, Miller claimed that it was on a "Sunday in November" of 1975, when the Goldblum restaurant arson took place, that Goldblum, Miller, and Thaddeus Dedo, a key land-fraud conspirator, were all in the basement of Goldblum's restaurant, the Fifth Avenue Inn. Miller claimed that Goldblum began talking around the possibility of arson, casually explaining that the building was in bad shape, but that it was well-insured. According to Miller, Goldblum then proposed that Miller and Dedo burn down the building, detailing the entire crime and its plan without any indication from the men that they would agree to the proposal.

Miller claimed Goldblum spoke of cans of Sterno stored in the basement. Further, he detailed a plan to pour it on the rugs, to drill holes in the 3rd floor walls and pack them with fire accelerant, and topping off the plan, by pouring accelerant on the stairs so firemen would not attempt to enter the building.

At this point, the detectives failed to ask obvious follow-up questions.

What was the relationship between these three men? Why had they gathered in the basement? What was being discussed before this proposed arson came up between these social acquaintances (particularly Dedo, who claimed to not even know who Goldblum was, let alone be aware of his criminal plan)? Why had Goldblum detailed the arson? How had Miller become aware of so many details of the arson's execution?

The detectives asked none of these questions

At this point in the interview, Miller claimed he told Goldblum he "wanted no part in this" and left to go to the Penthouse Theater to see the strippers. Around 7 p.m., he heard the fire engines. Miller then claimed that at a later date he could not recall, that Wilhelm told him that he had burned down Goldblum's restaurant for him. The detectives did not seem at all suspicious why Miller was so well acquainted with the details of the arson, nor concerned with the fact that his story was completely without any verification, corroboration, or physical evidence.

A thorough examination of the timeline and progression of events during this interview with Miller make his story ridiculous.

According to him, he and Dedo were allegedly at the restaurant around 5:00 p.m. the afternoon of the arson. Then, with no warning, Goldblum first suggested that Miller and Dedo burn down the restaurant that same evening. Then, in the one hour and 22 minutes after Miller said "no" and left and when the fire started, as documented in the official Fire Prevention Bureau report, Goldblum managed to convince Wilhelm to come over and burn the building.

This is implausible to the point of impossibility, yet the detectives took it at face value.

Continuing, Miller stated that his friend Wilhelm informed him that Goldblum agreed to pay him $3,500 for the arson when the insurance settlement came through.

According to Miller, Wilhelm said he had received $2,000 of the money Goldblum had promised and had been pressing him for the rest. Miller claimed Goldblum had reached out to him and explained the same predicament Wilhelm had told him on a different day. He then asked Miller to help him set Wilhelm up to quiet him about the arson debt. Miller said he had agreed to set up an assault on his friend of eight years for just $50.

Capping off their report, the detectives noted that, "Clarence then related about the incident (murder) this of course was the same as earlier statements given to the above officers." They made no mention of any details of Miller's second recollection of the crime, the erratic changes in his story, nor its elements of suspicious improbability.

At 6:10 p.m. the interview ended, and Miller was taken back to a cell in the Public Safety Building.

Attorney Murovich, perhaps to find out for himself whether Miller was innocent, requested that he be given a polygraph test. After the polygraph test, Attorney Murovich was told by Detectives that Miller passed but the test was shaky. Murovich believing that Miller had passed the test allowed the Detectives to continue questioning Miller without his presence. In reality, Miller failed the test and had Murovich known that, he would not have allowed his client to continue with the questioning.

This first examination was administered on Friday, February 13 by Sgt. Joseph Modispatcher, the most experienced polygraph administrator in the police department, as noted in the report prepared by Detectives Condemi and Amity.

According to the report, Modispatcher failed Miller.

Unfortunately, the only remaining record is the Master Polygraph Log and the final paragraph of Condemi and Amity's report which ends, "...for further details on this check with Joe."

A police report filed on January 27, 1978, after Goldblum's conviction and just before Miller's trial, mentioned that on May 15 and 25, 1976, two additional polygraph examinations were administered to Miller by Detective Joseph Stotlemyer, who only recently had been trained to operate a polygraph. This report also mentions Miller's confession to being involved in the murder.

The reason these polygraph examinations cannot be examined is because all five copies of the police file of this case have mysteriously vanished. Despite this, it is known that Miller gave disparate answers as to his role in Wilhelm's assault and even Stotlemyer noted in his report that he believed Miller was involved in the arson.

It should also be noted that Storyteller's primary job at the time was investigating homicides in the same unit as Freeman. As the investigation wore on, Sgt. Modispatcher claims he repeatedly approached Freeman stressing his belief that Miller was the lone assailant but was always brushed off.

On February 12, 1976, Miller was treated by doctors at Southside hospital for possible brain problems due to the pressure and pain in his head.

On February 16 and 17, 1976, Miller was examined by Allegheny County Behavior Clinic Psychiatrist/Medical Doctor E. H. Davis. Dr. Davis reported that "Miller was also very anxious to relate the entire incident that transpired in order to protect himself and to excuse responsibility for what transpired." Dr. Davis also reported, "It simply becomes a matter of whether you wish to believe him or the co-defendant, Charles Goldblum. Goldblum, of course, is denying any participation in the incident, except to imply that he didn't do it but this defendant did." Miller claimed that he took a polygraph test and that he passed the test. The polygraph test was administered 4 days prior to this report and Miller failed the test. Miller was diagnosed by Doctor Davis with having a Personality Disorder, Emotionally Unstable Type with Congenital Reading Defect. Miller was again examined by the Behavioral Clinic Psychologists on February 24 and 25, 1976.

At this point Miller had been psychologically examined 5 times and all of the Psychology Reports were available to the Detectives and Prosecutor at the time of Miller's interviews.

On Tuesday, March 2, 1976, Miller was finally brought in to make a recorded statement.

By this point, Detective Freeman had assumed the role of lead interrogator during this interview. His role was likely influenced by several factors; his senior status in his group of homicide investigators, his reputation as a strong interrogator and "closer," and his desire to make the case his own after criticism of his handling of the early stages of the investigation.

The interrogation began with Freeman explaining Miller's self-incrimination rights for the record. For some reason, Miller's defense attorney permitted his client to be interrogated without his presence and advised him to answer all questions. Miller's tone was indulgent, submissive, willing, and eager.

Miller started with a lie. Freeman asked, "Is there any reason, any medical or physical reason that you can't tell us the truth?"

Miller responded, "No, No," despite knowing he had suffered brain trauma as a child after being struck by a trolley car which led to his tendency towards confabulation. Throughout this interview, many key details and facts of Miller's recounting changed, yet Freemen, a detective recognized as a skilled and aggressive interrogator, questioned none of this.

As the interview proceeded, Miller said Goldblum had contacted him the day of the murder and asked him to arrange an appointment with Wilhelm for the purposes of an assault, because Wilhelm was "shaking him down" for money.

Miller's intricate web of lies continued to change. In his February 10 statement, Miller claimed that he and Goldblum had met at the garage on February 8 to plan the assault. In this version, Miller alleged that Goldblum called him at 8:00 the morning of the murder and asked that Miller set up the meeting with Wilhelm, to "put a Jewish curse on him" and "beat the hell out of him." Miller went on to tell Freeman that after having coffee at McDonald's, Goldblum requested that Wilhelm drive him up to his car in the Smithfield-Liberty Parking Garage.

Miller claimed that once they got in Wilhelm's car, Goldblum asked if he could wear a pair of gloves Miller happened to have on him. Miller changed this recounting from his original statement in which he claimed Goldblum asked him to bring the gloves specifically from home. Likely realizing how little sense this made, Miller tweaked his statement. After undergoing laboratory analysis, it was determined that hairs found inside of the glove were consistent with samples taken from Miller, but not from Goldblum. In the interview transcript, Freeman did not note or question any of this.

Miller continued his story, claiming that Goldblum directed Wilhelm to drive until they got to the garage's 8th floor. Then he told him to pull into an empty spot right next to the elevators and stairwell exits, and, at the moment the car stopped, hit Wilhelm "on the back of the head" with a wrench. At that point, Wilhelm fell forward, struck his nose on the steering wheel and immediately fell out of the car.

Wilhelm's autopsy detailed the injuries he received. All of this was available to Freeman at this interview. There was no abrasion on the back of Wilhelm's head and no tissue or blood found on the wrench in his car. Freeman did not question the discrepancy between the physical reality of the evidence and Miller's recounting.

Continuing his recounting at Freeman's prompts, Miller alleged that after Wilhelm fell from the car, Goldblum exited and while repeatedly stabbing him, backed him against the wall of the garage, at which point Wilhelm fell over the edge.

Another key piece of physical evidence directly conflicts with Miller's version of the attack. The abundance of blood on both his pants, which were subsequently scrubbed clean, and his jacket, which he felt necessary to dispose of contrasted with the complete absence of blood on any of the clothes Goldblum wore the evening of Wilhelm's murder.

To explain the lack of blood on Goldblum's clothing, Miller alleged that he showed up for the meeting wearing a secondary topcoat and fishing coverall waders. Miller went on to claim that after they left the murder scene, Goldblum disposed of the bloody overcoat and fishing waders in a garbage bag he had in the trunk of his car. Aside from its simple ridiculousness, this obvious fabrication was disputed by witness Kurutz, who described Goldblum as wearing a topcoat. There was no mention of fishing waders nor a bloody overcoat, an outfit that would stand out in any context.

Yet Freeman did not press Miller about the incredibility of his statement nor its inconsistency with the statements of an eyewitness.

Miller claimed Goldblum then left the garage, and he followed. He told Freeman that Goldblum intimidated him into presenting the alibi that they had met Wilhelm for coffee and left him alive and well.

Miller then admitted that after he got home, he took off his overcoat and threw it into a city garbage truck. At this point in the interview, it is clear that Miller is the prosecution's favored son. Miller did not admit to Freeman that his coat was bloody or go into any detail, but merely stated, "I - was ah- I took my clothes, it was a topcoat I had. I took it and I ah, put it in a bag and I took it up the top of the hill and I put it in the garbage truck, city garbage truck."

Freeman asked Miller, "Why did you do that?"

He responded, "Well I was - I don't know why I did it. I just threw it - and ah, I just did it, that's all." Rather than pressing Miller for a reasonable explanation or touch upon the fact that this was suspicious behavior for a supposedly innocent man, Freeman guided the interview back to painting Goldblum as the guilty party.

Freeman continued, "Well getting back to...when did Zeke first call you to tell you that he wanted to see George?"

This is a glaring example of bias shown toward Miller throughout the investigation. Facing a conviction due to the physical evidence and Wilhelm's dying declaration, Miller was desperate to do anything he could to mitigate the severity of his circumstances. Recognizing this, the detectives allowed him to distort, revise, and outright lie throughout his interrogations. They failed to question the inconsistencies in his story or even probe blatant admissions of a deeper involvement by Miller. The prosecution needed Miller's testimony to secure Goldblum's conviction, and they were willing to overlook myriad inconsistencies and manipulations to do so.

At this point in the interview, Freeman prompted Miller to recount the entire day leading up to the assault. Miller obliged, describing himself as the go between for Goldblum and Wilhelm throughout the day. Miller claimed that he fielded a total of four calls from Wilhelm and three from Goldblum in order to arrange the meeting. Again, Freeman failed to question the glaring inconsistencies of this assertion.

If as Miller contended, Wilhelm and Goldblum already knew each other and had a financial and criminal connection through both the land fraud and arson, why didn't Wilhelm have a direct way to get in contact with Goldblum?

If Wilhelm had no way to contact Goldblum or was too afraid to even call him, how was Wilhelm "shaking down" Goldblum for money?

The simple answer is that the two men had no such connection. Despite Miller's claims to the contrary, no other witness ever testified to any relationship between Wilhelm and Goldblum.

Employees of Goldblum's restaurant who testified on issues related to the arson could never identify Wilhelm nor establish any relationship between the two men. Additionally, members of the District Attorney's office have subsequently stated that they never believed Wilhelm was involved with the arson. Yet throughout the investigation and at Goldblum's trial, this was the exact story the prosecuting attorneys chose to present to the jury.

According to Miller, after the meeting was arranged, Wilhelm picked him up just after 8 p.m. to go to McDonald's downtown in order to meet with Goldblum. After Miller and Wilhelm arrived at the McDonald's, Miller excused himself, explaining that he was going to get some tobacco. Miller told Freeman that he went outside and stood by a pay phone to wait for a call from Goldblum.

Even this simple statement is rife with inconsistencies. Why would Goldblum, having only called Miller that morning to set up the meeting, memorize the number of the phone booth in front of the McDonald's so he could reach Miller? Why would Miller lie to Wilhelm when going to get Zeke if the meeting was meant to be between Wilhelm and Zeke in order to work out their issues? This bears no particular weight to the issue, other than highlight that even in the simplest recounting of details, Miller impulsively and seemingly uncontrollably, distorted reality.

Eventually, Miller alleged to Freeman that Wilhelm looked to Goldblum and asked, "You got anything for me?" To which Goldblum responded, "Yeah...take me up to my car." Miller described getting into the car, at which point Goldblum asked if he could wear Miller's gloves.

Miller then went on to recount the assault itself. According to Miller's interview with Freeman, Goldblum directed Wilhelm to drive to the top level and "...Soon as he shut the ignition off that's when everything started."

Miller claimed that the moment Wilhelm shut off the engine, Goldblum came up with the wrench from the backseat and hit Wilhelm on the back of the head. Directly after being struck, Wilhelm opened the driver's door and fell from the car. Miller alleged that Goldblum then got out of the vehicle and immediately began to stab Wilhelm. Miller claimed, presumably to paint himself in a positive light, that he attempted to assist Wilhelm a couple of times as he was lying on the ground being stabbed, but Goldblum pushed him away.

Miller concluded his statement to Freeman by describing how he and Goldblum took the exit near the elevators right after Wilhelm went over the ledge, walking two flights, then taking the ramps to the ground. He said that Goldblum drove him home while developing the oddly simple alibi of "We met with Wilhelm for coffee, and we left him there alive." When asked why he did not go straight to the police,

Miller claimed that Goldblum told him the police would show favoritism to Goldblum because his father was a prominent rabbi and he was an attorney, while Miller was just an uneducated street punk.

Freeman asked, "Did you believe that, ah, we would show any special consideration because of that?"

Miller responded in an amicable way, "Not you two guys, no."

Goldblum then dropped Miller at his home between 9:30 and 10 p.m. Miller recalled that his wife saw him when he got home.

It is important to recollect the February 10 report in which it was noted that Miller had scratches on his wrists, arms, and face, in addition a finger laceration, which he explained by claiming that he had been playing with his cat.

Cognizant of his need for a witness to secure a second conviction, Freeman did not mention the defensive wounds nor the weak explanation behind them.

Miller then alleged that Goldblum called the next morning around 7:30 and told him not to worry, to stick to the story that the three of them had coffee together, then the two of them left, taking the route over Mt. Washington because the Liberty Tunnel was closed, and Goldblum dropped him at his home.

Ignoring the constant discrepancies and unbelievable claims made by Miller throughout this interview and his other reports, the physical evidence and witness testimony at trial ultimately debunk Miller's recounting to Freeman.

1. It was not recorded in the police reports that Miller suffered defensive wounds, while Goldblum had not.
2. Miller admitted, and the Wilhelm family corroborated, that Miller and Wilhelm had been friends for years leading up to the homicide, while no witness other than Miller could create a tie between Wilhelm and Goldblum.
3. Gloves which Miller admitted owning were found near the parking garage soaked in Wilhelm's blood. Hair found inside these gloves was analyzed and found to be consistent with Miller's and inconsistent with Goldblum's
4. Miller admitted to Freeman that he had disposed of the clothing he'd worn the night of the murder, but Freeman never pressed him on the issue. The clothes which

Goldblum wore the evening of the assault were recovered by the police department and, save from one microscopic speck on one sleeve, they were free of blood.

5. Although Miller claimed that Goldblum initiated the assault by striking Wilhelm on the back of the head with a wrench, the wrench was free of blood, hair, and skin tissue, and there was no abrasion on the back of Wilhelm's head reported in the autopsy.

6. In this interview, Freeman never questioned Miller about any of this physical evidence which contradicted his story. Nor did he reference or question the many discrepancies between Miller's February 10 statements and those made in his March 2 interview.

7. This is police work that was either motivated by a predetermined agenda to create the appearance of Goldblum's guilt or one of extreme incompetence.

Miller's description of the day of the homicide and the circumstances surrounding the meeting at the McDonald's are more ridiculous in light of his recounting of why the meeting came to pass and why it turned so violent. After recounting the day of the homicide, Freeman questioned Miller regarding the backstory to the meeting and began to delve into the motive behind the homicide.

At the March 2 interview, Miller claimed that Goldblum owed Wilhelm money for the burning down of his restaurant, the Fifth Avenue Inn. Miller described a scene that was slightly different yet equally unbelievable as the one described in his February 10 statement regarding the arson of Goldblum's restaurant. According to Miller, Goldblum called him, Wilhelm, Dedo, and Orlowsky two weeks before the fire was set on November 30, 1975 and requested they come to his restaurant for dinner.

It should be noted that Dedo claimed to have never met Goldblum. Nor had employees of the restaurant been able to identify Wilhelm nor recall having ever seen him at the restaurant.

Again according to Miller, one week before the meeting, Goldblum allegedly told Miller he owed the IRS $9,000. Miller then alleged that following this dinner, Goldblum explained to all of these men, two of whom we know Goldblum had never met, that he needed a "torch" to burn down his restaurant.

Miller claimed that he, Dedo and Orlowsky all refused Goldblum's offer.

At this point in the fabrication, Miller explained that Dedo and Orlowsky left after Goldblum's alleged invitation to help him burn down his restaurant and Wilhelm arrived. According to Miller, Wilhelm and Goldblum went off in a corner, where they discussed the details of burning down the restaurant before Wilhelm agreed to do it.

Ignoring the laughable nature of this improbable tale, that Goldblum invited four men, two of whom he did not know, to his restaurant in order to openly discuss the commission of a serious felony, it is important to note the glaring discrepancies between the March 2 recounting of how the arson came about and the one Miller gave on February 10.

In his first version, there was no organized meeting two weeks before the arson. Rather Goldblum, on November 30, 1975, the day of the fire, invited Miller and Dedo to take part in his plan. According to the February 10 police report, after Miller and Dedo refused to participate, Goldblum allegedly remarked, "I'll just get George to do it."

In addition to not questioning the unbelievable nature of Miller's story, Freeman never noted nor interrogated Miller regarding the drastic changes in his story. According to the transcript, Freeman merely accepted Miller's claims without corroboration and moved on with the interview.

Miller went on to allege that nearly a month after the fire, Goldblum came to him and said Wilhelm was shaking him down, pestering him for the money he was owed for the arson. Wilhelm was threatening to go to the Arson Squad and the Insurance Commission and inform them that Goldblum had burned down the restaurant. I have to ask myself, does this sound like a man who is frightened of Goldblum?

Once again, Miller twisted the more rational and believable reality, that he helped Goldblum to set the fire in a way to portray himself as innocent. While shifting blame onto Goldblum, he simultaneously manufactured a patently false motive for Goldblum to want Wilhelm dead.

Why would a man who had committed an arson and who relied on that felony remaining a secret for payment, threaten to tell the police about the arson? If Wilhelm was one of the two perpetrators involved, then this empty threat would have drawn police attention to that crime. Additionally, if money had been the main motive for Wilhelm's anger, why would he report the arson, thus guaranteeing the insurance would not be paid and, therefore, neither would he?

This story simply makes no sense, and a veteran investigator such as Freeman, a detective known for his intelligence, relentlessness, and savvy, should have realized this and interrogated Miller until the truth came to light.

The fact that he never questioned the legitimacy or rationality of this manufactured and constantly evolving string of lies raises suspicions whether Freeman was pursuing the truth or simply using Miller to secure Goldblum's conviction. Having secured from Miller the story necessary to further his prosecution of Goldblum, Freeman ended the interview, leaving all of the unanswered questions, manipulations, and inconsistencies to lay dormant.

After the interview, Freeman saw Miller as a person with a mental problem he could manipulate. Miller became Freeman's tool to build a case against Goldblum. When confronted by homicide detectives about the disparities between his and Goldblum's version of what had happened, Wilhelm's dying declaration, and the blood spatter evidence, Miller was easily intimidated. He felt that he had no choice but to acquiesce and put himself at Freeman's mercy. This initial interrogation with Freeman struck so much fear into Miller, he fainted due to the stress and required hospitalization.

After his release from the hospital, Freeman began using Miller to build a case against Goldblum, manipulating the evidence to fit his theory of the crime. Goldblum was never interrogated nor given the opportunity to present his side of the story or respond to Miller's assertions. Freeman ultimately succeeded, securing first-degree murder convictions for both Goldblum and Miller.

Miller's defense attorney, Vincent Murovich, handed Miller over to the police and received no written assurances of any deal in return. Freeman got unlimited access to Miller without his attorney being present. How did Freeman manage to convince Miller and his attorney to agree to this arrangement? In 1978, during Miller's murder trial, both he and Murovich claimed Miller had been promised a plea bargain deal of a sentence of 10 to 20 years for his cooperation. While it was not official or put into writing, there appears to have been a verbal agreement.

At that time, this was a common practice among prosecutors so that, on cross examination, their witnesses could truthfully testify that their testimony was not being offered as part of a plea bargain, thus granting their testimony more weight and believability. The District Attorney's Office and Freeman both denied there had ever been any plea bargain arrangement. Neither Freeman nor Dixon has ever addressed this beyond expressing general surprise.

For prosecuting attorney Dixon, the ultimate question of who physically assaulted George Wilhelm is irrelevant.

In his mind, Goldblum and Miller formed a criminal conspiracy to intimidate and assault Wilhelm. The assault had spiraled out of control, and Wilhelm was killed. As a result, this murder occurred in furtherance of a criminal conspiracy and therefore, under Pennsylvania law, both parties are guilty of first-degree murder.

Aside from the previously established problems with Goldblum's motive (or lack thereof), the disorganized, impromptu nature of the assault disproves this assertion.

These are not the hallmarks of a calculated assault, but of a sudden, emotionally driven attack. Miller's sworn, 1980 post-conviction affidavit is further validated as his recollection of the homicide coincides sensibly with the reality of the nature of the attack.

Considering the nature of the attack, the lack of motive by Goldblum to harm Wilhelm, and the wealth of evidence pointing towards Miller, this recounting of the homicide is more reasonable and believable than the elaborate story told at Goldblum's trial. The prosecution's recounting painted Goldblum as a criminal mastermind and a murderer who planned to assault Wilhelm after allegedly spearheading two separate and previous criminal conspiracies. Miller, having temporarily lost his mind, mentally blacked out in a rage over a money disagreement and viciously attacked and killed Wilhelm. There simply was no planned murder.

Miller felt betrayed that his cooperation with Freeman and Dixon during Goldblum's trial did not yield a more merciful deal with prosecutors, and he wanted to avoid conviction for murder at all costs.

Although a natural reaction, this does not take away from the fact that Miller was aggressively interrogated and intimidated into constructing a murder case against Goldblum; not for the sake of justice or to ensure the punishment of all guilty parties involved, but for the sake of a second conviction.

Freeman committed further actions that call into question the nature and appropriateness of his relationship with Miller, a prime suspect in a brutal murder.

After being arrested and charged, Miller was unable to pay his bail bond, and so he remained in jail. Freeman contacted the pastor of Miller's parents' church to ask for help to raise money for Miller's bail.

A police detective committing an act such as this is beyond unconventional. At a hearing before Miller's trial, Freeman disclosed his efforts to assist Miller in securing bail. Then later in a sworn deposition, Freeman denied assisting Miller in the bail issue.

During Miller's trial the year after Goldblum was convicted, the pastor of St. Mark's Church and his wife both testified that Detective Freeman had contacted them on the telephone and requested help from their congregation to make bail for Clarence Miller.

Freeman went so far as to assure them that he was "100 percent certain" that Miller did not kill Wilhelm. Freeman also told the pastor that Miller had passed a polygraph test, which was not true. Based on Freeman's assurance, the congregation took-up a collection and secured enough money for Miller's bail bond.

Freeman also went to the District Attorney's Office and asked them to contact the Pennsylvania Supreme Court to request that Miller's bail be reduced. Under oath during Miller's trial, Freeman denied any involvement in the bail issue and denied initiating any conversation with Miller's pastor. Either both the pastor and his wife are lying, or Freeman lied under oath during Miller's trial.

Prior to this point in the investigation, the prosecution, in all likelihood, learned that Miller suffered a brain injury as a child and had been diagnosed as a confabulator. At the very least, the prosecuting bodies should have known something was mentally wrong with Miller after reading the Southside Hospital's report as well as reports of brain tests at the Allegheny County Behavior Clinic dated February 16,17, 24, and 25, 1976.

Helping Miller post bail allowed Freeman to continue manipulating, controlling and deceiving Miller, which was necessary to build his case against Goldblum. Miller's freedom gave Freeman more control over him and Miller's relationship with ADA Dixon.

Additionally, Freeman spent an inordinate amount of time with Miller in contexts that call into question the nature and legitimacy of their relationship. Once Miller was out on bail, they frequented topless bars and houses of prostitution that Freeman claims they were investigating. With no cases brought as a result, it must be questioned exactly what it was they were investigating during these meetings.

Another detective, who asked to remain anonymous, refused to allow Freeman onto his crime scenes because of his questionable methods. Miller, a diagnosed confabulator who was very malleable and impressionable under the pressure of those in authority, was the perfect individual for Freeman to mold as a prosecution witness.

Goldblum, in a fit of desperation and moral weakness, tentatively agreed to a solicitation to murder Clarence Miller, a solicitation which was initiated by police informant Andrew Kinser Bey.

Although the facts of the solicitation seem clear, the background circumstances surrounding the charges raise questions.

A review of the Master Polygraph Log indicated that Bey was never administered a polygraph to determine the truthfulness of his allegations concerning Goldblum's interest in contracting a hit man.

The record establishes that Bey contacted Goldblum shortly after the former's release from the Allegheny County Jail. Prior to that, Goldblum had not been shopping around for a hit man. While Goldblum did not initiate this process, he was culpable in going along with the suggestion. At a second meeting, Bey introduced Goldblum to John Mook, an undercover Pittsburgh police sergeant, who played the role of the hit-man.

There was a discussion of how the murder might be done and what it would cost, but no final decision was made. Goldblum claims he phoned Mook to call it off, but shortly afterwards was rearrested and charged with solicitation to murder.

Issues of entrapment aside, it is curious why Bey was released early from jail while he still facing serious criminal charges.

Considering the many odd circumstances surrounding this case, other questions about this murder solicitation come to mind:

1. Who facilitated Bey's early release?
2. What prompted Bey to contact Goldblum?
3. After meeting with Goldblum, Bey visited Goldblum's defense counsel, H. David Rothman. Why? Was he trying to turn Rothman into a witness and force Goldblum to find another attorney?
4. Why, during Goldblum's trial, was Bey unable to be found to testify and answer these hard questions?

These questions are not posed to absolve Goldblum of the first solicitation. He was wrong to even think along these lines.

Although the facts of the first solicitation were never determined, Detective Freeman's role in a second solicitation for murder was nothing short of sinister.

After Goldblum was rearrested for violating his bond, Freeman commissioned Ronald O'Shea, a violent convict serving a long sentence, to fabricate further charges against Goldblum. O'Shea claimed, but subsequently recanted, that Goldblum had solicited him to murder Detective Ronald Freeman, Lieutenant Ralph Pampena, Clarence Miller, and Detective Sergeant John Mook, who had played the role of hit-man in Goldblum's first murder solicitation.

These charges were completely fabricated by O'Shea at Freeman's urging. While on death row years later, O'Shea admitted to this in writing, issuing a sworn affidavit. Freeman's direct involvement in this second solicitation casts suspicion regarding his involvement in the first solicitation and adds weight to the questions above.

The prosecution presented both solicitation charges at Goldblum's trial to discredit his character and prejudice the jury and media against him.

As it turned out, however, several months after Goldblum was convicted of the murder, he stood for a non-jury trial in front of Judge Dauer on the first murder solicitation. Represented now by Attorney Charles Scarlatta, Goldblum was found guilty and sentenced to an additional one to two years. However, that sentence was subsequently reversed by the Superior Court under speedy trial rules violation. He was never tried for the second solicitation, and the District Attorney had the charges dismissed.

Even after Goldblum was convicted of first-degree murder, Freeman continued his aggressive and unethical pursuit to extract as many convictions as possible from Wilhelm's death. Still reeling from his murder conviction and life sentence, Goldblum and his parents were escorted to an office in the Public Safety Building.

Freeman approached them and requested that Goldblum testify that Thaddeus Dedo and Fred Orlowsky, the other parties in the land fraud, had roles in Wilhelm's murder.

During an interview on November 23, 2012, Evelyn Goldblum, Zeke's mother, clearly remembered the meeting and expressed general shock and disbelief that an officer of the law would make such a request.

Goldblum refused to testify against these men for a crime they did not commit, but Freeman persisted. He demanded Goldblum simply state this on record, implying that he would help during sentencing. Mrs. Goldblum recalled Freeman's words. "He said just give me, just give us, Dedo and Orlowsky, and we'll make it easier for you. Those were his words."

Police detectives can become aggressive when working on high-profile cases.

When a detective is convinced a defendant is guilty but lacks sufficient evidence for a conviction, there is a temptation to cut corners or act dishonestly. Some detectives draw ethical lines based on the seriousness of the charges involved in a case they are working. In summary and misdemeanor cases, for example, the truth seemed to matter less.

Good homicide detectives who worked on homicide cases did not engage in this kind of deception. In cases involving major felonies, too much is at stake. Some detectives "look the other way." While not actively participating, they do nothing to stop an action. They may fear reprisal and isolation, or they "go along to get along." They feel that as long as they were not the perpetrator, they did nothing wrong.

Yet when particularly unusual occurrences arise, such as five copies of the official case files and records disappearing from different archive locations, it legitimately raises the question whether official misconducts occurred during the investigation and actions were taken to hide them.

This is an important point to keep in mind, because without those two murder solicitations, the prosecution case against Goldblum was relatively weak. In fact, absent those solicitations, Goldblum would have likely been acquitted of the murder.

Eventually Freeman was promoted to the rank of Commander, a political appointment comparable to the Chief of Police, and he was placed in charge of Homicide Investigations. This gave him access to all police department case files and records. He could go anywhere and take any file or record at any time.

Throughout Goldblum's trial, Freeman's name came up in connection with the following irregular circumstances:

1. When the facts concerning the second solicitation came to light, O'Shea implicated Freeman as being the mastermind behind the falseaccusations against Goldblum.
2. When Dedo refused to talk to Goldblum's lawyers after offering to testify at trial, he expressed a fear of Freeman.
3. Freeman involved himself in securing bail for Miller, who had been charged with murder. He both took steps to get the bail reduced and solicited funds from the church where Miller's family belonged. Both actions were highly unorthodox. Freeman later denied his involvement, despite the sworn testimony of Miller's pastor and his wife contradicting this assertion. In all likelihood Freeman did this to help control Miller.
4. After Miller had been released on bail, Freeman spent a lot of time with him "investigating" matters that never led to an arrest. They frequented bars and houses of prostitution. This kind of relationship between a detective and a witness is unusual and cause to question.
5. After Goldblum's guilty verdict for first-degree murder, fraud, arson, and conspiracy to commit arson was handed down, Freeman approached Goldblum, offering leniency at sentencing if he would falsely testify that Dedo and Orlowsky were involved in Wilhelm's murder, despite knowing this was untrue.

6. During his own murder trial nine months after Goldblum had been convicted, Miller and his defense attorney, Vincent Murovich, asserted that Freeman had promised him a sentence of 10 to 20 year rather than life in repayment for his help building the case against Goldblum.

There are simply too many questionable circumstances in this case, and Freeman appears to have been involved in most of them. Due to this, his credibility is highly suspect.

Ultimately the flaws in the investigation into Wilhelm's murder boil down to an essential disparity between the theories the prosecution presented at Goldblum's trial and the physical evidence and witness testimony.

The assertion that Goldblum owed Wilhelm a debt due to his role as the torch in the burning of his restaurant is unreasonable, unbelievable, and unsupported by the evidence. In fact, many of the individuals behind this theory have subsequently admitted to its glaring holes.

Charles Goldblum was convicted of murder based entirely on Clarence Miller's testimony, which manipulated the facts and was often contradicted by the evidence. Miller was a desperate man with a penchant for deceit enhanced by his confabulatory amnesia and other weaknesses, and the homicide detectives were more than willing to use this to their advantage.

If the investigators of Wilhelm's murder had followed the facts of the case and the trail of evidence, Goldblum still would have served a reasonable sentence for his wrongdoings. Justice would have more properly been served on the party who actually committed his murder.

That guilty party was Clarence Miller.

The Prosecution and Trial

Edward "Ted" Fagan, second Assistant District Attorney for Allegheny County, was initially in charge of prosecuting the Wilhelm murder case.

However, Fagan was nearing retirement and hesitant to take on the burden of a lengthy trial. Recognizing the Goldblum trial would be an exhaustive and complicated proceeding spanning many weeks, involving evening and weekend sessions, interviewing numerous witnesses, and untangling an intricate and complicated series of connected crimes, Fagan withdrew as lead prosecutor a few months before the trial began.

Fagan was the more experienced and senior member of the District Attorney's office, and he had worked closely with the detectives involved in investigating the case.

While Assistant District Attorney F. Peter Dixon had been involved in preliminary trial preparations alongside Fagan, he did not take over as lead prosecutor until 3 or 4 months before the trial began.

After graduating from Duquesne University School of Law and passing the Pennsylvania bar examination, Dixon began his career in the private sector, practicing civil law with his three uncles in Pittsburgh. He married, had two children, settled in the Pittsburgh suburb of Bethel Park, and pursued a career in the family firm.

Yet Dixon found private practice to be a prolonged grind and came to believe his true talents were under appreciated and underused.

Many years later, during a recorded interview with Jim Ramsey, who was investigating the Goldblum case, Dixon described the experience:

"What I discovered over that time was that while these men were outstanding trial lawyers, the practice we had was kind of everything. You have an accident case, that's fine. Estates, wills, you know, wills, everything. We handled anything. So, I'm the new guy, right...What it meant was, that I did all the groundwork and legal research and all the things that involved no court appearances.

Now, after some years of that, I was very unhappy and I did get to try a few cases, but... This was not my idea of a very glamorous lawyer, uh, so, what can I do? I'm, I'm the heir apparent. I have to carry on the tradition and so, all of my other uncles are retiring and so, I kind of felt obligated... I felt trapped in it and so, I asked God, Lord, do you want me here and, if so, you know, make me satisfied with the work or do something? Where do you want me to go?"

Dixon worked at the family firm with these nagging thoughts at the back of his mind until 1974, when he felt the urge to explore a career in the District Attorney's office. According to Dixon:

"...This is in the era where all the guys and women who were hired by the DA are political friends and these are rewards for political assistance in him getting elected... so there is no such thing as going and applying at the DA for a job. That's ridiculous. No one has ever done that, and I kept explaining that to God, and he kept telling me to go anyway."

During his interview with Ramsey, Dixon recounted that the DA at the time, Robert Dugan, had recently committed suicide and had been replaced by Jack Hickton, a fellow graduate of Duquesne University whom he knew. He went to the Court House and called on Hickton, then acting District Attorney. In a brief interview with Hickton, Dixon learned that an experienced trial lawyer had recently dropped out, and the DA was seeking a qualified replacement.

Hickton decided Dixon fit the bill and hired him as an Assistant District Attorney. Eventually, Hickton ran for District Attorney and was defeated by Robert Colville, who kept Dixon on.

Like most new Assistant District Attorneys, Dixon went to the Public Safety Building in Pittsburgh for preliminary hearings. That was where he would learn part of his prosecutorial trade. Dixon worked in Crimes against Persons and other sections before landing in the Homicide Section of the District Attorney's Office.

Based on his experience as a trial lawyer, Dixon was given the responsibility of serious cases straight away. After his first trial, involving an involuntary death in a traffic accident, Dixon's opponent, a veteran defense attorney, praised his capabilities by sending a letter of praise to Hickton. During his interview with Ramsey, Dixon recalled the experience fondly:

"Unbeknownst to me, he writes a letter to Jack Hickton, the D.A. and he says this guy is a good trial lawyer. He should be trying every murder case. So, the next thing I know, I'm getting heavy murder cases, two murder cases a month. No matter what, you know, and that worked out pretty well. So, I guess over the seven years I was there I tried maybe 150 murder cases, more or less. They weren't all jury trials, but most were, because of the nature of them and, and, I thought to myself, 'This is where I belong.' When I tried a case, to me, I had found my home…"

Dixon worked as a prosecutor for about seven years before he resigned and returned to his family's practice. During his time as Assistant District Attorney, Dixon earned a reputation as a talented and effective litigator.

During his interviews with Ramsey, Dixon admitted that after returning to the private sector, he lost his way and his world began to crumble. This loss of purpose and the relentless minutiae of work in the private sector took its toll. Eventually the tediousness and pointlessness of daily office life got to him. He began to experience depression and, to cope, he began drinking. As Dixon described the experience:

"And, so I thought, well maybe, maybe now it can work. Well, it didn't. I was depressed very soon. I not only missed what I used to do, but I hated what I was doing. Now even though everyone that I worked with was outstanding and I loved them, it was the work that I hated: the nature of the work; the paperwork; the endless answering of interrogatories… So I kept on trying and trying and trying and, and I was still not drinking, but I was getting more and more depressed. So within a couple of years, of course, I started to drink again…So, I'm hating now, myself. How stupid I was to leave a job I loved. So now, the hatred turned inward is the definition of depression. So, I'm taking this hatred on myself, hating myself, hating my work, and so, I'm medicating all of this sadness and hatred with alcohol."

A sense of purpose and achievement is recognized as one of the most essential elements of human existence. In leaving the District Attorney's office, Dixon lost this and, in doing so, lost himself to self-loathing and alcohol abuse. He struggled on in this state until personal agony led him to check into a hotel with the intention of committing suicide on what Dixon described to Jim Ramsey as, "...a beautiful, sunny afternoon, September 23, 1996."

As Dixon sat on the bed of a motel room, prepared and fully committed to taking his own life, he described being overcome by an impulse to call his doctor, a therapist who tried to help him through these dark times.

Dixon misdialed and was put through to a random office in the UPMC Health System. When he asked to speak to his therapist, he was told by the receptionist that he had just happened to walk past her office. Putting Dixon on hold, she ran after the doctor, and returned him to her office. He kept Dixon on the line until the police could respond to this attempt at suicide and transport him to the Western Psychiatric Institute.

To Dixon, this coincidence was too much and, as he said during his interview, "Right then, I knew that I was experiencing a miracle from God. It was not an accident that I dialed the wrong number."

The experience was enough to inspire Dixon to continue living and to get the help he needed. After entering a recovery program, rediscovering religion, and regaining control of himself, Dixon was a changed man.

Though, in light of him viewing his years at the District Attorney's office as the most meaningful and accomplished of his life, it is difficult for Dixon to examine his role in the Goldblum trial objectively, particularly considering his description of the case as, "...probably the most important case in the time I was in the DA's office."

While Dixon lays claim to strong principles and an innate desire to do the right thing, conflicts between his moral standards and his ego arise, particularly when discussing this case. Dixon attaches a strong sense of pride to his time at the District Attorney's office and the convictions he secured.

The Goldblum case in particular, which garnered much attention from the Pittsburgh newspapers and television, generated a reluctance in Dixon to confront the fact that he played a role in securing a life sentence for a murder of which one defendant was innocent. Honest, objective analysis of his theory of the case was hard for him, and the possibility that his prosecution was ethically unsound was extremely difficult for him to confront.

Dixon honestly admitted to the suspect nature of the prosecution against Goldblum, specifically in 1996, when he wrote an affidavit on Goldblum's behalf and in 1999, when he testified at a 1999 Board of Pardons hearing, recommending that Goldblum be released.

Ultimately, however, Dixon backtracked and redacted his statement supporting Goldblum's innocence. The motivations behind these reactions were no doubt nuanced, but, as detailed below, the shift in Dixon's views was abrupt and contradictory.

While well intentioned, Dixon remained conflicted about this case.

In his interviews with Jim Ramsey, he elaborated extensively on the importance of his religious values in his personal ethos. He delved into the importance of a moral individual recognizing his own flaws and mistakes so that he might correct them.

While such sentiment is admirable, it does not appear that he applied these principles to Goldblum's prosecution. Although when he was contacted to review Goldblum's case by Goldblum's defense team in 1996, Dixon's principled side initially rose to the forefront regarding the skewed and flawed prosecution. At the Board of Pardons hearing, he spoke on Goldblum's behalf and spoke thoroughly and scathingly against the prosecution's theory and handling of the case.

Yet after this hearing, he underwent a sudden and unexplained change of heart. Following a tense meeting with Goldblum and his defense attorney, and a subsequent antagonistic telephone conversation with Goldblum, Dixon seemingly decided to dismiss the essential morality of his principles.

He began to justify the glaring flaws and gaping holes in Goldblum's murder conviction with equivocations and limp legal justifications. Dixon now claims that Goldblum may have been guilty of the homicide, but did not receive a fair trial because Thaddeus Dedo, a key witness and conspirator in the land fraud, was not granted immunity to testify at Goldblum's trial.

At the time of Goldblum's trial, Dixon had to work with evidence the police investigators gave him, including the contradictory and constantly evolving testimony of his star witness, Clarence Miller.

Although Dixon may have been brought into the case a few months into the investigation, in preparation for the trial, he had access to all of the physical evidence against Goldblum, or, more accurately the lack thereof, as well as the glaring inconsistencies of Miller's statements.

These statements evolved every time new evidence was uncovered that conflicted with Miller's story. He always worked to paint Goldblum as a criminal mastermind intent on murdering Wilhelm.

In his preparation for the trial, Dixon certainly had adequate time to familiarize himself with the obvious inconsistencies in Miller's account of the killing, as well as the wealth of physical evidence that pointed to Miller being Wilhelm's killer.

On the other hand, Detective Ron Freeman worked the Wilhelm murder case from the beginning and spent a lot of time with Miller.

While Freeman had no problem engaging in dubious investigative tactics in the name of a conviction, Dixon wanted at some level to be honest.

While Dixon did things that crossed the line, he was not as blatant about it as Freeman. Dixon's denial of wrongdoing exists through his justification of positions unsupported by the facts. These illogical rationalizations allowed him to summarily dismiss all who disagreed with him.

Dixon's culpability for Goldblum's wrongful murder conviction came into play at several key points during the trial.

One was his failure to notify the defense of Miller's diagnosis of confabulatory amnesia, a neurological disorder in which the sufferer involuntarily produces fabricated, distorted, or misinterpreted memories about oneself or the world. This diagnosis did not come to light until Miller went to trial nine months after Goldblum had been convicted.

Aside from Miller's obvious motive to manipulate the situation to his advantage and falsely testify against Goldblum, Dixon admitted to recognizing, even at the time of trial, the ever-changing, conflicting, and false nature of Miller's testimony.

When questioned during a March 8, 2007 deposition by Goldblum's attorney, Lee Markovitz, on the extent to which Dixon had vetted Miller as a witness, Dixon recognized the true nature of Miller's testimony, saying:

"But the other thing is - that entered into this was that I could see from already the multiple statements that Clarence Miller had given, various versions and everything that, that his - it was in his best interest and the best interests of the Commonwealth if I gave him a basis to tell the truth."

How did Dixon discern what the truth was? He admitted to noticing the flaws, holes, and conflicts in Miller's many disparate statements to the police. Yet, rather than being principled and digging into the veracity of Miller's statements, Dixon decided to work with him and give Miller "…a basis to tell the truth."

To an outsider, after reviewing the glaring inconsistencies between Miller's recorded statements to the police, his testimony at the pre-trial hearings, and his testimony at trial, it appears that Dixon was really giving Miller the opportunity to iron out the kinks in his obviously false testimony against Goldblum in an attempt to solidify the Commonwealth's case.

After ultimately backtracking on his testimony at the Board of Pardons hearing, Dixon maintained that presenting the conflicting, obviously false testimony of Clarence Miller at trial was justified.

During the same March 8, 2007 deposition, Lee Markovitz confronted the issue head-on, asking Dixon: "And you have all of this physical evidence in the case that - and combined with the dying declaration, that seems to point toward Miller and away from Goldblum?"

In the face of this question, Dixon equivocated and washed his hands of responsibility. He claimed he was not culpable for presenting Miller's lies at trial because he had qualified Miller's testimony with the jury, replying:

"No, I don't agree with that...And the - the way that I saw the case was that my job was to take everything that I had, Clarence Miller with all of his liabilities, and every other aspect of independent corroborative evidence, present it to the jury, and then it's their job to decide what, if anything, to believe that Clarence Miller says and the same with any other witness. That's the jury's job. It's not my job to - to be a juror or a judge with any witness, no matter who he is. I don't decide the case."

If, as Dixon frequently claims in his interviews and deposition, he truly was a man of principle, should he not have had a dedication to the truth? This is especially important when dealing with a capital murder prosecution that would ultimately put a man in jail for the rest of his life.

It must also be pointed out that the law simply does not support Dixon's view of his role in the process. Attorneys in any proceeding, no matter what side they are on, are not permitted to present testimony they know to be false, especially not criminal prosecutors. In one breath, Dixon claimed to be a man of strong ethical values. In the next, he rationalized that he did nothing wrong under the standards of the system.

In a less abstract vein, it must be questioned the extent to which Dixon was justifying unethical behavior and was, at the time of trial, merely going along to get along.

In this statement, Dixon turned a blind eye to his own responsibility in securing Goldblum's conviction by allowing a witness to present false testimony. He also recognized that Miller's testimony needed qualification in order to feel justified in presenting it.

If Dixon truly believed Miller's testimony to be true, why would he not present the evidence which solidified it, rather than raising his hands and offering the lame excuse that it was "not my job" to vet a witness and ensure that the truth was being presented in court?

If a district attorney, as representative of the full power of law and justice, knows or suspects that a witness is lying, it is an ethical responsibility to step forward and prevent such testimony from being presented. At some level, Dixon knew that.

Unless ignorant by way of negligence, the prosecution knew of the brain injury suffered by their star witness and of his tendency towards constant lying. The prosecution should have called for a sidebar to explain that Miller perjured himself when he denied under oath that there was anything that could potentially interfere with his ability to testify truthfully.

Anticipating Miller's subsequent homicide trial in 1978, two separate experts conducted examinations and noted that Miller had been struck by a trolley car as a child, and that this accident resulted in brain trauma which influenced his mental development. These examinations were conducted by Dr. James R. Merikangas on April 28 and Dr. Arthur J. Van Cara on May 3.

In his report, Dr. Van Cara noted: "As a child, Mr. Miller reports having sustained a closed head injury from being struck by a streetcar. He demonstrated a scar in the left front temporal region and a scar in parietal-occipital area. He recalls nothing of the accident, though reportedly was out of school for two months during which period his vision remained blurred."

Miller was treated for these injuries at Washington Hospital in Washington, Pa., and the records of this treatment were accessible by the Commonwealth. While being cross-examined at Goldblum's trial, Miller lied to the defense attorney and denied having ever been hospitalized. If Dixon was aware of Miller's condition or hospitalization at the time of trial, he was required to notify the court and defense counsel.

Additionally, in a prior examination by a Dr. Merikangas, Miller's head injury and brain trauma were noted. More disturbing, his report also recorded that: "[Miller] said that he would have told the police anything to get out of the situation. They told him if he confessed, he would be allowed to go home. He claims he doesn't remember what he told them and that he fainted afterwards...It is clear that he has facility for lying, and I don't know much of anything he told me is reliable and believable."

If the Commonwealth had done its due diligence in vetting its key witness in an important murder prosecution, such facts related to a key witness's mental competence should have been recorded. The options are either a negligent and inadequate vetting of Miller, or, more disturbingly, a withholding of such diagnoses.

An honest and objective prosecutor would have prioritized the truth over securing a conviction. If the prosecutor was aware of Miller's diagnosis, he had a clear obligation to inform Goldblum's defense counsel H. David Rothman and the court, particularly when the issue had been raised directly by Rothman during cross examination.

When Rothman asked Miller if he had ever suffered any injury in the past that would interfere with his ability to present testimony, Miller perjured himself by claiming he did not. If Dixon was aware of Miller's condition and chose not to alert the court to Miller's perjury, his conduct was indefensible and he deceived the court. Surely, the District Attorney knew Miller had mental issues based on his reading of the Southside Hospital's brain tests and the Allegheny County Behavioral Clinic Psychological reports on Miller, dated February 16, 17, 24, and 25,1976.

Miller frequently perjured himself during his testimony, and the prosecution consistently permitted him to mislead the jury. As a result, Goldblum did not receive a fair trial.

There is a vast difference between a brief explanation of an individual's attempt to deceive or manipulate the facts compared with the testimony of an expert at trial, explaining Miller's brain injury, exactly what confabulatory amnesia is, and how it affects an individual's ability to recall events. Dixon was and continued to be invested in the lies told by Miller.

No conspiracy between Goldblum and Miller to murder Wilhelm can be proven unless Miller's twisted contentions of the truth are relied upon exclusively.

Dixon claimed that he was unaware of the confabulation diagnosis at Goldblum's trial. Additionally, he states that even if he was aware of the diagnosis, it would have been irrelevant.

In his mind, his warning to the jury of Miller's dishonest nature, supplemented by his belief that there was a conspiracy between Goldblum and Miller, made the withholding of this diagnosis inconsequential.

During the same 2007 deposition conducted by attorney Markovitz, Dixon claimed to have properly explained to the jury to Miller's penchant for dishonesty, thus appropriately qualifying his testimony.

In this deposition, Dixon claimed that, "...in this particular case I spent considerable time vilifying Clarence Miller to the jury..." Yet a review of Dixon's opening statement reveals that he only very briefly touched on Miller's near-constant lying and the many versions his statement against Goldblum went through before it adequately matched up with the progression of events to secure his conviction.

The record shows that Dixon's qualification of Miller's testimony in his opening statement consisted merely of recognizing that the witness lied during his initial police interview and that he continued to distort events to his benefit.

Ultimately, Dixon appears to assert that Miller's account is the true one. As quoted from the August 1977 trial transcript, Dixon told the jury that during the police investigation:

"Clarence Miller begins now with the renewed interrogation - although not all at once - he still tries to cover up and distort, but the story begins to come out bit by bit - the story comes out from Clarence Miller that what really happened that night is as I have outlined it to you."

By stating that Miller tried to "cover up and distort," Dixon seemed to think he appropriately qualified the testimony to the jury, and thus absolved himself from all culpability in presenting patently false testimony to a jury during a homicide trial.

In an objective review of this case, a one-sentence recognition of Miller's distortion of the truth and covering up of his own involvement and obvious guilt does not constitute a "considerable time vilifying Clarence Miller."

Additionally, in the conclusion of his qualifying statement, Dixon claimed that Miller ultimately outlined "what really happened that night." This can only mean that Dixon claimed Miller's testimony should be believed as truth. He was an experienced and capable litigator. He knew where the ethical lines were, and it is hard to imagine that he didn't sense the contradiction built into his position.

During Goldblum's 1999 Board of Pardons hearing, Dixon ultimately recognized these facts, detailing them to the members of the Pardon Board.

In the opening moments of his testimony, Dixon recounted how he came to be involved once again in Goldblum's homicide conviction, only this time, on the other side of the aisle. Dixon told the Board:

"I lived with this case for months, and recently when I was called in for a deposition by defense counsel in an ancillary matter in this case, he asked if I would review the transcript over the years, looking at the whole case from this perspective as to whether there was any injustice, whether there was any irregularity, whether there was anything in the trial of this case that indicated that there was an unfair result.

I had very little hope, feeling, or expectation that I would find any such, but I had declared to counsel that I had always conducted myself in the hundred or so murder trials that I prosecuted over seven years that if I found such, I would let it be known. I have dismissed murder charges in the past when I found that to be necessary for what is wise and just. And, when I agreed to review the transcript, he said, fine, and he hands me a box with 18 volumes and 5,000 pages...That is an idea though of the magnitude of this case. And what I have found in that review are as follows. Number one, I am convinced that Charles Goldblum did not participate in any active way in the murder of George Wilhelm."

In his statement, Dixon admitted that he skeptically and reluctantly agreed to undertake a review of the case, and this review led him to unmistakably conclude that Goldblum was not responsible for Wilhelm's murder.

When asked by the Board of Pardons to explain the reasoning behind this bold claim, made by the prosecuting DA after an extensive review of the trial transcript and investigative materials, Dixon delved into the prosecution's theory as a series of causal events, beginning with the land fraud, exactly as it was presented at the time of trial.

During Goldblum's trial, Dixon painted a picture of an elaborate criminal conspiracy for the jury. At its center, Goldblum was the orchestrator behind the land fraud that bilked Wilhelm out of thousands of dollars.

At Goldblum's trial, Dixon contended that once the fraud came to light, Wilhelm demanded repayment. That led Goldblum to burn down his restaurant, supposedly using Wilhelm to strike the match. Then, finally, when Goldblum did not collect on the insurance and could not pay his debts, the prosecution claimed Goldblum arranged for Wilhelm's murder.

Yet at this Board of Pardons hearing, after an extensive review of "18 volumes and 5,000 pages," Dixon, finally confronted with the truth behind this catastrophe of justice, admitted:

"[Goldblum] did not participate in the land fraud...he had no motive. And he had nothing to gain from the murder of George Wilhelm. And that is tied into the conclusion that I drew that he had no motive. He had nothing to gain because he was not involved in the land fraud...He has no motive and nothing to benefit."

Dixon would go on to detail Goldblum's complete lack of involvement in the land fraud, and thus eliminate any motive for Goldblum to harm Wilhelm.

He explained that no witness, other than Miller, ever put Goldblum at the meetings in Pittsburgh, Washington, PA, or Washington D.C. that occurred in furtherance of the land fraud.

He noted that Goldblum had never been mentioned in the FBI's files concerning the fraud, and that it was Dedo's and Miller's prints that were found on the fraudulent land deeds.

Additionally, he noted that Goldblum received a large settlement offer from the insurance company for the fire at his restaurant, yet turned down the money which could have paid the supposed debt to Wilhelm which provided the alleged motivation behind the murder. Dixon testified before the Board:

"If Charles Goldblum was desperate for money because he was involved in the land fraud, so desperate that he was going to burn down his restaurant and murder a man, wouldn't he have said, thank God, I'll take the $40,000? Here, Wilhelm, is your money, the matter is over. You see it doesn't fit. It doesn't fit."

Ultimately, Dixon recognized that the entire theory behind Goldblum's guilt relied exclusively on the testimony of Clarence Miller. He concluded dismantling the Commonwealth's case by stating:

"He doesn't have a motive once the land fraud falls. Don't you see it's a house of cards? Without the land fraud, if Charles Goldblum is not involved in cheating the victim in this case, he has no motive to murder the man."

Years later, after the falling-out between Dixon and Goldblum and Dixon's subsequent change of heart regarding Goldblum's guilt, Dixon attended the previously mentioned March 8, 2007 deposition.

While unwilling to discuss Miller's testimony and its truth, or lack thereof, Dixon was willing to offer insight into the denial of Use Immunity to Thaddeus Dedo.

Dedo, through his attorney, had come forward during Goldblum's trial and offered to testify that Goldblum had no role in the land fraud. This would have also removed the basis for Goldblum's alleged motive to kill Wilhelm and contradicted the testimony of the prosecution's star witness. Dixon stated during the deposition that this would have strongly damaged the prosecution's case.

During Goldblum's trial, Dedo's attorney approached H. David Rothman, Goldblum's defense attorney, and offered Dedo's testimony, provided his client was granted Use Immunity for his upcoming trial for the land fraud.

Dixon was then advised of the proffer, as was the Court. Dedo would have testified that Goldblum was not involved in the land fraud, but not wanting to make statements that would be used to convict him in a later trial, Dedo insisted that he would testify only if granted Use Immunity and his testimony sealed.

While this would not have prevented the Commonwealth from trying Dedo for the land fraud crime, it would have prohibited the Commonwealth from using his testimony against him at his own trial. Use Immunity was denied, so Dedo did not testify.

Dixon still felt strongly that because Dedo did not testify, Goldblum did not receive a fair trial. He told Ramsey that this issue remains so important that all the other problems behind Goldblum's conviction are irrelevant.

Dixon places the blame for this oversight firmly and unjustifiably on the presiding judge Donald Ziegler. In reality, Dixon was responsible for Dedo not testifying as he was the only party who had the authority to request Use Immunity. Dixon should have had the courage to step forward and request immunity for Dedo so that Goldblum could receive a fair trial.

According to Dixon, Dedo's attorney met in chambers with Judge Ziegler to discuss whether Dedo would receive immunity. Dixon contended it was Judge Ziegler's responsibility to use the King's Bench Power to grant Dedo immunity if his testimony was important enough to the case.

The King's Bench Power, in this context, is the supervisory power of a judge to compel officers of the court to perform duties required of them by law that they object to performing. Based on statutes carried over from British law during the colonial period, King's Bench Power is invoked only under the rarest and most specific circumstances in which officers of the court are in blatant violation of legal procedure.

In this case, the duty would be to present the exculpatory testimony of Dedo to ensure Goldblum due process and a fair and balanced trial.

When Judge Ziegler refused to grant Dedo immunity under the King's Bench power, Dixon arguably could have requested immunity. If he sincerely prioritized truth and justice over securing a conviction, he would have made the request. Dixon uses the excuse that nobody specifically requested that he issue Use Immunity to Dedo. He claims that if he had been asked, he may have granted the immunity.

The court record shows Goldblum's defense attorney H. David Rothman, Dixon, and Judge Ziegler debating this issue on the record. Rothman opened the issue at sidebar during Miller's cross-examination by pleading to Judge Ziegler as to the necessity of Dedo's testimony, saying:

"Your Honor, I want to make this request. The immunity statute in Pennsylvania, which Mr. Dixon and I have just gone through maybe three weeks ago before Judge Schwartz in the Shoemaker-Todd case. It was a case in which the Commonwealth has, as the statute allows, sought immunity as to a particular witness's testimony. There is no similar provision in the law that allows the defense to seek the immunity of a particular person so that the defense can get the benefit of the particular testimony. In that regard the statute is patently unconstitutional in denying the defense the protection of the law because immunity may work to the benefit of the defense."

Seeking a legal basis for allowing Dedo to testify, Judge Ziegler asked, "Has this been litigated in Federal Court?"

Rothman was forced to confess that, "No, it has not been litigated anywhere."

Later in the discussion, Judge Ziegler sought to know if Dedo was, indeed, willing to testify specifically that Goldblum was not involved in the fraud. In doing so, Dedo would also offer testimony that could incriminate himself. At the time of Goldblum's trial, Dedo was under indictment for the land fraud. Judge Ziegler, for the purpose of clarification, put to Rothman, "The witness represented to the Court that he was going to testify."

To which Rothman responded, "To my knowledge, Mr. Dedo, who has counsel here, will not testify under his privilege to remain silent. If he got immunity, he would testify and I believe..."

At this point Rothman was interrupted by Dixon, who asked what basis Rothman had for this representation.

Rothman replied that Dedo's counsel had indicated Dedo's testimony would be helpful to Goldblum if he could testify. After a brief back and forth between Dixon and Rothman, Judge Ziegler intervened and asked Rothman to clarify his request.

To which Rothman replied:

"I feel that in this case, Mr. Dedo's testimony could be taken and sealed and not used against Mr. Dedo and still give Mr. Goldblum the benefit of that testimony. And if the Court doesn't have the power to do it, then the defendant is deprived of his right to summon witness..."

The judge had no authority to compel Dedo to testify under the King's Bench power. The next day, before Miller's cross-examination resumed, Judge Ziegler ruled on Rothman's request, stating:

"I would like to put on the record that the Court has discussed the testimony of Thaddeus Dedo with his counsel, and I have been advised by his lawyer that he does not intend to testify, that he intends to invoke the privilege under self-incrimination under the

United States and Pennsylvania constitutions... Mr. Rothman has asked the Court to request Mr. Dedo to testify and seal his testimony and prevent the Commonwealth from using it in a criminal case against him. The Court is unaware of any statutory, constitutional, or common law power which would permit the Court to compel Mr. Dedo to testify when he is invoking his privileges, and the immunity statute of Pennsylvania clearly does not apply to this situation."

Judge Ziegler correctly ruled that he could not grant immunity on his own. It could only be granted if the Commonwealth made the request, which Dixon did not volunteer to do.

During Dixon's statement at the Goldblum's 1999 Board of Pardons hearing, he addressed this issue directly, stating:

"...not only did [Goldblum] not have any motive or nothing to gain from the murder, but he also did not receive a fair trial. And the reason that he did not receive a fair trial was that he begged the court, through his counsel, on the record, please let me call Thaddeus D[e]do. He's the only person in the world that knows Goldblum didn't have anything to do with the land fraud. D[e]do was the only person he had to call. The key witness...And I say you this, and I mean it with all of my heart, if Mr. Goldblum had the opportunity to call Mr. D[e]do and Mr. D[e]do would have said, Clarence Miller is a liar. He was never involved in the land fraud, the jury verdict would have been different. That's why I'm here."

If Dixon felt as strongly about this issue as his recorded statement at the clemency hearing suggests, then why did he not use the authority of the Commonwealth to seal Dedo's testimony and give him the opportunity to testify?

As detailed in Judge Ziegler's ruling, the Court did not have any authority to compel such Use Immunity. The ethical and legal imperative fell squarely on Dixon's shoulders. While Dixon has maintained that no one expressly and directly asked him to request use immunity, he was present when Rothman asked the court to grant immunity and heard Judge Ziegler's response.

The record of that conversation has Rothman pleading that Dedo's testimony be sealed and his story be heard, saying:

"The request here is for the Court to confer with Mr. Dedo and his counsel, and particularly his counsel, so Mr. Dedo might be made available as a witness in this proceeding and that his testimony be sealed, that it not be used against Mr. Dedo in any other proceeding so that Mr. Goldblum has the benefit of his constitutional right to summon witnesses on his own behalf, and the one-sidedness of the immunity statute deprives Mr. Goldblum of that opportunity. To my knowledge the Commonwealth has not cited immunity for Mr. Dedo."

In response, Dixon simply stated, "No."

In his 2007 deposition, Dixon, having drastically shifted his stance on Goldblum's innocence, was asked by Goldblum's then counsel, Lee Markovitz, why Dedo was not granted the opportunity to testify. Dixon responded: "The only thing that was said to me was has Mr. Dedo been granted immunity...To which I responded no. We didn't grant him immunity."

This flimsy and arbitrary distinction only attempts to justify his inaction. If Dixon truly adhered to his principles, if as a representative of the prosecutorial powers of the Commonwealth, he was honestly seeking the truth behind a crime rather than gunning for a conviction because it was possible, he would have requested immunity and, in doing so, provided Goldblum a fair trial.

Dixon obviously regarded Dedo's testimony as detrimental to his case. Had Dedo testified that Charles Goldblum was not part of the land fraud, then the jury would not find motive for Goldblum to kill George Wilhelm.

As previously noted, Dedo's testimony would have had a "house of cards" effect on the Commonwealth's entire case against Goldblum, as admitted to by Dixon. Had Dedo testified, a series of cause-and-effect breakdowns would have led to the discrediting of the prosecution's theory of Goldblum's guilt. Whether intentionally or not, in not granting Dedo immunity for his testimony, Dixon contributed to the unfair trial and false conviction of Goldblum for murder.

It must be recognized that Judge Ziegler had no legal basis for invoking King's Bench power and was not in a position to grant immunity. While the immunity statute in effect at that time required a request by the Commonwealth, it was restricted to organized crime cases only.

It is hard to imagine that Dixon was not aware of this. In his deposition, Dixon attempted to use Dedo's testimony as a red herring that carries no legal impact and amounts to nothing more than a distraction from the fundamental problems with Goldblum's prosecution and eventual conviction.

Furthermore, shortly after Goldblum's trial concluded, the land fraud charges against Miller, Dedo, and Orlowsky were dismissed under the speedy trial rule, or Rule 1100, after the District Attorney's office allowed the deadlines for prosecution to elapse. After this dismissal, Dedo refused to talk to Goldblum's attorneys or investigators, even though he was no longer under risk of being prosecuted.

During these refusals to cooperate, Dedo expressed a fear of Detective Ronald Freeman. Investigator Ramsey believes that Dixon intentionally allowed the speedy trial rule time to lapse because he did not want Dedo's testimony to come out.

At the time, had the fact that Goldblum never participated in the land fraud conspiracy been made public, in all likelihood Goldblum would have been awarded a new trial based on after-discovered evidence. The prosecution's easy way out was to allow Rule 1100 to come into play and later go through the exercise of appealing Judge Ziegler's decision, knowing the appeal would not prevail.

Dedo has since passed away, and his truthful testimony is forever lost.

This was not a simple oversight. Prosecutors are always careful about observing the time remaining to bring a criminal defendant to trial. It was not a minor detail. The District Attorney's office appealed Judge Ziegler's dismissal of the land fraud charges against Dedo and Orlowsky, however the fact that an appeal was taken is not dispositive. Once the time expired, there was little chance the Superior Court would reverse the decision.

It is curious the level to which Dixon later became preoccupied with this specific issue. He stated that the forensic evidence, Miller's confabulation and false testimony, and the potentially dishonest and unethical investigation, are all a waste of time.

That Dixon wanted to pursue this time issue to the exclusion of all others must be considered in conjunction with the fact that the time under the speedy trial rule expired and that Dedo later refused to communicate.

While this may all be another coincidence, so many unusual coincidences in one case is highly unlikely.

Dixon felt Dedo's inability to testify on Goldblum's behalf was the most important issue in the case, and he claimed frustration that Goldblum's lawyers never pursued it. Dixon referred to two cases in support of his claims, *Virgin Islands v. Smith* and *United States v. Straub*.

Nearly all the favorable cases on this issue involved federal prosecutions where immunity was granted to prosecution witnesses but not to defense witnesses who could contradict the testimony of the immunized prosecution witness. In the overwhelming majority of appeals court decisions, this claim has consistently failed. The two cases cited by Dixon represent a small minority position.

The decisions in the Pennsylvania courts are not favorable. In *Commonwealth v. Johnson* and *Commonwealth v. Hall,* the court denied the claim. In almost all situations, courts do not want to grant Use Immunity unless it is requested by the prosecutor. Between this and the fact that Dedo has passed away, this issue offers little or no hope for resolution.

It must be asked why Dixon would insist that the sole legal issue on which Goldblum's defense teams should have been focusing has proven to be little more than a waste of time.

Aside from shifting any burden of blame for Goldblum's wrongful conviction away from himself, Dixon's insistence that the lack of Dedo's testimony is the sole issue of Goldblum's unjust trial is disturbing as it does not, legally speaking, carry water.

Dixon appeared determined to shift the blame for Goldblum's wrongful conviction away from himself and his willingness to present the obviously false testimony of Clarence Miller, and onto the Dedo issue, despite it being, both legally and literally, a dead-end. The unwillingness of Goldblum and his defense team to concentrate on this is a key reason for the eventual falling-out between Goldblum and Dixon.

No reason, other than Dedo's fear of Freeman, was ever given for his refusal to communicate with Goldblum's investigator once he was free from the possibility of criminal conviction for the land fraud.

Why would he offer to help during Goldblum's trial only under the protection of Use Immunity, then refuse to testify when it was no longer any risk for him to do so?

Dedo's about-face is troubling. He initially displayed a strong willingness to testify by coming forward without even being asked. Coupled with his subsequent refusal to help once he was out of jeopardy, this strongly suggests that something else was influencing his decision.

After escaping prosecution for the land fraud, Dedo simply wanted nothing more to do with testifying.

This is hard to accept for two reasons. First, because of all the other suspicious anomalies in this case, and second, because there was no selfish motivation for Dedo to come forward in the first place. The most protection Dedo could have received for testimony at Goldblum's trial was Use Immunity. Had he testified at Goldblum's trial, it would have limited his ability to testify at his own trial later.

In the absence of any other credible explanation or other evidence, the most likely reason for Dedo's subsequent silence was his explicitly expressed fear of Detective Ronald Freeman. Goldblum's attorneys failed later to pursue this issue. After the land fraud charges were dismissed, they could have asked the courts to compel Dedo to testify. Goldblum's change of attorneys following his conviction explains this possible failure.

We gain insight into the potential basis for Dedo's fear through a recollection of Goldblum's mother that Detective Freeman tried to coerce her son into testifying falsely that Dedo had been involved in Wilhelm's murder.

After Goldblum's conviction, Freeman arranged a meeting at the police station with Goldblum and his parents. As the family sat taking what little comfort they could in each other's presence, Freeman entered the room. He pressured Goldblum to testify against Dedo and Orlowsky, implying that if he was willing to testify and implicate them as being tangentially involved in Wilhelm's murder, then he might have his sentence reduced.

This recollection is not an accusation manufactured by Goldblum, but a memory vividly recalled by his mother, Evelyn Goldblum.

It became apparent through Freeman's aggressive and manipulative pursuit of Goldblum's conviction, that he was seeking to extract as much clout as possible from Wilhelm's murder. This, coupled with Dedo's expressed fear of Freeman and Freeman's attempt to solicit Goldblum's false testimony against Dedo, provide a likely explanation for Dedo's subsequent unwillingness to testify on Goldblum's behalf after the fraud charges were dropped.

Perhaps Dedo feared that if he stayed involved in the case, he could end up wrongfully prosecuted as Goldblum was for the crime.

It is also important to note that Goldblum's trial in general, and the issue of Dixon's refusal to grant immunity specifically, have bothered the presiding judge for many years.

Naturally the physical evidence, the stretches of logic, and the victim's dying declaration all contributed to Judge Donald Ziegler's feeling that this trial resulted in the conviction of a man for a crime he did not commit.

His conscience having been nagged by the case for decades, Judge Ziegler even wrote a series of letters to the Board of Pardons in support of Goldblum's claim of innocence during his 1989, 1994 and 1998 applications for clemency.

In these letters, Judge Ziegler emphasized the importance of George Wilhelm's dying declaration identifying Clarence Miller as his killer. He wrote that:

"...I have been troubled for years by the dying declaration of the victim: 'Clarence - Clarence Miller did this to me.' It is a moral and legal precept that a person is presumed to speak the truth when he is faced with death. The victim knew that he was dying, and he never mentioned the name of Charles Goldblum. In short, the murder conviction was based on the testimony of Miller and the jury's apparent dislike for Mr. Goldblum."

This quote touches upon one of the most fundamental arguments for Goldblum's innocence and the most confusing and unanswerable questions arising from this saga. If, in his dying breath, Wilhelm expressly identified his killer as Clarence Miller, then why was such an aggressive investigation and prosecution initiated against Charles Goldblum?

Additionally, Judge Ziegler succinctly quantifies the weakest and most condemnable aspects of the prosecution's case. He goes on to write:

"In my opinion, Mr. Miller's testimony was suspect and quite frankly, if I was the fact finder, I would have rejected as unpersuasive, much of the testimony of this individual."

Even the case's presiding judge was aware and doubtful of the prosecution's near total reliance on the ridiculous, self-contradicting, and untrustworthy nature of their star witness and his testimony.

As noted above, Dixon admitted years ago that Goldblum was not involved in the land fraud, even detailing the abundant evidence which supports this. Dixon has said he believes Goldblum could have been acquitted if Dedo convinced the jury that Goldblum was not involved in the land fraud.

Goldblum's lack of involvement in the land fraud is essential in analyzing whether or not the assault was, as Miller claimed, premeditated. If Goldblum did not defraud Wilhelm, and as previously established, Wilhelm had nothing to do with the arson, then there is no motive for Goldblum to have assaulted and murdered Wilhelm.

Without a motive, the idea of a conspiracy between Miller and Goldblum to injure or kill Wilhelm makes no sense; a fact admitted on record by Dixon himself at Goldblum's 1999 Board of Pardons hearing.

Premeditated murders are not planned unless there is something to be gained by the parties involved. If there was a planned murder, the only person with motive was Clarence Miller, the prosecution's key witness.

In addition to his statement at the 1999 Board of Pardons hearing, Dixon also drafted an affidavit asserting Goldblum's innocence. Dixon changed positions again, believing Goldblum was guilty, but that he did not receive a fair trial because Dedo was not given Use Immunity to testify.

Based on this, Dixon wanted to help Goldblum get a new trial, even though this issue had little chance for success. Dixon's strong urging to pursue this issue to the exclusion of all others remains questionable. For him to state without qualification that Goldblum was innocent, would have required admitting his role in a miscarriage of justice.

This would have been extremely difficult for him, especially in relation to a case he viewed as one of his life's greatest achievements. If Dixon accepts this case for what it really is, his major accomplishment becomes a painful personal failure and a great loss.

Dixon also harbored negative feelings for Goldblum, in part from the case itself. Additionally, Dixon and Attorney Lee Markovitz visited Goldblum before Dixon argued on Goldblum's behalf before the Board of Pardons in 1999.

This meeting did not go well.

When Goldblum called Dixon on the telephone after the Board of Pardons denied his appeal for clemency, Dixon hung up after a minute.

Goldblum then wrote a letter to Dixon, which went unanswered. Goldblum's criticisms of Dixon's testimony obviously offended Dixon. Dixon felt Goldblum should be contrite and appreciate his willingness to come to his aid, even if the desired result had not been achieved.

This conflict could explain Dixon's change of position from believing fully in Goldblum's innocence, to believing only that Goldblum did not receive a fair trial. Personal animosity should not factor into the decisions of ethical prosecutors. A prosecutor has a tremendous amount of discretionary power and only the evidence should dictate such conclusions.

It is not just Dixon's change of heart that is particularly troubling. It is also the facts he overlooked to come to his conclusions.

Dixon was uncertain if Goldblum participated in the fraud and never believed Wilhelm was the arsonist. In recognizing this, he also recognized Goldblum had no motive to murder Wilhelm. Yet Dixon still maintained his belief Goldblum could have been guilty of premeditated murder.

Dixon prosecuted too many murder cases to not see that lack of motive is highly problematic. In his 2007 video deposition, Dixon was asked to consider Goldblum and Miller's disparate accounts of what happened on the parking garage roof that evening, keeping in mind the forensic evidence, the dying declaration of Wilhelm, and Goldblum's lack of motive.

Dixon dismissed the consideration as irrelevant because of the conspiracy that had been established by Miller's testimony. Despite his previous recognition of the many glaring gaps in the prosecution's theory of Goldblum and Miller's alleged conspiracy, following his inexplicable change of heart, Dixon said:

"So what I kept telling the jury was: This is the case. You have the conspiracy to do a criminal act. It gets out of hand so blood spatter means nothing. Who did what means nothing. As long as the conspiracy is ongoing, they're both guilty of murder of the first degree."

The problem with this argument is, there was no conspiracy.

Despite the evidence contradicting Miller's account, the dying declaration of the victim naming Clarence Miller, and Goldblum's lack of motive, Dixon still claimed to believe that Miller and Goldblum conspired to assault Wilhelm.

He then claimed that, under Pennsylvania law, it does not matter which of the two physically stabbed Wilhelm. Due to the alleged existence of a conspiracy between the two to lure Wilhelm to the garage, Dixon believes they were accomplices and equally guilty of the murder.

When pressed on the disparities and illogical nature of this belief, Dixon changed the subject and dismissed the question.

Dixon presented the perfect Catch-22.

Why are the questions inconsequential to Dixon? Because there was a conspiracy.

How do we know there was a conspiracy? Because Miller claimed there was one.

Why are Miller's inconsistencies irrelevant? Because there was a conspiracy. Dixon's need to defend the verdict has made it difficult for him to be honestly objective.

Aside from Miller's, the only witness testimony Dixon feels grants credence to the claim of conspiracy was that of Richard Kurutz. Returning from night school on the evening of Wilhelm's murder, he exited the garage elevator sometime following Wilhelm's assault. When asked what he saw, Kurutz testified:

"I came out of the elevator. My car was parked right in front of the elevator and I heard a sound like a thud or something. I looked to my left and I seen two men standing over there by the wall about 30 yards away from me, and I looked at them and they seen me and I started getting into my car. I was watching them while I was getting into the car, and then I backed up and went down the ramp."

Kurutz continued to testify that he saw two men. While he could offer vague physical descriptions, he did not clearly see their faces, and stated that he would not have recognized them. In Dixon's mind, that Kurutz saw Miller and Goldblum together at the scene of the murder is indicative of their conspiracy to assault Wilhelm together. Therefore, Dixon believed that Goldblum's lack of motive and the physical evidence discrediting Miller's account should be dismissed.

While Dixon gave the testimony of Kurutz excessive weight, his observations were after-the-fact and provided nothing more than possible corroboration.

Without the conspiracy and motive behind Wilhelm's assault, the testimony of Kurutz was not the proof that Dixon wanted it to be. It is hard to accept that Dixon depended on one part of Miller's testimony to prove a conspiracy while dismissing the fact that Miller perjured himself about the true facts of the assault. Dixon would not explain this due to his inability or unwillingness to confront the issue.

Another key factor in Dixon's contribution to Goldblum's wrongful conviction was his failure to procure and turn over photographs of the interior of the vehicle.

At Goldblum's trial, the Mobile Crime Unit detective who photographed the crime scene was examined by Dixon regarding the photographs he took of the vehicle's interior.

Dixon asked Detective Crisanti, "Did you take photographs of the dashboard of the vehicle or the window of the victim's car?"

Crisanti responded, "I recall taking a photograph of the interior of the car. I would have to see the photograph of the dashboard again. I would assume it would be in that picture."

Dixon then followed up, asking, "All right. Other than that one photograph, did you take any other interior shots of the victim's car?"

To which Crisanti responded, "That's it."

In reading over Crisanti's entire testimony, it is interesting the clarity with which he recalls photographing the car's interior specifically.

Minutes earlier in his testimony, when asked to recall whether he took certain photographs of the crime scene, the detective testified that he could not recall the specific evening, but, did recall the photographs themselves. Crisanti stated, "Yes. I recall the photographs. Now, it has been that long since I have, but I recall seeing them again."

When asked about other photographs he had taken and whether he remembered shooting them, Crisanti replied, "The only way I can answer that is I would have to see the photographs and note if my initials are on the back."

Here, Crisanti admits that while he can't recall shooting the photographs, those possessing his initials were taken the evening of the homicide.

It is only when asked about the photographs of the interior of the vehicle that Crisanti's memory suddenly comes into sharp focus. After reviewing Crisanti's testimony, the only possibility is that such photographs were taken and were not shared with the defense.

It is not believable that an experienced Mobile Crime Unit detective would have taken only a single picture of the interior of a car where a homicide was alleged to have been initiated.

Throughout the investigation, Crisanti identified blood spatter by photographing it, scraping off a blood sample, then preserving it for crime laboratory analysis. There is no logical reason that he diverted from this process.

Years later both Sgt. Modispatcher and Detective Freeman claimed they saw the blood spatter photos from the dashboard of Wilhelm's vehicle. With Modispatcher and Freeman admitting they saw photos of the dashboard blood spatter, it proves the photos existed. Crisanti could not identify photos that were not shown to him by the District Attorney. Dixon should have shown the blood spatter photo with his initials on the back so Crisanti could identify it. Dixon withheld the exculpatory photos from the defense and thereby denied Goldblum a fair trial.

This physical evidence would have greatly assisted Rothman to discredit the testimony of the prosecution's key witness and dismantle its presented theory that Goldblum was the assailant. Without access to these key crime scene photographs, Goldblum's defense could not confront and disprove, through crime scene and blood spatter analysis, Miller's testimony that it was Goldblum who assaulted and killed Wilhelm.

In an April 24, 2008 deposition, the lead detective Freeman confirmed that such photographs did, in fact, exist.

Attorney Chris Eyster, then a member of Goldblum's defense team, asked Freeman, "And you recall today -- sitting here today, you recall that photographs were taken and they were used in this case?"

Under oath, Freeman responded, "I can't say what Pete Dixon used in the case. That 's going back a lot of years. I don't know what exhibits he used."

To which Eyster said, "But you recall there..."

Freeman interrupted, "There were photographs taken. Sure, there were photographs taken of the car."

Yet Goldblum's defense counsel never received such photographs from the Commonwealth. While these photographs may not have been used by the Commonwealth at trial, the distinction is irrelevant.

If, as required by law, the photographs had been turned over to the defense, the blood spatter pattern would have been forensically analyzed and used to show the jury, conclusively and incontrovertibly, that Miller's account of the evening of the homicide was physically impossible and obviously fabricated.

The blow dealt to Goldblum's defense in not receiving the photographs was considerable.

Dixon's final contribution to Goldblum's wrongful conviction, though less glaring than keeping Dedo from testifying, presenting Miller's perjured testimony during trial, and failing to turn crime scene photographs over to Goldblum's defense team, still contributes to an overall pattern of mishandling the prosecution.

Throughout the investigation by the homicide detectives, Miller was administered polygraph tests to verify the veracity of his statements. While inadmissible in court, the polygraph remains a tool used by detectives to determine whether a suspect was more likely to be lying or telling the truth.

Ultimately, Miller was administered three polygraph examinations, none of which were revealed to Goldblum's defense counsel.

The first was conducted on February 13,1976, at the behest of Miller's attorney, Vincent Murovich, and was administered by Sgt. Joseph Modispatcher. The police report, written by investigating detectives Condemy and Amity, recorded the following:

"Our conversation with Clarence and his attorney was concluded and he was conveyed to the number one cellblock at 6:10 p.m., arrangements were made to keep Clarence in the PSB so as we could take a tape statement and possibly a polygraph exam. On Friday, Feb 13, 1976, Clarence took the polygraph exam through the advice of his attorney and Sgt. Modispatcher failed him..."

This initial polygraph was administered to test the veracity of Miller's first two interviews in which he claimed his innocence and attempted to shift all of the blame onto Goldblum. The examination indicated that Miller lied in these first two statements.

The second polygraph test was administered by Detective Stotlemyer on May 15, 1976. After the test, in an interview with the examiner, Miller admitted participating in Wilhelm's assault, but only to hold him down while Goldblum stabbed him.

In the final polygraph test administered on May 25, again by Detective Stotlemyer, it was noted by the detective that he felt Miller was involved in the arson.

Oddly however, the records of the second and third reports were not filed until January 27, 1978, well after Goldblum's trial and conviction. In his summarizing report, the polygraph test's administrator, Detective Stotlemyer, wrote:

"...Miller admitted in the post-test interview that he, relative to the murder, had in fact prevented the victim from fleeing Charles Goldblum. Miller stated that he did this by blocking the victim's path of escape and holding the victim while he was stabbed by Charles Goldblum."

While this statement may not exonerate Goldblum, it does indicate that Miller was lying about his role in the assault and clearly contradicts his testimony at Goldblum's trial.

Dixon knew of this admission in May 1976, yet allowed Miller to falsely testify that he had nothing to do with Wilhelm's murder. Miller, in usual form, edged close to the truth without quite getting to it, forming his story to line up as closely to the facts as possible, while still shifting all of the blame onto Goldblum.

Additionally, the report goes on to state: "Miller was also advised at this time that it was the opinion of this examiner that he was involved in the arson of the restaurant. He denied any involvement at this time."

This again contributes to the ever-crumbling theory the prosecution presented to the jury at trial. If Goldblum took no part in the fraud and Wilhelm was not the arsonist, any debt or criminal relationship between Goldblum and Wilhelm was eliminated.

This being the case, why did the police and Dixon believe in their motive for Goldblum?

Though the belated polygraph report may not completely exonerate Goldblum, it does cast another layer of doubt on the validity of the Commonwealth's case, while raising some disturbing questions.

If, as it is detailed in the report, these examinations and revelations came about on May 15 and 25 of 1976, why was the report on the interrogations only filed in January of 1978?

Why was the defense never given transcripts of these interviews, or, at the very least, some report or summary of these interviews, in which Miller obviously lied about his involvement in the arson and admitted to Stotlemyer that he participated in Wilhelm's assault?

Why were the second and third polygraphs kept out of the Master Polygraph Log?

Why was there any cover-up at all?

The true motivations behind Dixon's insistence on Goldblum's supposed guilt cannot be definitively known since he died in 2014.

In order to cling to his belief in Goldblum's culpability, Dixon had to ignore Miller's near-constant lying, both during the investigation and trying of the murder case. He did so despite the physical evidence that contradicts Miller's testimony regarding the assault, as well as Wilhelm's dying declaration that Miller, not Goldblum, stabbed and killed him.

The records and facts of the case definitively show that Dixon played a key role in securing a conviction that was not just.

By withholding exculpatory photographic evidence, by failing to disclose multiple disparate statements made to Detective Stotlemyer by Miller during polygraph interrogations, and by denying Goldblum a full and fair trial by silencing Dedo, Dixon ultimately bore a significant share of the burden for securing a wrongful prosecution and conviction of Goldblum for Wilhelm's murder.

Although Dixon came to Goldblum's aide during the 1999 Board of Pardons hearing as a result of personal conscience and objectivity after an extensive review of the transcripts and available exhibits of Goldblum's trial, ultimately, he chose to continue to engage in willful blindness.

Whether motivated by an inability to embrace the concept that he may have contributed to a wrongful conviction, or the desire to preserve what he considers a key accomplishment of his legal legacy, Dixon was responsible for the lifelong imprisonment of a man for a murder he did not commit.

While he had the opportunity and briefly grasped at a means by which to clear Goldblum's name and correct his mistake, ultimately Dixon's inability to accept the invalidity of Goldblum's conviction prevailed.

It would have taken a man of real strength and principle to recognize and admit such an error. Dixon had the opportunity to become that man and, for the sake of justice and morality, return to the clear-minded and objective state he achieved in 1999, overcome his personal sense of achievement, and correct what he himself called "a tragic miscarriage of justice."

Unfortunately, he did not do so before he died.

The Cover-Up and Misconducts

In 2005, when he first became involved in the Goldblum case, retired Pittsburgh Police Detective Jim Ramsey doubted there had been an express plan to falsely convict Charles Goldblum of murder or to convict Clarence Miller of a higher degree of murder than he was truly guilty of. The prosecution's corrupt acts and subsequent cover-ups were probably not planned in advance, but decisions of expedience taken as events developed.

From his experience in the police, Ramsey knew Ron Freeman to be an ambitious detective who wanted to make a name for himself. The Goldblum case presented him with an ideal opportunity to do so.

Ramsey has come to believe that Freeman's ambition was the primary catalyst, but that over time, his ambition got the best of him. The other participants in the investigation and prosecution of the case simply acquiesced and most likely went along with decisions Freeman made.

Ramsey believes the vast majority of police detectives and prosecutors are honest public officials who want only to find the truth in their cases. There are, however, a distinct few who do not properly do their jobs.

There are signals or clues to watch for when determining whether improper acts or decisions have been made by investigators and prosecutors.

The first clue is corner cutting. This happens most often when a mistake or oversight has occurred, and the party responsible does not want it revealed. Normally a conscientious officer will admit to his mistakes, because there is no shame in making a mistake. After all, humans are imperfect. He or she corrects that mistake and moves on.

Less scrupulous officers will try to cover up or erase their mistakes. The mistakes can be the result of dishonesty, laziness, slothfulness, or simple oversight. Mistakes can be made because criminal situations are always evolving, and the detective has to adjust.

Deliberate mistakes are usually followed by unrealistic denials or flimsy excuses that place the blame on others. Ramsey believes that happened in the Goldblum case.

The second signal of malfeasance is excessive zealousness or obsession with a single case. Under normal circumstances, detectives and prosecutors are involved with several cases at any given time. When one case starts to command too much of a detective's attention, especially when it is done at the exclusion of other responsibilities, it is a sign that something is amiss, that something out of the ordinary may have happened.

The third clue is a departure from normal routine, procedure, or process. If conventional protocol or procedure was not followed, there must be a logical explanation.

The fourth clue is acts of dishonesty or unexplained inconsistency. When these happen, there really is no satisfactory explanation.

Unfortunately, that seems to be what happened in this case.

For Ramsey, the facts too strongly suggest that this case was pursued dishonestly, followed by a variety of maneuvers to cover-up significant wrongdoing and mistakes.

At the beginning of this investigation, there were no unusual procedural circumstances. However, during the investigation's first 48 hours, several situations point to cover-ups that eventually resulted in Charles Goldblum's unjust conviction and Clarence Miller being over charged with premeditated, first-degree murder.

Ramsey does not take lightly the accusations he makes in the following **11 Count Indictment.**

The cold evening of February 9,1976 was like many others in Pittsburgh that winter. Snow had fallen that day and the temperature hovered in the low 20s.

Around 9:35 p.m., the police dispatcher contacted the homicide unit for assistance regarding what appeared to be an attempted homicide.

COUNT 1: Within two hours, the Pittsburgh Police Crime Lab detectives, known as the Mobile Crime Unit were called to the crime scene to collect evidence. Detectives Crisanti and Hill photographed the scene and collected blood evidence which was sent to a Crime Laboratory for analysis. Both detectives were interviewed by defense investigators and claimed that the entire crime scene was photographed, including the pattern of blood spatters across the dashboard of Wilhelm's vehicle.

Detective Freeman was interviewed later and recalled seeing photographs of the blood spatter on the dashboard, but he could not remember when and where he saw the photos. In 2011, Ramsey interviewed Detective Sgt. Joseph Modispatcher, who recalled seeing the blood spatter photos in the homicide case file only days before Goldblum's trial.

So there is no doubt that these blood spatter photos existed. In light of the opinion of the experts, and Freeman's testimony describing the blood spatter, these photos were clearly exculpatory evidence, or what is referred to as "Brady" material.

The law requires Brady material to be turned over to defense attorneys so they can examine the material and, if necessary, call expert witnesses.

This was not done in this case. To make matters worse, by the time of Goldblum's trial, many photos of the crime scene had mysteriously vanished. There has never been an explanation by the police or prosecution regarding why the exculpatory photos were never turned over to the defense or how they vanished.

This is an important point. In his testimony at Goldblum's trial, Freeman acknowledged he could read a crime scene. He testified that he noticed the tails of the blood spatters which moved from left to right across the car's dashboard. He also knew that no blood spatter photos were available at Goldblum's trial. That made it impossible for the defense to secure forensic specialists before trial to help determine who in the vehicle was Wilhelm's assailant. Both Freeman and prosecutor Dixon knew that if experts had access to the photographs before trial, it would have been nearly impossible to allow Miller to testify that Goldblum was the assailant.

In his interview, Freeman claimed that Assistant District Attorney Peter Dixon also saw the blood spatter photos but that he did not know what Dixon did with the photos.

Keep in mind that the forensic experts only looked at the evidence and testimony many years after Goldblum had been convicted. They all agree that the blood spatter pattern as described in Freeman's oral testimony meant it was Miller in the passenger seat who inflicted the initial wounds on Wilhelm, not Goldblum, who was in the back seat.

Even the prosecution's expert witness conceded that if Freeman's testimony at Goldblum's trial was correct, then Miller was the assailant. However, the prosecution expert further claimed that without the photographs of the blood spatter pattern on the dashboard, no one could definitely assert that it was Miller who stabbed Wilhelm inside the car.

That is why the photographs and their absence were crucially important.

At his trial, Goldblum's defense was never given the blood spatter photographs. Nor were they even informed of the existence of the blood spatter on the dashboard until Freeman testified during the trial itself. As a result, the defense was never able to properly argue that Miller was the assailant.

Who had anything to gain by the disappearance of the exculpatory blood spatter photos?

This question must be asked in conjunction with the fact that all copies of the official police files of this case, as well as Coroner's Reports, vanished from different official archives.

While the evidence is circumstantial, the disappearance of the blood spatter photos was more likely to have been an intentional cover-up. Only the police and prosecutors were in possession and control of the photographs, and only they had something to gain by misplacing them. It is the responsibility of police and prosecutors to maintain custody and preserve all evidence, including exculpatory evidence.

Should the disappearance of the blood spatter photos and case files be considered a cover-up? You decide.

COUNT 2: The next questionable event in the investigation also took place within 72 hours of Miller's arrest.

On February 13, four days after the murder, Detective Freeman ordered a polygraph test for Miller, which was administered by Sergeant Joseph Modispatcher, who was trained to conduct polygraph tests.

In 2011, when Ramsey interviewed him, Modispatcher insisted he had told Freeman that Miller failed the polygraph test and suggested that Freeman should consider Miller as Wilhelm's lone assailant.

At the end of the interview, Modispatcher was shown a copy of the Master Polygraph Log as well as the single report that Detective Stotlemyer had prepared after two subsequent polygraph tests of Miller. Freeman ordered these test's on May 15 and 25, but curiously, these two tests were never entered into the master log and a report was not prepared until 20 months later.

Asked for his thoughts, Modispatcher said:

"There is something wrong here, somebody is trying to hide something. If I had administered the two polygraphs, I would have entered them in the Master Log the same day, prepared separate reports of each, and made sure a copy was placed into the homicide file... I would have made mention of the questions and answers, and I would have kept the polygraph instrument sheet safe for future review....There is no reason to delay preparing a report for 1 year and 8 months."

In addition, each individual polygraph test requires a separate report, and the original copy is placed in the homicide case file. The existence of the two subsequent polygraphs and an official report were kept from the defense until 20 months later, well after Goldblum had been convicted.

Ramsey finds this interesting because the second and third polygraph tests were administered by Freeman's friend and fellow homicide detective, Joe Stotlemyer, rather than by Sgt. Modispatcher, who was a senior polygraph operator.

In an interview, Freeman claimed he did not like the results of Modispatcher's polygraphs because they leaned toward innocence.

But if the Modispatcher polygraphs leaned toward Goldblum's innocence, what motivated Freeman to venture into the unknown with tests administered by Stotlemyer?

Almost from the case's beginning, Freeman had learned that the person Miller named, Charles Goldblum, was an attorney and that his father was a prominent rabbi at Beth Shalom Synagogue in Pittsburgh. From this point on, Ramsey became suspicious of the decisions Freeman made in this investigation.

If Freeman intended to make Miller his star witness in a case against Goldblum, he would not have wanted Miller to fail any additional polygraph tests. Freeman had to have known that if he returned to Modispatcher for further testing, Miller would most likely fail again.

Were the results of the second and third polygraph also kept from the prosecutor? Or was the prosecutor also aware of the second and third polygraph tests and deliberately withheld this information from the defense?

Following the second polygraph test, Detective Stotlemyer wrote in a police report that, "In the Post Polygraph interview, Miller admitted he was involved in the murder."

Miller's statement was never put to a polygraph test. In the third polygraph Miller failed, Stotlemyer reported that Miller was involved in the arson.

Remember, each polygraph test should have had a separate report that is promptly filed, but Stotlemyer did not file the report on the second and third tests until 20 months after they were administered, and when he did, he combined both tests into a single report.

Furthermore, the questions Stotlemyer asked during both polygraph tests of Miller were never entered into the log, nor made available to Goldblum's post-conviction defense team.

At Goldblum's trial, Miller denied he was involved in the murder and blamed everything on Goldblum. Miller also denied being involved in the arson of Goldblum's restaurant.

The misconduct in this act is very serious, and it denied Goldblum a fair trial.

The prosecutor and detectives knew of the second and third polygraph tests, and they withheld that information from the defense for their own reasons.

The prosecutor knew his star witness was perjuring himself at the Goldblum trial.

The prosecutor and detectives were aware of this information in May 1976, more than a year before the beginning of the Goldblum trial in August 1977. Why did they initially withhold this information and keep it out of the Master Polygraph Log? Why was the official report withheld for 20 months?

So, within three months after the murder, at least two very questionable and significant events had taken place and were followed by attempts to cover them up.

These lapses must be also be considered in light of the fact that all of the case files on the murder and Coroner's Reports subsequently vanished from official archives under circumstances that have never been explained.

COUNT 3: Miller claimed that between February 10 and June 1976, the police and prosecutor made an unofficial agreement with him and his attorney.

In return for his cooperation and testimony against Goldblum, Miller said he was led to believe he would receive a 10 to 20-year sentence rather than life or worse. Miller was told by Dixon that his "only chance to stay alive was to cooperate." According to Miller, after Goldblum was convicted, the prosecutor failed to uphold their end of the agreement.

At Goldblum's trial, no one was told that Miller was testifying pursuant to an official or unofficial agreement. Even if no written deal had been made, it is likely Miller was under the impression that he would get a more lenient sentence of some sort.

However, shortly before his own trial began in 1978, Miller was unable to prove that he had a deal with the prosecution. Miller claimed that "the prosecutor got amnesia when it came to his sentencing." He was subsequently convicted of first-degree murder and received a life sentence.

Over the years, the Commonwealth has maintained that no deal was ever offered to Miller. In light of the facts and how easily manipulated Miller was, this contention is probably false.

Shortly after Miller's arrest and his first failed polygraph test, Miller's defense attorney, Vincent Murovich, gave the police *carte blanche* access to Miller, and he did not insist on being present during Miller's interviews and debriefings with Freeman. Prosecutor Dixon also had several meetings with Miller without Murovich being present.

Why would such an experienced and respected defense attorney such as Murovich, simply hand his client over to the police and prosecutor with no agreement in return? That is very unlikely.

It is hard to believe Miller would testify as to what he did without some kind of understanding with the police and prosecutor. Miller's testimony both made him part of an alleged conspiracy and placed him at the scene of the murder.

Murovich must have realized this. Why would he let Miller put himself in such a bad position for his own trial unless he felt that he had an advance agreement for a lesser sentence?

In all likelihood, there was an oral agreement, but Murovich foolishly failed to get it in writing or on a tape recording.

COUNT 4: Between February and June,1976, Miller was also examined 3 times by the Allegheny County Behavioral Clinic Psychologist and several psychiatrists. He was also examined by brain specialists at Southside hospital. After reviewing the results of Miller's analyses, it had been determined that he suffered from brain impairment. The results of the testing were available to only the prosecutor and the investigating detectives.

The prosecutor and police knew prior to Miller's testimony in Goldblum's trial that his testimony was untruthful and unreliable, yet they allowed Miller to perjure himself in court as long as his testimony was harmful to Goldblum's case.

It must be asked how often police and prosecutors proceed with a witness or informant who has failed several polygraphs.

Later before his own trial, Miller was tested again by a psychologist and a psychiatrist who then testified on Miller's behalf.

Miller's trial counsel, Harry Stump, used the testimony of the psychologists in an attempt to suppress Miller's previous statements to the police. The experts testified Miller had suffered a brain injury in a childhood accident and diagnosed him as a "confabulator." The diagnosis was supported by brain scans.

By definition, a confabulator is "a person who will chat, gossip, converse to compensate for the loss or impairment of memory by fabrication or invention of details." A confabulator fills in the memory blanks with fabrication and the invention of details.

The prosecutor never disclosed this at Goldblum's trial or to his post-conviction defense team.

While the prosecution claimed lack of this knowledge, during his opening argument at Goldblum's trial, Dixon warned the jury that

"Miller lied a lot, sometimes unconsciously," precisely the definition of confabulation.

Apparently, the prosecutor expected the members of the jury to be able to distinguish on their own when Miller was being truthful and when he was lying. Since Miller did not actually know that he was lying, the jury's task was even more difficult.

The prosecutor and police used dishonest tactics to cover up the truth. Miller was manipulated into admitting things that were not true as a means to convict Goldblum of a murder he did not commit. They were also used to convict Miller of first-degree murder, when in all likelihood, he was guilty of manslaughter or third-degree murder.

The prosecutor expected the jury to distinguish when Miller was telling the truth, which was an impossible task. The prosecutor used Miller's brain injury to hide the truth.

COUNT 5: Between February and June 1976, Freeman interviewed Miller numerous times and ordered three polygraph tests. By this point, Freeman was apparently trying to gain as much control over Miller as he could.

In May or June, Freeman complained to Dixon that he had to get a court order every time he wanted to interview Miller at the Public Safety Building.

Freeman also asked Dixon whether he would oppose a bond reduction for Miller if Miller's attorney made a motion. Dixon said he would not oppose the reduction.

A motion was placed before Judge Samuel Strauss to reduce Miller's bond from $50,000 to $30,000. The motion went unopposed, and Miller secured his bail the following day.

In a 2013 interview with Ramsey, Dixon's supervisor, Joseph Steele, reported that he would have opposed any bond reduction for Miller and was shocked by Dixon's behavior.

The interesting thing is that according to the minister of St. Mark's Methodist church to which Miller's mother belonged, Freeman telephoned him on two occasions and asked if the church would take up a collection to help secure bail bond for Miller.

In other words, Freeman became actively involved in getting Miller's bond reduced and then helped to raise the money needed for Miller's bail.

This is highly unusual. Police officers simply do not assist defendants to secure bail, especially in homicide cases.

Furthermore, Freeman lied when he assured the minister that Miller had no part in the murder. Freeman knew that following his May 15 polygraph test, Miller had admitted that he took part in the murder.

The second time Freeman called the minister, his wife answered the telephone.

Freeman identified himself, and the minister's wife took a message for her husband. At Miller's trial, Freeman denied under oath that he ever contacted the minister, but both the minister and his wife swore under oath that Freeman contacted them first.

Aware it was against police regulations to help a defendant secure bond, Freeman not only assisted in getting the bond amount reduced, but also helped raise bond money for Miller. Then, in Ramsey's opinion, Freeman lied about it under oath.

Why did Freeman act so recklessly?

Was this part of the unofficial agreement that Miller and his attorney claimed was made?

Why did Freeman really want Miller released from custody?

Was this a sign to Miller that Freeman could deliver on his promises, that he would uphold the unofficial plea agreement?

These questions are not speculative; they are raised by the facts of the case. It is hard to imagine an innocent explanation.

COUNT 6: The prosecution and police were clearly aware within the first few months after the murder, that Goldblum really had no motive to attack or kill Wilhelm.

As the investigation proceeded, it became increasingly clear that Goldblum had not been involved in the land fraud. Once the FBI file concerning the land fraud was obtained, there was little doubt. The FBI file was secured by Goldblum's defense team, rather than by the prosecution. No reason has been given for this oversight.

Furthermore, the prosecutors and police had strong cause to doubt Miller's version of the arson, the only testimony that implicated Wilhelm as the arsonist.

During their background investigation of Wilhelm, the police learned that he was an honest man. Years later, Assistant District Attorney James Gilmore publicly apologized to the Wilhelm family for allowing Miller to testify that Wilhelm had been the arsonist, when no one in the District Attorney's Office believed it to be true.

This included Dixon, who also subsequently admitted openly that he never believed Wilhelm was the arsonist. Neither Dixon nor Gilmore ever expressed any moral regret for using a false motive against Goldblum in a capital murder case.

Ramsey finds this unethical oversight unforgivable and part of the cover-up.

Dixon used Miller's testimony regarding the land fraud and arson, that he clearly knew to be untrue, to create a false motive for murder against Goldblum. Dixon knew that both the testimony presented and the motives suggested were equally false.

Keep in mind the undisclosed polygraphs administered by Stotlemyer that suggested Miller was involved in both the arson and the murder.

Had Miller's polygraphs been disclosed, Goldblum's defense team most likely would have done its own investigating. That would have led to evidence which would have helped them argue more forcefully against Miller's lack of truthfulness and honesty.

While the polygraph test results themselves would not have been admissible at trial, they were important exculpatory evidence. What happened amounts to a dishonest cover-up by the police and prosecutor.

To recapitulate, by understanding the cumulative effect of the cover-ups, we know that:

- The photos of the blood spatter vanished shortly before trial.
- After Miller failed the first polygraph test, Sgt. Modispatcher told Freeman, the case's lead detective, that Miller was the lone assailant.
- Miller's second and third polygraphs were administered by Detective Stotlemyer, but he filed no report on these tests until 20 months after they were administered.
- Furthermore, Stotlemyer then failed to properly record the second and third polygraphs in the Master Polygraph Log.
- In all likelihood, Miller had been led to believe that he would receive a lenient sentence, which was not

disclosed to Goldblum's defense. Not only was there lack of disclosure, but facts strongly suggest Miller was manipulated into acting against his own best interests. What did Miller think he would receive in return for his cooperation and testimony?

- The prosecution was fully aware of Miller's brain injury and confabulation amnesia diagnosis well before Goldblum's trial, but it did not disclose this information to his defense team.
- Dixon and Freeman helped to get Miller's bond reduced from $50,000 to $30,000.
- Freeman was involved in both the bond reduction and raising money to secure bail for Miller. This vital information was not disclosed to Goldblum's defense counsel.
- Freeman lied under oath about his involvement in the bond reduction. Miller's family minister claimed Freeman lied about Miller's innocence when soliciting them to raise money for Miller's bail.
- By their own admission, the police and prosecutors did not believe that Wilhelm was the arsonist of Goldblum's restaurant, yet they presented it to the jury as Goldblum's motive for his murder.

These points make a strong case for official dishonesty, misconduct, and subsequent cover-up in the murder prosecution of Charles Goldblum.

Regrettably, there is more.

COUNT 7: While Goldblum was incarcerated in the Allegheny County Jail, he was kept in the Selective Housing Unit (SHU) and separate from the general population of inmates. After several months in custody, Goldblum's family was able to raise bail.

Andrew Kinser Bey, a prisoner in the SHU, first met Goldblum a few days before he was released.

A few weeks later, Bey was also released and shortly afterwards, he telephoned Goldblum and proposed a meeting. At the meeting, Bey told Goldblum that if Miller was killed, he could not be prosecuted. Bey also intimated that he knew someone who could do the job.

Several days later, Bey brought John Mook to meet Goldblum. While there was some discussion of the murder and how much it would cost, there was no firm agreement for Mook to act. Mook turned out to be an undercover Police Sergeant and within hours after they met, Goldblum was re-arrested.

Prior to Bey's suggestion, Goldblum claimed he never thought of harming Miller.

After reviewing the Master Polygraph Log, it was determined that Bey was not administered a polygraph concerning Goldblum's willingness to contract a hit man.

Suspiciously, at the time of Goldblum's trial, Bey was not available to testify. According to the police, he had disappeared and could not be found.

Also suspicious, Bey had also paid a visit to the office of Goldblum's defense attorney, H. David Rothman. Rothman suspected the police were behind the visit and that Bey was attempting to turn him into a witness. Had that happened, Goldblum would have had to secure new counsel.

Is it credible that a principal informant of a solicitation to murder would be missing at the time of trial or that the police would not be able to locate him?

What prompted Bey to contact Goldblum?

Why did Bey go to the office of Goldblum's lawyer?

Was he perhaps sent there by Freeman or the prosecutor to learn Goldblum's defense?

Why did Detective Freeman fail to have a polygraph test administered to Bey?

It is also fair to note that Goldblum's solicitation for the murder charge was subsequently overturned on appeal, again a violation of the speedy-trial rule. A major issue is that the jury heard this incriminating testimony at Goldblum's trial.

COUNT 8: After being charged with attempting to arrange the murder of Miller, based on the suggestion of police informant, Andrew Kinser Bey, Goldblum was arrested and returned to the Allegheny County Jail. This time, Goldblum was housed in the prison infirmary.

Another inmate identified as Ronald O'Shea was also housed there. After a few days, O'Shea approached Goldblum in an overly friendly way and tried to engage him in conversation. Goldblum rebuffed O'Shea and said to leave him alone. That same afternoon, however, Goldblum was charged with soliciting O'Shea to murder Freeman, Miller, Mook, and police Lieutenant Ralph Pampena.

These charges were totally untrue. Ultimately, O'Shea revealed it was a lie, and that it was all Freeman's idea.

Ironically, Goldblum and his father, Rabbi Moshe Goldblum, figured O'Shea's lies out from a small piece of circumstantial evidence.

When Goldblum was charged with the solicitation for murder, the name of the undercover detective, John Mook, had never been released to the media. The Goldblums realized that if O'Shea knew Mook's name, there must have been police participation in the fabrication of the false charge. It also must be pointed out that Goldblum had nothing to directly gain if the three police officers were killed.

When Freeman allegedly received news of the death threats from O'Shea, he should have ordered a polygraph examination to determine the truthfulness of the accusations?

In a sworn affidavit dated January 20, 1996, O'Shea claims he was never administered a polygraph test by the Pittsburgh police concerning the false information provided to detective Freeman concerning the solicitation. O'Shea claimed that Det. Freeman put him up to falsely accusing Goldblum with solicitation to murder the officers.

Yet, a recent review of a copy of the original Master Polygraph Log does show an entry for a test administered to a Ronald O'Shea on December 30, 1976. Unfortunately, the record does not indicate whether that polygraph test was for the burglary that O'Shea was involved in. The Master Polygraph Log indicates the test was for a conspiracy, not a solicitation for murder.

So it is fair to assume that O'Shea was telling the truth, and Freeman did not have a polygraph administered to O'Shea concerning the solicitation nor a list of questions O'Shea might have been asked.

Ramsey believes the reason for this omission was that Freeman knew O'Shea would not pass the polygraph test, and that would prohibit additional sensational charges to be filed against Goldblum. Ramsey also questions why was there no polygraph for Bey?

After Goldblum was convicted on the murder charge, the court ruled he also had to be tried on the two solicitations for murder within 180 days.

Now represented by attorney Charles Scarlatta, the non-juried case on the first solicitation charge was brought to trial on September 13, 1982, and heard by Judge Dauer, who on October 28, 1982, found Goldblum guilty and added an additional one to two years to his sentence. However, Scarlatta appealed to the Superior Court on the grounds the case had not been brought in a timely matter (Rule 1100), and the guilty verdict was overturned. The Commonwealth then decided it would NOT prosecute Goldblum for the second (O'Shea) solicitation. However, Goldblum countered, saying he would waive Rule 1100 in this case, and requesting a jury trial. Knowing they would lose, the prosecutor, Joseph Steele, was forced to dismiss the charge.

Goldblum used this tactic to bring light to his corrupt prosecution. The courts determined that both solicitation were baseless, their damage was doubly done. The decisions won him no new trial, while the embarrassment won him no friends in the District Attorney's office.

These are examples of the devious nature of Detective Freeman. How can he be believed? Was this part of the cover-up?

COUNT 9: In this count, the prosecutor is responsible for a violation of Constitutional Due Process.

Ted Dedo, one of the members of the land fraud, came forward during Goldblum's trial and offered his testimony exonerating Goldblum of any involvement.

Through his attorney, Dedo said he would testify that Goldblum played no part in the land fraud perpetrated on Wilhelm, which was being used as the prosecution's motive for Goldblum to kill him.

But Dedo needed Use Immunity to testify so that the prosecution could not use any incriminating statements against him at his trial for the land fraud, which was scheduled to take place shortly after Goldblum's trial.

H. David Rothman, Goldblum's attorney, asked the trial judge, Donald Ziegler, to grant Dedo immunity under the King's Bench Power, but the judge responded that he was not legally able to do this.

Dixon admitted years later that he knew if Dedo did not testify, there would be a due process violation. At that point in Goldblum's trial, Dixon was at a moral and ethical crossroads, and unfortunately he chose the low road.

Dixon further claimed that, he was not asked specifically to grant Dedo immunity and that if asked, he might have granted the immunity. Dixon continued to blame the judge for not granting immunity to Dedo, even though the record does not corroborate his account. He was far more responsible than the judge for keeping Dedo's testimony out of Goldblum's trial.

Dixon did subsequently concede openly that, "if Dedo testified that Goldblum was not part of the land fraud conspiracy, he could have lost the case." He admitted that, "the jury most likely would have disregarded Miller's account of the fraud." Rather than accepting his share of the blame, Dixon placed all the blame on Judge Ziegler. When asked if he could have been responsible, Dixon ignored the question.

It is also important that Dixon did subsequently concede he knew that most likely Goldblum had nothing to do with the land fraud, and that the episode with Dedo left him even more doubtful. Yet, even after this immunity issue was raised, Dixon continued to argue to the jury that the land fraud had been the motive for Goldblum to kill Wilhelm.

Dixon fervently believed this immunity issue was very important. Decades after the trial, Dixon advised Goldblum in prison to disregard everything else in his pursuit of a just verdict, and pursue this issue alone.

However Dixon still maintained he did nothing wrong, and that fault for the failure to grant Dedo immunity lies entirely with Judge Ziegler. But he could not explain why it is wrong if the judge didn't grant the immunity and it was acceptable if he denied the same.

On this count alone Goldblum should be given a new trial.

COUNT 10: What happened next indicates there simply had to be some kind of cover-up. It involves Speedy Trial Violation Rule 1100.

Prosecutors must always keep a keen eye on speedy trial dates, because they know if defendants are not brought to trial by a certain date, the case will be dismissed.

When it came time to try Dedo and Orlowsky for the land fraud case, the prosecution failed to bring the case to trial in a timely manner. That failure resulted in a dismissal of the charge.

Had Dedo come forward after the land fraud was dismissed, Goldblum would have been granted a new trial as a result of after discovered evidence, under the decision in *Commonwealth* vs. *Fiore*.

The combination of Dedo's refusal to talk and the dismissal of the land fraud strongly suggests a cover up. These two events cannot realistically be viewed as a coincidence.

It is likely that the prosecution deliberately failed to bring the land fraud case to trial in a timely manner because they knew that Dedo would have testified that Goldblum had not been part of the land fraud conspiracy, and he may have received a new trial.

When interviewed by a defense investigator after his charges were dismissed, Dedo claimed he was afraid of Freeman and would not talk. Dedo also claimed that he had been punched by a detective in the courthouse. The prosecution did not want to go to the expense for a new trial for Goldblum or risk having his conviction reversed, so they covered-up by allowing the time to expire on Dedo and Orlowsky's case.

COUNT 11: Without the preparation and maintenance of official records, files, and evidence, the police can be prohibited from bringing charges against a criminal suspect. In some cases when evidence is lost, the charges are dismissed. That is known as the Spoliation of Evidence Rule.

In our personal lives, we are careful about safeguarding tax, property, health, and insurance information. We know that we may need to prove facts to some authority. Our records enable us to do that. In much of the same way, it is fair to state that maintaining police records in safe locations is crucial in criminal cases.

This is pertinent in Goldblum's case because all of the official files and records of the case mysteriously vanished from separate archive locations.

The homicide squad has always made and maintained three copies of each case file. This is done so that even if someone checks out one copy of the file, the office still has at least one. When a case goes to trial, one copy is sent to the District Attorney, leaving two in homicide. After the trial, all copies of the case file go into homicide archives.

It would be very unusual if all three copies of a case file were to turn up missing from homicide. According to police detectives who Ramsey interviewed, the Wilhelm case file was physically large. The Wilhelm murder was a big case, involving two defendants, three offenses, and a long time span. That makes the disappearances of all three copies from police archives much more out of the ordinary. All three copies in police archives disappeared without any explanation.

In early 1995, Rhoda Shear Neft, then Goldblum's attorney, sent a subpoena for the case file. She was told that all copies of the case file were missing.

Neft then asked to see the Mobile Crime Unit's report file. That file, too, had vanished.

Neft then asked for any records that the Police Photo Lab had for this case. Again, the Wilhelm case file was missing from that location.

These files were kept in separate locations. Someone with access was able to take these records and presumably get rid of them. Common sense suggests that "someone" was a member of the police department.

Finally in November 1995, Ms. Neft issued a subpoena to the Allegheny County Coroner's Office and sent crime scene investigator Jon Balshy to review the Coroner's report for the Wilhelm homicide.

On November 22, when Balshy went to the Coroner's Office, he was shown parts of the file but was told he could not inspect the rest without a court order. Under Pennsylvania's Open Records Law, the whole file should have been disclosed. Rather than going to court to gain quick access to the entire report, Neft made an arrangement with the newly elected coroner, Dr. Cyril Wecht. Scheduled to take office in January 1996, Dr. Wecht told Ms. Neft that he would allow her complete access to the file after that.

Shortly after taking office, however, Dr. Wecht discovered that both copies of Wilhelm's Coroner's report were now also missing. Dr. Wecht called in the Allegheny County Police to look into the matter, but after a week of investigation, they determined that no crime had been committed.

Several years after that, Goldblum's attorney requested a copy of the police report on that investigation. Lt. Elizabeth Hoover who had worked on the issue was deposed. She testified that after a week of investigating the office, no file was created. Instead, she had prepared a memo stating that no crimes had been committed. This memo, called a "blue special," was purged from the police files.

These missing files have made it much more difficult for Ramsey to establish a timeline and investigate the case. It has been frustrating to not be able to follow up on all the inconsistencies of the case.

What happened to the photographs of the blood spatter evidence from Wilhelm's car?

The missing polygraph files are also highly suspicious.

In 2005, after years of questioning how so many files could go missing from so many locations, Zeke's younger brother, Dr. David Goldblum, contacted a professor of Statistics and Social Science at Carnegie Mellon University for answers.

Dr. Stephen E. Fienberg determined the probability of the different files being innocently missing to be at 0.00000001 percent. The case files did not disappear as a result of innocent inadvertence. They were not lost at random.

Why would someone want the files to disappear? Because, without the files, it is difficult to reconstruct the facts of the case and fully investigate its inconsistencies, cover-ups, and misconduct of the police and prosecutors.

There may be other reasons, but it is highly unlikely that the records just vanished independently at random.

These eleven points of indictment represent Ramsey's professional opinion for advocating that Charles Jacob Goldblum should be awarded a new trial.

Ramsey's favorite is COUNT 2. The deliberate act of keeping the two polygraphs out of the Master Log and not reporting them until 20 months later can't be explained away.

The dishonesty, abuse, and misconduct in this case needs to be addressed. Has our justice system failed to protect a citizen? Ramsey's opinion is that in this case, it has.

The irony is that Detective Freeman always had a solid case against Goldblum, due to his providing Miller with an alibi for Wilhelm's murder. Freeman did not need to manufacture motives.

There was no premeditated murder in this case. The murder was the result of an argument between two friends, Miller and Wilhelm, that escalated into an assault.

The mitigating argument was over a land fraud scheme perpetrated by Miller, Dedo, and Orlowsky who had bilked Wilhelm out of $21,000.

Wilhelm understandably wanted his money back.

The evening of the murder, as Wilhelm drove to the top floor of the parking garage with Miller sitting in the front passenger seat and Goldblum in the back, Miller told Wilhelm he could not repay the money any time soon. Wilhelm became upset, which is understandable, and he punched Miller in the face. Miller responded by grabbing a half of a grass shear from somewhere in the front of the car.

In a fit of rage, Miller mentally blacked out, as corroborated by Miller in his 1980 PCRA petition. He stabbed Wilhelm 24 times, and tumbled him over the edge of the roof.

There was no elaborate scheme, no plot, and no premeditation to murder Wilhelm.

When investigators and prosecutors try to manufacture motive while investigating a crime, mistakes occur. That is when the cover-up begins.

The facts that Goldblum was an attorney and his father was a prominent Rabbi, promised to make the case newsworthy, and both Freeman and Dixon capitalized on it.

Both men enjoyed considerable public exposure for the Goldblum case, and the more sensational the revelations, the more frequently their names appeared in print or on television.

At one point, Dixon was so out of control, he broke the judge's gag order.

Freeman leaked information about the case to newspaper reporters.

In a 2013 interview with Ramsey, former DA Supervisor Joseph Steele claimed he would not have charged Goldblum with the land fraud, because he did not believe Goldblum was a part of that crime. Mr. Steele also believed that Wilhelm was not involved in the arson.

Detective Jim Ramsey's Summary and Opinion *

During my long career as a police detective and drug enforcement officer, I worked on many complex investigations, with parties acting as go-betweens and facts learned second-hand. Furthermore, while taking courses in criminology at the University of Pittsburgh, I developed an interest in following complex cases and studying their outcome.

When presented with a case that has many moving parts and often little direct evidence, I learned to look for subtle clues and patterns when building a case. I also learned how important it is to be cautious, being careful to neither jump to conclusions nor misinterpret evidence.

For example, shortly after becoming involved with this case of Charles Goldblum, I interviewed the primary prosecutor, Peter Dixon. During the course of several meetings, I discovered things that shocked me. Dixon believed he crossed no ethical line when he allowed Clarence Miller to make statements to the jury that Dixon did not believe to be true.

The first statement was Miller's claim that Wilhelm had been Goldblum's arsonist.

That reminded me of white-collar and fraud prosecutions, where a business executive claims to have no direct knowledge of wrongdoing by employees. Prosecutors build entire cases based on the theory of "willful blindness" or "conscious indifference."

This was a large part of the strategy in several high profile criminal prosecutions, such as the Enron case. It also explains how the original concept of "knowing use of perjured testimony" evolved into the "knew or should have known," concept.

It is a practical solution, a means by which courts have allowed claimants to prove through circumstantial evidence and/or surrounding circumstances that someone must have known of negligent or criminal activity.

I believe that the Wilhelm murder case falls into this category.

In some investigations, judgments are made too early. Decisions get made before the facts are known or understood. Good detectives use circumstantial evidence carefully when building a case. Everything has to fit, and any contradiction is always an important warning.

Thoughtful investigators never ignore these signals, especially when there are many of them. Clues must be investigated and disparities reconciled. The more serious the criminal charges, the greater the need for care. Investigating a conspiracy with several suspects is always difficult, but it is important to sort through the outer layers to get to the core.

Detectives with separate agendas are prone to misinterpret evidence, to see what they want, as opposed to what is there. Then, once an investigation has developed momentum along a particular path, mistakes become hard to admit or correct.

I believe the facts strongly suggest this kind of failure in the investigation and prosecution of Charles Goldblum for the murder of George Wilhelm.

There is no doubt Goldblum was way out of his element. When pressures made him desperate, he let himself disregard his normal sense of right and wrong.

He did commit arson, participate as an accessory after the fact to Wilhelm's murder by providing an alibi, and considered a proposal to have Clarence Miller killed. However he did not enter into a conspiracy to murder George Wilhelm.

By making himself legally vulnerable, Goldblum was convicted of a murder he did not commit. After serving nearly four decades in prison, he admits he brought this sentence on himself by his own poor decisions.

Within hours of Wilhelm's murder, the prosecution had identified Clarence Miller as the suspect. Within days, they were aware Miller had suffered brain trauma as a child and was a confabulator. Although devious in his own right, Miller was also malleable in the hands of Detective Freeman. His willingness to defraud a longtime friend out of thousands of dollars is revealing of his true nature. He also actively involved himself in other less-than-honest activities.

Freeman was a motivated, goal oriented, and up-and-coming homicide detective. He appears to have been willing to cut corners to achieve his goals. Perhaps his ego and desire to advance his career initially kept him from dealing with this investigation properly. It appears on at least two occasions in this investigation, he fabricated false charges and testimony.

Assistant District Attorney F. Peter Dixon became lead prosecutor of the Wilhelm homicide several months before Goldblum's trial began. He also wanted to make a name for himself and apparently recognized that winning a high profile case could enhance his professional visibility.

Keep in mind that thoughts like these often happen at a subconscious level.

Several members of Goldblum's family came to court every day to support him and witness the proceedings. It goes without saying that they were under considerable stress.

The courtroom was full nearly every day due to the case's high publicity, but without notifying, Dixon arranged to have a daily seat reserved for his own mother next to Goldblum family members.

The Goldblum's were never told who she was. In fact, Dixon never disclosed this to Goldblum until he visited him at SCI Mahanoy shortly before the 1999 Board of Pardons hearing where he spoke in his support.

Dixon claimed he had done this to help bring comfort to the Goldblum family. It is hard to see how they could receive comfort from either a complete stranger or the mother of the prosecutor arguing to imprison their son and brother. Why would he subject his mother to the revelations of a brutal murder?

Perhaps he wanted to show his mother his own importance and level of professional accomplishment. It is also possible that he was willing to use his mother to sit and listen, to perhaps hear something he could use to further his prosecution. If that was the case, he was as bad as Freeman.

A small point perhaps, but here is another.

Dixon relied on the information provided by Detective Freeman, and he tried to make the case conform to testimony of other witnesses, particularly Miller.

It is possible that at the time, Dixon was not consciously aware Freeman was providing him with false and misleading information. Dixon later claimed this to be the case.

The problem is that Freeman also admitted separately that he never believed Wilhelm had anything to do with the burning of Goldblum's restaurant.

Dixon wanted to do the right thing at these later interviews, but he was conflicted.

It was and remained hard for him to admit he might have been used and misled by Freeman. His pride understandably got in the way. His affinity for law-enforcement as well as the passage of time were also factors. It is hard for him to be objective when faced with the possibility he was wrong in bringing Goldblum to trial for a murder he did not commit.

Three factors may help understand the motivation for the prosecution's initial case. First, it was a lurid, high-profile murder. The police had exclusive and abundant access to a very malleable Miller. Finally, Goldblum made for a perfect "trophy defendant."

During the investigation, the police never made a cooperation overture to Goldblum, either directly or through his attorney. These overtures are fairly routine, because there is no downside for police to contact every defendant and ask for their cooperation. In light of the many contradictions in Miller's many accounts, this would have been the next logical step in the investigation.

Had Freeman followed normal procedure and done this, he risked losing control of the case. It appears he was seeking a guaranteed verdict to generate headlines and advance his career.

Also conspicuously absent from the investigation's initial stages is the usual vetting process that always occurs before detectives commit to using an informant or witness.

Detectives are aware of the high degree of importance that an informant provides to a particular case and know how much a case relies on an informant, so they check them out thoroughly. There are two possibilities involved, neither of which constitutes a thorough, professional, objective investigation.

This level of vetting does not seem to have been done in this investigation, but no explanation has been given. Perhaps the vetting was done but not shared with the defense, as per the Brady requirement.

Freeman cannot deny his knowledge of:

- Wilhelm's dying declaration
- Miller's failed initial polygraph test
- Miller's bloody clothing
- The defensive scratches on Miller's wrists, arms, and face, as well as a finger laceration
- The lack of blood on Goldblum's clothes

- The absence of defensive wounds on Goldblum
- The missing photographs of the blood spatter pattern on the dashboard
- The unrevealed second and third Miller polygraphs and the results of his failures
- Miller's confession to participating in Wilhelm's murder

To overlook all this and still claim that Goldblum was the assailant and Miller merely an unwitting accomplice, is difficult, if not impossible, to innocently explain.

There were simply too many clear red-flag warnings that Miller was lying.

Freeman must have noticed that Miller changed his story about what Goldblum was wearing after being told of the blood spatter and other evidence.

For Freeman to maintain that Miller was telling the truth in spite of all the contradictions, strongly suggests that Freeman was deliberately dishonest. These questions must be asked.

How much of Miller's testimony was his own account and how much was fabricated by Freeman and fed to Miller? As noted above, Freeman's conduct seems to have been driven more by a personal agenda, as opposed to conducting an objective investigation.

Early in the investigation, the standard procedure would have been to confront Miller with the numerous and significant discrepancies in statements he had made. No reason has been given for this failure.

Normally, Miller would have been asked the following:

1. Mr. Miller, you seem to be shifting guilt for the murder of George Wilhelm away from yourself and toward Charles Goldblum. Explain why, after searching Goldblum's car and home, we did not find any hair, fiber, tissue, or blood evidence?
2. Why do you have blood on your clothing and numerous scratches and abrasions to your skin which look like defensive wounds?
3. How can you explain that your hair was found in a bloody glove near the scene of the murder?

4. How do you explain why George Wilhelm made a dying declaration that you murdered him?
5. How can you explain the fact that the forensic evidence contradicts your account?
6. How can you explain changing your story concerning the clothing Goldblum wore at the murder?
7. How do you explain why an eye-witness, Kurutz saw Goldblum wearing a topcoat, not fisherman's coveralls as you have alleged?
8. Are you aware that the police examined Goldblum's topcoat that you later described and could not find any traceable blood, hair, or fiber evidence placing him with Wilhelm?

The undisputed facts strongly indicate that from the very beginning, Miller was trying to shift blame for the murder away from himself and incriminate Goldblum.

The police cannot deny recognizing the discrepancies between Miller's account and what the witness Kurutz saw, especially regarding what Goldblum was wearing.

How likely is it that Goldblum participated in the murder, considering Miller's clothes were drenched with Wilhelm's blood but none was found on Goldblum, his clothes, his home, or vehicle? Furthermore, Miller was covered with scratches, but none on Goldblum. When Mrs. Miller was interviewed, she never mentioned that her husband had been playing with their cat, and that is how he received what appeared as defensive wounds.

It is hard to imagine why the police did not see these glaring discrepancies, yet no logical explanation was offered.

Analyzing the facts objectively, it seems that someone in the police department was actively and consciously assisting Miller to create a false account. Had the detectives been conducting the investigation honestly, Miller would have been confronted with the discrepancies and contradictions in his various statements. The failure to challenge Miller strongly indicates dishonest collusion.

An honest, professional detective would have presented the whole story to Dixon. Dixon should have been expressly apprised of the many problems and contradictions with Miller's many accounts. Freeman had no intention of weakening his case. The facts and circumstances strongly suggest that Freeman turned Miller over to the prosecution without a complete and honest appraisal in order to facilitate false testimony.

I have seen no other case where detectives faced so many contradictions and kept going forward, certain that a suspect, Miller, did not commit the crime.

How did they ignore Miller's statement following the second polygraph on May 15, 1976, that he held Wilhelm down during the murder?

Why ignore so many red flags?

Did evidence disappearing from police archives allow false testimony to be given? The missing photographs of the blood spatter support this conclusion. The disappearance of entire files concerning the case from official archives also indicates someone wanted to hinder future investigations into the facts.

It must also be pointed out that at the time, Goldblum and his attorney should have approached the police and confessed his culpability in the lesser crimes of which he was guilty.

Goldblum accepts this. Wanting to hide his involvement in the arson, combined with the deteriorating relationship with his defense attorney, accounted for Goldblum's unwillingness to do the right thing. He had committed arson and agreed to provide Miller with an alibi for the murder to keep the arson hidden.

That put Goldblum in a serious predicament. The arson gave the police good reason to suspect him, but it must be emphasized, their initial suspicion, as reasonable as it was, does not accurately explain what happened. Goldblum had his faults, but that was no reason to fail to thoroughly and honestly investigate a crime.

The investigation was likely corrupt from the start. Its one-sided nature is too clear.

Why did this happen? Were the investigation findings slanted at someone's request or insistence?

In some respects, this makes more sense. The homicide squad consisted of experienced and reasonably capable detectives. Why did they go along with Freeman's unorthodox activities?

Freeman had to have known that something was wrong early in the investigation.

Within the first week, he knew of the dying declaration, the initial forensic evidence, and the failed polygraph.

Goldblum made matters worse by denying his part in the arson. In doing so, he could not admit why he had covered up for Miller after the murder, which compounded his appearance of guilt. The jury could not understand why he had tried to provide an alibi for Miller if he had not been involved in the murder. On top of this, revelation of Goldblum's alleged solicitation to have Miller killed was devastating. When they heard that evidence, it was hard for the jury to consider Goldblum anything but guilty.

Goldblum was guilty of lesser crimes, and his actions were clearly wrong. This does not justify his conviction for crimes of which he was innocent, namely, the murder/conspiracy and land fraud.

I cannot overemphasize how important it is for police and prosecutors to never look the other way. Criminal convictions are valid only when actors are guilty of the offenses for which they are charged.

In 2005, when I first became involved in this investigation, before I read any transcripts, police reports, or other evidence, I presumed Goldblum was guilty. My initial inclination was and always is to give both police and prosecutors the benefit of the doubt. As a Pittsburgh police detective for many years, I believed that nearly all those convicted of a crime are guilty. I believed that the Commonwealth tries to convict only guilty parties.

So I came into this case with a skeptical attitude toward Goldblum's claims of innocence.

One of the first things that made me uncomfortable about the case was who some of the key players were. It helps when you are familiar with the investigators involved and to what length they were willing to go to achieve goals. This is especially important in a complicated case like this.

Having worked in drug enforcement for many years, I rarely saw detectives cut corners in the process of securing warrants or writing reports. I came to realize how important it was to know if an individual was always honest. I worked with cops I could trust. They told the truth, never rationalized, and saw things for what they were. They never let their personal likes, dislikes, or goals preempt their integrity.

We had a saying, "We can make a million mistakes, but the criminal has to make only one." If I lacked enough evidence to make a case against a particular individual, I knew that there would be another day, and the suspect eventually would make a mistake.

We know that Freeman decided to present Miller's account that Goldblum was the assailant, even though he was aware of the forensic evidence, the victim's dying declaration, Miller's admission to participating in the murder, Sgt. Modispatcher identifying Miller as the lone assailant, and the two failed, but hidden, polygraph tests.

During Freeman's initial interview with Miller, he should have asked questions about Miller's mental health, and Miller would have disclosed that he had a brain injury as a child, and that he suffered with a diagnosed condition of confabulation. Freeman would have had access to the Allegheny County Behavior Clinic report identifying Miller with a Personality Disorder as well as other mental issues prior to his March interview.

If you spoke with Miller for ten minutes, you could see something was mentally wrong with him. Sgt. John Mook, who was involved in the investigation, claimed that Miller had the intelligence of a 10 or 11-year-old child. It would be hard to see how Freeman was not aware that Miller was a malleable confabulator.

How much stake do you put into a man's child-like intelligence without seeking strong corroboration and verification, especially when a man's life and liberty are at risk?

Freeman's interpretation of Wilhelm's dying declaration, that Goldblum had set Wilhelm up, is troubling. He had the victim's expressed declaration, corroborated by forensic evidence and a failed polygraph test. Common sense strongly suggests his interpretation was contrived.

It is hard for me to imagine an honest detective fabricating charges or playing with the truth to achieve a dishonest goal, especially in a potentially capital case. Examining the evidence available to the police makes it hard for me to conclude otherwise. Freeman's investigation had a secondary agenda, and it was pursued dishonestly.

Goldblum's attorney, for the most part, concerned himself with the trial's proceedings rather than taking a critical eye toward the investigation.

Reversible errors do lead to new trials, but this case is too unusual. For me as a detective, the trial was not the place to look for errors. Trials result from crimes, crimes require investigations, which must be reviewed to understand the outcome.

The missing case-records complicated my analysis. It bears mentioning that the file for the Wilhelm murder was a large one, and multiple copies of the investigative file were created and maintained. Three copies of this large file vanished. The Mobile Crime Unit and Police Photo Lab files also came up missing. Finally, nearly two decades after the crime, both copies of the file in the Coroner's Office also turned up missing under very suspicious circumstances.

Do not be misled by Freeman's actions in this investigation. He was a capable investigator, an aggressive and single-minded closer with a reputation for securing confessions and convictions. After this case, he had a successful career, rose to the rank of Police Commander, and has since taught at Duquesne University.

I do not suggest that the Wilhelm case was typical of his investigating abilities or tendencies. In my opinion, Freeman became so invested in Miller's lies that he never considered other paths. Freeman defended his decisions to the point of embarrassment.

I believe that when Freeman sent Miller to the Behavior Clinic and learned of his brain injury, he should have given the case an honest look and taken another direction. He should have relied on corroboration and verification concerning any statement given by Miller. He should have presumed that Miller, with an intelligence of a 10 or 11-year-old, would lie, just like any child. When investigating homicide cases, the consequences are higher than other crimes.

As an experienced homicide investigator, Freeman should have gone to the Behavior Clinic and consulted with them, when he saw and acknowledged all of the lies Miller was telling. Freeman knew that he could not prove his case against Goldblum without Miller's lies, and he permitted them to be told to a jury.

We know Wilhelm was an innocent man who came into a significant sum of money as a result of a disability settlement and wanted to use that money to acquire a parcel of land in North Carolina.

As previously discussed, Dixon and Freeman were aware that Wilhelm had no propensity towards criminal behavior. ADA Dixon admitted he never believed Wilhelm was the arsonist, as Miller stated in his sworn testimony. Dixon believed Goldblum was not involved in the land fraud based on the testimony that Dedo would have provided. This means Dixon did not buy into either of the two motives he presented at trial for Goldblum to commit murder.

Retired Detective Salvatore Crisanti, formerly of the Pittsburgh Police Mobile Crime Unit, worked the crime scene in this investigation. He recently provided a written statement to the effect that his partner never would have scraped off the blood spatter from the dashboard of the victim's car without first taking photographs of it.

As previously discussed, several detectives on the case, including Freeman himself, gave statements to the effect that they had seen such photographs. Yet somehow, at Goldblum's trial, not a single photograph depicting the blood spatter on the dashboard could be found. Detective Crisanti also stated that he would never remove blood spatter without first photographing it. The investigative reports that survived, indicated that Crisanti photographed each object first before removing it as evidence, and forwarding it to the Allegheny County Crime Lab for analysis. The point I am making is that Crisanti would have photographed the blood spatter on the dashboard before removing it and sending it to the Crime Lab and, that these important photographs were missing at Goldblum's trial.

As an experienced homicide detective, Freeman knew how to read a crime scene and would have realized that the tails on blood spatters on the dashboard of Wilhelm's car proved the direction from which they came. He made detailed notes and testified at Goldblum's trial regarding the tails of the blood spatter. He also knew that without the photographs, forensic specialists would not be permitted to identify the person most likely to have stabbed Wilhelm inside the vehicle. Therefore, Miller's testimony would not be challenged.

Why is this important?

Had crime scene photos of the interior of the Wilhelm vehicle been available, they would have been analyzed by a crime scene specialist or a pathologist. That specialist would have said that the blood spatter came from the passenger side of the vehicle and not from behind the victim as the prosecution alleged. This appears to be another instance of Freeman working to manipulate the evidence to fit his case, rather than letting the evidence guide his investigation.

Detective Sgt. Joseph Modispatcher was the chief polygraph operator. He tested Miller three days after his arrest to determine whether he was involved in Wilhelm's murder. Miller failed, but the questions asked during that test are missing.

In late July 2011, Sgt. Modispatcher told me he was certain that Miller was the lone assailant. He claimed he kept telling Freeman about his findings, but Freeman ignored them and insisted on putting Miller through two more polygraphs, to be administered by his fellow homicide investigator, Detective Joe Stotlemyer

Following the second polygraph test, Miller confessed that he held Wilhelm down, implicating himself in the murder. This important revelation was covered up and kept from the defense. In fact, even the existence of the second and third polygraphs was not discovered until shortly before Miller's trial, a year after Goldblum had been convicted, and even then by chance. An investigator hired by Goldblum overheard them being discussed.

We only know of these two polygraphs because of the master polygraph log, which was kept separate from the case file. While the disappearance of one case file might not be noticed until someone asked for it, making the master log for all polygraph examinations vanish would not be easy to accomplish.

Stotlemyer reported that Miller had passed the test when asked about killing Wilhelm, but afterwards admitted to holding the victim down. Without knowing what questions Miller was asked, there is no way to determine whether he truly passed the polygraph. Test questions can be asked in such a manner as to elicit double meanings. It is also difficult to determine what role Miller's confabulation would play into his answers.

The important thing is that after the second polygraph, Miller admitted to being involved in Wilhelm's murder. More importantly, this polygraph was withheld from the defense at trial because it would have damaged Miller's credibility.

No reason was given for never entering the second and third tests into the master polygraph log.

Considering all the anomalies of this investigation and prosecution, either separately or in combination, there are a number of difficult questions.

What other case has this many irregularities followed by a mysterious disappearance of all criminal investigation files?

As previously noted, there is a real difference between Freeman and Dixon. I talked to Dixon several times on the phone and in person. One meeting, on March 8, 2007, was video-taped. He was well intentioned and willing to discuss the investigation. I believe he was fundamentally decent and wanted to do the right thing.

I cannot say the same thing for Freeman. I asked Freeman several times to discuss the case and he always declined. For him, I suspect, Goldblum was a means to his ends.

While I did not know him in 1976, I have had time to get to know Goldblum since. I have interviewed him in prison on several occasions, and I have spoken to him on the telephone many times. He understands the huge consequences of poor decisions he made and feels considerable remorse. He recognizes he let his family down and caused them a lot of pain.

Goldblum also feels tremendous regret for having misread the situation between Wilhelm and Miller. Goldblum had no idea that Miller was capable of that kind of savagery and wishes he had done something to stop the fight. There is a very strong possibility that Miller did mentally blackout during the murder, as he claimed in his 1980 PCRA Petition, and that unleashed his savagery.

This case deserves a fresh look without preconceived ideas. What Goldblum may have done decades ago fairly reflects on him as a person at that time. It was not, however, a reason to convict him of a murder he did not commit nor a land fraud in which he was not involved.

This case reveals a clear pattern of contrivance. The investigation and prosecution raise too many questions to be left alone. The facts support the following conclusions:

1. There was no conspiracy between Miller and Goldblum to lure Wilhelm to the garage roof that night. The story given by Miller is simply too implausible and lacks corroboration. Its acceptance by the Pittsburgh Police and prosecutors is questionable.

2. The forensic evidence strongly suggests a one-on-one assault. The defensive wounds on Wilhelm's hands and arms indicate he was not held down while attacked.

3. The evidence strongly suggests Miller was the sole killer, as verified by Wilhelm's dying declaration. Miller's defensive wounds, the arm hairs forensically matched Miller's hair found in a pair of bloody gloves near the scene, the lack of blood on Goldblum's clothes, Goldblum's lack of defensive wounds, Sgt. Modispatcher identifying Miller as the lone assailant after his polygraph, and Miller's 1980 post-conviction application indicating temporary insanity, all contribute to this conclusion.

4. Goldblum was wrongfully convicted of the land fraud perpetrated against Wilhelm.

5. Goldblum was wrongfully convicted of murdering Wilhelm and conspiracy to kill Wilhelm.

6. Goldblum was guilty of accessory after the fact to murder for helping Miller leave the scene of the murder, and for providing Miller with an alibi.

7. Goldblum was guilty for arson, and conspiracy to commit arson with Miller.

8. Wilhelm was wrongfully accused of arson to give a false motive for Goldblum to murder him. Both Dixon and Gilmore, who both worked at the District Attorney's office at the time of this trial, have openly admitted to knowing Wilhelm played no role in the arson.

9. Miller was guilty of the land fraud, for Wilhelm's murder in the second degree, and for arson and conspiracy to commit arson with Goldblum.

10. Miller was guilty of perjury for falsely accusing Goldblum in the participation of the murder and land fraud of Wilhelm.

11. Miller was manipulated by Detective Freeman. Miller's attorney, Vincent Murovich, gave the police carte blanche access to Miller believing his client would receive a prosecutor- recommended prison sentence of 10 to 20 years for his cooperation.

The evidence strongly suggests that in fact, Miller was promised a reduced sentence in return for his perjured testimony against Goldblum. Miller maintained this at his trial and stuck to it throughout his lifetime.

Goldblum was convicted of the first murder solicitation charge, but the case was overturned on appeal. The charges against him for the second solicitation were dropped by the DA. All of these proceedings occurred after his trial.

Why, with all of the police resources, were they not able to find Andrew Kinser Bey at the time of Goldblum's trial?

Was he conveniently misplaced so he would not testify about how he had been coached to approach Goldblum and entrap him into killing Miller?

Goldblum was under considerable stress when the solicitation was first discussed. Though out of jail on bail, he had lost his day job and teaching post. Only the day before the solicitation, his wife left him.

Still, he cannot be completely excused for all this. In fairness, this crime cannot be overlooked. While Goldblum's willingness to meet with Bey and Mook is far from excusable, the facts strongly suggest that Bey's release from jail was arranged with a clear motive to entrap Goldblum into a crime he had not previously considered.

I asked myself, what might have happened had Goldblum refused Bey's offer, then, inspired by the idea, subsequently found someone else to kill Miller?

Who would have been responsible for Miller's murder, the Pittsburgh Police who suggested this crime or the District Attorney's Office who supervised the detectives in their investigation? This type of reckless official behavior has consequences.

Goldblum's second solicitation for murder was clearly manufactured and instigated by Freeman. The police falsely claimed O'Shea took a polygraph concerning the solicitation to murder the officers. The Master Polygraph Log clearly shows that O'Shea took a polygraph for a conspiracy, however not regarding the solicitations to murder. After Ronald O'Shea, the accuser, was confronted with discrepancies in his story, he implicated Freeman. The second solicitation was dismissed by the District Attorney's Office after Goldblum insisted on taking the case to trial and refusing to ask for dismissal under the Speedy Trial Rule.

I do not believe that Charles Goldblum would have sought a hit-man to kill Miller had Bey not been inserted into the picture. Freeman sent Bey to entice Goldblum at the time when Goldblum was extremely emotionally vulnerable.

As noted above, this had a significant impact on the trial and the jury's perception of Goldblum. While Goldblum was in the wrong, so were the police who initiated the process.

Justice and fairness demand that this case be carefully re-examined. I am embarrassed by the conduct of the Pittsburgh Police in this case. Several things were allowed to happen that never should have occurred.

My pre-conceived notion did not turn out to be correct.

Not all convicted defendants are guilty.

* The opinions expressed in this chapter have been approved by Ramsey Consulting LLC.

Detective Jim Ramsey's Timeline and Conclusions *

To get a better understanding of the case and its evolution, Jim Ramsey created the following timeline, which starts at the earliest pertinent event.

- In July 1971, George Wilhelm, a driver for Purolator Armored Car Company, was injured on the job and placed on workmen's compensation pending a disability settlement.
- Sometime in late 1973, Fred Orlowsky, a mutual friend, tells Clarence Miller that Wilhelm is coming into some money and wanted to buy a parcel of federally-owned land in North Carolina to mine semi-precious stones. (Speculation: Wilhelm and Orlowsky had lived together previously following a fire at a bath house on the north side of Pittsburgh. Might Miller have had anything to do with that fire? This was not part of this investigation, so we have no idea whether this was an arson or not, but it is interesting to speculate. Did Miller have any history of arson?)
- In April 1974, Miller contacted Thaddeus Dedo, another friend, who agreed to pose as Ken Manella, an aide to Senator Schweiker. Miller told Wilhelm he could help get him the land.
- In May 1974, Miller, Orlowsky, and Dedo (posing as Manella) met with Wilhelm in Pittsburgh to convince him that Miller could use his political contacts to arrange the sale of the land.
- On 7/24/74, Miller and Wilhelm flew to Washington DC to meet with Dedo, posing as Ken Manella. Wilhelm gave Dedo around $7,000 as a deposit for the land purchase and Miller received $500. There was at least one subsequent ground trip to DC.
- On 8/07/74, Miller and Wilhelm drove to a hotel in Washington, Pa. to meet with Dedo. Wilhelm gives him the balance of the $21,000 and receives a false deed for

the property dated 7/24/74. Miller takes $500 commission.

- In August 1974 Wilhelm traveled to N. Carolina and met a friend. When Wilhelm told him that he owned the land, the friend said it was impossible because the land was in a National Forest and could not be sold. They checked with the recorder of deeds who says there had been no transaction filed.

- On 10/07/74, Wilhelm visited Senator Schweiker's Pittsburgh office and learned he was being swindled. He was advised to contact the FBI.

- On 10/08/74, Wilhelm met with the FBI for an interview on the land fraud. Later that day, Wilhelm filed a complaint at the Pittsburgh FBI Office, accusing Miller, Orlowsky, and Manella (the impostor Dedo) with land fraud. Later that day, he confronted Miller and told him of the FBI complaint. Miller convinced Wilhelm to withdraw the complaint or the land deal would not go through.

- On 10/11/74, Wilhelm and Miller went to the FBI, and Wilhelm withdrew the complaint saying it was a prank to politically embarrass Senator Schweiker. Subsequently the FBI wanted to prosecute Wilhelm for filing a false statement, but the Assistant U.S. Attorney demurred.

- Over the next 13 months, Wilhelm continued to pressure Miller to either get him a valid deed for the property or return his money.

- 11/30/75: Miller later claimed that on this afternoon, Goldblum propositioned him to burn down his restaurant, but he refused. Miller further stated that he witnessed a meeting between Wilhelm and Goldblum that same afternoon. (Note: witnesses testified seeing Miller and Orlowsky at the restaurant, but Wilhelm had never been seen there.) Later that evening, the Fifth Avenue Inn burned down. The destruction was so extensive that neither the Pittsburgh Fire Department nor ATF agents could determine whether or not it was arson.

- 2/08/75: This is the day Goldblum claimed he was first introduced to Wilhelm by Miller at a downtown McDonald's, where they discussed Miller re-paying

Wilhelm the money he owed him for the land deal. When he realized Miller was not being truthful with Wilhelm, Goldblum left, but then agreed to another meeting the next evening.

- On 2/09/76, Wilhelm met again with Miller and Goldblum at the downtown McDonald's around 8:00 pm. An hour later, on the 8th and top floor of a nearby parking garage, Miller attacked Wilhelm with the blade of a grass shear and threw him over the edge of the building. Wilhelm survived long enough to make a dying declaration to the police officer who found him. "Clarence. Clarence Miller did this to me."

- On the morning of 2/10/76, Miller was interrogated by homicide detectives. Pittsburgh Police Sgt. Jack Mook claimed that after speaking with Miller for 10 minutes "you would believe that you were talking to a person with the intelligence of a 10 or 11 year-old." Mook's opinion was shared by other homicide detectives. (Note: so the bar has been set, and the police knew that they were questioning a child in the body of a 38-year-old man. One key was Miller's behavior after being vigorously questioned. He became very nervous, shaking, stuttering, changing statements, attempting to assist the police. Complaining of a bad headache, he fainted twice and was transported to Southside Hospital for treatment. These are symptoms of Confabulatory Amnesia, which corroborate Miller's 1980 PCHR Application. During the interrogation, Miller also stated that he had met with Goldblum on 02/8/76 to discuss the Wilhelm situation, and Goldblum instructed him to arrange a meeting with Wilhelm for the following evening. Neither this first meeting nor the conversation were corroborated or verified. No one ever testified seeing Wilhelm and Goldblum together prior to 2/9/76.

- That same morning, Freeman and Superintendent of Detectives Curran argue at the crime scene. Freeman is initially transferred, but then is returned to the case two days later.

- Also on 2/10, ADA Ted Fagan was assigned to the Wilhelm murder case. Finally, that evening, Miller was taken to Southside hospital for treatment and observation.
- On 2/12/76, the hospital doctors refused to release Miller into police custody. He complained of terrible headaches, and they wanted him to have brain scans.
- On 2/13/76, Miller met with his defense attorney Murovich, Detective Ron Freeman, and ADA Dixon. Later that day, Miller is given his first polygraph test, which he fails. Sgt. Modispatcher, who administered the test, claimed he told Freeman that Miller was the lone assailant. Miller subsequently asserted that a deal was made for him to get a 10 to 20-year sentence if he testified against Goldblum. Murovich gave the police unfettered access to Miller. When the police took a recorded statement from Miller later that day, they were already aware of the confabulation/amnesia issue and the implications of accepting uncorroborated statements made by someone with the intellect of a 10-year-old child. (Miller had just been released from the Southside hospital after being treated for pressure on the brain).
- On 2/16 and 2/17/76, Miller was examined at by the Allegheny County Behavioral Clinic, an arm of the Allegheny County Health Department, and given brain scans. Miller's health records would have been available to the District Attorney and the investigation team, as rules concerning the privacy of health records were not as strict then as now. At that time, sending a person to the Behavioral Clinic was tantamount to a request for their medical opinion on the mental state of the patient/accused.
- On 2/17/76, Miller was diagnosed with Personality Disorder and other maladies. So the police knew of his propensity to be dishonest and his inability to tell the complete truth.
- On 2/18/76, the following day, Miller testified without corroboration at the Coroner's Inquest and accused Goldblum of being Wilhelm's assailant. (In 2007

deposition, former ADA Dixon stated " basically, I told Clarence from the beginning, the only chance you have to **stay alive** is to cooperate.") Following the inquest, Attorney Ernie Orsatti witnesses police detective Charles Lenz sucker punch Ted Dedo in the hall outside the coroner's office.

- On 2/21/76, three days after the Coroner's Inquest, Miller was examined again by the Behavior Clinic psychologists. He had now been examined four times, but Goldblum's defense was not notified.

- On 3/02/76, Miller's statement was tape-recorded by Freeman.

- Between February and June 1976, Miller was frequently removed from the County Jail and interviewed by Freeman. During this time, Freeman also met with Dixon. On June 23, Freeman asked Dixon to not oppose a bail reduction for Miller. Freeman also contacted the minister of St. Mark's church, where Miller's parents belonged, requesting financial assistance for Miller's bond. DA Dixon claimed Freeman asked him not oppose to the bond reduction. (Note: Freeman later denied assisting at all in Miller's bond reduction.)

- On 4/07/76, the Pennsylvania Supreme Court set Goldblum's bond at $50,000. His family made the financial arrangements, and he was released.

- On 4/29/76, Judge Ziegler issued an order to case participants to refrain from making public statements. Dixon later violated the gag order without consequence.

- On 5/15/76, Miller was given a second polygraph test. After the test, he told Det. Stotlemyer that he had held Wilhelm down during the murder. Neither the polygraph results nor Miller's confession were entered into the Master Polygraph Log until 20 months after they had been administered.

- On 5/25/76, Miller was given a third polygraph test. Stotlemyer failed Miller concerning the arson and gave Freeman his opinion that Miller was involved in the arson. In an effort to hide the unfavorable opinion, this test was not entered into the Master Polygraph Log nor was a report prepared.

- On 6/23/76, the Pennsylvania Supreme Court reduces Miller's bail from $50,000 to $30,000, which at an 8-percent bond rate, required a cash outlay of $2,400. Miller's attorney, Murovich, obtained the money from the minister of St. Mark's Church, and Miller was released on bond. At night court that same evening, Miller testified concerning the arson of The Fifth Avenue Inn, accusing Wilhelm and Goldblum with no corroboration. Was his false testimony repayment for the bond reduction and help with financing the bond? From this point to the beginning of Goldblum's trial, Miller meets regularly with Freeman and Dixon. (Note: Miller's bail reduction was unopposed, as corroborated by the record.)
- On 11/23/76, Goldblum's bond is revoked, and he is returned to jail on a charge of solicitation to murder. Earlier that week, Goldblum had been contacted by Andrew Kinser Bey, a prisoner he had met in jail. Bey suggested the idea of having Miller murdered, and he set up a meeting with a "hit man," who was an undercover cop.
- On 12/31/76, again in jail, Goldblum is charged with five additional counts of solicitation to murder several police officers, as well as Miller. This second charge was eventually dismissed under speedy trial rule 1100. (Note: Years later, Ronald O'Shea, the prisoner who made the charges, revealed that it was Freeman who engineered this false claim against Goldblum. The DA eventually dismissed all five of these charges.)
- On 8/15/77, Goldblum's trial began. He claimed innocence and argued that the DA should file a complaint against Miller for lying to the FBI on 10/11/74 concerning the land fraud.
- On 8/31/77, Goldblum was found guilty and sentenced to life in prison plus 30 years. Goldblum's appeal process began immediately.
- On 9/14/77, Goldblum's appeal for a new trial was denied.

Fast forward to 1978 prior to Miller's trial for George Wilhelm's murder

- On 4/28/78, Miller was examined by a psychiatrist, Dr. Merikangas.
- On 5/03/78, Miller was examined by a psychologist, Dr. Van Cara. Both doctors described Miller's symptoms in great detail as Confabulatory Amnesia, the same symptoms he exhibited while under questioning on 2/10/76. This corroborated Miller's prior diagnosis that was not disclosed to Goldblum's defense team.
- On 5/25/78, Miller's trial began. Miller argued that since he testified against Goldblum, he should not be tried for first-degree murder, and that he had mental problems.
- On 6/08/78, Miller was found guilty and sentenced to life. His appeal process began.

Fast forward to 1980 and Miller's post-conviction affidavit

- On 5/09/80, Miller filed a PCRA application, which stated that the police engineered the false claim against Goldblum and that he had been temporarily insane during the assault and never saw Goldblum stab Wilhelm. Miller also claimed his defense counsel had been negligent for not informing him that he could have pled temporary insanity.

It was then four years and one month since Wilhelm's murder. Miller was complaining about his legal representation and promises broken. He questioned his mental condition when he made recorded statements on 2/13 and 3/2/76, claiming that they were invalid because they were the product of the police and not his own. Miller's outline of his illness and hospitalization corroborated the psychologists and psychiatrists description of Confabulatory Amnesia. In a sworn affidavit, Miller denied that he saw Goldblum stab Wilhelm, and he insisted that his actions were those of a person in the state of temporary insanity.

This assertion corroborated Goldblum's version of the murder. Miller claimed that the police and prosecutor "had amnesia" when he came to trial. He was of the opinion that a deal had been made with the prosecutor in exchange for his testimony, and that his attorney,

Vincent Murovich, witnessed the offer made for a reduced sentence of 10 to 20 years in prison.

In a Pittsburgh Post-Gazette article dated March 4, 1980, Miller's defense attorney, Harry Stump, confirmed that Miller had the impression that he had a deal. Furthermore, Det. Freeman stated that he had not been opposed to offering Miller a deal because everyone in the homicide office liked him.

If everyone in homicide liked Miller so much, why didn't Freeman arrange a deal for his cooperation?

Ramsey believes that Miller was offered a 10 to 20-year prison sentence in the presence of Murovich, that the deal was orally made and accepted, but later, the prosecutor reneged. The police and prosecutor clearly took advantage of and manipulated this 10-year-old child in a grown man's body and used him to secure the spurious murder conviction of Charles Goldblum.

Return to the trial of Charles Goldblum

District Attorney F. Peter Dixon spoke to the jury and told them that Miller sometimes lied not knowing he was lying, which happens to be the definition of Confabulatory Amnesia. It is clear that Dixon knew, based on all of the above, that Miller was suffering from Confabulation Amnesia. When he did not reveal it to the defense or explain confabulation to the jury, Dixon defrauded the court.

Proof and Corroboration that Miller had a deal with the police and prosecutor

- On 2/10/76, Miller and Goldblum were arrested and charged with the same degree of Capital Murder, which at that time was death-qualified. (NOTE: Legal observers knew that the statute was going to be struck down, but at the time, the crime was still death-qualified.) Between 2/10 and 12/76, Miller was hospitalized at Southside Hospital, due to extreme headaches and what appeared to be pressure on the brain.
- On 2/13/76, Miller met with Murovich prior to his polygraph test. Miller failed a polygraph test concerning the murder. He claimed he and Murovich came to an agreement with the police and prosecutor that if he cooperated and testified against Goldblum, he would be

exposed to only a 10 to 20 year prison term. Miller began to tell the truth as best as he could as a confabulator. Miller was questioned several times, and notes were taken by the police.

- On 2/16/76, Miller was examined by the Behavior Clinic.
- On 2/17/76, Miller was examined by the Behavior Clinic.
- On 2/18/76, Miller accused Goldblum at the Coroner's inquest.
- On 2/21/76, Miller was examined by the Behavior Clinic.
- On 2/23/76, Miller was examined by the Behavior Clinic.
- On 3/2/76, Miller was questioned and tape recorded by Freeman. (20 days Post Arrest). As of this date, Miller had been examined 5 times, and the reports were available for Freeman to know that Miller was a confabulator.

Prior to Miller's trial (5/25/78), his attorney Murovich claimed that there was a deal for a 10 to 20 year sentence for Miller. A hearing or a conference had also taken place with Judge Ziegler concerning this matter. Murovich was unable to prove that a deal had been made, because there was nothing in writing and the police and prosecutor denied any deal existed.

For proof there was a deal, consider a deposition taken of former prosecutor F. Peter Dixon on March 8, 2007. Those present included attorneys Stanton Levinson and Lee Markovitz and detective Jim Ramsey.

Q: (Levinson or Markovitz) - Now, when you met with him (Miller), was he accompanied by his attorney?

A: (Dixon) - No. No. In fact, his lawyer Vince Murovich had contacted me ahead of time and said I'm going to have Clarence come in and see you, and he's already talked to the police. You've got the file. You know what he's told the police. He's testified under oath at the Coroner's Inquest.

This is where Dixon slipped up. He continues,"I told Clarence from the beginning, the only chance you have to stay alive is to cooperate. So he (Murovich) said I'm letting you know that anything that you do with Clarence is okay with me. You've got *carte blanche*. I don't need to be contacted or be there."

"You know, he's facing the death penalty. So, you know, he's -- he's there to cooperate."

Why is this important and what does it prove?

It is important to know that both Miller and Goldblum were both charged with Capital Murder which was death qualified.

Dixon clearly stated he told Clarence from the beginning that his only chance to stay alive was to cooperate, which indicates he had spoken with Miller even prior to Murovich conversation. Both Dixon and Murovich refer to the death penalty.

When Dixon said "Stay alive," he revealed to Miller that by cooperating, he could be tried for a lesser degree of murder, avoid the death penalty, and serve a lesser sentence of 10 to 20 years. Goldblum continued to face the death penalty.

When Dixon said, "I told Clarence from the beginning, the only chance you have to stay alive is to cooperate," he indicated he had prior conversations with Miller. Dixon indicated that Miller was cooperating by testifying at the Coroner's Inquest, and that he had also given statements to the police. This tells Ramsey that Dixon was satisfied with Miller's cooperation at that point, and Miller expected to avoid the death penalty for his continued cooperation.

The problem is this deal with Miller was never shared with Goldblum's defense.

Prior to Miller's trial, Murovich had a conference with Dixon and Judge Ziegler and stated that Miller had a deal for a reduced, 10 to 20 year sentence. The prosecutor denied any deal had been made.

Two months prior to his PCRA application in 1980, Miller's defense attorney, Harry Stump, stated to a newspaper reporter that Miller was under the impression that he had a deal with the prosecutor if he cooperated and testified against Goldblum.

On May 9, 1980, Miller filed a PCRA application under oath claiming he had been promised a deal of 10 to 20 years for his cooperation. Even if it is true that there was no written agreement between the prosecutor, police, and Miller's defense team, some deal must have been implied. When Dixon told Miller if he wanted to stay alive, he had to cooperate, and he did cooperate, that is proof that there was, at the very least, an understanding that Miller would not face the death penalty and therefore he would be prosecuted on a lesser charge of homicide.

Ramsey uses these timelines to answer important questions he frequently gets about the case.

When did the police and prosecutor learn of Miller's confabulations?

All of the symptoms were present on 2/10/76 and confirmed by Miller's examinations at the Behavior Clinic on 2/16, 2/17, and 2/21/76. Additional confirmation was provided on 4/28 and 5/3/78, when Drs. Merikangas and Van Cara examined Miller and read a brain scan identifying the lesion caused when, as a child, he had been struck in the head by a streetcar.

What we haven't discussed is the importance of a person suffering from this serious mental condition. When questioning Miller and knowing he suffered from this condition or other maladies such as personality disorder and childlike behavior, an investigator should have been careful to seek corroboration for any claims he made. By not verifying the facts when dealing with a confabulator, an investigator fails in his duty to conduct an unbiased investigation. The doctors who examined Miller had a difficult time sorting out his confabulated truths, and that was a signal to look for corroboration and verification.

Had the jury heard from experts describing Miller's mental illness, they would have delivered a different verdict. If a psychologist found it hard to determine Miller's truthfulness, how could a jury separate truth from fiction in his testimony, especially with no corroboration or verification of his statements?

Seeking the truth is often difficult but seldom impossible. The police and prosecutor both have a responsibility to search out the truth, not a false answer to support a chosen motive.

What about those missing dashboard blood spatter photos?

On February 9 and 10, 1976, crime scene detectives Al Crisanti and Ed Hill collected, photographed, and processed evidence at the George Wilhelm murder scene.

The best way to explain the crime scene process is to understand that there is no set number of photos that the evidence technician is required to take. He or she can take a thousand photos if they feel it is necessary. The rolls of film negatives are treated as evidence and need to be protected from spoliation.

Detective Sal Crisanti did the photographing with a standard police-issued 35mm camera. He has no idea how many photos he took of the crime scene. He turned the rolls of film over to the photo lab for processing which they would return as photographs. Detective Crisanti would then turn the photos over to the detective in charge of the case, and he would place copies into the case file. Additional copies were often ordered from the original negatives. The photo lab would print additional copies, and Detective Crisanti would write his name on the back of the photo and the date it was taken, then move onto the next case.

Months and sometimes years could go by before the photos that were taken would be used as evidence. (Note: All of the photos are turned over to the DA who decides which photos to use at trial. The DA might use only one or two of the photos to make his case, but the photos that were exculpatory should have been given to the defense attorney, which they were not.)

Crime scene detectives work numerous cases simultaneously, which makes it difficult for them to remember every photo of every case. That is why they write their name and date of the case on the back of the photos. This helps to jog the detective's memory. If other photos were not used by the DA in a case, then the detective would believe the photos shown as an exhibit were the only ones taken.

It should be noted that it is the responsibility of the police department to maintain a chain of custody, protect evidence, and to provide the defense with copies of all evidence.

Detective Crisanti was deposed on several occasions, and also gave a written statement as recently as September 30, 2015. He maintains that in ALL cases, he would have photographed a blood spatter before removing it and sending specimens to the crime laboratory for analysis. He could not remember a single time that he did not follow this procedure.

This is important because it confirms that the blood spatter on the dashboard was photographed, cleaned off, and sent to the crime laboratory as standard procedure.

The photographs would have been placed into the case file, and a copy would be provided to the prosecuting attorney, in this case ADA Dixon. Dixon was responsible for providing a copy of all exculpatory photos to the defense.

During a deposition with defense Attorneys Stanton Levinson and Chris Eyster, Detective Freeman admitted to having seen the dashboard blood spatter photos, but he could not remember when or where, but he also believed that ADA Dixon saw them. Freeman stated that he could not remember which photos Dixon used at trial. Several days before Goldblum's trial, Sgt. Modispatcher was going through the file, and he recalled seeing the dashboard blood spatter photos.

The blood spatter photos of the dashboard were not presented at trial.

Who would benefit because the blood spatter photos went missing?

The only benefit would go to the prosecution, because the photos in question would have been exculpatory evidence, and without them, experts have subsequently not been allowed to voice their opinions.

The unanimous decision by all of the experts including the prosecution's, is that Miller did the stabbing inside the car from the passenger's seat and not Goldblum, who sat in the rear left side. Should the accused be penalized because the prosecution withheld exculpatory evidence? Is it not the duty of the American justice system to seek out the truth?

In Ramsey's opinion, the prosecution would have to admit that Miller, their own witness, was the person who killed Wilhelm, which was why they were determined to keep the truth from being told.

It is clear from the recount above, that blood spatter photos were taken in this case. The police failed to prevent spoliation of the evidence or someone from the prosecution side removed the photos to deny the accused an opportunity to argue who inflicted wounds on Wilhelm in the car. The defense was never given a copy of the photos. Now, the defense is suffering due to either spoliation of evidence or the deliberate withholding of evidence. Either or both would be grounds for a new trial for Goldblum. If they are truly seeking justice for Wilhelm, then they should set aside prosecutorial ambitions and let the truth be spoken.

What is the District Attorney's office afraid of?

Why do they refuse to admit that Goldblum was denied a fair trial?

Why do they not just say, "We were responsible for the spoliation of exculpatory evidence, so we will use Freeman's description of the blood spatter that he saw at the crime scene, and the defense would stipulate that Freeman's observation is accurate." Let the experts testify, including the District Attorney's own expert, based on Freeman's description of the blood spatter. Then allow an independent judge to determine whether Wilhelm was stabbed in the car by Miller or by Goldblum.

In Ramsey's opinion, the District Attorney's Office wrongfully stood by while a citizen was falsely accused and convicted and has now served nearly 40 years in prison for a crime he did not commit.

Why are you so sure that Wilhelm was not the arsonist?

Charles Goldblum was in the restaurant business for less than one year.

In January 1975, he purchased the Fifth Avenue Inn. On the evening of November 30, 1975, a fire destroyed the building.

We have established by corroborative police documents and statements that Goldblum did not know George Wilhelm during the time of the land fraud scheme. Goldblum's name is absent from the FBI report on the fraud; co-conspirators Dedo and Orlowsky stated he was not involved. The prosecution's only proof were the ramblings of a grown man, a diagnosed liar with the intelligence of a child.

We all know that to avoid punishment, children will make up stories and routinely blame their bad behavior on siblings or other innocent people. That is why parents must corroborate or verify their children's claims; call it, checking up on the story.

One must never lose sight of this when considering any of the crimes involving Miller.

Clarence Miller was a 38-year-old man with the mental capacities of a 10-year-old child, and his statements should be treated as such. We should look at Miller's statements as those of a child shifting the blame, and they should not be accepted without corroboration or verification.

Now here is where it gets interesting.

The investigation by the Pittsburgh Police of the arson, as it related to the homicide, was also a clear demonstration of Willful Blindness.

Ramsey believes they looked the other way to avoid conclusions they did not want to make: that Charles Goldblum was innocent of the land fraud charge, that George Wilhelm was innocent of the arson, and that both claims were based on statements made by a confabulator.

The police knew that Miller had limited mental capacity, yet they accepted his statements without corroboration or verification. When the police did not like statements Miller made, they simply looked the other way, concealed, or ignored the facts (Willful Blindness). They hid statements by Miller that disproved allegations he had made against Goldblum and Wilhelm, and deliberately made sure they were not presented at Goldblum's trial.

In reading all the available police reports, Ramsey could not find one person who ever claimed to see Goldblum and Wilhelm together, anywhere or any time prior to February 8, 1976. Employees of the Fifth Avenue Inn testified they had never seen Wilhelm in the restaurant. No other witnesses claimed to have seen Goldblum and Wilhelm together.

Knowing that, an investigator would have been compelled to seek out anyone to corroborate Miller's incriminating statements.

In fact, Miller destroyed any hope of making himself look like an innocent bystander on May 15, 1976, when, in an effort to explain why he had Wilhelm's blood on his clothing, he told Detective Stotlemyer that he had participated in the murder by holding Wilhelm down.

Stotlemyer told Freeman that information the same day.

Recognizing this would be a problem at trial, Freeman concealed the admission, so that Miller could testify he played no part in the murder. Furthermore, after Miller testified falsely, Freeman made no attempt to correct the record.

In Ramsey's opinion, by doing this, Freeman crossed the line because it was inconvenient and damaging to his version of the crime. He intentionally disregarded the truth and ignored facts that did not fit his desired motive.

On May 25, 1976, Freeman ordered a polygraph test for Miller concerning the arson, and Stotlemyer, who administered the test, failed Miller and offered Freeman an opinion that Miller was involved in the arson.

Freeman was faced with another dilemma. If he ignored the failed polygraph test, covered it up, looked the other way, or made no mention of the test or its findings in any report, then he could allow Miller to testify that Wilhelm was the arsonist. Or he could have been honest and reported the actual findings to the District Attorney.

Unfortunately, Freeman choose the low-road. He both concealed the failed polygraph tests and neglected to prepare reports on them.

At Goldblum's trial, Miller testified that he played no part in the arson and claimed that Wilhelm was the arsonist. Again there was no corroboration or verification of his allegations.

In Ramsey's opinion, Freeman chose to engage in obstruction of justice and spoliation of exculpatory evidence.

Both examples point out that conscious decisions were made to deny exculpatory information to the defense. Furthermore, those decisions themselves were probably criminal.

In Ramsey's opinion, had the jury learned of these two examples alone, their verdict would have been different.

Further proof that Wilhelm was innocent of the arson charge alleged by Miller is that nothing mentioned anywhere in all of the police reports attempted to link Wilhelm to Goldblum and the arson.

The police engaged in Willful Blindness and chose to use Miller's statements because it offered an easy way to get what they wanted, a high-profile conviction.

Wilhelm was dead and could not defend himself. Cops call this "blame it on the dead guy" theory. The police had a responsibility to conduct an honest investigation into Wilhelm and his record if they were going to claim he participated in an arson. If there was an investigation, it would have determined that Wilhelm was a good person without a criminal history.

The arson took place on November 30, 1975, just 69 days before Wilhelm's murder. The police were successful in recreating the movements of Miller, Wilhelm, Dedo, and Orlowsky in the land fraud, which took place almost two years earlier. Surely, they could have recreated Wilhelm's movements on the day of the fire. After their investigation found that Wilhelm was not involved in the arson, another one of their motives for Goldblum to kill him would have evaporated.

This issue alone demonstrates that the police had no intention or desire of disproving Miller's incriminating statements. If the police had conducted an honest and truthful criminal investigation into Wilhelm's murder, they would have found Miller's statement against Wilhelm to be false. And that would have damaged the case they were making against Goldblum.

This is another demonstration of Willful Blindness and bad decisions made during the police investigation into the arson. Had they investigated Miller's accusations against Wilhelm, they would have again discovered there were problems with his ability to tell the truth.

It is the duty of the police to sort out the truth by corroboration and verification. They knew they were dealing with a childlike person, and this was literally a life and death situation. The police should never act so cavalierly when dealing with the lives of people who are wrongfully accused.

The District Attorney's office later admitted that no one in their office believed that Wilhelm played any role in the arson. The problem is, Goldblum has paid for their bad decisions with nearly 40 years of his life, and he continues to pay.

If the District Attorney at the time of Goldblum's trial publicly admitted that they did not believe Wilhelm was involved, would that have made a difference in the jury's decision?

Had the police publicly admitted that Miller failed a polygraph concerning his involvement in the arson, and that it was the opinion of Det. Stotlemyer that Miller was involved, would that have made a difference in their decision?

If your answer is yes, then Goldblum deserves a new trial. In the interest of Truth and Justice, the present District Attorney should re-visit this entire case and go over every crime to determine whether Goldblum received a fair trial.

The District Attorney did re-visit the case approximately 20 years ago, but he was not convinced that Goldblum should receive a new trial. He did not share his feeling why not.

Since then, additional revealing information has come to light.

Ramsey hopes the current District Attorney will take a fresh look at the case, considering all that has been discovered since Goldblum's conviction. He believes the purpose of the District

Attorney's office is to dispense justice. If there is a possibility that justice has not been served, they have a responsibility to correct it.

How do you prove that there was no conspiracy to murder Wilhelm?

A conspiracy requires two or more people to plan a crime.

We have established that Goldblum was not a part of the land fraud conspiracy.

We have established that Goldblum conspired with Miller, not Wilhelm, to commit arson, and that he is guilty with Miller of conspiracy to commit arson. Wilhelm had nothing to do with the arson, and he was falsely accused by Miller.

We have established that Wilhelm and Goldblum did not know each other on November 30, 1976, the day of the arson, so Wilhelm could not have been a part of an arson conspiracy with Goldblum.

The prosecutor subsequently admitted that Wilhelm was not part of any conspiracy to commit arson.

If Wilhelm was not the arsonist, who was?

We know Goldblum had an alibi for his presence during the arson, but years later, he admitted his involvement and identified Miller as his co-conspirator. At Goldblum's trial, the jury was convinced that Wilhelm was the arsonist, and they convicted Goldblum on that false motive theory.

The current District Attorney should consider overturning the verdict on that issue alone. The Commonwealth should stop fighting Goldblum's commutation, and either give him a new trial or release him because of a bad verdict.

Simply put, if Goldblum was not part of the land fraud, and Wilhelm was not part of a conspiracy in the arson with Goldblum, there was no reason for Goldblum to injure or kill Wilhelm.

The conspiracy to kill Wilhelm existed only in the minds of the police who manufactured and manipulated Miller into falsely testifying that there was a conspiracy. Miller swore in his 1980 Post-Conviction appeal that the police manufactured the conspiracy.

We have established with the statements made by Goldblum and corroborated by Miller's sworn affidavit, that it was Miller who killed Wilhelm while in a state of temporary insanity. There is absolutely no proof that there was a conspiracy to kill Wilhelm and no motive for Goldblum to injure Wilhelm, much less to murder him.

Was the Wilhelm homicide investigation and prosecution dishonest?

Ramsey asks you to judge whether Goldblum and Miller received fair, honest, and truthful trials, as guaranteed by the United States Constitution.

When accused of a crime, every American citizen has the right to a fair, honest, and truthful trial. No matter what the crime, police and prosecutors have a duty to try the accused using truthful evidence. Evidence can not to be manufactured, hidden, or cherry-picked because it fits the presumed motive. If the evidence is not there or insufficient, the accused is set free. Consider that:

Miller's psychological profile of confabulatory amnesia was discovered by the police and prosecutor within days of his arrest and was further confirmed during the investigation. The profile was never turned over to the defense.

Miller's damaging statements went uncorroborated or verified and were used as fact despite knowing he had been diagnosed as a confabulator.

Miller admitted he was involved in the homicide, and the police never turned this exculpatory evidence over to Goldblum's defense.

Miller testified under oath at Goldblum's trial that he was not involved in the homicide. This was perjury, but the police and prosecutor suborned him.

Miller took three polygraph tests, and the prosecutor never notified the defense.

Miller failed the first polygraph, and the polygraph operator told Freeman that Miller is the lone assailant.

Miller was given a second and third polygraph test, but neither was ever entered into the Master Polygraph Log, nor was any report made of the tests or their results. Nor was the defense informed of these tests. This is spoliation of evidence and obstruction of justice.

Miller failed the third polygraph concerning his involvement in the arson, and the police hid this important exculpatory fact from the defense and never filed a report during the Goldblum investigation. This is also spoliation of evidence and obstruction of justice.

Detective Freeman corrupted the Polygraph Master Log System by not reporting Miller's last two polygraphs.

Dixon then stated that Freeman was involved in the reduction of Miller's bond, yet at trial, he permitted him to testify under oath that he was not involved. This is subornation of perjury, a criminal act.

At his own trial, Miller claimed he had made a plea agreement to testify against Goldblum, but the Goldblum defense was never told.

Important exculpatory blood spatter photos went missing, which hindered the defense from presenting expert witnesses as to who killed Wilhelm. This is spoliation of evidence and, if deliberate, obstruction of justice.

No polygraph test was given to Andrew Kinser Bey. Or if there was one, there is no mention of it in the Master Polygraph Log.

Bey entrapped Goldblum into briefly considering the murder of Miller. That is obstruction of justice.

The polygraph test administered to O'Shea on December 30, 1977 was for a conspiracy charge, not the solicitation to commit murder. This corroborates O'Shea's affidavit that he was never given a polygraph test concerning his involvement in the entrapment scheme with Freeman. He also stated that Freeman propositioned him to make the false allegations against Goldblum. Obstruction of justice occurred once again.

The prosecution allowed Miller to testify that Wilhelm was the arsonist without corroboration or verification, when it was clear that Wilhelm was not involved.

The police rarely sought to corroborate or verify Miller's statements, all the while knowing they were dealing with someone who had the brain of a 10-year-old child.

By the time of Goldblum's post-conviction hearing in 1997, all of the case files had disappeared. That is spoliation of evidence and obstruction of justice.

How many other polygraph tests did Miller take that were unreported? We will never know, because we can't trust the word of the investigators after they failed to report the second and third polygraph tests and their results.

How many times did the police in this investigation give polygraph tests to other actors involved in this case without reporting them?

How many times in the past have they circumvented the Master Polygraph Log?

Do the police log-in only polygraphs they favor? If they do not like the results of a particular polygraph test, do they just not enter it into the Master Log and pretend no test was taken.

Detective Freeman has forevermore corrupted the system, because there will always be doubts about any conviction in which he was involved.

The system is a good system, assuming polygraph operators are honest and follow proper procedures. The system identifies the person taking the polygraph, the polygraph operator, the date, the crime, and the results of the polygraph (Pass/Fail). Simple and effective, it is easy to go back and find details about who took a polygraph by reviewing the Master Log.

Ramsey believes that if even one of these points is correct, then Goldblum and Miller did not get fair trials and should be retried.

After all this time, why should anyone care who murdered George Wilhelm?

After a decade of investigating this case, Ramsey is confident that serious miscarriages of justice were perpetrated on Charles Goldblum.

In his opinion, the police and prosecutors not only violated the defendant's constitutional right of Due Process, but they also committed serious criminal acts while doing so:

- They knowingly allowed perjured testimony to be presented at trial, defrauding the court.
- They deliberately excluded or destroyed exculpatory photographs, an obstruction of justice.
- They intentionally violated the chain of custody by not turning over photographs, polygraph test results, or defendant confessions.
- They failed to maintain proper control of evidence, which violated spoliation rules and further denied the defendant's due process.
- They rigged their investigation and prosecution to support their false theories.
- They based these theories on the testimony of a frightened, childlike individual knowing he was lying to shift the blame away from himself.

friend of Wilhelm's in North Carolina, and they also located and opened a safety deposit box Wilhelm had in North Carolina.

So it is apparent that early-on the Pittsburgh Police planned to use the land fraud as a motive for the murder, even though as the prosecutor later admitted, they never believed Goldblum was actually involved in that earlier crime.

It is interesting to speculate how the outcomes of the case might have been very different had Thornburgh approved the false swearing and land fraud prosecution in 1974.

With a strong case to make and Wilhelm still alive to identify the perpetrators, Miller, Dedo, and Orlowsky could have been charged, tried, convicted, and imprisoned.

With Miller in prison and not knowing another criminal to burn down his restaurant, Goldblum would likely have filed for bankruptcy rather than opting for arson when he could not sell the Fifth Avenue Inn.

Most importantly, George Wilhelm would not have been murdered. With the balance of his $40,000 injury settlement to begin a new life, perhaps he would have relocated to North Carolina to fulfill his dream of digging for semi-precious gem stones.

Both Wilhelm and Goldblum were victims of unforeseen consequence.

Is there any new evidence?

Even after 40 years, new puzzle pieces of the dishonest prosecution of Zeke Goldblum are still being discovered.

The issue of Thaddeus Dedo being unwilling to testify that Goldblum had played no part in the land fraud perpetrated on Wilhelm has been attributed to his not being granted immunity. While that must certainly have been a factor, there was an even more primal reason: fear.

Dedo said several times that he was afraid of getting beaten up **again** by police.

His fear was documented at least twice.

An investigator who served Dedo with a subpoena on June 24, 1977 noted, "This witness states he was physically attacked and beaten by Det. Lenz at coroner's inquest. Is very fearful of further abuse."

Seven years later, on April 9, 1984, John Portella, an investigator working on the Goldblum case, filed this report:

On 4/9/84, I located Mr. Thaddeus Dedo at 1721 Plateau Street, Carrick, Pgh., Pa. This is a private home and had 3 old autos parked in the driveway.

As I pulled into the driveway area, a white male with a baseball cap on, no shirt, came to the front door stoop and while I was in my car I asked if he was Thaddeus Dedo and he replied "yes, who are you?" I gave him my name and indicated I was a private investigator and started to open my car door. Dedo asked me not to do that so I invited him to come to my car. He did and I gave him my business card and said I needed his help to aid someone who is in prison and that I assured him that he was not in any danger, that he could not be involved, except as a witness and that no one was going to arrest him. Dedo exploded and said he did not want to be harassed, had nothing to say, he was sucker-punched in the court room and ordered me off his property or he was going to call the police and his attorney. I left.

On 4/10/84 at about 10:30 A. M., I called Dedo at 885-1742 in an attempt to try to explain who I was and what I wanted and he agreed to listen. I said I wanted to talk to him about the land deal in North Carolina and whether Zeke Goldblum was involved. Dedo shouted I don't want involved. I do not know anyone named Goldblum and hung up.

Then most recently, on May 5, 2016, during a visit to see Zeke in prison, Ernie Orsatti, a law school classmate of his, long time supporter of his cause, and now a highly respected labor lawyer, had a revelation.

As a close friend (Zeke had been an usher in his wedding) and young lawyer, Orsatti also attended the coroner's inquest for George Wilhelm on February 18, 1976.

As Ernie explained in a notarized affidavit on May 27, 2016:

"I was a law school classmate of Charles J. Goldblum and have been a close personal friend of his since that time. I have been licensed to practice in Pennsylvania sine October 15, 1974, and my area of concentration is labor and employment law.

Prior to my discussion with Jim Ramsey, Marc Simon, and David Bear on May 5, 2016, I never saw a connection between an incident that I observed on February 18, 1976, the day of the coroner's inquest regarding the death of George Wilhelm and Zeke Goldblum's case.

Let me describe what I observed. I attended the coroner's inquest regarding George Wilhelm's death. After the inquest, I returned to my office which was in the Lawyer's Building, a short distance away. While leaving, I was outside the County Morgue, where the inquest took place, and I noticed a white-haired detective, who I identified shortly thereafter to be Charles Lenz, as he calmly but viciously punched a smaller, dark-haired, and younger white male. The one punch knocked the man to his knees. He got up and quickly scurried away, and Lenz calmly walked away as if nothing had happened.

I remember that I knew at the time that the assailant was a police officer, although I don't recall why I knew that. I may have seen a badge on his belt or I may have seen him before. But I am certain that the assailant was Charles Lenz.

The incident stuck in my head because it made me concerned about Charles Lenz and his willingness to assault someone in broad daylight in front of witnesses. I made a mental note to watch out for him, in case he was involved in any other incidents.

However, prior to May 5, 2016, I thought the incident that I observed was just an unrelated example of police abuse of power. Also, since I did not observe what preceded the punch, I was not completely certain that the conduct was not justified.

I don't know what Thaddeus Dedo looked like. But if Dedo said that he was assaulted by Lenz on the day of the inquest, as indicated in investigator reports dated June 24, 1977 and April 9, 1984, which I have just seen for the first time, then what I observed would very likely have been that incident."

While it is no longer possible to know what provoked the brazen punch Orsatti witnessed and both Lenz and Dedo have long since died, it is fair to speculate both about what brought Dedo to the Inquest and what prompted Lenz, a senior homicide detective nick-named "the Silver Fox," to attack him so openly.

This much we do know.

Wilhelm's inquest was held on February 18, nine days after his murder. While the Land Fraud was not public knowledge at that time, both Freeman and Lenz, his immediate superior, would have known about it. The FBI had passed on its investigative file on the land fraud case file to Police Superintendent Robert Coll on February 12, six days earlier. They had already decided to prosecute Goldblum for Wilhelm's murder, using Miller's uncorroborated testimony to do so.

What brought Dedo to the inquest? There was no reason for him to be summoned to testify about Wilhelm's murder, but perhaps he was concerned about how the murder might affect Miller and, by association, implicate him through his involvement in the land fraud.

At any rate, we know, Dedo showed up at the Coroner's Inquest and likely heard Miller testify that "Dedo was with him and Zeke when they did a walk-through."

We know from Zeke that when he and Miller walked through the 5th Avenue Inn prior to the fire, they were alone.

Perhaps, knowing that Miller was lying, Dedo made a comment that someone overheard. Whatever happened, Lenz saw Dedo outside the Coroner's Office and felt compelled to deliver so forceful a message in a public place.

We know that Dedo could and would have testified both that he had played no role in the purported arson nor had Goldblum been involved in the land fraud. Miller was the only person he knew anything about.

Apparently, the Silver Fox decided that Dedo needed to keep his mouth closed and not say anything that might impugn the police's star witness.

At very least, this shows that the police collusion was broader than just Freeman. Why is this important?

When Dedo was silenced by Dixon not granting immunity nor dismissing the Land Fraud charge (a case later dismissed without trial), Zeke was denied due process. Dixon later claimed that he was trying to be "creative" at Zeke's trial and allow Dedo's testimony, but he knew there was a Due Process issue.

Witness intimidation, Assault and Battery on a defense witness, Obstruction of Justice, on these issues alone, Zeke should be granted a new trial.

In all my years in law enforcement, this is the only case I can remember that the police and prosecutor committed more crimes than the accused.

Can the injustice be corrected?
Ramsey challenges the current Allegheny County District Attorney to use the same decision-making process as the National Football League.

Arguably the central issue in the case is who killed Wilhelm; Goldblum or Miller?

In the NFL, referees are on the field to make calls that can be supported by the evidence provided by video backup. In this legal case, there is one expert eyewitness, still alive, who could clearly exonerate one of the two men found guilty of murdering Wilhelm.

That person is former detective Ronald Freeman.

Freeman is not an amateur nor someone unfamiliar with details of the case. In fact, he managed the investigation and testified at Goldblum's trial, describing the pattern of blood spatter on the dashboard of the victim's car. We know that Detective Crisanti would not have removed the blood splatters without photographing them. The blood spatter evidence scrapped from the dashboard was sent to the Crime Lab for examination. Proof of this can be found in item #27 in a document prepared by the Allegheny County Crime Laboratory dated August 25, 1977, which was hand-carried to the Goldblum trial by Detective Freeman. For further corroboration, Detective Edward Hill, Detective Crisanti's partner, testified at Goldblum's trial that blood spatter was removed from the dashboard of Wilhelm's vehicle.

So we know the blood spatter was photographed, and on two separate occasions both Freeman and Modispatcher claimed to have seen the photographs prior to Goldblum's trial. Freeman said he thought Dixon also saw the photograph, but decided not to use them at trial.

If Dixon had used the photos at trial, he would have lost the case against Goldblum.

If Freeman had given the photographs to Dixon, he would have lost the case against Goldblum.

Ramsey believes that either Dixon, Freeman, or both destroyed the exculpatory evidence. There is no other reasonable explanation.

Since the photographs were destroyed and the chain of custody violated, the most practical way to resolve this important issue is to use Freeman as an eyewitness, including his description at Goldblum's trial regarding the blood spatter on the dashboard. Freeman testified that the blood spatter pattern traveled from left to right, with the tails facing the passenger's side of the vehicle.

If people are truly interested in determining who killed George Wilhelm, this proposition should be put before expert witnesses, with a stipulation on the prosecution that they would not argue against Freeman's ability to describe the blood spatter.

Ramsey's guess is that the present District Attorney will not accept the challenge, knowing if expert witnesses were allowed to address key issues, Charles Goldblum would be given a new trial. Rather than facing the truth and righting an old wrong, the expedient decision is to keep in prison for the rest of his life a man who has already served time far in excess of any crime he committed.

* The opinions expressed in this chapter have been approved by Ramsey Consulting LLC.

Detective Jim Ramsey's Comparative Investigation ∗

Cynics say hindsight is always 20/20. They're right.

The dictionary defines 20/20 hindsight as "Perfect understanding of an event after it has happened; - a term usually used with sarcasm in response to criticism of one's decision, implying that the critic is unfairly judging the wisdom of the decision in light of information that was not available when the decision was made."

You have to admit that having a historical perspective does offer distinct advantages when trying to get your head around a complicated crime. Not only are the facts more clear about what really went down, it is also easier to identify and follow the consequences of decisions that were made and paths of inquiry pursued. Same for those that weren't.

In fact, sometimes hindsight is the only way to recognize realities that were always right in your face.

Since you have read *Willful Blindness* this far, you know the broad details of the case that evolved from the murder of George Wilhelm on February 9, 1976.

Of course, no one back then had that perspective. All most people knew about the crime was what they read in the papers or saw on TV news.

Even though I was a Pittsburgh Police detective back then working the narcotics beat, I was caught up in my own investigations and had only a vague awareness of the crime at best. I heard the detectives working the case had good reputations and assumed they would solve the case.

In fact, I didn't get into the case until nearly 30 years after the crime. Then long retired from the force, I was working as a private detective helping attorneys track down evidence to make their cases. An attorney friend asked me to read the Goldblum file, interview several witnesses, and give him my honest assessment.

During my long career as a detective and drug enforcement officer, I worked on many complex investigations, often with various parties acting as go-betweens and facts learned on the fly or second-hand. Furthermore, while taking courses in criminology at

171

the University of Pittsburgh, I developed an interest in following complex cases and studying their outcomes.

I learned that when presented with a case that has many moving parts and so little direct evidence, to look for subtle clues and patterns. I also learned how important caution is, being careful to neither jump to conclusions nor misinterpret evidence.

After my initial reading of the Goldblum file, I was shocked at how many dishonest steps the investigating detectives took. I was not surprised to discover that years after Goldblum was found guilty, both the presiding judge and prosecutor publicly admitted he did not get a fair trial for the murder.

So I looked more deeply, and with my knowledge of proper police procedure and the tremendous advantage of hindsight, I discovered much more that was not right.

That bothered me. Understand my definition of detective is "Seeker of Truth." Being a police detective is serious business, and the reports we file document the truth we find.

When mistakes or lies are found in an investigation, an honest detective is obligated to note them. They're part of the process of discovery. When the evidence is gathered, an honest detective is obligated to separate truth from lies, and only then to conclude who committed the crime.

On the other hand, a dishonest detective has no conscience and is willing to let an innocent person be convicted on false premises, be sentenced to life imprisonment, or even condemned to death.

Willful Blindness chronicles a prosecution that was dishonest from the start, but in addition to chronicling what went wrong, it also can be instructive to compare what actually happened with what should have happened.

First, a bit of background on how homicide investigations unfold in a large police department. The homicide investigation section is called in when someone is discovered dead or dying and the circumstances seem suspicious. Until homicide detectives arrive, police officers secure the crime scene and keep everyone away. The less disturbed the scene, the better the chance of gathering incriminating evidence.

When a call comes into the homicide office, a rotation system automatically assigns the case to the next detective in line. Supervisors are free to assign any investigation out of rotation, but since there better be a good reason for doing so, it rarely happens.

The detective who is assigned the case is called the Primary or Constable, and it becomes his or her duty to manage the investigation and assign tasks to the other detectives involved. It's also important to understand that for all detectives but homicide in particular, a high case-clearance rate is the primary indicator of competence.

Detective Ronald Freeman was eventually given the primary role, although there is nothing in the record to explain how that happened.

Detectives Diggs and Carter, who were the first to get to the crime scene, were initially assigned this task. Freeman arrived at the crime scene that night and, as a senior detective, assumed control. The next morning, Freeman had a disagreement with Assistant Superintendent James Curran, who immediately reassigned him. "Garage Slay Case Detective Shifted, Spats with Boss" read the headline of the Post-Gazette article that ran on February 12, 1976. Yet, two days later, Freeman was back in charge.

In the normal case-flow, once the initial testimonies are taken, photography, polygraphs, forensic evidence gathered, criminal and medical backgrounds investigated, and witnesses identified, the Primary prepares the case to take to the District Attorney's office to make decisions about criminal prosecution.

The record also shows that on February 13, Freeman met with Assistant District Attorney F. Peter Dixon to discuss the Wilhelm murder and made suggestions concerning what charges to bring and against whom, according to the evidence that was available and presented to him at the time.

Following the coroner's inquest, on February 18, ten days after the killing, both Miller and Goldblum were ordered held on charges of first-degree murder.

Although all of the official police files have inexplicably vanished, other available records document how the case proceeded from that point. So many questions arose about this investigation and how it was handled, it seems prudent for another detective to offer an opinion on Wilhelm's murder and how its investigation should have gone, had it been conducted in an honest and truthful manner.

While I have little direct experience with homicides, I did manage the investigation of many notable drug conspiracy cases, some far more complicated than this. In addition, I've had years of other training and experience during my career.

Murders are not that different from other investigations. The objective, comparative investigation and prosecution should proceed without preconceived objectives. Truth has no agenda.

Had I been assigned to be Primary on the Wilhelm case, here's how I would have proceeded, starting with the first police intervention.

Around 9:30 p.m. that snowy Monday, February 9, 1976, Officer Tom Pobicki was investigating a minor traffic accident downtown, when radio dispatch reported a man seriously injured at the nearby Smithfield/Liberty parking garage. Pobicki arrived and was directed to the rooftop, where he looked over the short wall and saw a man lying on a ledge one floor below. Pobicki and Sgt. Reynolds climbed over the wall and down to the man, who, though covered in blood, was still breathing.With Wilhelm lying on the rooftop, Pobicki went to his head and Reynolds to his feet. Finally, desperate to identify his killer before slipping away, and as Officer Pobicki did his best to keep Wilhelm from thrashing around, Wilhelm managed to gasp to Officer Pobicki, "Clarence – Clarence Miller did this to me"

An ambulance arrived, but it was too tall to fit into the garage, so a nearby station wagon was used to ferry the victim down to the ground floor. While being transferred from the rooftop to the station wagon, Wilhelm continued to repeatedly lament, "I'm gonna die! I'm gonna die!."

In the ambulance, Pobicki comforted the injured man, now identified as George Wilhelm.

But even before Wilhelm expired, Officer Pobicki would have notified homicide about the attack and the victim's dying declaration about who did it.

Here is where the normal rotation of detectives would have brought me into the case.

174

As Primary, I would have visited the garage right away, that night, if only to make sure the crime scene had been secured. The Mobile Crime Unit would have been notified to collect evidence and photograph the crime scene, including the vehicle that appeared to be involved in the investigation. I would have made sure they noted the half of a grass shear, which appeared to be covered in blood, the wrench found in the vehicle, the blood trail from the car across the snowy deck to the cement wall, as well as the interior of the vehicle, which we discovered was registered to Wilhelm. I would have directed the MCU to photograph the blood spatters on the car's dashboard and to collect samples.

I then would have gone to the police criminal records bureau. Finding files for several Clarence Millers, I would have pulled their mug shots, along with a few other, similar looking men. Informed that members of the victim's family had come to Mercy hospital, I would have gone there to see if they could identify Clarence Miller. When Wilhelm's brother picked one out and said, "that's my brother's friend, Clarence," I would have immediately sent detectives to watch Miller's residence which was listed as Groveland Street in the Brookline neighborhood.

Early next morning, I would have knocked on Miller's door and begun questioning him about his friend's murder. I would have noticed scratches on his fingers, wrists, face, and neck, plus a laceration the second finger of his left hand, and had them photographed. Miller would have admitted to having met Wilhelm for coffee at McDonald's downtown the night before. He would have said his lawyer friend, Charles Goldblum, was also there. With the victim's dying declaration in mind, I would have taken Miller down to the Public Safety Building for further questioning.

I would then have identified Goldblum and gone to his office to question him regarding what Miller had said. Then, because Miller had used him as an alibi, I would have also taken Goldblum in for further questioning. I would have kept the two of them apart to identify discrepancies that might emerge from their stories.

Next, I would have had search warrants issued for both of their residences, as well as Goldblum's vehicle and office. Then I would have returned to the Public Safety Building and, based on Wilhelm's dying declaration, charged Miller with the murder.

We know from the testimony that during this second interrogation, Miller fainted and was taken to South Side Hospital. I would have followed him there, and once he had been examined by the medical staff, had him placed him in protective custody.

Interestingly, we know that on February 12, the U.S. Attorney passed along the FBI report on the 1974 land fraud to Police Superintendent Robert Coll, who would have immediately notified homicide. So, in addition to the victim's dying declaration, the police already had a second item of evidence linking Miller to questionable activities that involved Wilhelm.

The record shows that on February 13, Freeman and Dixon met with Miller and his lawyer, Vincent Murovich, a well-respected criminal defense attorney.

We know from subsequent testimony that Miller wanted to work out a plea deal for a reduced sentence in exchange for his cooperation and testimony against Goldblum.

Freeman and Dixon both deny they offered Miller any plea agreement, but using hindsight, that seems unlikely.

Although no offer was put into writing, it must have been implicitly understood. Otherwise, why would Murovich agree to let the police and prosecutor question Miller without him being there?

What makes little sense to me is how early in the investigation this agreement seems to have been brokered between Miller and the police/prosecution. Within three days of Miller's arrest, Murovich gave Freeman permission to interview Miller at any time without counsel being present. handed him over to Freeman. It seems implausible that Murovich would have done this had an agreement not been struck. Furthermore, how could police even broker a deal like that so quickly without investigating the case more fully?

Once deals are made, they can't be taken back, so police and prosecutors seldom rush to make them. They pin down major points first. Also remember that a police detective cannot make a deal on their own without the prosecutor's consent.

The usual process for a plea deal begins with a proffer from the defendant's attorney. Then detectives investigate the proffer to determine whether or not the information is truthful.

This did not happen in the Wilhelm case. Miller was handed over *carte blanche* by Murovich. It is hard to believe there was no *quid pro quo.* Murovich would not have handed Miller over based only on the hope of a deal.

At any rate, this agreement lead to Miller's first polygraph, also on February 13. It was conducted by Sergeant Joseph Modispatcher, a trained polygraph operator, and focused on the murder. Now polygraphs are good tools for the police, but they are not to be depended on solely, nor are they admissible in court as evidence.

Miller failed the test, and Modispatcher told Freeman that he believed Miller was the only killer.

That first polygraph result should have been a key factor in deciding whether to actually accept Miller's proffer of a plea bargain. Instead, Freeman and Dixon made a deal with Miller to testify as the accomplice even though, based on the evidence they had, they had to at least suspect he was the actual assailant.

Like Freeman, I would have had the prosecutor writ Miller out of the County Jail and brought to me at the Public Safety Building for questioning. I would have focused on his story about Goldblum's involvement in the murder, because I sensed that something didn't fit right and needed to be cleared up before any deal could be made.

I would have prompted Miller to talk about his criminal background, because it is important to know everything about a key witness. I would have noticed the peculiar way he spoke, dressed, and behaved. I would have discussed his health background, so there would be no surprise mental illness.

It's hard to believe that Freeman didn't recognize Miller's issues. He spent a lot of time with Miller and found him very compliant.

If I had pressed Miller, he would have admitted to the several minor charges on his record that resulted in arrest. He would have told me he suffered a brain injury as a child, and I would have immediately requested an additional clinic examination. The behavioral clinic diagnosed Miller as a confabulator with a personality disorder along with other less serious problems. At that point, I would have gone to a medical dictionary, as I had never heard that term and would have wanted to know how it might damage Miller's credibility.

After researching the term confabulator, I would have recognized a major problem. I would have not have considered anything Miller said without solid, independent corroboration. In all fairness, how can you allow a person with this diagnosis to testify in a murder case without warning the court?

I would have also questioned Miller about his involvement in the land fraud and who all of the participants were. Miller would have said that Goldblum had been the mastermind, Dedo the impostor, he and Orlowsky just helpers, and Wilhelm the victim. He claimed Goldblum collected the money from Wilhelm and dispersed shares to the various co-conspirators. Miller later said that Wilhelm gave the money to Dedo; so now there is a conflict in his statements.

For Miller's story to be true, Wilhelm would had to have known Goldblum back when the land fraud began in 1973 or 1974, when the later was still a law student. I would have asked Miller why, when Wilhelm went to the FBI, did he not mention that Goldblum had any involvement in the fraud, let alone being the mastermind behind it?

Why did Wilhelm only mention you and the impostor? Miller would not have been able to answer that question, but I would have let it be for the moment.

I would have approached Dedo and Orlowsky separately. I would have told each that I intended to arrest him for the land fraud and then offered him a chance to come clean in exchange for leniency. I would have emphasized that I only needed one of them to confess, so they should own-up sooner rather than later. I would have also reminded them that while the fraud charge by itself might normally entail a significant sentence, a brutal murder could have even more serious consequences.

While neither would be offered immunity, one of them might have gotten himself less jail time and restitution. Considering that Dedo later came forward voluntarily during Goldblum's trial, in all likelihood, he would have taken me up on my offer. Orlowsky probably would have too.

For the time being, however, let's say that Orlowsky declined my offer. Now, after receiving approval from the DA, I would have approached Dedo through his attorney, and he would have said, that if not arrested or given Use Immunity, he would be truthful. His truthfulness would have exonerated Goldblum, because Goldblum played no part in the land fraud.

I would say I'd get back to him. Since I know Dedo's honesty would exonerate Goldblum in the land fraud, there was no motive there for him to injure Wilhelm. So he was not part of that crime, and

Miller was directing the blame away from himself. Hindsight shows that other than Miller's false statements, there was never any independent testimony that Goldblum ever played any part in the land fraud. I would have had to disclose Dedo's statements to Goldblum's defense. It was required by the Brady rule.

I understand why an ambitious detective might still be tempted to believe Miller. If Goldblum did murder Wilhelm, it would be a more sensational case and newsworthy, the kind of case that could advance a career. On the other hand, the tactic was also risky. If a case like that blows up, it could kill a career. Most detectives are cautious and do not stick out their necks. Freeman deliberately skipped a lot of basic steps that a detective would normally take. Why was he trying so hard to build Miller's credibility?

My next best hope for finding a motive would lie in the second crime that Miller brought up.

Miller claimed Goldblum conspired with Wilhelm to burn down his restaurant in November 1975. He said Goldblum solicited him to be the arsonist, even walked him through the building and showing him holes drilled in the walls where Sterno would be placed to accelerate the fire. According to Miller, when he told Goldblum he would not burn down the restaurant, Goldblum immediately said he'd have Wilhelm do it.

At this point, I would have looked into Wilhelm's background. After some digging, I would have discovered he was known as a law-abiding citizen with no criminal involvement in his life. Everyone I interviewed said he would be the last person on earth to get involved in an arson.

While Freeman accepted Miller's account of the fire, I would have found it unbelievable. I would have pressed Miller to tell the truth about this. I would have asked him why he was seen at the restaurant shortly before the fire, while Wilhelm had never been seen there. By Freeman's own account, he did not believe Miller's claim that Wilhelm had set the fire. It makes no sense to me that Freeman did not follow up on this.

I would have also checked with the Pittsburgh Fire Department who investigated the fire and did not rule it as arson. ATF was also called in, and they also could not determine arson as the cause.

Even after Miller's testimony, the Fire Department re-opened their case on the fire but found nothing.

Here again, Freeman failed to question Miller's story that he was not involved in the arson.

I would have. I would have made clear to Miller that any deal was contingent on him being totally honest about everything. I would have reminded him that, of the list of charges he was facing, arson was not the most serious.

I now would have been convinced Miller was again shifting the blame from himself and this time, onto the innocent victim, Wilhelm, who was dead.

There was other proof. On May 15, Freeman had Miller take a second polygraph test administered by Detective Joe Stotlemyer. After the failed test, Miller admitted to Stotlemyer that he had participated in Wilhelm's stabbing. On May 25, Freeman had Stotlemyer give Miller a third polygraph test concerning the arson, which he again failed. Stotlemyer stated that Miller was lying and he believed Miller was involved in the arson. Curiously, records of the second and third polygraph were never entered into official logs.

Ethically, I would have been unwilling to present the arson as a motive for Goldblum to murder Wilhelm, when I did not believe it to be true. My hope to find a motive for Wilhelm's murder based on his participation in the arson had also flamed out.

By this point, neither I nor anyone else in the District Attorney's Office believed that Wilhelm did the arson, as Miller was still claiming. There was still no motive for Goldblum to injure or kill Wilhelm.

I would now question Miller concerning the murder. Since he had already lied to me on at least two key issues, I knew I had to be careful about anything he said.

Miller claimed that the day before Wilhelm's murder, a Sunday, he went to Goldblum's downtown Pittsburgh office in the Koppers Building, and called him downstairs. According to Miller, Goldblum suggested strolling over to the Smithfield/Liberty parking garage a few blocks away. He said that they went to the garage's rooftop level, where Goldblum walked around kicking the snow. Miller said that Goldblum was looking over the wall when he suggested that he was going to lure Wilhelm up to the roof the next day to beat him up.

Why? Because Wilhelm kept calling Goldblum's office, threatening to expose him for starting the restaurant fire and hounding him for the money that had been promised. Freeman accepted all of the above and never challenged Miller's account.

I could not have left it at that point. It was all too implausible. I had already ruled out Wilhelm as the arsonist, so I knew that Miller is lying to me again about another important fact, but I would have wanted to listen to the rest of his story.

However, I would have asked some hard questions and made him understand I would not accept stories that made no sense.

I would have asked Miller if anyone else was present when Goldblum made this suggestion, and he would have said no.

I would have asked him why he ever agreed to such an impractical plan to confront Wilhelm in such a public place. I would have told Miller that his account made little sense to me. When he gave a typically passive excuse like he gave at trial, I would have told him he had to do better. At Goldblum's trial, he came across as someone who didn't like to do any thinking and just went along with what he was told. Freeman seems to have accepted his line, but I would not have given in to it.

I would have asked Miller why a strong, 6' 2" tall man like Goldblum would need his help to beat up the much smaller Wilhelm? Miller would have said he did not know.

According to Miller, Wilhelm drove downtown the next evening, February 9, to meet with him and Goldblum. Wilhelm parked on the street a short distance from the McDonald's, entered the restaurant, and had a conversation with him and Goldblum about Goldblum re-paying the money taken in the land fraud.

At this point, we knew that Miller lied about Goldblum's involvement in the land fraud, so in reality, Wilhelm was there arguing with Miller to repay the money. Nor was there any mention about Goldblum paying Wilhelm for the alleged arson, which occurred just two months prior. All they talked about was the land fraud?

After some time, Wilhelm, Miller, and Goldblum left the restaurant and climbed into Wilhelm's blue Plymouth Fury, with Wilhelm driving, Miller in the front passenger seat, and Goldblum in the back, behind Wilhelm. Miller claimed it was Goldblum who suggested that Wilhelm park in the public garage a short distance away, the same garage Miller said he and Goldblum had visited the previous day.

Miller said that Wilhelm entered the garage and drove to the top floor, where he parked.

Miller claimed an argument had ensued, and Goldblum clocked Wilhelm on the back of the head with a wrench. However, the medical examiner found no indication that Wilhelm had been hit on the head inside the vehicle, as Miller suggested. Nor does the autopsy report mention any wound to the rear of Wilhelm's head, nor was any blood, human tissue, or hair found on the wrench to suggest it had been used to hit someone. These are not clues detectives overlook.

According to Miller, Goldblum then began stabbing Wilhelm from the back seat.

Amazingly, rather than challenging Miller's account, Freeman accepted it without question. This has to be considered even more in light of what he already knew.

He was aware of Wilhelm's dying declaration, that Miller's clothing was covered with Wilhelm's blood, and that Miller had defensive scratches on his wrists and face. From his testimony, we knew that Freeman knew about the blood spatter on the dashboard of Wilhelm's car.

Yet he did not challenge Miller.

I can not imagine overlooking these discrepancies.

Freeman's skewed analysis doesn't end there.

One of the crime scene detectives, Sal Crisanti, attested that the Mobile Crime Unit took photos. If Miller was telling the truth, those photos would help corroborate his story. If the blood spatter pattern was as Freeman described at Goldblum's trial, Miller was lying. Then the only person inside the vehicle who could have stabbed Wilhelm would have been Miller.

At this point, I would have had the photos taken by Detective Crisanti in the case file. I would also have independently observed the blood spatter and cast-off on the dashboard, and knowing how to read blood spatter, I would have caught Miller in another lie. When blood spatter travels from left to right, as Freeman described, only the person to the right of the victim could have done the stabbing.

Miller continued his confabulation, saying Wilhelm tumbled out of the driver-side door and tried to escape. According to Miller,

Goldblum also got out of the car and followed after Wilhelm, continuing to stab him. Miller said that when Wilhelm reached the low wall at the edge of the floor, Goldblum hoisted him over the wall.

Miller claimed that just as Wilhelm disappeared over the wall, a garage elevator door opened. The man who got out said he heard something that sounded like ice falling from the roof.

Most importantly, Miller said he did not participate in the murder. Yet in a statement following a second polygraph he was given on May 15, Miller admitted to participating in the murder.

I would have asked Miller to describe again the clothing that he and Goldblum were wearing at the time of the murder. Earlier, he had claimed Goldblum had been wearing hip-high fishermen's wading boots and an outer coat over his business suit.

Without the benefit of hearing Goldblum's version of the event, I would have spoken with Mr. Kurutz, the witness who was exiting the elevator shortly after the assault. I would have asked him to describe the clothing both men were wearing, because I had nothing other than Miller's statement to connect Goldblum to the murder. Kurutz identified Miller's clothing, then described Goldblum's clothing as business wear, a suit, top coat, hat, and glasses.

Here is another discrepancy between Miller's description of Goldblum's clothing and Kurutz's recollection. It again appears that Miller was deflecting the blame away from himself.

I think that with all of the blood at the scene, some would surely have gotten on Goldblum's clothes or shoes. We had already searched Goldblum's home, office, and car. The clothes he wore the night of the murder were confiscated and examined by the Allegheny County Crime Lab. No blood or any forensic evidence relating to Wilhelm was found on Goldblum's clothing or shoes. No fishermen's waders or bloodstained overcoat were found.

Finally, I would have reviewed the entire case and the notes from the other detectives several more times, looking for any connection that would link Goldblum with Wilhelm's murder.

Then, armed with all of the investigative findings, I would have made an appointment with the assigned prosecutor at the District Attorney's Office, to go over the case and get recommendations.

In a complex case like this, prosecutors often ask for more investigation and follow-up. More importantly, Miller posed serious problems as a witness that had to be resolved. Lastly, we would have had to decide what charges to file against Goldblum.

Problems with Miller as a Witness

Our conversation would have started with the reliability of using Miller as a witness. I'd tell the prosecutor that Miller had a brain injury and had been diagnosed with a personality disorder known as confabulation. I would have explained that a confabulator will compulsively lie, fabricating imaginary details to compensate for loss or impairment of memory. This made it hard to know when Miller was lying or being truthful.

The prosecutor would have confirmed what I already knew; that in any trial in which Miller testified, the defense would have to be apprised of Miller's condition, as required by the Brady Disclosure Rule.

I would have explained about Miller's three failed polygraphs; that Modispatcher, who administered the first test, told me Miller was the lone assailant. Let's assume I also knew about the second and third polygraph tests, that Stotlemyer, who administered them, told me Miller had failed when asked about the arson. He also reported that after the second test, Miller stated he had participated in the attack.

The prosecutor would have disclosed this information to Goldblum's defense. The prosecutor would not have been comfortable letting Miller on the stand, knowingly allowing perjured testimony to be presented. Getting the truth from Miller would be crucial.

If Miller testified that he did not play any part in the killing, the prosecutor knew about his admission to Stotlemyer, in addition to the forensic evidence and the dying declaration. The prosecutor would have asked me to talk more with Miller, and he would also have wanted to interview him personally.

Throughout it all, Miller would have been told in no uncertain terms that if he lied to us, there could be no plea deal. I'd explain the evidence and make sure he knew whatever he said had to be consistent with it.

Freeman did none of this. He never second-guessed Miller.

This does not get ADA Dixon off the hook. He also met with Miller many times. It is hard to imagine he was not aware of the problems of using Miller as a witness. In fact, Dixon eventually warned Goldblum's jury that Miller might sometimes lie and not be aware of it, the definition of confabulatory amnesia.

There's another curious issue.

After they were arrested and charged, both Goldblum and Miller managed to get released on bail, but under very different circumstances.

Goldblum had to get a ruling from the Pennsylvania Supreme Court, which set bonds for both men at $50,000. Goldblum's family posted his bond on April 7.

Two months later, Miller also made bond, but his release was orchestrated by Freeman, with Dixon playing a supporting role. Freeman engineered getting Miller's bond reduced from $50,000 to $30,000 and then convinced the pastor of the church that Miller's parents attended to put up the cash necessary to free him.

Freeman's course of action was not only highly suspicious, it was definitely against the police rules of procedure.

If Miller had asked me to help him make bail, I would have refused outright. However, what made this situation more criminal was that Miller did not ask Freeman or Dixon to assist in reducing or procuring his bail. This was the dark and shadowy idea of Freeman and Dixon.

From Wilhelm's dying declaration and Miller's own admission to participating in the murder, we knew he was involved in a brutal murder. If I helped him make bail and he got into any trouble, I could kiss my job good-bye. Miller was jailed only two blocks away from the Public Safety Building. I would have had him placed in a cellblock there while investigating his leads. So it made no sense for me to help him make bail.

Finally, it is interesting to observe, through the power of hindsight, that Dixon did let Miller present testimony at Goldblum's trial which he knew at the time was false. Furthermore, neither of the Stotlemyer polygraphs nor Miller's statement that he had participated in the murder were not entered into official logs or shared with Goldblum's defense until nearly a year after he had been convicted.

These oversights played major roles in this miscarriage of justice, but it's now important to look at the three crimes in more detail.

The Land Fraud

My next step in building this case would be to break down the three crimes for the prosecutor, looking for a motive for the murder that implicated Goldblum or anyone else. In first-degree, potentially capital murder cases, motive is paramount.

I would have used the basic elements to frame the case.

Starting with the land fraud, I would have told the prosecutor that Miller claimed Goldblum was the mastermind, Ted Dedo was the impostor posing as Ken Manella, and he and Big Fred Orlowsky were just helpers. I'd point out that the incident had taken place in 1973 or 1974, one to two years before the murder.

We'd consider this carefully, because if Goldblum had been a co-conspirator, he might have had a motive to kill Wilhelm.

I would have explained how Wilhelm got furious at Miller when he discovered that Dedo was an impostor and reported the incident to the FBI for investigation. The FBI are thorough investigators, but nowhere in the 302 Reports they filed is Goldblum's name ever mentioned. As angry as Wilhelm was, he fingered the impostor and his friend Miller to the FBI, yet never mentioned Goldblum, the so-called mastermind who Miller said had taken the money.

Although we agreed this was significant, the prosecutor would have asked me to question Miller further about this issue. In light of the FBI reports, we could not proceed against Goldblum based solely on Miller's assertions.

Furthermore, we had recently discovered that the falsified land deeds had been prepared on Dedo's typewriter using Pennsylvania forms. It's doubtful a trained attorney like Goldblum would have done such a sloppy job.

With Wilhelm dead and Miller telling lies, we realized we needed to talk to both Dedo and Orlowsky. I would have sought the prosecutor's permission to offer a plea deal to one or both of them regarding the case against them in exchange for the truth about what happened. We needed only one to flip, but if either named Goldblum as part of the fraud, we'd have a motive for him to murder Wilhelm.

While the land fraud wasn't as important with Wilhelm dead, the crime could be used to convince either Dedo or Orlowsky to talk. Knowing about Miller's confabulation, we had to get corroboration about anything he said.

Having worked with many prosecutors, I know they all would have emphasized the need to find out what really happened. Apart for any veneration for the law, prosecutors prefer straight forward cases with little or no doubt. They do not like parsing the truth and hate being surprised.

We know Dedo and Orlowsky were likely to flip in return for lenient sentencing, and that the fraud itself was not as important as whether it was a motive for murder. We needed to know who killed Wilhelm and why. The dying declaration and forensics made clear who the assailant was. What we needed to determine was why Wilhelm was killed.

If their testimony confirmed that Goldblum was not involved in the land fraud, that would have eliminated that crime as a motive for him to murder Wilhelm.

The police record shows no attempt by Freeman or Dixon to reach out to Dedo or Orlowsky. That is hard to understand. Freeman accepted Miller's word for nearly everything. When Freeman had contradictory evidence, he never challenged Miller in any way. In all my years as a detective, I never experienced anything like this.

After Goldblum's trial, Dixon allowed the speedy trial time to expire against the land fraud, and the case against Dedo and Orlowsky was dismissed. I would have asked the prosecutor how he allowed this to happen. I would have also contacted the FBI and U.S. Attorney to see if Federal charges could still be brought for the land fraud. Freeman and Dixon did not do this. I have to question their motives Was this payback to Dedo and Orlowsky for not testifying that Goldblum was not involved in the land fraud? If so, it would have blown the prosecution's false motive that Goldblum murdered Wilhelm out of the water.

Even after Goldblum had been convicted, he would have received a new trial had Dedo or Orlowsky's testimony come out. If they had been successfully prosecuted, Wilhelm's family might have received some restitution.

The Arson

If the land fraud wasn't a motive for Goldblum's involvement with the murder, might the restaurant fire have been?

I'd remind the prosecutor we have Miller testifying that Goldblum brought him into the restaurant the afternoon of the fire and solicited him to burn it down. Miller said he declined, and at that point, with no other corroborating witnesses present, Miller said Goldblum told him he'd have Wilhelm burn the restaurant because he owed him some money.

If that statement was true, then it should be used in trial. The problem is that other evidence was not consistent with Miller's story. After the fire, witnesses were found who said they saw Goldblum and Miller, talking together, but they could not verify what was said. That only corroborates they were together, not the truthfulness of Miller's testimony. No one saw Wilhelm.

I would have told the prosecutor that Stotlemyer had administered a second polygraph test to Miller on May 15 concerning his involvement in the murder, and after failing the test, Miller admitted participating in the assault. So he participated in the murder, but he was going to testify that he did not participate. On May 25, Stotlemyer administered a third polygraph which Miller failed when asked if he participated in the arson. Stotlemyer's opinion was that Miller was involved in the arson but Miller was prepared to testify that he was not involved.

I would have told the prosecutor that a background check of Wilhelm found he was known as a law-abiding citizen who never would have gotten involved with criminal activity. Furthermore, the fire had been investigated, and no one could determine whether it had been arson. How could someone with no experience burn down a multi-story building so cleanly and leave no evidence behind?

When the prosecutor asked whether I believed Wilhelm was the arsonist, I would have said no, that it was only another example of Miller's blame-shifting.

If he asked why, I'd explain that Miller knew too much about the fire and was also seen at the scene of the crime. I'd still think Goldblum might have been involved, but that he had hired Miller or Orlowsky to be his torch.

Based on this, the prosecutor would have told me to interview Miller again. He'd also ask me to reach out to Goldblum through his attorney.

The detectives never did this, which is as hard for me to understand as their total acceptance of Miller's story.

In talking to Miller, I would have told him I knew he was involved with the fire, but Wilhelm was not. If he wanted to help me convict

Goldblum, he had to tell the truth about the arson. If he didn't, there would be no plea deal.

While I would have been unwilling at that point to charge Goldblum with murder, I would want to charge him with arson. That is part of why I'd want to pressure Miller. Once I had an arson case against Goldblum, I might have leverage with Miller concerning the murder and maybe the fraud. This might not have panned out. Miller was an unreliable witness with a lot of negative baggage, and Goldblum was represented by a respected criminal defense attorney.

We would have concluded that if Wilhelm wasn't involved with the arson, it could not be used as a motive for murder against Goldblum. This would have been fundamentally dishonest. While police and prosecutors have been known to stretch the rules, this step would have been too far for any prosecutor I have dealt with over the years.

The Murder

We would then turn our attention to the murder itself. Even though we still had not found a motive for Goldblum to kill Wilhelm, there was more evidence to examine.

Playing the devil's advocate and knowing involvement in a conspiracy could pull someone into a murder, we'd double check for any hint of one.

We already knew Goldblum had nothing to do with the land fraud. We had enough background and supporting evidence to know that Wilhelm had not been the arsonist.

However, we also knew Goldblum did lie to the police in abetting Miller and providing an alibi the night of the murder. We strongly suspected he had hired Miller to burn down his restaurant, even though no evidence of arson had been found.

But these assumptions did not provide a valid, realistic motive for an attack. Evidence, experience, and common sense all indicated that Goldblum was an onlooker to the murder, rather than perpetrator. Motive to cover up for Miller is not the same thing as motive to attack Wilhelm.

While we concluded that Goldblum was not Wilhelm's assailant, he was clearly culpable as an accessory after the fact for hindering apprehension. We also could charge him for unsworn falsification, for lying to the police.

How would Freeman, an experienced homicide detective, have missed submitting charges this clear?

While we were able to corroborate that Miller called Goldblum at his office that Sunday and that they left together to meet with Wilhelm, we found no actual evidence to indicate the murder the next day was premeditated.

We would have rejected Miller's account that he and Goldblum visited the garage the day before the murder as fantasy contrived to create premeditation. It may have been a result of his confabulation, but the story did not help his case, only incriminating him and making him part of a conspiracy. His other lies to deflect blame did not hurt him legally.

If not confabulation, then the story might have been suggested to him by others.

Furthermore, I would have asked why Goldblum would have planned an attack in such a public place. Why the open air roof top, rather than a less visible part of the garage where evening shoppers might be less likely to witness the assault? For that matter, why not drive to an even more secluded place, a park, down by the river, or out of town? In my opinion, Miller was trapped in his confabulated story.

Miller's description of what occurred in Wilhelm's car is also discredited by the crime scene evidence. The photos I had seen of the dashboard blood spatter clearly showed Wilhelm's stab wounds were inflicted by the person sitting in the front passenger seat, Miller, and not Goldblum, who was sitting in the back.

Even without photos, Freeman's detailed description at Goldblum's trial of the blood spatter would have been enough to discredit Miller's testimony. Dr. Wecht and Dr. Herbert McDonnell were willing to render opinions based on that description alone. Why did Freeman not share his description with anyone until he testified at Goldblum's trial? He had access to the coroner and medical examiner, and he knew the significance of the blood spatter.

Had I shared those photos or that description with the prosecutor, he would have sent me back to squeeze more truth out of Miller. These inconsistencies had to be explained before the case against Goldblum could proceed.

I would remind Miller of the forensic evidence that indicated his guilt, and the bloody clothes he had tossed in to a garbage truck near his home after the murder. How did he explain changing his story about why Goldblum had no blood on his clothes or shoes, saying he had been wearing an outer coat and fisherman's waders? This was contradicted by the eyewitness, Richard Kurutz. Then there were the scratches on Miller's wrist and face, plus the finger laceration.

And the wrench that Miller claimed Goldblum used from the back seat to hit Wilhelm in the back of his head, the crime lab examined it and found no trace of blood, tissue, or hair on it. Furthermore, the Coroner's Office stated that there was no wound to the back of Wilhelm's head, which contradicts Miller's statement.

The prosecutor would have wanted to know more about Kurutz's statement. He said when he came out of the elevator and saw two men standing at the rail, he heard a noise that sounded like the thud of falling ice.

This could be considered evidence that Goldblum was at the wall when Wilhelm went over, but it would not have been enough for me. First, if Goldblum was that close to Wilhelm, there would have been blood on him.

Second, Kurutz reported hearing a sound like ice falling from a roof. A thud could be caused by anything from someone slamming a car door or trunk, or many other sounds. On the open area of a garage roof, sound travels in all directions. Miller said the sound Kurutz heard was Wilhelm hitting the ledge, but because of all his lies, I can't believe him.

An equally plausible explanation is that Miller and Goldblum were looking over the wall some short time after Wilhelm fell, and a car door or car trunk closed which sounds like a thud. Kurutz might also have been mistaken about the timing.

Based on our conclusions, we would have charged Miller with Wilhelm's unpremeditated murder, but not Goldblum. He was an accessory after the fact and lying to the police. We also saw Goldblum and Miller guilty of the arson of Goldblum's restaurant, but it would be difficult to prove, because Miller accused the innocent dead victim. We'd want to find if Orlowsky was involved with the arson, as he had been seen at the restaurant the day of the fire. We'd still try to get Miller to come clean about his participation in the arson. If he did, we could confidently charge Goldblum with the arson. Finally, we saw Miller, Dedo, and Orlowsky committing the land fraud. If we let Dedo testify under a plea bargain, he would have verified that, as well as the fact that Goldblum had played no role in the fraud.

But we would see no evidence of a conspiracy to attack or kill Wilhelm. Since Miller was named in the dying declaration, he was clearly trying to shift blame for the murder onto Goldblum. He did the same thing with the land fraud and the arson, naming Goldblum as the fraud mastermind and Wilhelm as the arsonist.

We knew that Miller enjoyed being associated with politicians, and he knew a lot of them. He ran errands for them, and he and Wilhelm worked together posting campaign signs. Their tools for that trade include a staple gun, a hammer or wrench, and a grass shear blade to pry up the staples. We were confident Miller knew the murder weapon was already in Wilhelm's car, which was more circumstantial evidence of the lack of previous planning. It also pointed another finger in Miller's direction, since he knew about the shear blade, while Goldblum had no reason to know. Doing the attack on the roof also indicated a lack of prior planning. I would tell all this to Miller when I pressed him to tell the truth.

If that didn't work, I would have approached Miller's attorney and told him I needed his help getting the truth. I'd remind him that if Miller was part of a conspiracy, he would be guilty of first-degree murder. If he came clean and as part of that, admitted he was the lone assailant, his sentence could have been third-degree murder.

The prosecutor would want to know more about Bill Hill, the union president who knew Wilhelm and testified he'd heard Wilhelm claim to know Goldblum.

We know that both Miller and Wilhelm liked to boast about knowing important people, attorneys, judges, and politicians. Miller regularly introduced people to politicians. It's possible he also boasted to Wilhelm about knowing Goldblum.

When Bill Hill mentioned that while riding in a car with Wilhelm, Wilhelm said he knew Attorney Charles Goldblum. But it's not clear whether Wilhelm really knew Goldblum or only knew of him. Hill also said that Wilhelm boasted about his importance and told a lot of stories that were not true. We have interviewed a lot of people, and no one ever saw Wilhelm and Goldblum together.

I would have also asked the prosecutor whether he had a problem if I reached out to Goldblum's attorney, David Rothman, to see whether he'd let me interview his client.

Before I did that, however, I'd check out Goldblum's background. I would have found no police record, nor anything else that might have indicated trouble. The 26-year-old Goldblum had graduated from Duquesne Law School in 1974, passed the bar, and found work as a tax specialist at a downtown accounting firm. Married shortly after college, he also taught a course at Pitt. The second son of prominent rabbi, Goldblum also taught religious school and tutored Bar Mitzvah candidates.

He certainly didn't fit any profile of a murderer.

Rothman probably wouldn't have let me at Goldblum before trial, but he might have made a proffer, one that would have been consistent with Goldblum's trial testimony.

I would have asked Rothman what Goldblum's version was of what happened inside Wilhelm's car. He would have said his understanding was that when the three men in the car reached the garage's top level, an argument broke out between Wilhelm and Miller in the front seat.

I'd have asked Rothman why they went to the garage roof, and he explained it was not planned, that they just ended up there continuing their discussion from the McDonald's restaurant.

I would have asked for more detail about what happened in the car.

Rothman explained that Wilhelm and Miller were friends who worked together hanging political campaign posters. That evening Wilhelm was driving his car, a blue Plymouth Fury, Miller was in the passenger seat, and Goldblum in the back. While Wilhelm drove higher in the garage, he and Miller argued about the money Miller owed him.

When they got to the top floor, Miller admitted he couldn't pay back the fraud money because it had been spent. Wilhelm then punched Miller in the face. Miller went crazy with a half of a grass shear that he found and began to stab Wilhelm, the same tool they used to pry up staples when taking down political posters from wooden utility poles.

193

After being stabbed several times, Wilhelm tumbled out of the driver's side door and tried to crawl away. Miller got out and continued his enraged attack. Goldblum exited the rear driver's side door and backed away from the brutal assault.

When Goldblum reached the stairwell, he looked back and saw Miller tumble Wilhelm over the wall. When Miller saw Goldblum watching him, he turned and dropped the half of a grass shear.

Goldblum screamed at Miller, asking why he had attacked Wilhelm. For some reason, Goldblum then walked over to Miller at the cement wall. Together they looked over the wall and saw Wilhelm lying on the ledge one floor below. That's where they were when the elevator door opened and a man got off, whereupon Goldblum quickly walked away down the exit ramp, with Miller following close behind.

Rothman said that it was his understanding that Goldblum did provide an alibi for Miller, but he did not know why.

I would have asked whether Goldblum would admit to being involved in the murder. Rothman said no, because he was not involved other than providing an alibi. That's a crime, but at this point he would not proffer a plea.

When I asked him whether Goldblum would admit he had been part of a land fraud against Wilhelm, he said that it was his understanding that Goldblum was not part of any land fraud.

I asked him if Goldblum would admit to hiring Wilhelm to burn down his restaurant.

Rothman said it was his understanding that Goldblum did not hire Wilhelm to burn down the restaurant, and that he had first met Wilhelm just one day before the murder.

Finally, I asked him whether Goldblum was going to testify, and he said he believed so. Rothman would not go into any details concerning the arson.

Maybe my conversation with Rothman would not have settled anything, but it would have added pieces to a consistent story, one that was more consistent with the available evidence and less dependent on Miller's tale.

What is certain, however, is that Freeman did none of this, never approached Rothman to request an interview with Goldblum. That is also hard to understand.

I would have also consulted with both the Coroner, Dr. Cyril Wecht, and the Medical Examiner, Dr. Joshua Perper, who conducted Wilhelm's autopsy to help me figure out what really took place.

With hindsight, I know that many years after his trial, Goldblum's attorneys consulted with both Dr. Wecht and Dr. Perper. Both rendered opinions that, with a reasonable degree of medical certainty, it was Miller who inflicted the stab wounds that killed Wilhelm, not Goldblum. They based their opinions on the dying declaration; the nature, extent, and direction of the wounds; the pattern and direction of the blood spatters on the dashboard; the blood on Miller's clothes and the lack of blood on Goldblum's. Their analysis was thorough and without equivocation.

It is fair to assume their opinions would have been the same had they been consulted in the many months before Goldblum's trial. But no one did that at the time.

If I had this information, I would have shared it with the prosecutor. He in turn would have told me he could not allow Miller to testify that Goldblum was the assailant.

We already decided Goldblum had no reason to attack Wilhelm, and we knew he was not the assailant. While we could not charge him with murder, we could charge him with hindering apprehension and lying to the police. If Miller came clean, we could also charge Goldblum with arson. If not, the arson charge could have been difficult to prosecute, given Miller's confabulation diagnosis.

We could still have charged Goldblum with arson in the hope of getting leverage to make him agree to a plea bargain. We hoped to get him to testify against Miller for the murder, the land fraud, and the arson. While it wasn't predictable how this would work out for him, Goldblum, in all likelihood, would have faced some prison time.

It still was not clear whether we would have charged Orlowsky or Dedo. It depended whether one or both cooperated. As said earlier, I would have contacted the FBI and U. S. Attorney to help attain that leverage against these two.

To summarize: we would probably have initially charged Miller with murder and the land fraud. If Goldblum or Orlowsky cooperated, we would have also charged Miller with the arson. To begin, we would have charged murder generally (first-degree), but considering Miller's mental condition, a plea could have ensued for a lesser degree. It would have also required Miller to plead guilty to both the land fraud and the arson. Between third-degree murder, the arson, and the land fraud, Miller would have received a substantial sentence.

The prosecutor might have been willing to consider less than a life sentence for two reasons.

Miller had mental problems, and his attorney could have argued lack of capacity and intent. Murder trials require a lot of money and work to prosecute, and avoiding one is always tempting.

Second, in light of the facts, Miller may have been willing to accept a guilty plea to third-degree murder. Although Miller stabbed Wilhelm repeatedly, the fight was not planned, and Wilhelm threw the first punch. While a prosecutor might have accepted something less than life, the crimes still demanded a substantial sentence.

The problem is that so much of what normally takes place in investigations and prosecutions did not take place in this case. And things also took place that should never occur.

Something happened between Miller, Freeman, and Dixon very early in the case. Nearly all of the case files and official records have disappeared. We are left with too many serious questions and too few good answers. Miller and Dixon have passed away. Freeman is the only person who knows, and, though given several opportunities to clear the record, he isn't talking.

A second vein of prosecutorial chicanery involved the two charges of solicitation-to-murder that were brought against Goldblum at trial and used to discredit his character. Both incidents resulted from set-ups using jail-house snitches. Both charges were eventually dismissed, but the damage had been done.

I never placed much stock in using prisoners as resources, because inmates will do or say anything to get out of jail. You have to be very careful. If you have one inmate cozy up to another inmate and suggest something, say killing a witness, who is to say the idea would have ever otherwise occurred to the accused. And if, rather than using the undercover agent, the accused hires someone else who actually kills the witness, who is responsible? We planted the suggestion, and because we were unable to monitor the situation, the witness is dead. In my opinion, we just killed another person. No thanks.

In the end, we would have made an appointment with Miller's attorneys, Vince Murovich or Harry Stump, and told them we were not going to use their client as a witness against Goldblum, Dedo, or Orlowsky. Miller was a diagnosed confabulator with a personality disorder, and his testimony could not be relied upon to be truthful. We were inclined to believe Rothman's assessment of what happened in the car the night of the murder; that two acquaintances fought over money, and unfortunately Wilhelm ended up dead at Miller's hand.

Justice is served when the truth is revealed. If this version of the case had been presented to the District Attorney's Office, I believe the results would have been very different.

Two men would not have received life sentences for a murder that was not premeditated.

Everyone with whom I have had an opportunity to discuss this case, agrees that Charles Goldblum did not get a fair trial, that he was convicted of a murder with which he had no culpability, and that Clarence Miller was overcharged with premeditated murder.

Had Goldblum and Miller simply been truthful from the beginning, they both would have been free years ago after serving a substantial period of time in prison.

Three families were destroyed over greed, lies, and ambition.

Finally, since we're using the clarity of hindsight to reconsider the case, it is interesting to speculate how different the outcomes might have been if, back in 1974, Richard Thornburgh had approved the FBI's investigation into Miller's false filing about the land fraud.

With a strong case to make and Wilhelm still alive to identify the perpetrators, Miller, Dedo, and Orlowsky could have been charged, tried, convicted, and imprisoned. With Miller in prison and not knowing another criminal to burn down his restaurant, Goldblum would likely have filed for bankruptcy when he could not sell the Fifth Avenue Inn, rather than opting for arson.

Most importantly, George Wilhelm would not have been murdered. With the balance of his $40,000 injury settlement to begin a new life, perhaps he would have relocated to North Carolina to fulfill his dream of digging for semi-precious gem stones.

Post Scripts

In January 2011, after several personal visits with Dixon, I sent him an early version of this comparative analysis, asking him to review it. After I tried to reach him via e-mail several times, he phoned me on Easter Sunday. When I asked whether he'd read what I had sent, he said, "Yes. Very interesting."

"Knowing all that, would you have prosecuted the case the same way as I suggested?"

"Yes, I would have."

Finally, in late 2015, having learned of Dixon's death, David Bear, the editor of Willful Blindness, wrote to Commander Freeman, asking if he would settle some issues about the case raised during a 2012 video interview with Dixon. With all the other principals in the prosecution now deceased, these were questions only Freeman could clarify. Here is that correspondence.

Dear Commander Freeman:

By way of brief introduction, I am a writer and former Post-Gazette editor currently completing a book in which you play a prominent role.

Willful Blindness is an examination of the 1976 murder of George Wilhelm and subsequent prosecutions and convictions of Clarence Miller and Charles Goldblum. We expect the book to be published this spring, preceded by media coverage of the upcoming fortieth anniversary of the murder.

In a sense, *Willful Blindness* evolved from a comment made by the case prosecutor, F. Peter Dixon. During a series of interviews with Jim Ramsey several years ago, some of which were videoed, Mr. Dixon repeatedly stated his belief that Mr. Goldblum did not receive a fair trial, a claim that is supported by considerable documentation. It was Mr. Dixon who first suggested to Mr. Ramsey that a book be written about the case. *Willful Blindness* is that book.

During these same interviews, Mr. Dixon repeatedly found fault with the Pittsburgh Police investigation of the case and subsequent prosecutions, and he painted you and Judge Ziegler as the parties most responsible for Mr. Goldblum not getting a fair trial.

Mr. Dixon accepted no personal responsibility for any prosecutorial misconducts. However, other research has discovered that certain decisions which could only have been made by the prosecutor at least partly contributed to what has been called a "miscarriage of justice."

While *Willful Blindness* does not absolve Mr. Goldblum of all the charges against him, it does conclude he was wrongly convicted and excessively sentenced for crimes he did not commit.

Others have said you remained loyal to Mr. Dixon over the years concerning this investigation. That loyalty may no longer be necessary. As shown by the attached death certificate, Mr. Dixon passed away in Springfield, Ohio on January 25, 2014.

In reviewing the transcripts of the Dixon/Ramsey interviews, we identified eight primary issues that should be verified, as well as questions they raise.

At this point, you are the only person who can set the record straight. Both the issues and questions are detailed in the attached document. By answering these questions, you can settle these inconsistencies. With Mr. Dixon gone, there should be no dishonor in verifying the facts of what happened.

As you may know, Mr. Goldblum has consistently contested his original conviction and sentencing. Presently, he is petitioning the Pennsylvania State Supreme Court with recently discovered evidence in order to obtain a new trial. If that trial is awarded, he would likely be offered time-served.

Now nearly 67 and finishing his fortieth year in prison, Mr. Goldblum has always been a model prisoner. In poor health, he walks with a cane and presents no danger to any community.

Most importantly, he has repented and paid for the crime he did commit, as well as served most of his adult life for the crimes he did not.

You can help rectify that situation.

Please answer the attached questions as best you can and mail or email them to me at either of the above addresses. If you prefer, we can meet and discuss the matter in person.

Thanking you in advance for any assistance you can provide, I am

Sincerely,
David Bear

Issues regarding the Goldblum prosecution

1. On 2-9-76, the night of Wilhelm's murder, the Pittsburgh Mobile Crime Unit was called to the scene of the murder to collect evidence. Detectives Hill and Crisanti began photographing and collecting physical and blood evidence. Crisanti stated that he never removed blood evidence on any crime scene without first photographing the blood. You were at the scene before Crisanti and Hill, and you testified that you saw blood spatter traveling left to right on the dashboard of Wilhelm's car. You were an experienced detective and knew how to read a crime scene and blood spatter. You knew that blood spatter traveling left to right meant that the person to the right of the victim inflicted the wounds on the victim. At Goldblum's trial, you testified honestly and truthfully concerning your expert observation and description of the blood spatter. You later were deposed and admitted that you saw photos of the blood spatter on the dashboard which corroborates Crisanti. Crisanti claims that he always took a photo of blood spatter before removing it. The crime lab had the sample of blood spatter that was removed from the dashboard.

Sgt. Modispatcher stated that he saw the blood spatter photos several days before Goldblum's trial. You stated that you believed that you gave Dixon all of the photos in the Wilhelm investigation, but that you were not responsible for exhibits and Dixon never entered the blood spatter photos as exhibits.

Numerous experts have stated that based on your expert eyewitness observation of the blood spatter and the direction it traveled in, their opinion was the person in the passenger seat (Miller) inflicted wounds on the victim and not the passenger in the rear (Goldblum). Commonwealth witness Dr. Toby Wolson also stated that if your observation was correct, he would agree with Dr. Lee and the other experts that the front right passenger was the assailant.

Unfortunately with the blood spatter photo vanishing, the experts could not legally identify the assailant. The defense claimed that they never received the photos prior to trial. If the District Attorney did not furnish the defense with exculpatory evidence that he possessed, he violated Brady as well as Prosecutorial Misconduct.

Questions:

1. Did you give Dixon all of the photos that Crisanti shot of the Wilhelm murder scene?
2. Did you withhold any of the photos?
3. Was it the responsibility of the District Attorney to furnish the defense with copies of your file as well as all photos taken by the mobile crime unit?

2. On 2-12-76, Miller is examined by doctors at Southside hospital due to pressure on the brain, having passed out twice on 2-10-76 while being questioned, a symptom of confabulatory amnesia. Pressure on the brain causing extreme headaches is another symptom.

On 2-16 and 17, Miller is again examined by the Allegheny County Behavior Clinic. The examinations were extensively documented by your investigation and the doctors which examined Miller. So it is fair to say that the police and the prosecutor who would have read reports from you and the behavior clinic that Miller suffered from confabulatory amnesia you knew his statements could not be trusted. Jack Mook remarked in a statement that after talking with Miller for a few minutes "you would think you were talking with a child of 10 to 11 years old." Everyone who knew Miller at the time observed how he spoke and the clothing he wore and understood that he had mental problems and was childlike.

Question: Do you know whether Dixon came to the same conclusion as the doctors; that Miller was suffering from a childhood brain injury when he was struck by a trolley?

3. On 2-13-76, Miller was administered his first polygraph examination by Sgt. Modispatcher. Modispatcher subsequently stated that he failed Miller and that he told you that Miller was Wilhelm's lone assailant. Miller had a meeting with his attorney, Vincent Murovich. Both Miller and Murovich claimed that they met with you and Peter Dixon and discussed an unwritten understanding that Miller would receive a 10 to 20 year sentence for his cooperation against Goldblum. It is understood that it would have been strictly up to Dixon to make any plea deal and you were not

permitted to speak on behalf of the District Attorney's Office concerning any agreement. Dixon admitted that he spoke with Murovich and "I told Clarence that his only chance to stay alive is to cooperate." Operating under the understanding that there was an unwritten deal of 10 to 20 years for Miller, Murovich offered Miller's cooperation against Goldblum. Prior to Miller's trial, attorney Harry Stump stated that Miller was under the opinion that he had a deal. After his conviction, Miller stated that the DA got amnesia when it came to his sentencing. If the DA made an unwritten deal with Miller and did not disclose it to the defense, it is cause for a new trial and can be used as after-discovered evidence.

Question: Do you recall a meeting that involved Murovich, Miller, Dixon and yourself, where Dixon discussed an unwritten agreement with Miller for his testimony against Goldblum?

4. On 5-15-76, you ordered a polygraph test for Miller. After the test was over, Miller admitted to Detective Stotlemyer that he was involved in Wilhelm's murder. This polygraph and admission were never recorded in the Master Polygraph Log.

Questions:

1. Did you alert Dixon that Miller had confessed to being involved in the murder?
2. Did you tell Dixon that Miller should not testify that he was not involved in the murder as planned, because it would be perjury?

5. On 5-25-76, you ordered a third and final polygraph for Miller concerning the arson. Detective Stotlemyer conducted the polygraph and determined that Miller was involved in the arson. This finding and Stotlemyer's opinions were not entered in the Master Polygraph Log. The Miller confession and Stotlemyer's opinion were not reported for 20 months.

Questions:

1. Did you alert Dixon that Miller had failed the polygraph concerning his involvement in the arson and that Stotlemyer's opinion was that Miller was involved in the arson?
2. Did Dixon ask you to withhold reporting the existence of the confession and the opinion of Stotlemyer, that Miller was involved in the arson?
3. Did you remind Dixon that Miller intended to testify he was not involved in the arson?
4. Did you advise Dixon that you could not find anyone who would testify they ever saw Wilhelm and Goldblum together?
5. Did Dixon ask you to keep the two polygraphs out of the Master Polygraph Log?

6. The FBI investigation file into the land fraud dated 10-7-1974 mentions that the U.S. Attorney at the time shared the FBI investigative file with Superintendent Robert Coll, and that he shared it with your investigative team. According to FBI reports, this happened several days after Wilhelm's murder which would have made it 2-12-76.

That FBI file never mentions Goldblum's name, so within a few days after the Wilhelm murder, you would have known of the FBI investigation and that Goldblum's name was never mentioned. Furthermore, a review of all the written material in the police files revealed that no one could testify that they ever saw Wilhelm and Goldblum together prior to the murder.

During these 2010 interviews, Dixon admitted that he did not believe that Goldblum was involved in the land fraud. Ted Dedo attempted to testify to that fact at Goldblum's trial, but Dixon would not grant Dedo Use Immunity, so he would not testify. Dixon blamed Judge Ziegler for not invoking the Kings Bench rule and not ordering Dedo to testify. Apparently, Judge Ziegler researched the Kings Bench rule and found that he did not have the authority to order Dedo to testify.

Dixon admitted that he realized he would be violating Goldblum's constitutional right to summon witnesses. He chose not to offer Use Immunity to Dedo for his testimony, fearing he would lose the case against Goldblum.

If Dedo had immunity, he would have testified that Goldblum did not participate in the land fraud. Fred Orlowsky also later stated Goldblum was not part of the land fraud. Dixon used Miller's uncorroborated testimony to create a false motive for Goldblum's participation in the murder.

Questions:

1. Did you give all of your case file reports to Dixon?
2. Did you discuss the 1974 FBI Land Fraud Investigation with Dixon?
3. Did you mention to Dixon that Goldblum's name was absent from the complaint that Wilhelm filed?
4. Did Dixon ever ask you for independent corroboration for Miller's statements due to his mental problems?
5. Did you ever attempt to have Dedo or Orlowsky corroborate Miller's testimony?

7. On 11-30-1975, Goldblum's restaurant was burned down. Miller blames Wilhelm and Goldblum. Dixon claims that no one in the District Attorney's office believed that Wilhelm was involved. There was no corroborating witness to support Miller's testimony that Wilhelm burned down the restaurant. There was no follow-up investigation on the whereabouts of Wilhelm on the night of the fire. On 5-25-76 Miller failed a polygraph test concerning his involvement with the arson, and yet Dixon used this false theory as motive for Goldblum to murder Wilhelm.

Years later both Dixon and DA James Gilmore apologized to the Wilhelm family for claiming he had been an arsonist. However, the damage was done to Goldblum because the jury used this alleged motive to convict him when in fact Miller was the arsonist. This is why the truth is important and Goldblum and Wilhelm did not get justice.

Questions:

1. Did Dixon know that Miller failed his third polygraph test about being involved in the arson?
2. Did Dixon tell you that he didn't believe the Wilhelm arson theory as proposed by Miller?
3. Did you tell Dixon not to use the Wilhelm arson theory as motive?
4. After doing a background investigation on Wilhelm, did you discover any damaging information about any criminal tendencies he may have had?
5. Are you aware that the Pittsburgh Fire Dept. and the ATF did independent investigations and could not determine whether the fire was arson or not?

8. On 5-9-80, Miller filed a PCRA sworn affidavit. He is the same person the prosecution relied on to tell the truth during Goldblum's trial. Miller swore that any statements that he made against Goldblum were a product of the police and their imagination. He swore that he mentally blacked out during the murder and never actually saw Goldblum stab Wilhelm. He said he should have claimed temporary insanity, but that his attorney never advised him that plea was available to him. Much of what Miller swore to is corroborated by the circumstances of the murder and Goldblum's testimony.

The police reported Miller passing out several times while under pressure of questioning. This is a symptom of Confabulatory Amnesia, and the statements used to convict Goldblum, lying, fabricating, and believing his own lies, were part of that condition. Also, a person suffering from this condition feels it is important to impress and help those who are questioning him.

Miller placed the blame for his conviction and that of Goldblum on his attorney and the homicide investigators. There is little reason to disbelieve this sworn affidavit by Miller, because, unlike the police investigation, it was corroborated by other witnesses.

Miller claimed that he had been taken advantage of because of his easy nature and ability to be manipulated.

The night of the murder, Wilhelm, Miller, and Goldblum drove to the parking garage to continue their conversation from McDonalds, and when the car was stopped, Miller told Wilhelm he could not repay the money from the land fraud. Wilhelm lost it and punched Miller in the face. Miller and Wilhelm struggled in the front seat. (This is where Miller got the scratches on his face, hands and arms, rather than the cat story he concocted). Miller found the half of a grass shear and began to stab Wilhelm.

This account was corroborated by Goldblum, who was in the back seat, and further corroborated by you and the scientific community on the basis of your eyewitness observation of the path the blood spatter took, as well as physical evidence and forensic science.

This is why it is crucial to determine what happened to the blood spatter photos. Seeking the identity of Wilhelm's killer is important. There was no conspiracy to injure or murder Wilhelm, just two acquaintances arguing over money that Miller, Dedo, and Orlowsky stole from Wilhelm. It is clear Goldblum was not involved in the land fraud in any way, nor was Wilhelm involved in the arson.

Goldblum eventually admitted participating in the arson and subsequently providing Miller with an alibi after the murder. Goldblum should have been convicted for the arson and as an accessory after the fact to the murder, but not a false charge of first-degree murder. The science is particularly important in a case with no witnesses other than the possible participants.

Anyone interested in discovering the truth about who killed Wilhelm should rely on your expert observation and description of the blood spatter and allow the scientists to determine what happened, supported by crime scene evidence.

Questions:

1. Why didn't your team of investigators photograph Miller's facial, hands and arm scratches and compare them to scratches from a cat?
2. Why were the bloody gloves not examined and found to have Miller's hair in them and not Goldblum's, as Miller testified?
3. Why were no fishing waders found at Goldblum's home or in the trunk of his car?

4. Why was there no Wilhelm blood found on Goldblum's clothing or his shoes, in his car or home?

5. Was there ever a time that you doubted Miller's truthfulness or his ability to tell the truth?

6. Did you ever tell Dixon that Miller could not be believed and should not be relied on for the truth without corroboration?

7. Did you ever consider that Goldblum was innocent of the murder and Miller was attempting to shift the blame away from himself?

8. Did you consider telling the defense that on 5-15-76 Miller confessed to being involved in the murder, rather than withholding that information?

9. Did the revelation that Dedo and Orlowsky would have testified that Goldblum was not involved in the land fraud change your opinion that Goldblum should not have been charged in that crime?

10. With the revelation that the District Attorney never believed that Wilhelm was the arsonist (nor was any corroborative evidence discovered), do you still believe Wilhelm was involved in the arson?

11. Did the revelation that on 5-25-76 Miller failed the polygraph test concerning his involvement in the arson, coupled with Stotlemyer's opinion that Miller was involved, change your opinion that Miller, and not Wilhelm, burned down the restaurant?

With no participation in the land fraud nor Wilhelm being the arsonist, what motive did Goldblum have to injure, harm, or murder Wilhelm, who he met for the first time only the day before the murder?

The conclusion is that there was no motive for mayhem nor conspiracy for murder; just two men, Miller and Wilhelm, fighting over money.

Freeman's terse, email response came a few weeks later.

"I have no intention of answering any of your questions, based on your total lack of objectivity."

Commander Freeman had a chance to clear the record, but he declined. Considering all the dishonest decisions he and Dixon made, there is no doubt that Goldblum and Miller were not given fair trials, as guaranteed by the U.S. Constitution.

If the system treated everyone that way, there would be no justice.

* The opinions expressed in this chapter have been approved by Ramsey Consulting LLC.

Charles Goldblum's statement from his 1998 Application for Commutation

Personal Background

My name is Charles J. Goldblum. I was born in 1949. My nickname is "Zeke."

I have been in prison since the fall of 1976. During this time, I have maintained a good record as a prisoner and was recommended favorably by the Superintendent of my institution in my last three applications to the Board of Pardons.

In 1977, I was convicted of first-degree murder, arson, solicitation to commit arson, and conspiracy to commit theft. I was sentenced by Judge Donald Ziegler to life imprisonment for the murder, plus fifteen to thirty years on the other charges. Many years later, Judge Ziegler wrote several very strong letters on my behalf, questioning this verdict, and recommending my immediate release.

I come from a large, loving, and supportive family, the second of five children.

My father is a rabbi and in 1963, he came to Congregation Beth Shalom in Pittsburgh, PA where he served for more than 20 years before retiring in 1983. A few years later, he went back to work at a small congregation in Dover, Delaware, where he served for another decade. My father continued to work until he was 80 years old, primarily because of the large legal bills incurred in my defense.

My mother was always very involved in my father's career. In addition to raising five children, she kept very busy. In later years, after most of the children were grown, she did some substitute teaching and went back to school for her Master's Degree.

My older brother Simeon is a physician and professor of medicine at the University of Maryland. My younger brother David is a chemical/environmental engineer employed by the Federal Government. My sister Liba is a physician in private practice as a radiologist in Baltimore. My sister Orah is a teacher. She lives in Rehovot, Israel.

Throughout the many years of my ordeal, my family has always been totally supportive. Until my parents moved from Pittsburgh to Baltimore in 1986, they visited me every week, driving 270 miles each time. When they moved to Dover, Delaware, they continued to visit me every month. In the past few years as their health has declined, they have not been able to make the journey as regularly. They still come as often as they can, but now spend most of the year in Israel with my sister Orah. My brothers and sisters, in spite of their busy lives, have also kept in close contact with me. They visit often and are always there for me.

My family moved to Pittsburgh in 1963, the year that I started as a freshman at Allderdice High School. I earned my bachelor degree at Washington and Jefferson College in 1971 and graduated from Duquesne University Law School in 1974. I passed the bar exam and went to work for Arthur Young and Company, a major CPA firm now known as Ernst and Young. I was employed there until my arrest in February, 1976.

I was married soon after graduation from college in 1974. Several months after I was arrested in 1976, my wife left me and we eventually divorced. I feel certain that, had I never been arrested, we would still be happily married.

General Background

Three crimes occurred in this case. Their connecting link was Clarence Miller.

I first met Miller while I was a law student working as a summer intern for the Allegheny County Clerk of Courts.

Miller was a regular presence at the City County Building. He ran errands for the judges and constables in the courthouse, and we became casually acquainted. At the end of summer, I returned to classes and did not see Miller until some months after I graduated from law school. Miller learned that I had purchased a restaurant, and he stopped in one day at lunch time, while I was there to check in with the manager. After that, he came in regularly for take out orders and meals and we gradually became re-acquainted.

The first of these crimes was the defrauding of George Wilhelm in 1974 by Clarence Miller, Thaddeus Dedo, and possibly Fred Orlowsky. I was never involved in this crime and knew nothing about it until several years later.

The second crime is the fire by arson of The Fifth Avenue Inn, a restaurant I had purchased in January 1975 with significant financial help from my parents. I oversaw its operations, but quickly realized I was in over my head. A series of bad business decisions led me to a point of desperation, the consequence of which was the decision to have the restaurant burned down. On the evening of November 30, 1975, a fire destroyed the building, but no one was injured.

The third crime was the murder of George Wilhelm by Clarence Miller, a result of Miller's fear that Wilhelm would turn him into the authorities for the land fraud.

On the evening of February 9, 1976, Miller murdered Wilhelm in my presence and to my absolute surprise. However, I agreed to give Miller an alibi, because of my complicity in the arson. I did not want him to be arrested, fearing he would discuss the fire with the police. That would prevent my parents from recovering their investment and implicate me in the arson.

Wilhelm had absolutely nothing to do with the arson. At the time of the fire, I had not met him. Miller initially did not reveal the fraud to the police, and he attempted to convince them that the arson of the restaurant was my motive for murdering Wilhelm. Although unable to be truthful at my trial, Miller later admitted to the land fraud and his complicity in it.

Miller had reason to be worried. Wilhelm had already gone to the FBI about the land deal, as he understood at that time. When the initial FBI investigation reached out to Miller, he convinced Wilhelm to withdraw his complaint.

Wilhelm had earlier told the FBI about the deal for him buy the land in North Carolina through Senator Schweiker's office. On Miller's prompting, he went back to the FBI and told them that the complaint was a hoax to embarrass Senator Schweiker.

Interestingly, Gary Boutwell, the FBI agent involved in the case, testified at my trial that he did not believe Wilhelm when he withdrew his complaint and felt sure Wilhelm had been defrauded. According to his testimony, the FBI only discontinued further investigation because the United States Attorney for the Western District of Pennsylvania issued a letter of declination. At this point the matter rested, because Miller was able to keep placating Wilhelm until the killing in February 1976.

The rest of the story covering the land fraud, the arson, the homicide, the original trial, and post conviction procedures and appeals will be covered in more detail in the following sections.

The Land Fraud

In 1973 or early 1974, George Wilhelm, 42, received a settlement of $45,000 from a worker's injury settlement from an accident that had occurred when he drove an armored truck. Wilhelm became interested in using some of that money to acquire a parcel of property in North Carolina where he believed he could mine for semi-precious stones. The land was owned by the federal government.

Miller had been involved in Pittsburgh political circles as a small time operative of sorts. He would do errands and odd jobs around City Hall and work for republican candidates especially during campaigns. Miller and Wilhelm often drove around putting up posters for their patrons, and tearing down those of their opponents.

Somehow Miller convinced Wilhelm that he had a special connection with then Senator Richard Schweiker. From Miller's testimony at my trial, I learned that Miller got an acquaintance, Thaddeus Dedo, to pose as Ken Manella, an aide to Senator Schweiker.

Two secret meetings took place in hotel rooms; one in Washington, D.C. and one in Washington, Pennsylvania. At both of these meetings, Wilhelm gave several thousand dollars in cash to Dedo, believing he was Ken Manella. Miller was also present at these meetings. At my trial, Miller testified at that I was at meetings with Dedo and Miller in Pittsburgh. However, we were able to prove I had been out of town for my firm at the time.

When Wilhelm paid out a substantial amount of money, he obviously expected to receive a deed to the property in North Carolina. This did not happen and he became suspicious. He visited the Pittsburgh office of Senator Schweiker, he spoke over the phone to the real Ken Manella who worked in the senator's Washington office as an aide. When Wilhelm asked the real Manella about the land deal, he had no idea what Wilhelm was talking about. As a result of the conversation, Manella put Wilhelm in touch with the FBI in Pittsburgh.

At first, Wilhelm truthfully told the FBI about the land deal as he understood at that time. Miller was drawn into the FBI investigation at this point also. Miller somehow convinced Wilhelm to withdraw his complaint to the FBI on the premise that this would undo the arrangement for Wilhelm to quietly buy the land through Senator

Schweiker's office. At Miller's urging, Wilhelm went back to the FBI and told them that the complaint was a hoax to embarrass Senator Schweiker.

At this point the matter rested because Miller was able to placate Wilhelm until February, 1976.

The Arson

In January 1975, I arranged for the purchase of the Fifth Avenue Inn Restaurant, located near downtown Pittsburgh. The money for the transaction was provided by my parents, who invested nearly $70,0000.00 in the business and, using their own house as collateral, assumed a $100,000 mortgage on the building. This represented a substantial portion of their savings. The business did not do as well as I had expected and, consistently lost money through the summer months and into the fall. I became desperate.

I never should have asked my parents to make this investment. I had just graduated from law school, passed the bar, had a full time accounting position, and taught accounting part time at the University of Pittsburgh. The restaurant became the straw that broke the camel's back. There simply weren't enough hours in each day for me to get everything done. By late fall, I was completely worn out, needing to put more time into my career and marriage.

Something had to give. Originally, I made attempts to sell the restaurant but nothing developed quickly enough. It would have taken several months to sell the restaurant, and I was so frazzled that I felt I needed to find an immediate solution. In late November, I foolishly arranged to have the restaurant burned. I planned the arson, prepared the site, but hired Miller to actually light the fire. On the evening of November 30, the Fifth Avenue Inn was destroyed by a fire.

No one was injured as a result. I never told anyone, not my family nor my attorneys, that I had arranged the arson until many years later. By then, my parents had recovered a large part of their investment from insurance proceeds, and were no longer imperiled by the mortgage on the restaurant building. When I decided to have the restaurant burned, I did not have my normal judgment. I was worn out and grabbed for quick relief. I rationalized that no one would be hurt and hired Miller because I had no experience.

The Homicide

In early 1976, just two months after the fire, Miller came to me because I was a lawyer, and I was beholden to him. He needed advice in connection with a land deal that had gone bad. George Wilhelm had given Miller a considerable sum of money, had nothing to show for it, and was pressuring Miller. At first, I didn't believe Miller. I suspected he was trying to exact more money from me for burning down the restaurant.

The primary reason for my suspicion and disbelief was remembering that Miller had defrauded a friend who knew who he was. I couldn't see how Miller would defraud Wilhelm and nothing happen. At some point Wilhelm would have to realize that he had been cheated and would have to conclude that his friend Miller had been part of the scam. The other reason Miller's story puzzled me was that Miller kept making vague references to another participant.

This other person turned out to be Thaddeus Dedo who posed as Ken Manella.

I advised Miller that because Wilhelm knew who he was, his best chance for a quiet solution was to repay the money to Wilhelm. When I asked if he was in a position to do that, Miller said yes. I felt that if Wilhelm were repaid that he would not pursue the matter with the authorities again.

I agreed to attend a meeting with Miller and Wilhelm, with the understanding that Miller was going to come clean and offer to repay the money immediately.

There were two meetings.

The first took place on Sunday afternoon, February 8, 1976 at a McDonald's Restaurant on Smithfield Street in downtown Pittsburgh.

What was said during this first meeting confirmed my suspicion that another person was involved with Miller in the land fraud. More importantly, Miller did not do what he had agreed to.

First he told Wilhelm that he had been unable to contact Manella and suspected that the senator's aide had skipped with the money. As soon as I realized he was not heeding my advice to repay Wilhelm, I became very uncomfortable. Miller was bringing up an entirely new wrinkle and was most likely lying to Wilhelm. If I sat there quietly while Miller lied to Wilhelm, I would have been implicitly condoning Miller's dishonesty. I said I had to leave. I had my doubts at this point about whether the whole story was genuine. I half expected Miller to ask me for money to give to Wilhelm. I suspected that the two of them were trying to pull a scam on me by telling this inconsistent story that did not make sense.

Miller, knowing that I was disgusted with him, left Wilhelm at the table, and walked with me to the outside door of McDonald's. I told Miller that if he was not going to take my advice that he should not have asked me to help him in the first place. As I left, Miller asked me to meet with he and Wilhelm one more time the next day. Against my better judgement, I agreed.

The second meeting took place the next evening. Because I worked all day that Monday, and I taught accounting at the University of Pittsburgh in the evening, the meeting was scheduled after my class was over. I drove downtown from Oakland and parked in an alley near my office building where Miller met me. We walked to the same McDonald's where Wilhelm was waiting, we sat down and had coffee. Miller and Wilhelm immediately began to talk about the land deal, and when it became apparent to Wilhelm that we were going to be talking for a while, he said that he had to move his car which was parked at a meter.

Miller and I went with Wilhelm to his car. I got in the back seat and Miller got in the front passenger seat. Wilhelm drove the car to a public parking garage two blocks down Smithfield Street. During the ride and then proceeding upward in the garage, Miller finally told Wilhelm he was not getting the land. Miller still did not tell the complete truth about his own involvement. He did however, tell Wilhelm that he would make good on returning Wilhelm's money. Wilhelm became more agitated and asked Miller when his money would be returned. Miller hesitated and told Wilhelm that it would take a while, but that all his money would be returned.

At this point, Wilhelm had driven the car to the top of the parking garage and pulled into an empty space. By now they were yelling or more accurately, Wilhelm was yelling and Miller was trying to placate him.

They started to fight in the front seat, and after a brief struggle, I saw blood and realized that one of them had been wounded. Wilhelm then tumbled out of the car to try to escape. I was terrified and ran to the exit door on the opposite side of the roof. Miller chased Wilhelm and kept stabbing at him. Trying to escape, Wilhelm crawled to a wall and pulled himself up leaning forward over the rail. Miller pushed Wilhelm over the rail, and I heard a thud.

I froze where I was because I was afraid of Miller. Miller had used a weapon on Wilhelm and I wasn't sure what Miller would do to me because I had witnessed the assault. Miller saw my fear and held his hands out to show me that he no longer had a weapon. He beckoned me, I walked over, looked over the rail, and saw Wilhelm lying on a ledge one floor below. Wilhelm was not moving, and I was sure that he was dead.

I quickly walked away from the area back toward the door. Miller followed me. I just had to get away from the whole thing as fast as possible. I told Miller not to follow me, but he did. Miller had a lot of blood on him, and he wanted me to take him home. I was upset and scared and not able to think. Miller followed me to my car and got in the front seat with me. I foolishly went along with Miller's request to take him home and give him an alibi. Not thinking clearly, I agreed to place myself with Miller and Wilhelm at the meeting shortly before the homicide.

Even after all these years, I have not been able to come to terms with myself over my absurd conduct. The combination of my fear of Miller, witnessing the murder, and wanting him never to mention anything about the fire, led to my agreement to provide him with an alibi.

Wilhelm was still alive when the police found him. He made a dying declaration to an officer stating, "Clarence, Clarence Miller did this to me."

Wilhelm was taken to a hospital and died a few hours later.

The Arrest

Because of Wilhelm's dying declaration, the police brought Miller in for questioning the morning after the murder. Initially, he told the police our prearranged alibi; that Miller and I had met Wilhelm at the McDonald's. After the meeting, Miller and I left together, leaving Wilhelm there alone; then I drove Miller home.

Once the police interviewed Miller, they came to my office to corroborate the story he had given them. I spoke to two police officers and told them the story somewhat differently. The discrepancy concerned where we met before we went to the restaurant to meet Wilhelm.

The police left me, returned to the police station, and confronted Miller with the discrepancy. Miller broke down and told the police that he was present when Wilhelm was killed but that he was not the assailant. Miller told them that I was the killer. The combination of Miller's statement and my attempt to give him an alibi led to my arrest for murder.

The Trial

Because my attorney filed perjury charges against Miller in an effort to have him declared incompetent as a witness, my trial was not held until August of 1977.

His name appeared in the notarized affidavit Miller and Wilhelm filed with the FBI by claiming that original complaint had been a hoax. In Pennsylvania, at that time, a convicted perjurer was deemed not competent to testify. If convicted of perjury, Miller would not have been able to testify against me, and there would not have been a trial.

When my attorney filed these perjury charges through a private complaint on my behalf, the District Attorney declined to prosecute so that Miller could remain the chief witness against me. The petition for court approval of a private prosecution my attorney filed, then was turned down by the Court of Common Pleas. This decision was then appealed to the Superior and Supreme Courts of Pennsylvania which upheld the lower court.

I maintained my innocence for all the charges against me and never told anyone the truth about my involvement with the fire until several years after my trial.

My parents owned both their home and the restaurant building as entireties property, and there was a $100,000 mortgage on the restaurant. This meant that if there was a mortgage foreclosure on the restaurant, they could lose their home. I felt responsible for getting them into this mess, and I rationalized that if I admitted to having the restaurant burned down, they would be ruined financially.

I also suspected I would have to escape any criminal conviction in order not to be disbarred. Because I did not tell the truth, I had no valid explanation for providing Miller with an alibi. The jury logically concluded I must have had a motive to lie for Miller. Without admitting Miller had the arson hanging over my head, the jury believed that I was involved with Miller in the scheme to defraud Wilhelm and had a motive to want Wilhelm dead.

While I lied about my involvement in the fire, Miller lied also. He testified that I hired Wilhelm to set the fire and that Wilhelm was pressuring me for payment for both the fire and the land fraud. When Miller first talked to the police, he discussed the fire and the homicide. He made no mention of the land fraud. It was only after my attorney requested pretrial discovery in connection with the FBI file and the police questioned Miller, that he admitted the land fraud to the police. True to form, Miller implicated me. What is hard to explain is why the police accepted Miller's story with very little corroborating evidence.

Miller told the police:

- That Wilhelm was in the driver's seat, Miller was in the passenger seat, and that I was in the back seat.
- That I hit Wilhelm over the back of the head with a wrench and Wilhelm then got out of the car to get away from me.
- That I then got out of the car, chased Wilhelm, and continued to stab him.
- That I borrowed and wore a pair of gloves from him while committing the murder.

The physical evidence found at the scene totally contradicted Miller's statements.

Miller told the police what I was wearing that night, and when they searched my home the next day, they found the described clothing with no blood on them

According to the testimony of the pathologist who did the autopsy, there was no bump on Wilhelm's head. There was no blood or skin on the wrench that was recovered at the crime scene.

According to the testimony of one of the police detectives, there was a trail of blood spatters on the dashboard of the car with tailings on them showing the direction the blade had moved during the attack. This proved that the occupant of the right front seat had stabbed the victim who was seated in the driver's seat. This also meant that the victim had to have been stabbed in the car initially.

This is significant because it means that the prosecutor had knowledge through the police that the stabbing had to have started in the car. Notwithstanding this knowledge, the prosecutor went forward and put Miller on the stand to testify that the stabbing started outside the car. This was done to make it look like I could have been the one who wielded the knife;

Furthermore, Miller admitted to getting rid of the clothing he wore that night.

His gloves were recovered near the crime scene. They had blood on them from the victim. The crime lab also found one of Miller's hairs in the gloves. There was no evidence connecting me to the gloves. The prosecutor knew this when he presented Miller as a witness.

The police conducted a thorough investigation of the crime scene and took many pictures but did not take any pictures of the blood spatters on the dashboard of the vehicle. This is hard to explain in light of the fact that the rest of the crime scene investigation was so thorough.

According to the experts that we brought in while preparing this appeal, had the police taken pictures of the blood spatters on the dash board with a scale, they could have identified who the assailant was to a certainty. The crime scene was investigated thoroughly in all other respects. This investigation was conducted by the homicide department of a major police force of a large city. This unusual coincidence is hard to explain.

At a minimum, the prosecutor and the police prejudged this case and ignored forensic evidence which contradicted the theory of their case.

My lawyer had a strong feeling that Miller had something wrong with him psychologically. He filed a pretrial request to have Miller examined by a psychiatrist. The court denied this request. At my trial, my attorney asked Miller if he had ever had any medical problems and whether he had ever been hospitalized. Miller answered falsely that he had not.

The solicitation for murder charge brought against me was very damaging. This, coupled with no explanation for my trying to provide an alibi for Miller, led to my conviction for murder.

Several weeks after I had been released on bail, I was approached by a former inmate of the county jail who introduced me to someone he said could kill Miller. During a subsequent meeting with the supposed hit-man, I agreed to pay to have Miller killed. The hit-man turned out to be an undercover policeman, and I was immediately rearrested.

Several factors contributed to my participation in the solicitation. Soon after my arrest, I started seeing a psychiatrist. I had been taking tranquilizers and antidepressants in large doses under the psychiatrist's supervision. My wife left me a few weeks before the solicitation, and I was unable to work at anything meaningful while I waited for trial. I foolishly decided to abruptly discontinue taking all medications, convinced that my depression was the result of the medication and was a cause of my wife leaving.

What specific factor played the major role, I can not say for sure. They all combined to create a willingness on my part to participate in the solicitation. I felt that my life as I knew it had come to an end and that everything that could possibly go wrong had happened to me. I also was not getting along well with my attorney, H. David Rothman. He had delayed the trial, my wife left me, and Miller continued to blame me for everything he did. Because of this, I did not have faith in him, which made me feel that much more desperate.

Of the things I did, my participation in the solicitation for murder bothers me the most. That I allowed myself to go along with something like that, however briefly, has troubled my conscience more than any part of the whole story.

While housed in the county jail waiting to stand trial, I was accused of a second solicitation. This was very upsetting at the time, but it proved to me, my family, and my lawyers that the police were not acting honestly.

Another prisoner, Ronald O'Shea, claimed that I solicited him to murder Police Detective Ronald Freeman, Police Lieutenant Ralph Pampena, Clarence Miller, and the Police Detective John Mook, who was the undercover detective in the first solicitation.

As I said above, at first I was very upset at having to deal with more trouble, but then I realized that even though I knew that O'Shea was lying, I also knew from what he indicated, that there had been police complicity in his approach. When I was arrested on the first solicitation, the newspaper articles never mentioned the name of the undercover police detective, John Mook. This meant that either I gave Mook's name to O'Shea, or he got it from the Police.

I knew that something was wrong from the way that the Allegheny County jail handled the case. I was not placed in segregation or given a misconduct. I was allowed to remain in general population. This made no sense to me. Under normal circumstances in any prison or jail, a prisoner who tries to have someone killed is immediately sequestered to isolation. It is one of the most serious prison infractions.

This charge never went to trial for this case. The charges were dropped. After sentencing on the main charges I was sent to SCI (State Correctional Institute) Pittsburgh. That's where I next met Ronald O'Shea. I was surprised that he and I were allowed to be in the same institution. This too, is unheard of.

While I was at SCI Pittsburgh, O'Shea approached me and said that he was sorry. When I told him how I figured out how there was police complicity, he was shocked. I asked him who gave him Mook's name, and who put him up to it. He told me that it was Detective Ronald Freeman. He gave me a written statement which I immediately mailed to my attorneys. Within a few days, the police were informed. They contacted the authorities at SCI Pittsburgh. O'Shea then claimed that I threatened him. Again, no misconduct was issued. I was placed in isolation and then shipped to SCI Huntingdon.

Many years elapsed and Ronald O'Shea was convicted of first degree murder and sentenced to death. While he was housed on death row at SCI Greene, my attorney and investigator went to see him. He told them the story and signed an affidavit. A year or two later, O'Shea passed away of pneumonia where he was housed on death row. He was in his fifties.

Post Trial and the Direct Appeal

At Miller's trial, which took place one year after I was convicted, his attorney tried to have his many statements to the police suppressed. The basis for this application to the court was that Miller had been involved in an accident as a child from which he suffered brain damage. An expert psychologist and an expert psychiatrist testified to Miller's brain damage and resulting memory impairment.

The attempt to suppress Miller's statements was unsuccessful, and he too was convicted of first-degree murder of Wilhelm and sentenced to life in prison, plus 30 years.

My attorney at that time hired a private investigator to attend Miller's trial, which was where we first learned of my accuser's mental condition. We immediately filed a Petition with the Supreme Court of Pennsylvania, which had jurisdiction over my case on appeal. We wanted them to remand the case to the trial court for a hearing to determine whether or not I was entitled to a new trial based on after discovered evidence. The Supreme Court denied the petition.

Sometime later, the Supreme Court of Pennsylvania also denied Miller's appeal to have his previous statements about the case suppressed. Miller then filed a Petition under the Post Conviction Hearing Act. In this petition, Miller claimed that his lawyer was ineffective for not raising an insanity defense. Miller stated in his petition that he blacked out at the time of Wilhelm's homicide and could not remember what happened. We petitioned for remand again. This time the remand was granted. Miller later withdrew this petition on the advice of his attorney and the District Attorney's Office.

My remand hearing was held before Judge John O'Brien in the Court of Common Pleas. Normally, this hearing would have been held before Judge Ziegler, who presided over my trial. However, shortly after my original trial, he was appointed as a judge in Federal District Court.

This hearing was held to determine whether or not I was entitled to a new trial based on after discovered evidence. At the hearing, the psychiatrist and the psychologist who examined and interviewed Miller testified that he had a mental defect resulting from an injury suffered in an accident as a child. They testified that Miller had an impaired memory and, as a result, filled in memory lapses with what is known as confabulation. In medical jargon, confabulation means unconscious lying. According to the psychologist and the psychiatrist, when they tested Miller, they found a significant memory deficit.

The hearing went well. It went so well that my attorneys did not take the time to call up to testify an expert witness that we had retained.

A psychiatrist with a fine reputation, Dr. Sadoff was a professor of psychiatry at the University of Pennsylvania. He had flown to Pittsburgh from Philadelphia, but it was the end of the day. That meant the hearing would have had to be continued some weeks later, and we would have had to pay Dr. Sadoff a considerable amount of money to return. Accordingly, my attorneys decided that the hearing had gone well enough to forgo Dr. Sadoff's testimony.

Judge O'Brien denied me a new trial, and the Supreme Court of Pennsylvania affirmed his ruling. In his written opinion, Judge O'Brien stated that the psychiatrist had not recalled exactly what tests he had used to confirm his diagnosis of Miller. In the context of his testimony and all of the other evidence presented at the hearing, this reason lacked validity.

After the Supreme Court of Pennsylvania turned down my appeal, my family hired new counsel to pursue my appellate rights.

The Washington D.C. based firm of Arent, Fox, and Kintner represented me on direct appeal with Charles Scarlatta esquire, as local counsel. My next attorney, Robert Potter, was hired to pursue my appeal. Mr. Scarlatta remained loosely involved but was not active in any of the proceedings. Mr. Potter filed a Post Conviction Hearing Act Petition in the Pennsylvania Courts because all issues had to be exhausted in state court before an appeal could be taken to Federal Court on a Petition for Writ of *Habeas Corpus*.

After running its course through the Pennsylvania Courts, my Post Conviction Hearing Act Petition was turned down. A Petition was filed in Federal Court for Writ of Habeas Corpus. The Federal District Court turned down the Petition, and an Appeal was taken to the Third Circuit Court of Appeals, and later to the Supreme Court of the United States.

Potter and I disagreed on the issues to raise in my appeal, and much to my regret, I acquiesced to his perspective.

He would not raise the issues contained in my second petition, which dealt with the crime scene, destruction of evidence, prosecutorial misconduct, and ineffective assistance of counsel. His selection of issues led to a dismissal order without opinion everywhere, except for the Federal District Court.

Those issues were really no more than a rehash of the issues already raised on direct appeal. Because they really did not discuss anything new, there were summarily dismissed. I repeatedly told Potter that I wanted the case investigated. He would not do it.

In my second post conviction petition my lawyers requested the police records for the Homicide of George Wilhelm. They were informed that all copies of the case files were missing. Please keep in mind that this was one of the highest profile cases of the 1970s. The detective file, maintained in triplicate, was voluminous. That three copies of a major case file would turn up missing due to inadvertence or innocent happenstance is hard to believe.

The missing three copies of the main detective file is only the tip of the iceberg. My attorneys requested a copy of the Mobile Crime Unit file. They also requested a copy of the file in the Police photo lab. These two files, separately maintained, also turned up missing. No logical explanation has been offered beyond the fact that the Detective Branch of the Pittsburgh Police moved locations. We requested that the City of Pittsburgh disclose how many investigative files there were and how many were missing. They refused to provide the information.

In November of 1995, my attorneys brought in one of our experts John Balshy, to examine the coroner files. On the date of his visit, the coroner's file was intact. For reasons not provided, Mr. Balshy was only allowed to see part of the file. This was not in accordance with Pennsylvania law, which requires that the coroner's files be open to the public. We did not make an issue of this because Dr. Wecht had just been elected coroner and was to take office in January. He had previously written a letter on my behalf to the board of Pardons stating that in his opinion, I was not the assailant.

When Dr. Wecht took office in January of 1996, his staff discovered that the file was now missing. Dr. Wecht asked the County Police to investigate. Nothing was determined and no charges were filed. Recently, my attorneys sought a copy to the Allegheny County Police file of this investigation and they were told that the file had been purged a few years after the investigation was undertaken.

That all these files turned up missing due to inadvertence or innocent happenstance is not logically credible. From a common sense point of view, all one has to do is ask how all these separate archives could turn up missing in the absence of intentional acts. Dr. Stephen Fienberg, a professor of statistics, determined the probability of all copies of a case file to be innocently lost. He determined that "...finding four records missing is an extremely rare event. The alternative to assuming that we have observed such a rare event is to conclude that there is a connection among the files being lost, that is they were not lost at random."

In my second Post Conviction Relief Act Petition, I questioned the manner in which the police investigation of Wilhelm's killing was conducted. The experts we retained told us that if the police had conducted a complete and objective investigation, that the assailant could definitely have been identified. This was not done, and no good reason was ever given. My attorneys requested discovery, which the District Attorney vigorously opposed, and the Court did not allow. The trial court turned down my post conviction petition without a hearing.

The Superior Court reversed this ruling and ordered that an evidentiary hearing be held. The District Attorney delayed the expeditious movement of this case. First they asked the Superior Court to review this ruling en banc. Then they sought Allowance of Appeal from the Supreme Court of Pennsylvania.

This unnecessarily delayed matters by several months. It is only in rare cases involving significant legal issues that the Superior Court of Pennsylvania grants en banc review. There was also little to no chance that the Supreme Court of Pennsylvania would grant Allowance of Appeal, where the Superior Court had only granted a hearing and not finally disposed of a case. Nevertheless, the District Attorney filed these appeals to delay disposition and ultimately to keep me incarcerated as long as possible.

After my case was remanded to the Court of Common Pleas in Pittsburgh, it was assigned initially to Judge McGregor, who had a reputation for being thoughtful and fair. The District Attorney sought Judge McGregor's removal on the pretext that Judge O'Brien was the original judge from the first post conviction petition. After Judge O'Brien retired, the case was then assigned to Judge Donna Jo McDaniel.

Judge McDaniel decided that only Dr. Wecht, a prosecution rebuttal witness, and my original trial counsel would be allowed to testify. She based her ruling on a strained interpretation of the Superior Court opinion. It made little sense and distorted the nature of my ineffective assistance of counsel claim.

The essence of the ineffective claim was that my trial counsel had failed to investigate the crime scene and the forensic evidence. Judge McDaniel treated the claim as one for failing to call a specific witness, namely Dr. Wecht.

Where a court considers a claim of failure to investigate, it follows all legitimate leads that a reasonable investigation would create. On the other hand, a claim for failure to call a witness is more difficult. It involves deciding whether or not if a trial lawyer was objectively unreasonable to not call a specific witness after the attorney has spoken to the witness. The inquiry is always premised on the fact that counsel, after interviewing the witness and knowing what the witness would testify to, then decides that it is not in the client's best interest to call the witness in question.

Before trial, my attorney H. David Rothman never spoke to Dr. Wecht or any other forensic expert. He never made a conscious decision to call or not call Dr. Wecht as a witness at trial because he had not investigated. Rothman never spoke to Dr. Wecht before deciding not to call him as a witness.

Rothman claimed that after Detective Freeman's testimony concerning the blood spatter, he read a book on blood spatter by Dr. McDonnell. On the basis of what he read in the book, Mr. Rothman did nothing further.

We hired Dr. McDonnell as an expert in forensics and blood spatter. Please read over Dr. McDonnell's affidavits. They will show that Rothman was wrong to not consult with experts. Also read the affidavits of Stanley Greenfield Esquire, and Gary Zimmerman, Esquire. These two highly experienced criminal defense lawyers have opined that Rothman was not effective.

If Rothman never spoke to Dr. Wecht, there is no basis to cast the claim as a failure to call a witness. There is no credible, aboveboard explanation for Judge McDaniel's ruling. I have not come across a ruling like this in any other case.

At the hearing before Judge McDaniel, Dr. Wecht testified that he was confident to a reasonable degree of medical certainty, that Clarence Miller was the assailant. Judge McDaniel allowed the prosecutors to call as a rebuttal witness, Toby Wolson, a criminalist with the Miami Police.

Mr. Wolson testified that he could not make a conclusion on the meaning of the blood spatter without a picture of it. However, he did admit on cross examination, that if the blood spatter was as described by Detective Freeman in his trial testimony, then Dr. Wecht was correct in his conclusions. Judge McDaniel turned down my petition.

The Superior Court of Pennsylvania turned down our appeal of Judge McDaniel's ruling. Their opinion was short and conclusory. It offered no real explanation. It was not published. The Supreme Court of Pennsylvania denied allowance of appeal.

We next filed a request for permission to file a successive Petition for Writ of habeas Corpus in the Third Circuit Court of Appeal. Permission was granted and the case was sent to the United States District Court in Pittsburgh.

The case was assigned to Magistrate Lenahan who denied all our requests for discovery and an evidentiary hearing. Magistrate Lenahan issued a report recommending that my petition be denied. Her ruling was affirmed summarily by the United States district Court Judge Schwab.

We then appealed to the third Circuit Court of Appeal for a certificate of appealability. This was granted. The brief is due shortly.

Troubling Questions

There are several questionable facts and circumstances in this case, none of which alone, legitimately raises a question. But when taken together, the pattern is troubling.

I am sure that whatever happened in the beginning in 1974, had nothing to do with me. The original land fraud investigation was dropped in 1974, under unusual circumstances. In spite of the fact that the FBI felt that a fraud had been committed, the U.S. Assistant Attorney for Western Pennsylvania, Richard Thornburgh, issued a letter of declination, which meant that the FBI could not investigate further.

Mr. Thornburgh was a very partisan and ambitious Republican who went on to be Governor of Pennsylvania and Attorney General of the United States. 1974 was an election year in which the Republican Party was experiencing difficulties due to Watergate. Republican Senator, Richard Schweiker was up for re-election. Once Mr. Thornburgh was satisfied that the Senator's office had nothing to do with Mr. Wilhelm's loss, he was more than happy to let it go, regardless of whether or not a fraud had been committed.

The case was not turned over to local authorities to investigate, so the whole matter died. In my opinion this was because Senator Schweiker was up for re-election. Times were tough for Republicans. If the land fraud case became public, it might have proven embarrassing to Senator Schweiker, even if no one connected to his office had anything to do with it. Everything would have been fine from their point of view, if only Wilhelm had not been killed.

I have no solid proof that any one person did anything. However, the following facts cannot be disputed:

1. The declination by the US Attorney in 1974, after being told by the FBI that they felt that a fraud had been committed raises questions. Beyond this, neither the US Attorney nor the FBI saw fit to contact any local law enforcement that an individual may have been swindled out of $20,000.

2. The crime scene investigation was done by the homicide department of a major city police force.

3. The police detectives knew that Miller had scratches on his face and arms, as well as laceration on one finger.

4. The police detectives knew that Miller had failed a polygraph test.

5. The police had a dying declaration from the victim stating, "Clarence Miller did this to me."

6. The police interpreted the dying declaration to mean that Clarence Miller had set Wilhelm up to be assaulted by Charles Goldblum

7. Notwithstanding the fact that the police had a legitimate "whodunit" on their hands, they did not take pictures of the blood spatter on the dashboard in the vehicle. In the alternative, the pictures were taken but came up missing by the time of trial. When contacted by my investigator, the police photographer, Detective Crisanti, did not remember whether he took pictures of the blood spatter or not. It is possible that these pictures were taken but lost. Later in a deposition, Detective Crisanti emphasized how important it was to always photograph evidence before moving it.

8. The police lost all three copies of a large sized voluminous case file for one of their most important homicide cases.

9. The police also lost two other files related to this case, namely the Mobile Crime Unit file and the Police Photo lab file.
10. The coroner's file which was intact in the end of 1995, ended up missing when Dr. Cyril Wecht took office a month or so later. It was well known that Dr. Wecht had previously expressed his opinion that I was not the assailant.
11. When I applied for commutation in 1998, a public hearing was granted in 1999. At that hearing, the attorney for the Commonwealth, James Gilmore admitted that lawyers in the District Attorney's Office never believed Clarence Miller when he claimed that George Wilhelm was the arsonist of my restaurant. Mr. Dixon also admitted this to my attorneys. Notwithstanding this belief, no further investigation took place, and Miller was allowed to testify to this.

One or two of the above factors would not prove anything. However, there is a point where a series of unusual events or coincidences become so troubling that one has a right to ask why all of this has happened and who is the entity behind the curtain

Applications for Commutation

I have applied for commutation of my sentences to the Board of Pardons several times.

After I publicly admitted that I had committed the arson, Judge Ziegler, who presided over my trial, wrote a strong letter in support of my application. He has supported me strongly in each subsequent application. In my last application, Judge Ziegler also wrote to the Governor. Judge Ziegler has serious doubts about my guilt. It is not often that a trial judge writes such a letter. According to Judge Ziegler, this is the only time that he has done this.

When I applied for commutation the fourth time, in 1994, the Board of Pardons sat on my case for several months which they had never done before. Shortly before the election in October, a prisoner whose life sentence had been commuted moved to New York and was arrested for murder and rape. Soon after the story broke, all pending applications before the Board of Pardons were turned down, including mine.

What I Have Done With Myself

Now having served 20 years in Pennsylvania Department of Corrections facilities, I have kept myself busy and involved.

At SCI Huntingdon, I worked at the Dental Clinic, the Shipping Department, the Trade School, and the Electric Shop. In 1994, I transferred to SCI Somerset where I worked in the Library and the Activities Department. (In 1997, Goldblum was transferred to SCI Mahanoy where he is today.)

I have always been actively involved in organizational work. I participated in the Lifer Association, the Jaycees, the Jewish Congregation at Huntingdon, and the inmate organizations at Somerset and Mahanoy. I have held several elected offices and chaired many committees. I have served as a volunteer Lawback Literacy tutor for many years. I have derived a lot of satisfaction from tutoring.

(At SCI Mahanoy, he was assigned to the Library, participated in the Work Place Project, assisting inmates about to be released with occupational information, resumes, and cover letters. Due to his age and health problems, he only works part time.)

In my spare time, I read various newspapers and magazines such as Morningstar and The Wall Street Journal in an effort to keep abreast of current events. This helps me remain intellectually alert.

I am very involved with my family. They are a great source of strength for me. I keep in close contact with them and try to be involved in as many family affairs and matters as I can. They are all great that way and go out of their way to keep me involved. We speak on the phone regularly and they visit as often as possible. I know that when I am released, they will assist me in any way possible, including financial support and a place to stay.

I have tried to maintain a positive outlook despite my years of incarceration. I have made a few good friends over the years, and we have helped each other through the tough times. For the most part however, my existence has been a lonely one, and I have learned to make my own best company. I also have become used to a very simple style of living that most likely will stay with me.

Many years ago, I made some serious mistakes, the arson, not reporting Wilhelm's murder to the police immediately, and worst of all, for even considering a solicitation to have Miller murdered.

(added in 2015) I have been incarcerated for most of my entire adult life. Closing in on age 70, I am running out of time. Nonetheless, I am prepared to re-enter society and live what years that may remain as a productive, law-abiding citizen.

Doctor Cyril H. Wecht Provides Testimony

PROCEEDINGS: October 19, 2000
Before: Judge Donna Jo McDaniel
By Mr. Markovitz: counsel for Charles Goldblum
By Mr. Broman: counsel for the Commonwealth
Witness: Cyril H. Wecht, M.D. having been first duly cautioned and sworn, was examined and testified as follows:

Q. (Markovitz) State your name, please.
A. Cyril H. Wecht.
Q. What is your occupation?
A. Physician specializing in anatomic, clinical, and forensic pathology.
Q. Do you presently occupy any positions in the government of Allegheny County?
A. Yes.
Q. What position is that?
A. Coroner of Allegheny County.
Q. How long have you been Coroner of Allegheny County?
A. Since January 1, 1996. Previously, I served as coroner for ten years, from 1970 to 1980, and for four years as a chief forensic pathologist in the Allegheny County Coroner's office.
Q. Would you describe your education after high school?
A. Four years University of Pittsburgh, Bachelor of Science degree, 1952. Two years medical school, University of Buffalo, School of Medicine, then the third and fourth years at Pitt Medical School, with an M.D. in June '56. Year of general rotating surgeon.
THE COURT: Can we qualify Dr. Wecht as an expert in the area of forensic pathology? If there are other areas that you wish to qualify, you may also proceed on those areas, but at least in forensic pathology.
MR. BROMAN: No, your honor, I was given a curriculum vitae before the hearing yesterday, and I have no problem with that up to 1977, when he would have been testifying as an expert.
THE COURT: Okay.
Q. Dr. Wecht, let me show you what I have marked as Exhibit 1. Is that your curriculum vitae?
MR. BROMAN: What Exhibit number?

232

Q. 1.

THE COURT: I thought C.

MR. BROMAN: I thought C. 1 came in yesterday.

THE COURT: It was No.2, the affidavit, and it was admitted.

Q. I offer - Exhibit 1 into evidence.

MR. BROMAN: Only to the relevance of anything beyond 1977.

THE COURT: It would be admitted.

Q. Dr. Wecht, are you familiar with what we generally call blood spatter analysis?

A. Yes.

Q. Would you describe for the Court essentially what that is in general?

A. It has to do with hemodynamics, moving blood produced by some open laceration, tear of a blood vessel causing blood to emanate from the human body, the direction, the configuration, the physical location in relationship to a body or some incident of trauma, an assault, accident, whatever it might be, the combination of all of those things. In relationship to the body, and in many instances the kind of instrumentality that may have been used, the position of any third parties or sometimes even inanimate objects, et cetera, are all then put together, correlated for the purpose of arriving at some conclusions and opinions regarding what may have happened to have produced that outflow of blood. So we study all of those things in relationship to the human body in forensic pathology.

Q. Do you hold yourself out as having greater knowledge of blood spatter analysis or hemodynamics than lay persons?

A. Yes.

Q. And what is the basis of your knowledge?

A. This kind of a study is an integral part of forensic pathology. I studied this during my last two years of residency in courses at the Armed Forces Institute of Pathology when I was in the United States Air Force .

More fully, however, with the commencement of my fellowship and formal training in forensic pathology at the medical examiner's office in Maryland, '61 to '62. Of course, going to scenes, seeing bodies, working with, of course, senior forensic pathologists and my chief and people under him there at the medical examiner's office in Baltimore.

Since 1962 or to the present time, 38 years, I have had countless -- I don't know certainly in the hundreds, if not in the thousands, of instances which I have gone to scenes or I have studied photographs taken at scenes as well as diagrams, charts, and other narrative descriptions of those things. Goes back a long time. As a matter of fact, I recall quite vividly when I became medical legal consultant to the district attorney's office of Allegheny County and served as assistant district attorney, '64 into the summer of '65, about a year and a half, one of the very first cases was going to a scene of a shooting with then district attorney Robert W. Dugan.

A man had been shot and there was a question of whether or not it was a suicide or a homicide. Blood spatter evidence there at the scene on the walls in the room which he was found -- I remember that because the district attorney and his chief went with me and we drove in the car and then they took me home. That is why I remember it so well. So this is the kind of a thing that we do, and we do frequently in cases involving the Coroner's office.

Q. And you often have to analyze blood spatters on a body?

A. Yes. Let me say for the, sake of completion, we do do this in conjunction with criminalists who work in the forensic science laboratory division of the Coroner's office, and we do it sometimes in conjunction with the homicide detectives, the City of Pittsburgh or the County of Allegheny, but we the forensic pathologist have to correlate all of this and fit it into our final determinations. We happily and unhesitatingly reach out for additional input from other people. I don't want to suggest to you that we don't have such people around. Every large metropolitan medical/legal investigative office or forensic science laboratory should have and does have such individuals, but it is the ultimate responsibility of the forensic pathologist to make these kinds of determinations.

We have been doing this for many, many years. Indeed this subject was presented by me and by experts that I invited as members of the faculty at nine seminars funded by the LEAA in the early seventies at the Allegheny County Police Academy in North Park, so we were well aware of this and discussed these things on those occasions at extremely well-attended seminars by not only local law enforcement, but people who came from all over the state, and by the time we were into our second year, we had people wanting to come from New York, Ohio, and West Virginia.

Q. So the record is clear, by these things you mean blood spatter analysis?

A. Yes. That is what we are talking about. Or blood.

Q. I would offer for voir dire.

VOIR DIRE EXAMINATION BY MR. BROMAN:

Q. You stated, Dr. Wecht, that you first studied blood spatter evidence in the Air Force?

A. On a few occasions we had a couple of suicides on base, and then at courses at the Armed Forces Institute of Pathology, which I went to in 1960 and 1961. It was part of the overall subject material. It was not the sole subject; it was part of a week-long course in each of those two years given by the military forensic pathologists.

Q. In '61 and '62?

A. 60 and '61. I was in the service from 1959 to 1961, and these two courses, I think, were in the late winter or early spring of '60 and '61.

Q. And who at that time were the experts who were conducting scientific experiments on blood spatter evidence?

A. Well, at that time there were different forensic pathologists at the Armed Forces Institute of Pathology, and there were civilians whom they brought in to teach. I remember the civilians quite well because they were the leaders in the field, Dr. Milton Halpern from New York City; Dr. Joseph Spellman from Philadelphia, Dr. Richard Ford from Boston; Dr. Geoffrey Mann from Virginia and Dr. Russell Fischer, who later became my chief from Baltimore. Those are the civilians. I don't remember the military people. The ones I do remember were actually contemporaries of mine, so I don't think they were faculty at the time.

Q. And had they published treatises, these individuals?

A. I think everybody whom I mentioned has published some textbooks, others articles. I know that Geoffrey Mann had a textbook from the Commonwealth of Virginia medical examiner's office; Dr. Halpern's classical textbook with colleagues at the New York City medical examiner's office; others published many papers. I don't know that Spellman and Ford had textbooks.

Q. And these were all published before 1977, to your knowledge?

A. Yes. The books to which I referred were published before that time.

Q. Now, you stated you do things in conjunction with homicide detectives, were you referring to post-1977 or pre-1977?

A. Both. We worked closely with them. We receive calls, of course, from them; sometimes they from us, and it is a collaborative effort at the scene. And then they come to the autopsies to be in attendance and then in cases that have ongoing investigations and so on, there may be subsequent visits, a review of evidence, so these are the contacts that we have with them. Ultimately, of course, also at the trials of such cases.

Q. Are you referring to forensic pathologists going to the scene or criminalists?

A. Both. The criminalists go more frequently. I hesitate to say 100 percent of the time. It is 100 percent of the time when, of course, our office is contacted and such a request is made. The forensic pathologists go less frequently. They go in cases where there is a specific request where we think it is a complicated, potentially controversial kind of a situation; then the forensic pathologist will go.

Q. Have you yourself, Doctor, conducted experiments under a controlled situation with human blood and its results as far as splatters?

A. No. I have not conducted any original or basic research myself.

Q. Okay. Are you familiar with an individual by the name of Herbert McDonnell?

A. Yes.

Q. Are you familiar with the publication Flight Characteristics and Stain Patterns of Human Blood, which was published in November 1971?

A. Yes.

Q. Are you familiar with what the author's opinion is as far as to be qualified as an expert on blood stain patterns?

A. No.

MR. MARKOVITZ: Could I see that before the witness is shown that.

THE COURT: Yes you may.

Q. Highlighted section there, Doctor. Would you mind reading that? Please.

MR. BROMAN: I have no further questions your Honor .

A. "It is the author's opinion that before anyone is qualified to render expert testimony on the significance of bloodstain patterns, they must have conducted a variety of experiments under known conditions using human blood, preserve their results as standards for reference and have made a detailed study of these standards. "

Q. You have not done that?

A. No, I haven't.

MR.BROMAN: I have no further questions, Your Honor.

MR MARKOVITZ: I will ask that the Court accept Dr. Wecht as an expert in the field of blood spatter analysis.

THE COURT: Mr. Broman?

MR. BROMAN: I don't believe he is Your Honor, but given the fact that this is a remand for the hearing, given the fact that the standard to become an expert in Pennsylvania is rather low, I don't know that I have much of an argument.

THE COURT: Doctor Wecht will be accepted as an expert.

Q. (Markovitz)You were a Coroner when George Wilhelm was murdered on February 9, 1976?

A. Yes.

Q. You did not personally supervise that case as a forensic pathologist, is that correct?

A. That's correct.

Q. And you were also the Coroner when Zeke Goldblum was tried and convicted of that murder before a jury in August 1977?

A. Yes.

Q. Did any of the investigating police officers or detectives consult with you personally on the Wilhelm murder?

A. No, not that I have any recollection of, nor that I had any recollection of a few years ago when I was first contacted by another legal counsel representing Mr. Goldblum prior to your involvement in this matter.

Q. Did anyone to your recollection from the district attorney's office consult with you on the Wilhelm murder?

A. No.

Q. Is the Coroner's office in Allegheny County an independent office or an arm of the prosecution?

A. It is an autonomous independent office. I have made a very big point countless times in writing and speeches and discussions that our Coroner's office, and in my opinion, any medical/legal investigative office in the United States, medical examiner or Coroner, is not an and should not be an arm of the prosecution's office. It is an independent office; it is a medical forensic scientific embodiment for the community.

Q. As such, is your office open to inquiry or consultation from either prosecutor, police or defense lawyers?

A. Yes, it is. And I hold the same pattern for myself in my· consultations, so to speak, and performance of autopsies for Coroners in adjacent counties for whom I do autopsies. Whenever a defense attorney calls, of course, I refer them to the District Attorney's office of that county, making it clear that I have no problem, and that I will be happy to discuss my autopsy findings with them, but I want to make sure that all bases are touched first.

Q. And is it unusual for defense lawyers or defense experts in a homicide case to consult with you on a case?

A. No. I don't want to represent that it is done always or most of the time, but it certainly is not unusual. I think it should be done a lot more, but that is my own thought. I can't reach out to everybody and invite them, but it is not infrequent. It is not rare. And probably, you know, in recent years -- well, there is no question it has become now more of a frequent thing as people have come to learn a lot more about forensic science.

A. Do I know what?

Q. Do you know who defended him?

A. I think it was Attorney David Rothman. I know from the records.

Q. Did Mr. Rothman ever discuss this case with you.

A. Not that I recall.

Q. Did Mr. Rothman ever try to obtain your testimony in this case?

A. My testimony?

Q. Yes?

A. No.

Q. Have you reviewed certain materials with this case?

A. Yes.

Q. Can you describe some of the materials that you reviewed?

A. There is the original autopsy report. There were then portions of the transcript of the trial from several witnesses, Dr. Joshua Perper, then chief forensic pathologist in the Allegheny County Coroner's office who supervised the autopsy, which was participated by him and our then fellow in forensic pathology, Dr. Fombi Mallick.

There were autopsy photographs; there were summaries of some police investigative reports and crime lab reports. I subsequently received, by the way, reports that have been obtained from other experts, joint report by Dr. Michael Baden and Barbara Wolf, a separate report by Dr. Henry Lee. There was a real problem with regard to the review and study of all documents and records in the case because of the absence of such materials from the Allegheny County Coroner's office when I made the inquiry to see what not was there.

Q: The Coroner's file in this case is missing, is it not?

A. Yes, it is.

Q. Without explanation?

MR. BROMAN: Objection, Your Honor. This issue was attempted to be raised and Superior Court said it could not be raised.

THE COURT: I will sustain the objection.

Q. Dr. Wecht, let me show you -- I don't know if the Court wants me to mark this. This is just a portion of the trial transcript.

THE COURT: · You need not, I think.

Q. I'm referring to Page 1247 or -- I'm sorry. Yes, 1247.

A. You mean 1217.

Q. It looks like a four.

A. It is a four. 1247.

Q. 1247 of the original trial transcript, which includes the testimony of Detective Ron Freeman. In particular, the last question and answer of that page, which goes on to the next page. Could you just review that to yourself for the moment?

A. Yes.

Q. Does that testimony describe the blood spatter that was found on the dashboard of the victim's vehicle?

A. Yes.

Q. Now, based on that testimony, can a Coroner give an opinion as to who actually assaulted and committed a murder?

A. In certain situations, you might be able to, with additional information. If you mean by looking at a body only, no, you can only get sometimes an idea categorically, but not as to the identity of an individual.

Q. But based on your review of the testimony in this case and the other documents in this case, do you hold an opinion with reasonable medical certainty as to whether Mr. Goldblum inflicted the fatal stab wounds on George Wilhelm?

MR. BROMAN: I am going to object to the broad nature of that question. If he is asking Dr. Wecht if he is assessing -- if he is going to ask him about forensic evidence in the case, that is one thing, but to ask him about somebody's testimony and whether they are going to assess that and what have you, I don't think that is forensic evidence. I think at that point he is commenting on the credibility and assessing credibility under Seese (phonetic), I think that is impermissible.

THE COURT: I agree to some degree, but I think Dr. Wecht can still render his opinion if he wishes. So you may answer, Doctor.

A. Thank you, Your Honor. Yes, I have an opinion.

Q. And what is that opinion?

A. It is my opinion, based upon the forensic scientific evidence, the physical evidence and other related information in this case, from my perspective as a forensic pathologist, that Mr. Goldblum was not the individual who stabbed Mr. Wilhelm on this occasion.

Q. Dr. Wecht, is part of that conclusion based on certain forensic evidence in the case? For example, is part of that conclusion -- is your conclusion based partly on the evidence that Mr. Miller testified that there was blood on his clothes, that he had disposed of those clothes, and that Mr. Goldblum's clothes, as identified by Mr. Miller and seized by the police, had no blood on it?

A. Yes. That is part of it, because of the multiplicity and nature of the wounds sustained by Mr. Wilhelm, including the significant so-called defense wounds, which clearly then indicate a struggle, a discussion at that position of the two individuals to some degree, I find it very difficult to develop scenario in my mind whereby an individual who is inflicting all of these wounds on the victim would not get blood spatter back on to his clothes, him being the assailant. And based upon the information that you just set forth in your question with which I am familiar with the records, I therefore find it highly implausible that Mr. Goldblum was the individual who wielded the knife that inflicted these wounds on Mr. Wilhelm.

Q. And is your conclusion and your opinion also based in part on the evidence, forensic evidence, that gloves which were recovered near the scene of the crime containing blood that was of the same type as the victim's blood, that those gloves contained arm hairs or hand hairs that were consistent with Mr. Miller's hair but not consistent with Mr. Goldblum's or the victim's?

A. Yes. I am aware of that evidence. And that, too, is inconsistent with Mr. Miller's statement, as I recall, that Mr. Goldblum wore gloves. Mr. Miller's hairs were found in the gloves, not Mr. Goldblum's, so if anybody wore the gloves, it obviously then was Mr. Miller, unless somebody wants to suggest that the hairs were planted there.

THE COURT: That is only in California, Dr. Wecht.

THE WITNESS: Thank you, Your Honor. I certainly am not suggesting it here.

A. (Continuing) So yes. That is part -- that is a piece of the overall puzzle or fabric.

Q. In fact, there was no forensic evidence linking those gloves to Mr. Goldblum?

A. Not that I am aware of.

Q. Is your opinion also based in part on the testimony elicited at trial that on the day after the murder, when the police visited with Clarence Miller, they observed on him fresh scratches on his arms and on his face, and that there were no scratches or other signs of struggle observed on Mr. Goldblum?

A. Yes. I will not say that that would be considered in my first category of medical and forensic scientific evidence, but it certainly is a finding of relevance.

Q. You consider that part of the mosaic?

A. Yes. This is not something to be ignored. If there were other explanations, it is for other people to elicit and ascertain and evaluate them, but following this kind of an obvious struggle, the presence of scratch marks on one of two individuals who possibly may have murdered the victim and the absence of such scratch marks on the other individual is a relevant and significant finding.

Q. Now, turning your attention now finally to the blood spatter, and you have the testimony of Ron Freeman who described the blood spatters on the dashboard.

THE COURT: So that we are clear, this is the blood spatters on the dashboard?

MR. MARKOVITZ: Yes, ma'am.

Q. What did you find was the significance of that blood spatter testimony?

A. First, the fact that there is blood in that location on the dashboard. Second, that it had a left to right directionality. Third, that they would appear to have been what we call medium velocity blood spatters. These are the kind of spatter one finds in what we call a casting off, as when one is wielding a weapon repeatedly.

This man, Mr. Wilhelm, sustained 25 stab wounds overall. I don't believe that all of these were inflicted in the automobile, but many were. So that you had, obviously by definition, multiple strikes by whoever it was that was wielding the knife, so the directionality as ascertained by the tail; the medium velocity of the cast-off; the presence of the multiple stab wounds; the absence of a gaping laceration on the scalp or elsewhere that might have been caused by some blunt force instrument to suggest some other physical etiology; source of these wounds ultimately then correlated with the known and, as far as I understand it, incontrovertible positions of the three individuals in the car, Mr. Miller in the driver seat, Mr. Wilhelm in the right front passenger seat, and Mr. Goldblum in the back seat directly behind Mr. Wilhelm, putting all of these things together, those blood spatters therefore have great significance.

The significance is that these wounds are entirely consistent with and buttress and support the conclusion that a person sitting to the left of Mr. Wilhelm is wielding the instrumentality. That would explain the presence of these blood spatters on the dashboard in front of Mr. Wilhelm. If Mr. Goldblum, sitting in the back, were inflicting the wounds, I don't see how blood spatters then would be up in the front of the dashboard with a left to right directionality.

Q. Just so the record is clear -- maybe I misheard -- but Mr. Wilhelm was seated behind the wheel of the vehicle, correct, the victim?

A. Yes.

Q. And Mr. Miller was seated at the right front passenger seat?

A. Yes. Did I say?

Q. I'm not sure if you did or not. I may have misheard you. Now, the tails of the blood spatter you say indicate a left to right movement, and by that I assume you refer to a movement from the position in front of the driver over toward the passenger side of the car?

A. Yes.

Q. And the tails would have been pointed in that direction?

A. Yes.

Q. What do you, mean by medium velocity?

A. Well, gunshot wounds are high speed velocity. Medium velocity is the kind of things you see with these cast-offs as with somebody wielding any kind of a weapon instrumentality. Could be a knife, it could be something else.

And these are differentiated from the kinds of blood spatters that you might find if you sever a high pressure artery like the carotid artery, so we talk about high speed, low speed and medium velocity. Low velocity would be like if you -- I have a little cut or I started to just bleed on me a little bit if I drop some blood here and you saw it on the floor, you would say that would be on a low speed, a dropping, or if I put my hand over here (indicating) and it went on to the judge's desk, then that would be low velocity. There is no speed.

Q. When, if you can answer this question, when an assailant stabs a victim, would you normally expect the path of withdrawal from the victim to be the same as the path or roughly the same as path of the stabbing? If you could look at me for just a moment, Doctor, if I was to stab somebody like this, would I also pull out like this generally or if I was to stab somebody like this, would I not also generally pull out like that?

A. Yes. The motion of the arm whether it be the entire, arm from the shoulder or a forearm would be essentially in the same and, not to the specific degree.

That just follows anatomy as one reaches back. That could be somewhat different with moving assailant and moving victim. I am stabbing you here and you're running and I am running after you, it certainly -- with two people seated in the front seat of a car, it would be my opinion that the reverse movement, so to speak, of the arm would essentially follow the arc or pattern in the air, if one could envision that of the arc that was produced when the arm struck out to cause the wounds.

Q. Let me show you, Dr. Wecht, what I have marked as Exhibit 3.

MR. BROMAN: Your Honor I'm going to object to this Exhibit. This is the one that Mr. Markovitz showed me this morning. This is a summarization of things Dr. Wecht has said and the best evidence is Dr. Wecht. This type of document --

THE COURT: Well, I haven't seen the document so it is almost impossible for me to make a ruling.

MR. BROMAN: Very impossible.

MR. MARKOVITZ: Well, if I can have him identify it, then I will show it to the Court, you can rule.

THE COURT: Fine.

Q. Dr. Wecht, Exhibit J summarize the forensic bases of your conclusion that Mr. Goldblum did not stab Mr. Wilhelm?

A. Yes. In succinct, topical fashion it does.

THE COURT: Did you author this, Doctor?

THE WITNESS: No, I did not, Your Honor.

MR. MARKOVITZ: It is a demonstrative.

THE COURT: I will allow it for limited purposes.

Q. Dr. Wecht, based on your review of the materials in this case, your study of those materials, is there any physical or forensic evidence to indicate that Charles Goldblum participated in the assault of George Wilhelm in any way?

A. Not that I am aware of, from my review of the autopsy report and the various records and the portions of the transcribed testimony of the individuals involved and so on. I cannot think of any definitive, tangible, medical, physical, forensic, scientific evidence that would permit me, from a forensic scientific perspective, to say that Mr. Goldblum inflicted these wounds on Mr. Wilhelm.

Q. And is there any physical, forensic, tangible evidence that Mr. Goldblum acted as an accomplice in the murder of George Wilhelm?

A. That answer I think is in the legal arena really.

Q. I'm just asking you about physical and forensic evidence.

A. Well, the answer is the same, yes. But it is not for me to intrude on her Honor's domain here. Are you asking me from a forensic pathology standpoint? No. The same answer that I gave a moment ago would be applicable here.

Q. You have just gone through some testimony about blood spatter and how you analyzed and relate the blood spatter in the Wilhelm vehicle. Was this knowledge available in 1977?

A. Yes, it was. As a matter of fact, it is interesting that the district attorney showed me Professor Herbert McDonnell's treatise. Herb McDonnell was the individual that I had down to lecture on all nine occasions, three seminars a year as I recall with LEAA funds, as well as on subsequent occasions.

In addition to those seminars right here in Allegheny County, attended by a large number -- I can't tell you everyone; I don't know but a large number certainly of the homicide detectives from both the City of Pittsburgh and the County of Allegheny. We were also dealing with these things in the Coroner's office. Part of our teaching and training programs with our fellows, fellowship having been established in 1971, these were things that were being written about and discussed in the national and international forensic scientific literature.

I was, as I recall, the district attorney asked me the treatise to which the district attorney referred, I think he said, was published in 1971, which I thought it was around that time because I know that Herb was – he had a federal grant and so on, so it goes back to those years.

By the way, Professor McDonnell deserves a great deal of credit for the work he did; he is not the originator of this. He himself has referred to, and I remember personally hearing from him, about how he and his wife traipsed through places in Germany looking for original articles that went back to the 19th century on blood spatters and stuff, so it's been around.

Q. But the opinions that you have given today, had you been called as a witness in Mr. Goldblum's trial in 1977, would you have given those same opinions to that jury?

A. Yes, I can't think of anything which is modern day technology, nor can I think of anything that I have only come to have knowledge of and experience within the past 23 years that permits me to express opinions today that I could not have expressed back then in 1977. That everything we have talked about really is very, very basic.

Q. Now, just turning to a different subject for a moment, you described briefly some of the wounds suffered by Mr. Wilhelm. And I think you mentioned he was stabbed or cut in some manner approximately 25 times and that there were defensive wounds: he suffered wounds, did he not, to the front and back of his torso?

A. Yes.

Q. To the front and back of his head?

A. Yes.

Q. His hands, his arms were cut.

A. Yes.

Q. This pattern of wounds, do you have an opinion with reasonable certainty as to whether that is more consistent with being attacked by one man or is it more consistent with being attacked by two men?

A. In my opinion, based upon a reasonable degree of medical certainty, as I think about these wounds on the individual, I would definitely lean toward one individual inflicting all of the wounds. I don't see anything here that would cause me to think that it was likely that two people were doing this.

Q. Now, I take it you have worked with the police on many hundreds, if not thousands, of cases?

A. Yes.

Q. There was testimony in this trial with regard to the blood spatter, that the police never measured the spatter and never photographed the spatter. Do you consider that to be acceptable police work?

MR. BROMAN: Objection. This is yet another issue which was raised...

THE COURT: I will sustain the objection.

Q. If I can just have a moment, Your Honor.

(Whereupon an off-the-record discussion was held.)

Q. Dr. Wecht, again considering for a moment the nature, location and extent of the wounds in the victim, are those wounds, from your point of view as a forensic pathologist, would that be consistent or inconsistent with the idea that Mr. Goldblum held the victim while Mr. Miller stabbed him, and also keeping in mind what·you testified to earlier with regard to the lack of blood on the clothes?

A. Well, it is indeed the lack of blood on Mr. Goldblum's clothing, I believe, more than any other fact that I can think of that would lead me away from a conclusion that Mr. Goldblum was holding Mr. Wilhelm while Mr. Wilhelm was being stabbed by Mr. Miller. I can't think of anyone in which I can rule in or rule out somebody holding someone, at least not in this case, no sense discussing other things. They are not applicable here.

I would then just add this. Once the wounding commences with such severity at this and this amount of bleeding and so on, it is my opinion that there would be no physical need for the victim to be restrained. I believe that he becomes significantly and seriously incapacitated by this kind of an onslaught; however insofar as your question is concerned, the only thing I can point to having a physical nature would be the absence of blood and, in fact, then that becomes an even greater consideration than it was in the context of an earlier question.

The earlier question had to do with the stabbing and that kind of juxtaposition hypothetically of Goldblum to Wilhelm. The holding of a victim who is now being stabbed and who is bleeding and so on would lead, in my opinion, to closer, more protracted juxtaposition and is much more likely to produce a transfer of blood from the victim to the individual holding him.

Q. Dr. Wecht, there was testimony at the trial that the scratches on Mr. Miller which were found by the police the day after the murder -- they saw him the day after the murder -- which I referred to earlier were never photographed or analyzed by the police. Do you have an opinion as to whether that is acceptable police-work?

MR. BROMAN: Objection.

THE COURT: Sustained.

Q. Just to make the proffer, so to speak, Judge, the reason that I am asking this question as well as the previous one that was objected to is because I believe that Dr. Wecht has the qualifications to be able to give an opinion on the quality of the police work and could have given that opinion to Mr. Goldblum's jury.

THE COURT: The objection is sustained.

Q: Begging the Court's indulgence one last time.

THE COURT: All right.

Q: Just to fill out that proffer, so I can do a complete job, my client's position is that Mr. Rothman was ineffective for failing to present that type of testimony, that is, testimony regarding the quality of the police work to the jury.

THE COURT: Okay. Mr. Markovitz, the objection is sustained.

Q: Thank you, Judge. That is all I have of this witness.

THE COURT: Okay. Cross-examination.

MR. BROMAN: Thank you, Your Honor.

CROSS-EXAMINATION BY MR. BROMAN

Q. You indicated, Dr. Wecht, in assessing the forensic evidence here, that there were different levels of importance to you?

A. Yes, I said something about certain things have more forensic scientific substance than others.

Q. And you had said the scratches were not in the first level, so they weren't …

A. Yes. I will not place them, for specific example, at the same level as the blood spatter evidence.

Q. And probably this is a stupid question, but you don't number these levels?

A. No, I don't. I just said that here today for the first time in this case in response to Mr. Markovitz's question.

Q. Just wanted to make sure I'm being thorough. Now, as to the scratches, you're aware that there was testimony by Mr. Miller that they came from his cat?

A. Yes. I recall reading or hearing that somewhere.

Q. And if I'm not - - if I'm correct, weren't there fingernail scrapings which came back negative in this case?

A. Yes. I think that that was -- again, it is my recollection from the records.

Q. Now, you stated in regards to stab wounds coming into the body and the blood coming off the weapon as opposed that kind of cast-off, that if the person moves it wouldn't necessarily -- the presumption of being able to follow that line of direction would presume the person hasn't moved?

A. Yes. Not with total immobility and complete fixed rigid positioning of a victim and an assailant, but I was just contrasting a situation in which somebody might start stabbing me and I can run around this courtroom everywhere to the different situation where two people are in the front seat of a car.

Q. But there could be movement in the car as well?

A. Could be certainly some limited movement of the parts of the upper body.

Q. Back in 1977 and '76, I believe in your affidavit you incorrectly or perhaps it is a typo stated the homicide occurred in '77?

A. The homicide was in 76 and the trial, I think, was in '77. I'm sorry. Thank you for the correction.

Q. It may have been a typo.

A. Then no other attorney has pointed that out. Thank you.

Q. Just wanted to make sure we had it clear. Back then your chief forensic pathologist was Dr. Perper.

A. Yes.

Q. Was he appointed by you as chief forensic pathologist?

A. Yes.

Q. How many forensic pathologists in addition to yourself and Dr. Perper would there have been in the office at that time?

A. We had one person who was a trainee, a fellow in forensic pathology, so not -- well, just that. A trainee. And we had two or three people who were part-time, and I don't recall -- I know that one of them did become Board certified in forensic pathology later, but I don't think was yet at that time. I'm simply not sure.

And I think that there was one other person who was a full-time trained forensic pathologist, so myself, Dr. Perper, another person, a trainee, then two or three people part-time with some hands-on, practical experience in forensic pathology.

Q. Okay. The assignments to autopsies back then, did it happen to be pretty much a matter of who was on duty?

A. Yes. They rotated the call.

Q. You were aware of this case back then, were you not, Dr. Wecht?

A. Yes, I'm sure that I was.

Q. It was a rather famous case or well-known case?

A. I have no specific recollection, you know, where were you when John F. Kennedy was killed, that kind of thing, but I certainly knew of the case. Of course I did.

Q. Did you review your autopsy -- when Dr. Perper would come up with a protocol, would you review that in the autopsy report as part of your job?

A. No, I did not.

Q. You did not?

A. No.

Q. You state in Paragraph 13 of your affidavit that when the --
do you have a copy?

A. Yes.

Q. That when the case is assigned to another pathologist such
as the case here, that you would have been notified of a request for
information and would have had input into the request for
information and opinions. Would that have been -- are you talking
about written requests there?

A. No, very few – less such requests are in writing than come in
telephonically or by personal visitation. I wasn't differentiating here.
The answer to your question is that whatever the request form is, by
letter or by phone, my people then, as today, will tell me they got a
call from a defense attorney and so on, and they wanted to know
what I think and so on. Because we have to be certain that the
information we share is that which has been generated by us.

We do not divulge - it is not our responsibility, nor our right, nor
would it be ethical and I think even legal for us to give copies of
things generated by others such as police and sometimes the district
attorney's office or something like that. We can only talk about what
we have done, what we have generated and produced in our office.

Q. Have you talked with Dr. Perper to ascertain whether or not
Mr. Rothman informally inquired of him regarding this case?

A. I'm sorry.

Q. Did you inquire of Dr. Perper whether or not Mr. Rothman
had informally made any questions to him or of the like regarding his
autopsy?

A. No. I have no recollection of any such discussion.

Q. Dr. Wecht, do you remember reading Dr. Perper's testimony
that he testified he could not tell which of the 25 wounds were
inflicted first?

A. Yes.

Q. Would you agree with that?

A. Yes.

Q. Okay. Inside the vehicle, Dr. Wecht, would you agree with
me that in close quarters like that, that it would be more difficult to
have what you determined to be a mid-velocity cast-off, specifically
referring to the weapon that was used?

A. More difficult than what?

Q. Then if you were out in a less-confined area?

A. Well, everything is relative – it is a relative difference. It is not an exclusionary one.

Q. Maybe I misheard or -- the weapon was referred to as this being a knife. You're aware it is not a knife?

A. It was half of a shears, grass trimming shears.

Q. Single blade shear?

A. Yes. You're right. I shouldn't say knife; I should say stabbing or cutting instrument.

Q. And you're right, there are other things that can cause cast-off besides cast-off from a weapon; correct?

A. Yes. There are other kinds of things.

Q. For example, if I'm punched in the nose, get a bloody nose and jerk my head, that can cause a cast-off blood pattern, could it not?

A. It is not likely that that would produce blood spatters with equal velocity. This could even be measured physically, the thrust and withdrawal of an arm compared to the turning of the head after a blow. I don't think it would be the same. If you have a real violent, abrupt turn of the head, I hesitate to say it is impossible that you might get some kind of medium velocity, and of course, medium velocity has a range, too. It is not just one single, fixed speed. But I think it unlikely, but I can't say it is not possible.

Q. Maybe we can just get away from the word medium velocity. If I am in a struggle, and it's a violent struggle and I am bleeding from the nose and I jerk my head, it could leave, would you agree, a left to right blood pattern if I moved my head in that direction where I would have basically the tail that was described here?

A. I can't say that it is impossible. I just think it is unlikely.

Q. Likewise, Dr. Wecht, you had testified that there were defensive wounds to Mr. Wilhelm's hands?

A. Yes, there were.

Q. That would cause one to bleed?

A. Yes.

Q. And there is a violent struggle going on in the car. Could not the cast-off pattern have come from that defensive wound in the hand going in that direction, left to right?

A. Once again, I will say that it is a possibility I cannot physically exclude, but it is not one that would seem to be very likely.

Q. Well, you seem to think it is more likely that the cast-off came from the shear, if I am understanding?

A. Yes; that's correct. That fits in more with the location, the number, the directionality, and the amount of force that would be associated with these kinds of violent plows.

Q. You say the number. Do you remember how many that were described?

A. No. You mean the actual blood spatters. Gee, no, I don't have that number.

Q. Okay. This was described in trial as a small amount of blood. I don't know that they ever did. That was not a trick question.

A. I don't recall ever seeing a number.

Q. Okay. Isn't it correct, when you're talking about the blood coming off the cast-off from the weapon, is that what causes that cast-off is when -- the withdrawal of the weapon, which you would be talking about here it is, when you reach the maximum position out, as the hand comes out, the blood comes off it, that had the maximum arc of the arm corning out of the body with the weapon?

A. Yes. As the arm of the assailant holding the weapon is being withdrawn, then as it comes back, then that is when that kind of spatter would be produced.

Q. It is the corning to a halt of the hand that would cause the cast-off?

A. Most, I believe, would be produced at that time. You certainly could have some during the course of there are, but most would be associated with the cessation of the movement thereby resulting in a release, so to speak, of the blood from the instrumentality.

Q. Did you consider the fact, Dr. Wecht, that the front windshield was not broken or cracked in any way?

A. I am aware it wasn't cracked or broken, but I don't know when you ask me did I consider it. I don't recall factoring it into any question that's been asked of me.

Q. When you bring your hand out to the maximum point inside of an enclosed space and you're talking about a dashboard right there in front of the window, it might be logical that the hand corning out or the grass shear might hit that window?

A. No, I think not. No, I think not. You're in the passenger seat under the scenario that I deem most plausible, and you have a right hand coming back; you have the dashboard itself as a kind of a barrier to the window.

The side window is behind you. If you came back with great force and went all the way back, you might damage the window, but I don't see where the window would likely be broken, either front or right side.

Q. Okay. I was -- I just wanted to make sure, I was specifically addressing myself to the front window.

A. Yes. But I threw in the right front side for good measure.

Q. Now, do you remember any testimony regarding Clarence Miller having bruises on his hand as if he would have hit the windshield?

A. No. I just recall the scratches; I don't think I recall any bruises.

Q. In Defense Exhibit 3 or Petitioner's Exhibit 3, it states that the dying declaration -- do you have that, Doctor?

A. Yes, I do.

Q. Victim in dying declaration identifies Miller as his assailant. That was not forensic evidence, is it, Doctor?

A. No. I also, in retrospect, the measure -- it wasn't such a measure at the time of going to law school and I remember dying declarations. Is it forensic science *in* a hard sense, of course not. Is it part of the overall picture that we would deal with in evaluating cases, in arriving at opinions especially in the Coroner's system where we conduct inquests, and so on and so forth, it would be something. I just happen to believe that the Anglo-Saxon legal forefathers, they had some great psychiatric minds. Dying declaration, exceptions to the hearsay rule, makes the most sense to me.

Q. But the fact that it is an exception to hearsay, are you saying that it rises to the level of forensic science?

A. No . It would be something for the Court to deal with. I said in the context of the Coroner's office, I would want to know things like that from the homicide detectives and we would, of course, obviously permit that at Coroner's inquest that we conduct.

Q. I understand it would be evidence; I am just making clear it is not what we would generally consider.

A. N. It is not hard.

Q. You stated he identified Clarence Miller as his assailant. Do you remember his exact words?

A. I think he said Clarence did this or something like that.

Q. I can show it to you on Page 1528.

A. I think he said Clarence.

THE COURT: Clarence Miller did this to me.

THE WITNESS: Thank you, Your Honor. Clarence did this to me, yes.

Q. That is open to more than one interpretation in this case, is it not, Dr. Wecht?

MARKOVITZ: Objection. It is beyond the scope of his expertise and beyond the scope of direct examination.

THE COURT: I will sustain the objection. I think you can rephrase the question, however.

Q. You're aware that the Defendant, Mr. Goldblum, admitted to being at the scene of a homicide?

A. Yes.

Q. And I don't mean to be a wise guy with this question, but obviously you were not there?

A. I was not there. That's okay. I have been accused of worse things.

Q. Just for the record, I was making it clear, so the best you can do is look at this evidence and try to come up with a theory?

A. Yes. As I would in the consultations that I do in cases sent to me from around the country and in cases in our own office. Of course, it is not mathematics or chemistry or physics; it is part of medical science. We just use our reasoning and experience and training.

Q. Now, you're aware of -- going back inside Dr. Perper's testimony -- as to what could or caused the cast- off?

A. I did read his testimony. Could you tell me specifically what you're referring to, please.

Q. Okay. There was another weapon recovered in the vehicle, was there not?

A. Yes, there was. I forget something else that -- Pipe wrench? The question of whether the wrench was used, yes.

MR. MARKOVITZ: I object to the characterization.

Q. That I don't know if it was a weapon?

MR. MARKOVITZ : I object to the characterization of a pipe wrench as a weapon.

THE COURT: I think Dr. Wecht sustained objection.

Q. You're aware that a pipe wrench was recovered from in side of the vehicle?

A. Yes, I am.

Q. And you're aware that Dr. Perper testified that could have been -- could have resulted in a hit to his head causing a nosebleed?

MR. MARKOVITZ: Where are you referring to, sir? Which part of the transcript?

MR. BROMAN: If you will give me a minute, sir, I will find it. 1565.

MR . MARKOVITZ: Pardon me.

MR. BROMAN: 1565. I will withdraw that. Doctor, if we can refer to Paragraph 21 of your affidavit, you state that the presence of blood spatters on the dashboard establish the stabbing began while he was in the car?

A. Yes.

Q. That would be, of course, subject to the limitations that we have already talked about of possible nosebleed, possible cast-off from defensive wounds, but I guess it wouldn't contradict·the defensive wound cast-off?

A. Well, yes. And my reading of the·description of the nose wound indicates that that, too, would have been part of a cutting or stabbing. The nose was severed badly. It was almost transected, so even in talking about the nose bleed and so on, I think that would be associated with the stabbing as, of course, would the wounds on the hands.

Q. In Paragraph 3 you again refer to the stabbing and it seems throughout this you're presuming it was a stabbing and not a cast-off from, say, a bloody nose?

A. Yes. As we have discussed, that's right.

Q. Can we agree that the blood in those -- the way they are described by Detective Freeman would not be consistent with an aortic bleed?

A. Aortic.

Q. Aortic bleeding, that would be spurting out?

A. No; you're right. This is not from the aorta. The aorta is deep inside, and even when you have complete transection, unless you have a gaping chest wound as from a shotgun or something like that, you're not going to have any external bleeding from an aortic wound.

Q. Now, is there any other forensic evidence inside the vehicle, Dr. Wecht, which factors into your decision? Here again, there is a significant inconsistency, it seems.

A. Well, let me think. You asked about the wrench. To me, between what Mr. Miller said and the physical, evidence. I believe nothing was found on the wrench, hair, tissue, blood, anything like that, and there were no lacerations of the scalp caused by a blunt force instrumentality.

Blunt force instruments produce lacerations; cutting instruments produce stab wounds or incised wounds. So Mr. Miller, as I recall, said that Mr. Goldblum had struck Mr. Wilhelm on the back of the head with a wrench. A wrench is a pretty hard piece of equipment. The absence of anything on the wrench and the absence of a scalp laceration indicate to me jointly that Mr. Miller's story is false.

So that's an additional negative kind of forensic scientific evidence, so to speak, that I recall. Let me think if there is anything else, without repeating. I'm aware, of course, again, it is negative, that Mr. Miller had acknowledged or admitted that he had disposed of some of his own clothing which was stained with Mr. Wilhelm's blood. I don't have any evidence to evaluate them, but it is forensic scientific evidence in absentia that I would just factor into the whole scenario, just cited for completeness.

Q. Maybe my question·wasn't clear. I am referring, at this point, just to inside the vehicle.

A. Inside the vehicle there were blood stains on the...

Q. Let me ask you, on Page 1236 of the trial transcript, do you recall the testimony that there was blood stains found on the driver side window?

A. Yes. I recall. I don't remember the page, but do recall that there was blood found -- let's see -- on the outside of the driver's door, I think, and, well, outside of the driver's door, and inside of the driver's side of the window as I recall. Yes.

Q. On Page 1236, in the middle -- there is no lines, Your Honor, it says driver side, the inside window. And I'm not seeing it, but I think there was on the outside of the door.

Q. Okay.

A. of the driver's door.

Q. Is that not of some forensic significance Dr. Wecht?

A. Is what?

Q. The fact that there is blood on the inside of the driver's window, is that not of some forensic significance in reconstructing or attempting to reconstruct what went on?

A. Well, it just fits in with blows coming from the right side and blood from the assailant's hand, from the weapon, from the victim's hand and so on. I don't recall a description of the blood that was found there so - and I don't have any pictures.

Q. I think there is a description on the next page. Something about a horizontal line in here.

A. Yes. The bottom of Page 1237, Your Honor, referring to the blood stains on the inside of the window, the answer was a horizontal line on the window; no measurements given. Horizontal.

Q. And do you also recall, Dr. Wecht, that there was a description of a blood stain on the inside of the window directly behind the driver, where Mr. Goldblum was seated?

A. Not specifically. If it is there.

Q. All right. I will show you this.

A. Page 1201, yes, the top of the page, the answer, "On the inside of the window, the back left door or the door in back of the driver's seat, there was a small amount of blood on the inside of the window," a small amount of blood.

Q. That is the seat where both Mr. Goldblum and Mr. Miller admit that Mr. Goldblum was seated; correct, Dr. Wecht?

A. Yes.

Q. Is that pretty significant forensically?

A. No. That – first of all, I really don't know how much – a small amount – and what it looks like, whether they were just spatters or smudges as from a hand or so on. I just really can't express much of an opinion regarding that without knowing more about it.

Q. But you found the location on the dashboard over to the right to be significant because Mr. Miller was there?

A. Yes. But in conjunction with the fact that they were clearly spatters with tails, as they are physically described, that is the big, big difference. I'm not hedging or equivocating here for any reason other than what I have said. I just don't know, what did it look like? I mean, there is a lot of possibilities.

Q. Can you rule out that it was from Mr. Goldblum, that Mr. Goldblum got it on his hand in the assault and it got on the window as he was exiting the vehicle?

A. Can I rule it out? No. There is no physical way I can rule it out. Could it have been ruled out if all these stains had been collected and typed to determine whose blood it was? Can I do that today? No, I can't.

Q. Of course not. And at the time, did Dr. Marine work for you?

A. Doctor who?

Q. Marine, if I'm pronouncing that correctly. Marine, chief criminologist. Phillip Marine.

Q. Peter?

A. No. I don't believe that such a person worked for our office.

Q. Okay. Was the crime lab separate from the Coroner's then?

A. Yes, it was.

Q. You're aware that he attempted to test the blood and cannot get a type on any of these.

A. I can't recall. But if you tell me that, I certainly accept it. He said he could not get typing on the blood. No. I did not recall.

Q. And in fairness, it was tested right at the time of trial or close to it, and he would testify right at the time that the length of time could affect the ability to I want to make sure clear that your conclusion vis-a-vis the dashboard and two inside windows is not related to anybody's particular typing?

A. Not based on anybody's typing, of course, no. I don't have such information.

Q. Now, can you say you know if Clarence Miller is right or left handed?

A. No, I may have known this. I kind of think I probably did. In any event, right now, no. I'm not prepared to say.

Q. To be honest, I don't know either, but I was curious if you knew. What you're describing -- I will use Mr. Gilmore seated here as an example. He is seated in counsel table and I am standing next to him. If I understand your cast-off theory, that this was Clarence

Miller; he would be taking the grass shear, stabbing Mr. Gilmore, pulling it out to the right and the blood spatters go in a left to right direction?

A. Yes, It would be -- it would have been the right arm.

Q. Okay. Now, let's pretend I am seated in the back seat behind Mr. Gilmore, okay. And I reach up with the same grass shear, stab him and pull it out to the right. Would that not possibly create left to right blood spatters?

A. You could get some left to right directionality. If you were to hypothesize, No. 1, a reaching forward and then stabbing inward, then a pulling out that way as opposed to a pulling back. Is it within the realm of physical possibility as it relates to the range of angularity of our wrist, elbow and shoulder joints? Yes. Is it likely, in my opinion? No. I see no reason why such gyrations would be necessary.

Q. Is your likely opinion based upon Mr. Goldblum staying seated or, in my example, actually leaning – getting up and leaning forward, bending over the seat and doing it?

A. Well, if you stand him up and lean him forward, then that possibility does become greater; I would agree with you on that.

Q. Are you aware that Mr. Goldblum testified -- calling counsel's attention to Page 2657. Are you aware or do you remember reading that in Mr. Goldblum's own testimony he struck Mr. Miller in the face?

A. Yes, I remember vaguely. I don't remember the details of that, just a vague recollection.

Q. Okay. 2657.

MR. MARKOVITZ: Could we have the question read back that preceded the citation for the record.

(Whereupon, the reporter read from the record as requested.)

A. Mr. Miller, yes, which is what is set forth here on Page 2657.

Q. I'm sorry for the confusion. Mr. Miller was struck at least once in the face by Mr. Wilhelm, according to Mr. Goldblum's testimony?

A. Yes. At least once in the face, that's correct.

Q. And you have no way of knowing whether or not Mr. Miller got a bloody nose.

MR. MARKOVITZ: Mr. Wilhelm, you mean.

MR. BROMAN: No, Mr. Miller.

A. Whether Mr. Miller got a bloody nose.

Q. When Mr. Wilhelm struck him in the face?

A. No. I would have no way of knowing if Mr. Wilhelm bloodied Mr. Miller's nose.

Q. Okay. In this particular testimony, it says they were grappling and hitting each other?

A. Yes.

Q. So we have no way of knowing, and you have no way of knowing, if Mr. Wilhelm had suffered a bloody nose as a result of that?

A. Unfortunately, Mr. Wilhelm sustained such an injury to his nose that we can't know -- I can only tell you on Page 3 of the autopsy report where Dr. Perper described the stab wound of the lower portion of the nose, he only talks about a severance and does not talk about any contusion or bruise. So you know there is nothing here to suggest an additional injury.

Q. It was virtually cut off his face.

A. Well, it was almost, like, cut in half.

Q. You cannot rule out a bloody nose?

A. That's right.

Q. Now, you state regarding blood on clothes, Dr. Wecht, that it is unimaginable there was not a significant amount of blood on the individual doing the assault?

A. Yes.

Q. Have there not been beating cases stabbing cases, where there hasn't been a lot of blood, depending upon the type of struggle?

A. I can only talk, of course, about cases which I am familiar, and I can only tell you that where there has been an altercation with some kind of a stabbing or cutting instrumentality resulting in multiple wounds, including severance of the jugular vein, which is a substantial blood vessel that would produce a significant amount of external bleeding, plus the bleeding that you would get from the facial lacerations and the hand injuries, the time that it would take to keep stabbing somebody, I just find it very difficult to understand how there would not be blood on the assailant's clothes to a significant degree in more than one location.

Q. The amounts of blood transferred to clothes can depend on a lot of factors, one of which you're referring to is the type of wounds?

A. Yes.

Q. There are other things -- the position of the parties?

A. Yes.

Q. Whether or not more than one person was involved?

A. Yes.

Q. And not necessarily in holding the person, although that is possible, you can't rule that out here, can you?

A. I don't know what you mean by not necessarily holding the person. How would that second individual be involved other than...

Q. Pushing him back into the ring, so to speak, or something like that?

A. Oh well, yes. Yes. Sure.

Q. Now, you have stated that you consider it forensic evidence -- and correct me if I'm wrong; I'm sure you won't be shy, that Mr. Goldblum's admission that there. I'm sorry. Not Mr. Goldblum -- Mr. Miller's admission there was blood on his clothes you consider to be forensic evidence?

A. I think I said in absentia, a negative nature. Factoring it into the things that we have been talking about, just your recent line of questions about transfer of blood.

Q. Okay. Now, you stated there were no blood on the clothes seized from Mr. Goldblum.

A. I think, except for a little bit on the left cuff something like that.

Q. We will get to that. You're aware that the clothes from Mr. Goldblum were not seized immediately at the scene?

A. Yes, I believe I recall that.

Q. They were seized, in fact, the next day at 7:00 from his wife, based on Mr. Goldblum's directions?

A. I don't remember the details, but whatever is contained in the record.

MR. MARKOVITZ: I'm going to object to the form of the question. He may have misspoken.

THE COURT: The record will speak for itself; the objection is overruled.

Q. They were seized the next day. An individual certainly has time to change and disregard their clothes, as you have said Mr. Miller has?

A. Correct.

Q. Now, the police officer testified that the pants taken from the Goldblum house were freshly creased. Would that be considered forensic evidence or something different from that?

A. I can't think of any great significance one way or the other.

Q. Wouldn't that make it any more likely that they had been worn or not? Is that forensic evidence?

A. Could be. Let's say somebody says they slept in clothing for some period of time or so on. In certain situations, I wouldn't say it would never be of any significance. It would be an observation that could in some instances have relevance. In this particular case I can't think of any.

Q. Now, another means of keeping blood off yourself, so to speak -- let's refer to these pants. If someone were to put pants over top of those, then commit or be involved in the stabbing, and then take those pants off and their overcoat and discard them?

A. You mean both well, I was going to say the upper garments would be perhaps more important even than the lower one. If you are covered with two garments that you then discard, of course, you know the question contains the answer, then that would prevent blood from going on to the garments beneath them.

Q. And you're familiar that Mr. Miller testified that is precisely what Mr. Goldblum had done, are you not?

A. I have a vague recollection of that. I don't remember the specifics.

Q. Refer you to Page 667 of the transcript.

A. Yes, I read this.

Q. So there is forensic evidence, some similar to the evidence that you have cited, about Mr. Miller having blood on his clothes, that there was blood on Mr. Goldblum's clothing?

A. Well, the difference is, first of all, there is no blood mentioned here. Mr. Miller says that Mr. Goldblum put on a second pair of pants and had a top coat. There is no reference to blood on the page I just read, No.1. No.2, that's Mr. Miller saying that about Mr. Goldblum. The earlier reference that I made, as I recall -- and you will correct me if I'm wrong -- was that Mr. Miller acknowledged himself that he had gotten rid of his own bloody clothing. This came from his mouth pertaining to his clothing. There is a big difference.

Q. Likewise, are you familiar with Mr. Miller's testimony that the gloves which were recovered at the scene had been worn by Goldblum?

A. Yes.

Q. Now, you're not telling me that any time I put on a glove I am necessarily going to leave a hand hair in there, are you?

A. Depends on how hairy your hands are and probably what the inside of the glove is. Probably in this case we are talking about knit gloves; am I right? Knit gloves?

Q. I think Mr. Goldblum had knit gloves, but these were different.

A. Different gloves. You know, I can't be sure with 100 percent certainty. I will 'say more often than not, if one were to then lay open, fillet gloves, and spend hours looking for them, more often than not, you would find a hair from a man's hand who had worn those gloves, more often than not.

Can I say always, no, because I'm just not sure, but I think that kind of transfer would occur more often than not, if one were to conduct that kind of examination.

Q. Is there a reason -- I guess this is somewhat flippant, but it is somewhat serious, too -- is there a reason by the end of the winter that my hands weren't bald?

A. Bald?

Q. That all the hair isn't inside the glove, if it always comes off?

A. Well, my hair doesn't come back in the summertime, I will tell you that. No. I am not aware -- I don't know. I don't think I become less hairy in the wintertime on my hands.

Q. You're familiar then with the different types of blood that are left as a result of -- blood can be left outside of the body, we will call it, in different ways. We have already talked about cast-offs. There are also impact spatters; correct?

A. Yes.

Q. And impact spatters tend to be smaller, little dots, that type of thing?'

A. Yes.

Q. And we also have transference.

A. Yes.

Q. Okay. Transference, would you agree with me, tends to be, assuming that there is more blood there and not just a dot, would tend to be more of what you have touched and a little bigger?

A. Yes. Generally they are going to be, yes, and the smudge category, depending upon how much blood, how much surface of the body and so on, came in contact with the object.

Q. Now, you remember that there was a little speck of 25 blood on Mr. Goldblum's cuff that was retrieved from the shirt, retrieved from his house?

A. Yes. As I recall they said an indistinguishable bit of blood on the left cuff is my recollection.

Q. Also as well there was a brownish speck on the tee-shirt, I think. I will show you 1652 and 1653, really beginning at the bottom of 1652. "One, I think, on a tee- shirt?

A. By one, I think he is referring back to the brownish speck or a tee-shirt. That was not as clear as the cuff.

Q. That's correct.

A. I'm just going to address the cuff, but thank you for reading that. In reviewing for this today, did you review Mr. Goldblum's testimony of how he believed that speck got on his cuff?

A. No, I did not.

Q. Okay. Call Counsel's attention to Pages 2688 and 2692 of the transcript.

MR. MARKOVITZ: What page was that, Mr. Broman?

THE WITNESS: 2688 and 2692 is what we will be referring to.

Q. All right. Mr. Goldblum states here that he went over to the railing where the body had been thrown over.

MR. MARKOVITZ: Objection to the characterization of thrown over, because there is no evidence presented at trial as to how the body got over the rail.

THE COURT: I will overrule.

A. He went over to the railing where the body made its way over the railing, and he then stated that that speck on his cuff may have come when he went over to the railing to look over. That is what I read.

Q. Well, that would be a transfer of a larger smudge, not a smaller impact splatter. Would that not be more consistent with that?

A. No. That would depend on just how you touch. It could have been a larger stain or smudge, but might also just be a speck. That would really depend on how much of a contact there was.

Q. If there is blood on the railing and he states he leans on the railing to look over, we are not talking about a quick bare, tiniest touch; we are talking about somebody leaning on something?

A. You're assuming then that the leaning is into the totality or significant portion of the smudge, but what if one just is at the very periphery, they touch one little contour of the stain, then you might just get a touch.

Q. So if you touched -- what you're saying, if I understand this, if you would lean against a speck, that could transfer a speck?

A. Well, if you lean against a speck, yes, or if you just almost totally miss in the contact of leaning on the rail, and just get the tiniest, tiniest transfer, which is possible. If you lean into a larger pool of blood, you will get a bigger stain.

Q. The likelihood of that, the likelihood is smaller that you would just get a speck as opposed to a smudge, would you agree with me on that, particularly given the amount of blood involved here?

A. No. I just couldn't give you any percentages on something like that. That is, you know, like when we are eating or holding a baby or cut a finger. There is so many variations, you almost miss this, whether it is blood or juice from a sandwich or something. I don't know what to tell you. That would just be pure chance.

Q. Assuming someone was wearing a coat over and -- a sports coat over top of this shirt, and they hit someone who was bleeding profusely, could that not cause an impact splatter?

A. Yes, it could.

Q. Can you rule out that this dot on the cuff was an impact spatter by Mr. Goldblum striking Mr. Wilhelm?

A. I can only go by the description that was given at the time of a brownish speck. It did not appear to have been described with the characteristics that would have even been suggestive of a spatter pattern. Inasmuch as the homicide detectives knew what they were looking for and described blood spatters on the dashboard, so on and so forth, I would think that they would have given more information if they thought -- more description if they thought that it was blood spatter.

I myself can only go from the description on paper today of a brown speck. It doesn't seem to fit *in* with a blood spatter pattern. Also I think they said one, so again, anything is possible. Can you just get one spatter, yes, at some physical point you might just get one spatter. Doesn't seem very likely, however.

Q. Finally, Dr. Wecht I appreciate your patience.

A. If I don't want to be held in contempt of Court, I darn well better be patient.

Q. It is difficult to be patient with thousands of cases. And you're aware that Mr. Miller, when we looked at Page 695, said that Mr. Goldblum took his pants off and put them in a plastic bag, the outer pants?

A. I have a vague recollection, yes, harkening back to what you said.

MR. BROMAN: That is all I have, Your Honor.

THE COURT: Mr. Markovitz, I don't want to limit redirect; however, if you can keep it brief, I would like to continue so that I could excuse Dr. Wecht rather than have him come back.

Judge.

REDIRECT EXAMINATION BY MR. MARKOVITZ:

Q. Let's go. I won't be very long,

THE WITNESS: Thank you, Your Honor.

Q. Let's go back to using Mr. Wilhelm, if I might, as the victim in this case, and I am Mr. Goldblum coming from the back seat as here raised by the prosecution in this case now, and stabbing him from behind. And the motion of my arm is what we would call in baseball a three-quarter's pitching motion, and the withdrawing being the same, it would not leave a blood spatter that was found which was essentially parallel to the ground; would you agree with that?

A. There would be a diagonal intention. I cannot rule out some left to right directionality, which I think is what I was asked before. I would agree that such a motion is indeed not horizontal; it would have a diagonal angularity to it.

Q. You're aware that no blood was found on the windshield of the vehicle?

A. Yes.

Q. And are you aware that no blood was found on the ceiling of the vehicle?

A. Yes.

Q. And other than the small spot which is not described on the inside of the rear door behind the driver, there was no blood found in the back seat of the vehicle?

A. Yes.

Q. And you consider that to be tending to be consistent or tending to be inconsistent with the idea that the person In the back seat committed the stabbing and then supposedly exited the vehicle and continued the stabbing outside the vehicle, meaning that he would have carried the knife in his hand to exit the back seat?

A. The absence of all blood from the ceiling and from the rear compartment except for that tiny bit on the inside of the left side back door, all of that would be very inconsistent with someone sitting or standing or crouching in the rear compartment of the car behind Mr. Wilhelm and stabbing him in the front of his chest.

Without going back through everything we have talked about, when you think about the arm and think about the cast-off as the weapon comes back, the absence of blood in the rear of the car and in the ceiling of the car and so on would be quite inexplicable. Then the getting out of the car and so on, with now a quite bloody weapon and blood from the victim and so on, the absence of blood in the handles and other parts of the left rear door, it would be very difficult to explain.

Q. Now, the prosecution during cross-examination here raised to you about the possibility that the blood spatter on the dashboard came from the nose of the victim. Would the nose -- would you expect a cast-off from a nose? I understand you have explained that you don't think this cast-off came from the nose, but in terms of the height of the blood spatter, could you expect – the nose is significantly higher than the dashboard of the car; would you agree with that? Somebody sitting in a normal position?

A. Yes. Of course, as you sit your head and certainly the nose's level is higher than the dashboard level. On a person of average height, it is a different level.

Q. If there was significant bleeding from the nose, would you not expect to find blood I suppose dropped blood or dripped blood or whatever on the seat the driver was sitting or on the floor where the driver, the front of the driver sitting position?

A. Yes. If one has a bloodied nose as from a blow, then I would expect there to be some evidence of a dripping. Gravity would see to it that the blood would come down, even from a nose that has been severed as severely as Mr. Wilhelm's was.

Q. You're aware that no blood was found in the locations I just described?

A. Yes.

Q. Mr. Miller testified at trial that there was no stabbing inside the vehicle. That testimony is belied by the blood spatter; is that your testimony?

A. Yes. In my opinion, that under any scenario or any variation on whichever theory has been discussed and presented here today is, I think physically impossible. No matter who did what and how, that there would have been no stabbing inside the car is forensically, in my opinion, unequivocally ruled out.

Q. Returning for a moment to this small, unidentified blood transfer of some type in the rear door, the door behind the driver, had that blood been photographed by the police, is it possible that some firmer conclusion could have been reached about the source of the blood?

A. Yes. Photographs, of course, capture and memorialize something, which is why we take so many of them at scenes and on bodies and so on.

Q. You're aware, are you not, from reviewing the materials in this case that the clothing seized from Mr. Goldblum's home the day after the murder were the clothes described to the police as being worn by Goldblum by Clarence Miller; are you aware of that?

A. It is a vague recollection. I take your word for it, if it is there in the record with regard to the -- to, Mr. Markovitz? 1653.

MR. BROMAN: What page are you referring to?

MR. MARKOVITZ: I'm now referring to 1653.

Q. With regard to 1652 , the bottom, going on to 1653, referring now to the spot on the cuff of Mr. Goldblum's shirt, that spot is not even identified as being blood is it?

A. No, not by the person testifying. His statement is that, quote, "I imagine it was checked at the lab." He giving the testimony -- who was he?

Q. Detective Herringer.

A. -- did not know and did not state that it was blood.

MR. MARKOVITZ : Nothing further, Your Honor.

MR. BROMAN: I have just a few more.

RECROSS-EXAMINATION BY MR. BROMAN:

Q. Let's start with Mr. Markovitz saying that there was no blood. I call your attention to, "This was not analyzed on the shirt," Page 1799, Dr. Marine's testimony down here at the bottom. It goes *over* into 1800.

A. Yes. By the way, they have their sides mixed up, too. Up *above* you will see it says on the right sleeve, and I think we have all been talking about the left. But I just wanted to point that out. It is not nothing that you or I haven't spoken of, but you're right. He did say, "I did determine that it was blood, but there was not enough of the sample for further analysis."

Q. Okay. And one final thing, Dr. Wecht, Mr. Markovitz stated that Mr. Miller said he did not see a stabbing inside the car. Are you aware that Mr. Goldblum himself said he did not see a stabbing inside the car? If you would like it is 2659, please.

MR. MARKOVITZ: Page number?

MR. BROMAN: 2659.

A. That's correct.

MR. BROMAN: I have nothing further.

THE COURT: Can we excuse Dr. Wecht?

MR. MARKOVITZ: Just one other question.

REDIRECT EXAMINATION BY MR. MARKOVITZ:

Q. That same page, Dr. Wecht, Mr. Goldblum did testify that he saw Mr. Miller who appeared to him to be striking Mr. Wilhelm inside the vehicle, isn't that right?

MR. BROMAN: What page are we on?

THE COURT: Same page. 2659, I believe.

A. No, that is not on that page. It is earlier, yes, when we talked about the fighting – yes. Let's see. 2658, now, Your Honor, yes. That is when they talked about the striking, yes. He did make that mention of the blows or striking, yes.

MR. MARKOVITZ: Nothing further.

RECROSS-EXAMINATION MR. BROMAN:

Q. But there is nothing in the striking that indicates it wasn't fist-a-cuffs.

A. He used the word strike or blow, that's right.

MR. BROMAN: Okay.

MR. MARKOVITZ: Nothing further.

THE COURT: Thank you, Dr. Wecht. You may be excused.

A. Thank you very much. And thank you, Your Honor, for permitting me to continue.

Transcript of Interview with Dr. Cyril H. Wecht
by James Villanova Esq. and James Ramsey
on November 22, 2012

JV: Dr. Wecht, my name is James Villanova. Seated to my right is James Ramsey. We would have a few questions to ask you. Mr. Ramsey, as the head investigator for Zeke Goldblum at this point, also some questions bearing on Zeke Goldblum's case. First of all, your credentials are pretty widely known, probably throughout the United States and throughout the world, but what, what are your qualifications? You don't have to give them all to us but...

CW: No, I understand. Relevant to this issue, I would point out that I am certified by the American Board of Pathology in Anatomic Clinical and Forensic Pathology. I have performed since I first started doing autopsies in 1957, my first year of residency to this time, approximately 18,000 autopsies myself. I have reviewed, signed off, or supervised approximately 38,000 other autopsies. I was an assistant district attorney and medical legal advisor to the District Attorney of Allegheny county 1964 to 1965, Forensic Pathologist in Allegheny County Coroner's Office 1966 to 1970. I was then Allegheny County Coroner 1970-1980 and I was Allegheny County Coroner for another ten year stint 1996 until 2006.

I have testified in, I'd say at least three dozen of the 67 counties in Pennsylvania, I would say, three dozen of the 50 states of America, and I have also testified in four, five, or six foreign countries, Canada, Israel, Australia, Taiwan, and the Philippines. So, I have been consulted in cases from various other foreign countries in addition to the ones I have mentioned.

I have published as author or co-author approximately 560 articles dealing with various aspects of forensic science, forensic pathology, legal medicine. I am the editor or co-editor, author, or co-author of approximately 45 books in the fields of forensic science and legal medicine. One of these is a five volume set at which I am the editor entitled "Forensic Sciences." These are the basic qualifications.

I am also certified by the American Board of Legal Medicine and I am certified by the American Board of Disaster Medicine. I have been a president of American Academy of Forensic Sciences and a president of the American College of Legal Medicine.

I am currently the chairman of the Executive board of the American College of Forensic Examiners International which is the largest forensic scientific organization in the United States in terms of total membership. I am an honorary life fellow of the International Medical Legal Society or the National Medical Legal Societies of France, Spain, Belgium, Brazil, and several other countries.

I've lectured throughout the United States before various professional organizations, and universities, including Yale University School of Medicine, Harvard University School of Law, the FBI, the medical division of the CIA. I've lectured at international societies over the world and pretty much all continents since 1965, and a variety of programs.

I've been consulted by families and news media and various kinds of cases and agencies, different kinds; John F. Kennedy assassination, Robert F. Kennedy assassination, Martin Luther King assassination, Mary Jo Kopechne and the case with Ted Kennedy, and then through the years Elvis Presley, Sunny Von Bulow, Waco Branch Davidian fire, Billie Jean Harris case, Ron Brown, Vincent Foster, Chandra Levy, Jonbennet Ramsey, O.J. Simpson, Phil Spector, Anna Nicole Smith, her son Daniel Smith, Whitney Houston, Sam Shepherd, and various other cases.

I also have various faculty positions. I am a clinical professor of pathology at the University of Pittsburgh School of Medicine and Department of Pathology. I am an adjunct professor in the Department of Epidemiology at the Graduate School of Public Health at Pitt. I am adjunct professor at three different schools at Duquesne University School of Law, Graduate School of Health Sciences, and School of Pharmacy. I am distinguished professor of pathology at Carlow University here in Pittsburgh. And I am an adjunct professor of a medical college in Georgia; and also at a medical college in Nigeria, Africa.

So, I think these are pretty much the highlights.

JV: Thank You. You are presently licensed to practice medicine in the Commonwealth of Pennsylvania?

CW: Yes, I have been, since my years of internship, 1956 to 1957, then took the state exam, it would have been in the Spring of 1957. I've been licensed in Pennsylvania since 1957.

JV: I'd like you to turn your attention to the case of Zeke Goldblum and ask do you recall when you first heard of the case in general?

CW: Well, the case occurred during the time I was coroner. The year was 1972. It was my first ten-year stint, so the autopsy was done there at the Allegheny County Coroner's office by one of my staff forensic pathologists, Dr. Joshua Perper. So that was the first time the case was handled, how shall I say, in a typical, routine fashion. I don't say that in a casual way, but I mean it was a case in which the autopsy was performed. Dr. Perper was called to testify. I was never contacted by anybody, from the district attorney's office, by defense attorney, by anybody else, and I was not involved.

The next involvement, as I recall, was not until 1995. I ran for coroner again, was elected in November 1995, was to take office January 1. Around that time, before I took office, I was contacted by the attorney who was representing Zeke Goldblum at that time, and was asked something about records, at the coroner's office pertaining to this case. I told them at that time that as far as I was concerned, what my policy had been when I was there from 1970 to 1980 and what it would continue to be, would be, that records there, other than anything of a confidential nature, and I didn't know what could be confidential in a case that had already been tried publicly, that the attorney would be welcome to come and look over those records, and I made that statement to them. And then when I became coroner, I was contacted by that attorney, as I recall, and they came over, and that was when it was discovered by me, brought to my attention and brought to their attention for the first time, that those records were no longer there, they had vanished.

JV: Is that something, that in your experience, is usual rare, very rare, or how rare?

CW: I would say very rare. And another thing of a highly suspicious nature that does not require someone to go off on a wild tangent of paranoia or conspiracy theory is that around that same time there was another very controversial case also involving a law enforcement officer and I subsequently became involved in that case too and I had been, I think before.

A police officer who was involved in the Johnny Gammage case, the very infamous case here where that African American gentleman, a cousin of Pittsburgh Steeler Ray Seals, was killed by policeman for no reason at all other than he was just driving a car while black, a fancy car that belonged to Ray Seals. In any event, that officer was involved in that case and he had also been involved in the very suspicious death of his, was it wife or girlfriend, I guess it was his girlfriend, and those records wound up missing too, around the same time.

For those two sets of records to wind up missing within that short period of time, both of which involved law enforcement, well the one case didn't involve the law enforcement officer and the Goldblum case involved them in a different way because of the activities of the police officers and the highly questionable tactics that they engaged in, for those two cases to wind up missing, I would say extremely rare.

JV: Ok, you know since this case is so old, sometimes these time-matters sort of become lost on us, but the Zeke Goldblum case occurred in the early seventies. The Johnny Gammage case occurred in the last several years, so I thought.

CW: Well, it wasn't the Gammage case files I was talking about missing, I just referred to the Gammage case ...

JV: Oh, I see.

CW: ....because that police officer is the one who was mostly responsible for Gammage's death.

JV: Ok.

CW: No, no, no, I'm sorry if I confused you, no, the case involved...

JV: I see.

CW: .... the highly suspicious shooting death of his girlfriend.

JV: Ok, so in the coroner's office, after a case is analyzed, are the files ordinarily kept within the office or are they sent to something, like, the federal government has a Rocky Mountain storage facility?

CW: The files were kept at the coroner's office.

JV: So, is there any explanation at all that you know of, other than your suspicions as to what happened to the file?

CW: No, there's no explanation at all. And I do not know, I do not know to what extent and with what degree of investigative passion and totality that people who were working in the office and who would have been in the position to do away with these records were questioned by other law enforcement agencies. I don't know that, but it's too late, of course, I guess, to do anything about it, I don't know if these people are still around, but in my opinion, if that had been pursued as one should have pursued something in such a serious nature, they would have been able to find out who was the most likely person responsible. And to my knowledge, while some questions were asked, that was never, never pursued with that kind of rigorous investigative intensity.

JV: You wrote a letter that covered that topic in November of 2004 which you have before you, right there.

CW: Yes.

JV: And I take it that letter summarizes your thoughts on the missing file mystery.

CW: It was written at that time and that is indeed the best documentation and representation of my thoughts and opinion which I have expressed here today, so, you see, I set them forth on paper, November 21, 2004.

JV: And those are your thoughts in general today?

CW: Absolutely.

JV: Ok. Now...

CW: If I were a betting man and there were a way of proving this, I would give 100 to one odds that these records didn't just simply get lost in some kind of fortuistic simplistic fashion. I'm not telling you that nothing was ever lost at the coroner's office, but off hand, I can't remember an entire file missing and I certainly don't remember any case of a controversial nature that was being pursued by attorneys and which required that kind of revisiting of files to wind up missing. I don't recall any such case.

JV: I don't know if you're aware, but that same file is also missing from other places, like the DA's files, gone.

CW: Yes, thank you, I do remember that and I recall that in going through that. What more do you need then that, that you've got the same file missing from three offices. Who, I mean what kind of person would have such a degree of naivety, what kind of person would dare to offer an opinion without being ridiculed and, and I don't know, by a judge or some other authority told to, you know, take that kind of malarkey and sell it somewhere else, that the same file in three different offices, the same case file is missing.

JV: Now what are the three? The DA's office, your office?

CW: And the third one was.......

JR: Pittsburgh Police.

CW: The Police, ah..the Police, the police.....ha, ha, ha.. (soft laughter).

JV: The Pittsburgh Police have their own separate problems...

CW: What, what more do you need?

JV: I don't know, I'm not in the file storage business but it seems unusual, at least.

CW: Well, unusual is really frankly a very benign characterization, really unusual.

JV: Have you ever heard of any other file being missing from three separate places like that?

CW: No, no, no, I haven't, no, I haven't.

JV: And, as you point out, you've been around for a while.

CW: Yes, look, look, even at the Federal level, with the games that were played, Nixon and Watergate, and the papers with Ellsberg, Daniel Ellsberg, I mean you could just go weary. I challenge anybody to find one instance like this, and the only way in which that could have been accomplished would have been that somebody in the police department, most probably, had seen to it, that the file was removed.
They had to have the opportunity, the desire, and the status by virtue of his position to see to it, that the files were also removed from the coroner's office and the DA's office and with the complicity of somebody then in the DA's office. You didn't just walk in surreptitiously in the middle of the night, you had to make contact with somebody who was employed at the coroner's office, make contact with somebody at the..

JV: Right....

CW: At the DA's office to have those files removed. I'm not saying that the same cat burglar..

JV: Right...

CW: Came in the middle of the night, into these three different locations and removed three files.

JV: Yeah, I was thinking about this, and of course to say something is missing is one thing, to say something is missing and if found would indicated someone another thing. But, what I was thinking was the only thing that I can think of is, it would sort of be like today with a NFL game you have a play, then all of a sudden you have a film that would disprove a call is missing so you have to rely on the call on the field and in this case that's the only thing I can think of because I can't think of anything in those files which would have necessarily disproven the prosecution's case except for maybe the photographs of the blood spatter.

CW: Well, I would agree with you for the most part, but I think I would add to that, in addition to photographs to the blood spatter, I think that what was perhaps more of a vexatious nature for whoever it was that was concerned, would have been some statements, maybe, that were made, some things that were obtained by way of original investigative inquiry, some comments, some contacts, and so on. I think that, that might have been even more important than the photographs of the blood spattering and the front part of the car.

Think about that, things like that, which came to be issues subsequently, who said what to whom, what was done with regard to Miller, in terms of how things were worked out with him, that he not totally walked away but to a very great extent dumped everything on Goldblum. The whole business of Miller and being held in prison, and the deal, money being raised for him and so on and so forth. I think that area of investigation conducted initially and originally was of greater concern to them than just some photographs.

In fact, this is just conjecture on my part, but you gotta think, as you have pointed out, what would have been the purpose of removing the files?

Not the autopsy report, not the photographs of the body, not anybody's sworn testimony, what would be the purpose? What do you care? A lot of those things were not of great moment, I mean, you can't undo them that which have been set forth and so on. And that which could be in a way reproduced by way of testimony, whether it was by the pathologist who did the autopsy or somebody else involved in the investigation, but those things which got to beat that time probative and highly relevant to what transpired on that fateful day when Wilhelm was killed and to what happened thereafter, especially (inaudible) Miller, I think that's concerned them.

JV: I mean that makes sense. Ok. But all those things that would have been there would have been known to some law enforcement officer either in the police department or district attorney's office, in other words, the, whoever set this in motion to get rid of the files, wasn't doing it to prevent law enforcement officers from learning the truth, who would have already reviewed the files, it was to prevent somebody from looking at the files in the future.

CW: Well......

JV: So, it seems like somebody in law enforcement, someone along the line knew what was in the files and chose to ignore it.

CW: I agree with you. But, I would just point out one small additional fact. You said that law enforcement officers would have known. Not necessarily, so that law enforcement officers A, B, and C, would have known everything that D, another law enforcement, investigative officer in the case, would have written down would have commented upon. Eventually, yes, but, and maybe they did know, it requires number one, you to accept the fact that they were all cognizant of everything that had been set forth on paper back then, number one, and number two, that many years later, and remember, we're talking many years later, aren't we that they would of remembered what was there, and most importantly number three, there would have been documentation thereof.

So not only a matter of what somebody knew and what someone might have remembered, but where's your proof? You know, I've got a saying that I always tell my wife and my kids, we talk about the different things and so on, and my staff, and talking with other people. It's maybe a bit exaggerated, but it makes a point, it's a Wecht comment. "That which is not in writing does not exist." What I mean to say is not that I don't believe it doesn't exist, but it is highly arguable and always susceptible to total renunciation, rejection, and certainly obfuscation if it's not in writing. The fact that somebody might have known, what does that have to do with it, that 24 years later, most of these people are dead, they're dead, they're resigned, they're gone, they're retired to Florida, and what are they now. Ah.. so if you take it out of there, it's as if it does not exist; it's as if it never existed.

JV: Yep. So, now you mention, maybe I brought it up, another point, the blood spatters, and the blood in general. And to me as a lay person, it seems almost inconceivable that somebody could kill someone with a sort of a half of a garden shear and have not blood on them. Could you comment on that, is that a lay person talking, or do you agree with that sentiment?

CW: I definitely agree with the statement you have made, and I have set this with regard to the blood spatters and that forensic scientific issue in this case. Let me point out a couple of things. First we'll address them, then what you have said.

Number one, that if you have, let's reduce it to the prosecution's theory at that time, that Zeke Goldblum sitting in the back of the car was the one who stabbed Wilhelm repeatedly. So picture that Zeke Goldblum is in the back and he's got garden shearers and he's thrusting forward, thrusting forward, well you go in, and you come out, you go in and you come out. There's no way in the world that some blood does not come back upon you. It's just impossible with repeated stab wounds, especially instrumentality of that size producing very substantial wounds, it's just not possible.

Number two, correlating with that or the corollary to that point is, it is my understanding there was no blood on Goldblum's clothes. Now talking about blood on clothing, it also is my understanding that there was blood on Miller's clothing, and that he changed his clothing, and nothing ever was done to pursue that point and emphasize it and make it clear that there was blood on him.

And that ties in with the next point that the blood spatters definitely move from left to right. So Wilhelm's the driver, he's seated in the front seat then, behind the steering wheel, and then Miller to his right. The blood spatters come left to right, so here's Miller and he's stabbing, and out comes the knife, the shearer, in goes the shearer, out comes the shearer, in goes the shearer, out comes the shearer, left to right, left to right, it all fits, it all fits.

JV: I don't know if you can speculate on this or you actually know this but, the blood that comes out of a body while being murdered in this manner, would it be mostly from an aorta, like a geyser or ....

CW: Well, it could be from, the, no, well, the, the, aorta would be, is the major artery, and the hemorrhage of course, is greatest from a laceration of the aorta, but the aorta is back a little bit. You do have blood as the aorta is pierced on the shearer, but remember, there's a lot of blood vessels between the epidermis, the skin, and the aorta, back in the chest wall.

So, the answer to that is, it would of been various blood vessels, there would been a tremendous amount of bleeding. We're not talking about just a little bit of hemorrhage, there was a lot of blood, and you've got multiple wounds, and you've got a large instrument producing large irregularly shaped wounds from which blood can easily emanate.

So with repeated blows inflicted by the assailant utilizing this particular instrument, you are definitely going to have the pattern of blood coming back with the instrument as it is removed from the victim and then plunged back into the victim.

JV: Ok, would the blood mostly be from the action of taking the shearers out and the blood that comes with that, or would it be a situation where it could be, you know, literally squirting out like a geyser?

CW: Ah.. in this case, I would say, it would of been more from the instrument going in and out um.. because the spurting would have been more in a forward projectile fashion once the opening was there if the individual would had remained in that position. Blood spatters, as we have talked and described, moving from left to right, would have been more consistent with the movement of the shearers in and out of Wilhelm's body then in an aortic spurting from the wound itself.

JV: And you use the word in which people rarely use in any kind of a statement, impossible, you said it was impossible, and usually people ah....

CW: Well, I don't like to. You mean when I talked about all...

JV: You usually say within a reasonable degree of medical certainty or whatever but...(inaudible).

CW: Well, I always give my medical testimony in a court of law with a reasonable medical certainty. But I understand that and I believe that but we're having a discussion here....

JV: Right.

CW: And, I want to make it clear, not to be a wild-eyed partisan-type advocate and go beyond the realm of a forensic scientists, but I want to make the point that, you know, look, impossible, we can always talk about something at the end of the bell-shaped curve, etc. What I'm saying and will repeat is that somebody who is sitting in proximity to the victim, who repeatedly plunges an instrument like the garden shear into that individual and then brings it back out by definition, obviously the arm is flexed, and then the arm is extended, that blood has to come back with it. And then I find that it is impossible to understand how some drops of blood and really I would say with reasonable medical certainty, a very substantial amount, I would say in terms of whether some blood would be there, I would say that it is impossible for me to conceive how it could happen that no blood would come back on the assailant.

JV: Interesting. At the time that this trial went on, did it strike you as unusual at the time of the trial or does it become even more unusual later?

CW: To my recollection, I was not made aware of anything of a controversial nature at the time I was there as coroner. I want to say, and this is a matter of record, my worst enemy couldn't refute this, it is well known, that my office was always open for a defense attorney to come and talk and look. And all the records, other than those which have been prepared by other agencies, those he would have obtained pre-trial, from those other agencies, those I could share with him. As far as what we generated are finding, and in terms of our opinions and so on, and I was always available.

I did not at that time think of it. Yes it was not until later I came to know and questions had been posed. It's not a matter of too little too late or that I was indifferent or insensitive, or that I changed my mind, not at all. Nobody ever came to me, not at all.

Matter of fact, the lawyer who represented Zeke Goldblum at that time was somebody that I knew personally, then going back to graduate days at the University of Pittsburgh as I recall.

JV: You're talking about David Rothman?

CW: Yes. We knew each other well. He knew, he knew that he could talk to me. Not to have contacted me at all to have asked about this case or to have posed questions to Dr. Perper which would have then shared with, if not directly with me then through Perper, he should have known that.

And what then what needs to be said further, and again it's not just sitting here and being critical with hindsight, it's a matter of clear understanding that a freshman in law school would appreciate, if he wasn't going to contact us for whatever reason and so on, where, where was he, in terms of reaching out for appropriate experts of an independent nature then? Criminalists, blood spatter experts?

I certainly had no problem, later on when I was asked to review this case, I contacted my colleagues, Dr. Henry Lee, the international renown criminalist, who agreed with me completely, Herb McDonald, who is one of the original people to do blood spatter evidence and the whole patterns that one gets under different scenarios and so on. So these people and many others were available to them and other forensic pathologists were available, including even in this community and certainly anywhere else in America.

For David Rothman not to have reached out to other experts and not to have pursued this further with Dr. Perper on the witness stand before the trial began, and then in the trial, or to have come to see me is, is inexplicable, it truly is.

JV: Cause, this, this case is at the time, it's hard to, you know, recollect how, because so many things have happened since then. This a real cause celeb, it was sort of like a Pittsburgh version of the O.J. Case.

CW: Yes, yes...I...

JV: This was, this was a big, big news item....

CW: I would agree, I would agree....

JV: ...In Pittsburgh.

CW: And, and keep in mind, and I might as well make this statement, this is a good point to make, it became an even bigger cost of labor, much bigger than it would have been if a somebody who was a loser, what better single word to use to characterize Clarence Miller? If Clarence Miller had been the only person on trial, it would not have been anywhere near as big a case as it was with the son of a rabbi and an attorney on trial, that made it a much bigger case.

JV: He was, it was not just a rabbi, he was a pretty well-known rabbi ....

CW: Very distinguished. I knew Rabbi Goldblum, a very, very fine gentleman, and so, you know, this needs to be said, there's no question, anybody, that if you don't recognize, and accept that, then you are being deliberately, deliberately obtuse, then you are deliberately choosing to ignore the realities of this case. This is what it all comes back to. You could have Clarence Miller to dine upon any day of the week as a District Attorney, so who cares? But give me an attorney, a rabbi's son, and his restaurant has been torched, and so on and so forth, now I've got myself a big case. This is something special.

JV: Now, seated to my right here is a James Ramsey who I would say at this stage knows more about this case than any living person.

CW: Yes, I know, I've talked to Jim before. Yes.

JV: He has a couple questions.

JR: I have a couple questions, I wanna try and keep it right in the same vein.

CW: Yeah. Go ahead. Anything, Jim.

JR: I understand you also have a legal degree, also?

CW: Yes, I have a law degree, and as I said, I am an adjunct professor at Duquesne University School of Law and have been since 1962 and continue to teach a course in forensic science and legal medicine there.

JR: Ok, now the inside the automobile where this incident began, there's some evidence and testimony from Detective Ron Freeman that there was blood spatter on the dashboard. He describes the blood spatter in such a fashion, that in his description alone, shows that there was the blood, you said, moving from left to right?

CW: Yes.

JR: Yes, his description of the tails of the blood are pretty important ...

CW: Yes.

JR:...and they show that, that's the direction the blood was going. Now, there was some controversy about some photographs of the interior of the vehicle. I personally spoke with one of the two people who saw the photographs just days before the trial began, and these photographs never showed up at trial. The initial detective who took the photographs would of been a detective by the last name Hill, Edward Hill and his partner, Sal Crisanti. Now Sal gave us a deposition, or at least gave us a...

JV: Statement?

JR: Statement. And say that his partner, Ed Hill, would definitely with all the experience that he had, would of taken photos of the interior of the vehicle. Ron Freeman claims in a couple of different statements that he made that he believes that he saw photographs of the blood spatter on the dashboard. Joe Modispatcher, who was the sergeant in charge of the crime unit, claims that he had gone through the file days before the trial and he noticed that he'd seen the photos there before and then he noticed that the photos were missing.

So I guess my question is, do you feel that there is any significance or importance to, if there were photographs there and they were suddenly missing at time of trial, would that have aided or assisted anybody, a pathologist, or yourself, as the coroner, would that have aided you in being able to show that it was, it could not of, those blood spatters could not have occurred from a person in the back seat who also, by the way, a lot of people have missed this, but Miller claims that Goldblum struck Wilhelm on the back of the head with a wrench. Now, how does he got a wrench in one hand and a shear in the other hand? It just seems to me pretty improbable that something like that could happen, but primarily, what I guest I'm getting at is the photographs that they would be important.

CW: Well, your question contains the answer. Obviously, they were removed deliberately by somebody. Why would these several officers all state that these photos had been there a few days before trial, and then they're no longer there? How is that possible? In what way, physically even, how does that happen?

And the second part of your question is, would it have helped would it have been of assistance? Absolutely, and let me add to that, should it have been utilized by attorney David Rothman? Did he do any work? Did he do any study and preparation for this case at all? Did he ever come to me and talk about it? He should have seen those photos too. Number one, did he raise a question about their being missing? I don't know.

Let me ask that question back to you guys, if you know, did he raise a question at trial then, "Hey, where are these photos?"

JR: He didn't.

CW: Well, that's again, totally, totally, totally incomprehensible and unacceptable, and from the standpoint of a criminal defense attorney, unforgivable. It is gross, gross malpractice, there is no other way to say it, there is no other way to say it, gross incompetence. But this was from a veteran attorney, I don't know where he was, I don't know what happened, asleep at the switch. I don't understand, I really don't. He was no dummy. He'd been around a long time, and David was not a shrinking violet, he could, he could speak up. I remember I had a confrontation or two with him on other matters unrelated to this case, so he wasn't somebody to just, you know, sit back and, accept something, I, I, I don't know, I don't know the answer to that.

But getting back to your question, yes, it was something that we call demonstrative evidence. It's the old way of saying a picture is worth a thousand words. You take that picture, and you demonstrate it, and you blow it up, and you even bring, what I would have done, I would of even brought in, I would have gone to a junkyard and I would of gotten the paneling, of the whole front section of a car, I would of brought it into the courtroom, and I would of shown, in fact, it was something that could have been demonstrated. Using a mannequin with some red paint.

JV: Melvin Belli-style?

CW: I've done this in courtrooms. I did it in a stabbing case just a year or so ago in New York City, a very fascinating case that's been on television about someone charged with stabbing an individual, and I demonstrated it. They came here, and they had a car right across the street in a parking lot, and we had a collapsible rubber knife, and I was demonstrating something. What I'm telling you, you know, is not something that is wild, or so on, or that only I have thought of, it's something, you know, that people have utilized, have incorporated into their workup of a case countless times.

JV: Dr. Wecht do you have any other thoughts on this whole.......

CW: I think, I've pretty well, said, I don't recall if I said this before we started to put this on the record, that this case is truly, I use the word unique, in the literal Webster dictionary definition of the word, you have a case in which the trial judge, a very distinguished judge, who went on to become the Chief Judge of our local federal court, writing a letter saying that he doesn't believe that Goldblum was the murderer, and this is the judge who presided over the trial. Who, you know, he only had to deal with what he knew at the time, he didn't know all the things we've been talking about. Don Ziegler was a very experienced trial attorney, a very bright guy, a very decent ethical person, none of these things were brought to his attention at that time, and when they were in later years, he wrote a letter.

You got Pete Dixon, who was a veteran trial attorney, assistant DA who tried the case, and he has written a letter, and pointed out these things, and acknowledged them, they've been brought to his attention by you and other attorneys who have preceded you, representing Zeke Goldblum. And then you have everything we've been talking about, the whole business involving Clarence Miller and all these other things which get off into other areas for other people to deal with and so on.

I mean this, I truly must say, that this is the greatest travesty of justice that I have ever, ever experienced in 50 years, not only in cases in which I have been involved, but cases that I have followed, cases I am aware of, and I follow these, and I hear the discussions at our national conventions, and I talk with my colleagues and so on, I've heard of cases where lots of shenanigans have gone on, or a lot of things surreptitious or rotten nature have taken place.

I can't think of one case in fact. I would challenge anybody to come up with one case in which the trial judge and the DA who handled the case, both subsequently write letters saying they don't believe that the person who was found guilty at that time, was indeed guilty of the murder and where you have all this other stuff with missing files, missing evidence.

How this case has not reached the level of the Pennsylvania Supreme Court and one justice, one justice just spending a couple of hours, his/her clerks reading this stuff and then presenting the distillates, the crystallization of the facts, that we've been talking about here, has failed to address this, has not been intellectually insulted as a judicial person is astounding to me.

I do not understand it, and I do not understand whatever happened at the Superior Court back in 1997, the panel, the tribunal unanimously found that there should be a post conviction hearing that the decision made by the lower court was wrong, and so on.

I don't know; I just do not understand it. If someone came today and put a gun to my head and asked me to explain how this horrible injustice has continued for all of these years, I can't answer them, I'm a dead man. I mean, for somebody not to grab hold of this, for the state Supreme Court not to look at this case and say, hey enough is enough, and then to have this man sentenced to life without parole. Even that, get into that, people are committing murder all the time, and so on, and we're all opposed to murder, and one can argue capital punishment, one can argue this sentence, or that sentence, but it's not the great percentage that are sentenced to life without parole, without ever having the opportunity to have a parole down the road, whether it's 30, 40, or 50 years, and not to have a post-conviction hearing.

Let me say I have reviewed a couple dozen cases regarding post-conviction hearings, and I've testified at maybe half a dozen over the years. For this case not to have become the subject of a post-conviction hearing, again absolutely, I continue to use the word, inexplicable.

I don't consider myself a great legal scholar. I am a lawyer, and I know a little bit about these matters as they relate to my field and because of my experience over the years as a consultant in forensic pathology, and I do not understand. And I would love somebody to explain to me, how this case, given the gross incompetence of the trial attorney, David Rothman, and that is really what those post-conviction hearings are based upon, the incompetence of trial counsel, that is clear, it is obvious.

And then you throw in everything else. That's just bringing in some condiments, some salt and pepper, and gravy and flavor, to make that dish absolutely more appetizing, and absolutely impossible to set aside, that is unbelievable.

I hope that yet in our life times, thus more importantly, the life time of Zeke Goldblum, that, that opening of the door will be permitted. Let new judges look at this and come up with their answer as to what was done, what was not done, why it was done, what is most likely and whether justice was served. That is the minimum.

New judges review this in full, examine the record and say, well sorry, nothing to be done, all of this doesn't rise to the level of having a new trial or having him at least be considered for parole, then fine, let that happen.

But until or unless that happens, new judges at the appellate court level looking this case over and all the details that we have talked about, then as far as I'm concerned justice is not being served in the Zeke Goldblum case.

JR: Dr. Wecht, your affidavits, do you still stand behind the affidavits?

CW: I stand by every one of those affidavits and if necessary for me to attest to that, under oath or in writing, do I stand by that and so, absolutely, yes.

JV: Ok, at some point in the future I'm going to present you with the transcript of this and the affidavits and then you can sign.

CW: Absolutely.

JV: Ok.

JR: I did need to ask you one more question. There was a diagnosis of confabulation. I never heard that term before until I got involved....

CW: Well, it just means lying, confabulation, it's a fancy word for lying, and Miller was said to be a confabulator, pathological confabulator related to a brain injury he'd sustained before, so what? What does that got to do with anything? That doesn't change, that doesn't explain missing records (soft laughter)......

JR: No, it doesn't.

CW: That doesn't have anything to do with blood spatters, what does that got to do with anything?

JR: Do you think this was a dishonest prosecution on the part of perhaps the Police Department?

CW: Oh, yes, absolutely, absolutely, I think it was dishonest, because I think they came to know these things. They should have raised questions. Absolutely. Go and look at the code of ethics of the National District Attorneys Association. Go look at those. I just had an occasion to review them. I was consulted on a case in Ohio in which a woman was charged with the murder of a child. And I pointed out some things, and indeed they went back to the original pathologist, and she even reached out for a colleague of hers, another board-certified, forensic pathologist, and the DA reached out yet for another expert and so on. And the three of them then agreed with the point that I had made and so on, that District Attorney just last week withdrew the charges and dismissed the case.

Ok, that is ethics. Of, course, all DAs they'll pound their chest, we're interested only in justice and so on. OK, this is an injustice, justice cries out for somebody. And of course, we've got new DAs here and so on, and it's not for the District Attorney at this time. Not that I'm an admirer or a defender of the District Attorney, but I think, and you know better than I, from a procedural standpoint this doesn't commence in his office, it begins with whatever needs to be done procedurally in a court of law to try to achieve a post conviction hearing. Am I right? I think that's what's necessary here. Nobody is going to walk in and say he is innocent, goodbye, pack up your belongings, you're heading outta prison tomorrow. I understand, but let's have that post-conviction hearing, let's have these facts presented, and let's see what the court has to say.

JV: Thank you, Dr. Wecht.

Regarding the Homicidal Death of George Wilhelm

by Dr.Joshua A. Perper, M.D., LL.B., M.Sc. Forensic and Medical Legal Consultant - Submitted May 22, 2013

I have reviewed and evaluated the voluminous documentation regarding the homicide case in which two men, Charles Goldblum and Clarence Miller were tried and ultimately convicted of first-degree murder, Goldblum as being the assaulter stabber and Miller as a passive conspirator. The following documentary evidence was submitted for review:

1. Feb. 9, 1976 - Initial Police report
2. Feb. 9, 1976 - Mobile Crime Unit report
3. Feb. 10, 1976 - Wilhelm Autopsy report
4. Feb. 10, 1976 - Wilhelm Autopsy photos
5. Feb. 10, 1976 - Police report on witness, Richard Kurutz
6. Feb. 10, 1976 - Police report of Clarence Miller's arrest by Detectives Condemi and Amity
7. Feb. 10, 1976 - Supplemental Police Report by Detectives Condemi and Amity
8. Feb. 10, 1976 - Crime scene photos
9. Feb. 10, 1976 - Murder weapon photo
10. Feb. 11, 1976 - Mobile Crime Unit report
11. Feb. 11, 1976 - Goldblum clothing photos
12. Feb. 13, 1976 - Police report on Goldblum's clothes
13. Feb. 14, 1976 - Police homicide summary
14. Feb. 17, 1976 - Report on psychiatric examination of Clarence Miller by Dr. E.H. Davis
15. Feb. 18, 1976 - Testimony of Clarence Miller at Coroner's Inquest
16. Feb. 26, 1976 - Dr. Peter Marrone report of lab findings
17. March 2, 1976 - Report on Clarence Miller's interview report by detective Ronald Freeman (excerpt re: murder's commission and clothing worn during the same)
18. April 2, 1976 - Report of Clarence Miller's interview by detective Ronald Freeman

19. April 2, 1976 - Interview of Clarence Miller by detectives Gorny and Freeman
20. April 2, 1976 - Testimony of Clarence Miller at preliminary inquest, regarding fraudulent land deal
21. April 26, 1976 - Testimony of Clarence Miller's at inquest re fraudulent land deal
22. May 25, 1976 - Interview of Clarence Miller by detectives Gorny and Freeman regarding Goldblum's restaurant's fire.
23. Aug. 20, 1977 - Clarence Miller's trial testimony re: commission of the murder of George Wilhelm
24. Aug. 23, 1977 - Dr. Joshua Perper trial testimony
25. Aug. 25, 1977 - Det. Edward Hill (Mobile Crime Unit) - trial testimony re: crime scene
26. Aug. 23, 1977 - Det. Ronald Freeman- trial testimony Re: crime scene, evidence, blood spatter
27. Aug. 24, 1977 - Dr. Marrone (Chief Criminologist) - trial testimony Re: evidence
28. June 1988 - Affidavit of ADA F. Peter Dixon
29. Feb. 1994 - Commutation support letter of Dr. Cyril Wecht
30. Feb. 1996 - Affidavit of Dr. Cyril Wecht
31. Feb. 25, 1997 - Report of Forensic Laboratory
32. Three (3) consecutive letters by Judge Donald Ziegler, the sitting judge in Goldblum's trial, to Pennsylvania Board of Pardons
33. June 14, 2011 - Forensic report of Herbert L. McDonnell
34. Nov. 2012 - interview with Dr. Cyril Wecht
35. Affidavit of Dr. M. Baden and Dr. B.C. Wolfe
36. Affidavit of John Balshy, Investigator
37. Testimony of witness Cornelius Kelly
38. John Regan's statement to the police that he heard the victim's (Wilhelm) cries for help and approached him.
39. Statement of Richard Kurutz who observed Miller and Goldblum at the homicide scene.
40. Continuation Letter of Commutation Application by Charles Goldblum

The responsibilities of forensic pathologists and a short description of my forensic practice and experience in general and as applicable in this case.

The major function of forensic pathologists is the determination of the cause and manner of death of individuals dying as a result of violent physical or chemical trauma and environmental or industrial agents, and determining culpable or criminal actions by a person or legal entity under unclear or suspicious circumstance.

However, within the above universe of cases, forensic pathologists are required to evaluate and determine a complex array of findings including: the identification of whole or parts of human remains - relatively intact or decomposed, time of injury or death, post injury survival, the nature, severity and patterns of injuries, the significance of patterns of blood spots, whether a victim was conscious and for how long, whether there is evidence that a victim had the capability to protect themselves effectively during an attack, age of injuries, the time of death, how the clothing of the victim or assailant are congruent with the nature of the assault, their pattern as such and the evidence at the scene, whether the phenotype of the victim or the assailant may be pertinent in the case, determination of defense wounds on the victim and wounds of the assailant sustained during the attack, and whether statements of the victim, the assailant or neutral witnesses are congruent with the physical injuries.

For more than 40 years I was continuously engaged in the practice of forensic pathology and pathology, and performed thousands of autopsies. In the past I served as a Chief Forensic Pathologist and Coroner in Allegheny County for 22 years and for the next 16 years as Chief Medical Examiner of Broward County, Florida. During this period I was also active as a forensic and medico-legal consultant in civil and criminal cases.

During those periods, I also served as a Clinical Professor in Pathology, Forensic Pathology and Epidemiology Public Health at the University of Pittsburgh, University of Miami, and SE Nova University. For a number of years I was an adjunct professor of law at Duquesne University and an adjunct professor of psychiatry at the University of Pittsburgh.

I published 10 book chapters or books in the field of forensic pathology and more than 120 forensic publications, the vast majority in peer review journals. I also received the Milton Helpern Award of the American Academy of Forensic Sciences "*In recognition of outstanding contributions to Forensic Pathology,*" as well as other recognition awards.

During my years of forensic practice, I determined and continue to determine on the basis of objective forensic evidence not only the cause and manner of death, but all the related issues enumerated above, including whether criminal or civil charges are congruent with forensic evidence, or whether alleged statements of the defendant or accuser are congruent with evidence.

Initial investigation on February 9, 1976

On February 9, 1976, the initial report by Detectives Diggs and Carter indicated that they had been notified at 9:35 p.m. that a man had been stabbed at the Smithfield and Liberty Stanwix Parking Garage. Detectives Gorny and Freeman also covered the scene. At the scene, Detectives Diggs and Carter were met by Medic 4 who was putting the victim in the ambulance.

Also at the scene they met Officer Thomas Pobicki who told them that the victim had told him: "Clarence. Clarence Miller did this to me." The detectives were notified that the victim had been tossed over a wall from the 8th floor onto the 7th floor landing on the roof of a bridge that led into the adjacent building. The victim had been transported from that roof to the street level, and transferred to the Medics.

The detectives proceeded to the 8th floor, where they identified a blue Plymouth Fury belonging to the victim. There was a brown corduroy waist length jacket rolled up laying in the left corner of the back seat, a wrench with no handle on the driver's front seat, and a brown fur hat on the middle front seat with a set of keys to the right. There were drops of blood on the dashboard on the passenger side, as well as on the inside of the front window on the driver's side, and on the rear on the left side and left side rear window. The report noted: "*There was nothing else remarkable in the interior of the car.*"

There were more drops of blood 3½ feet in the rear of the car on the ground, 6½ feet to the right of the car, and 29 feet away toward the west wall. The car was parked facing the east wall with the front just about touching the wall. There was blood on the ground by the east wall about 8½ feet from the right side of the car. The railing was measured at 3 feet 8 inches high. A black men's shoe was found 2 feet from the left rear tire. The handle of the wrench was wrapped with grey plastic tape and was found 1 foot in front of the east wall. There was blood at the level where the victim was found that covered 22 feet from north to south. There was a half of a pair of garden shears recovered at the 7th level at the rear of the car which was on the 8th level. There was grey plastic tape around the handle (of the same type as the tape on the wrench handle) with blood on it. About 8 feet from the shears was partial piece of a lower denture plate containing 4 teeth, located on the 7th level. The height to the 8th level was not measured at that time.

The detectives then interviewed John Regan, who was working at the garage. He stated that he was on the 6th level when he heard someone yelling *"Help me, help me."* He stated he then ran to the 7th level and saw the victim lying on the concrete beyond the wall and the railing, and that the victim was almost going over the ledge. He instructed the victim not to move, and then went down to the lobby level to call the police. He then went back to the 7th level, removed the victim from the ledge, and where he was conveyed down to the ambulance on the street below. He stated he did not see anyone near the victim, and did not see any cars leaving the garage in a hurry.

Officers Crisanti and Hill from the Mobile Crime Unit had arrived by then, and photographed the scene. Evidence was also collected by them and transferred to their office. The victim's car was removed to the Public Safety building for processing by the Crime Unit. The victim was seen in the hospital by Dr. Kapnakas and listed as critical.

Follow-up investigation by Detectives Freeman and Lenz on February 10, 1976

On the morning of February 10, 1976, Homicide Detective Freeman came to the Crime Unit Office and at 8:45 requested that photographs be taken of the scene and to further the process now that it was daylight. At about 9:10 a.m., photographs were taken from the 8th level looking down to the 7th level, and the ledge where the victim was found. They were also given a pair of men's leather gloves turned in by employee Milton Loeher. The gloves were removed from a brown paper bag and were noted to have a large amount of blood on the outside and a small amount on the inside. Mr. Loeher claimed that they had been turned in by an unknown white male who claimed he found them in an alcove outside the garage. No description of the man was available.

An examination of the stairwells showed that the fire door from the 8th level was the escape route used, and a small amount of blood was found on the door and knob and photographed. A small amount of blood was noted on the handrail on the 8th floor stairwell, and a sample was collected. At the street exit level, there was blood on the door frame, which was sampled and photographed. The detectives then returned to the Crime Unit office, where they also received the larger portion of the denture transferred by Detective Lenz. This was submitted for testing.

The samples obtained in the search included the lower denture plate, several paper matches, a small white box containing suspected tobacco, a small white box containing suspected blood and paint scrapings and scrapings from the inside door frame, a round box containing suspected tobacco found at the front deck passenger side of the car, and black vinyl gloves containing suspected blood and hair fibers. Also obtained were a man's black shoe, grass shear, black tape wooden handle, blood scrapings and hair from the blue Plymouth, a brown man's fur cap, and sweepings from the backseat of the victim's car.

On February 10, 1976, Officers Condemi and Amity were advised that the victim had been fatally stabbed, and conveyed to the Coroner's Office along with the suspected weapon (½ a pair of grass shears) at 10:00 am. They then obtained a search warrant for the home of Clarence Miller, who had been identified by the victim in his dying declaration.

Mr. Miller was noted to be co-operative. There was a recently washed beige shirt in the washer with no stains noted, and no other items found in the remainder of the search.

In an interview, Mr. Miller stated he had known the victim since 1968. He stated that he had been home until about 7:15 p.m., and then taken a bus downtown to meet Charles "Zeke" Goldblum. They had then walked to Wood Street to meet George "Dodo" Wilhelm for coffee. Wilhelm left alone at about 9:10 p.m. to meet someone. Miller claimed that he went into Wilhelm's car before he left to get some matches. He claimed that he and Goldblum then left together in Goldblum's car, and that Goldblum drove him home and dropped him off. He stated that his wife and daughter met him at the door. He claimed that Wilhelm was a homosexual but that he "never tried anything with me."

The detectives noted that Mr. Miller had some scratches on the inside of both wrists and on the forearm of the right arm, which he claimed he had gotten playing with his cat, in addition to a finger laceration. They then called Detectives Cooper and Longacre who were interviewing Mr. Goldblum, and learned that Miller's and Goldblum's stories were not consistent.

The detectives then confronted Mr. Miller, and he stated that he did not stab the victim. He claimed that the victim was going to cause trouble for him and Mr. Goldblum, who hoped to get an appointment to become an Assistant DA. He stated that the he and Mr. Goldblum decided the victim would have to be silenced, and met on February 8, 1976, and discussed that they would stab him at the parking garage.

Mr. Miller called Wilhelm and they met him at 9:00 p.m. They then drove together in the victim's car with Mr. Miller in the passenger seat, and Goldblum in the rear. As soon as they parked, he claims that Mr. Goldblum struck the victim on the head with a wrench. The victim got out, and Mr. Goldblum began stabbing him with a shear type instrument. He claimed that he did not know that Mr. Goldblum was going to kill Wilhelm, and that had he known he would not have gone along. He stated that he knew the victim kept the wrench and shear in his car under the front seat, and that he saw Mr. Goldblum take these instruments from under the seat. He stated that he had gotten some blood on the cuff of his pants "from trying to help the victim," but that there was nothing he could do for him. He claimed that the black hat and black gloves belonged to him, but that Mr. Goldblum was wearing them at the time of the stabbing.

Mr. Miller was noted to have a scratch on his nose, a small laceration on his 2nd finger of the left hand, and several scratches on the arms and wrist. He claimed the scratches on his nose were due to psoriasis, and the other scratches were from his cat. He appeared to be very nervous during this second interview, and complained of a pain in his chest. While setting up to tape the interview, Mr. Miller was noted to pass out. He declined an ambulance, and was about to be interviewed when he passed out again. At that time, the ambulance arrived, and he was treated and transported to Southside Hospital.

Mr. Miller's physician, Dr. Mamula stated he was treating Miller for coronary disease and hypertension. He was admitted for observation overnight. Therefore he was not arraigned at that time. While he was being admitted, he stated that he thought Wilhelm and Goldblum were lovers. Also, the detectives were called by attorney Murovich, who claimed he was a friend of Miller, but not acting as his attorney. He stated that Miller had done some political work for him.

Autopsy findings

On February 10, 1976 at 11:00 a.m., an autopsy was performed on George Wilhelm at the Allegheny County Coroner's Office by associate pathologist Dr. F. A. Malak and myself and revealed the following findings:

General findings

The nude body of 42-year-old white male, well developed in good nutritional state, weighing 170 pounds and measuring 5'8" in length.

Evidence of injury

The deceased's head, body and extremities were stained with blood and showed more than 20 stab wounds, four of them potentially lethal, particularly a stab wound lacerating the thoracic aorta.

Distribution of stab wounds

- There were nine (9) stab wounds on the front of the body, including a stab wound on the forehead reaching the bone, but not perforating it.
- There were nine (9) stab wounds on the back of the body.
- There were multiple defense incised wounds of the fingers of the left hand consistent with the victim trying to defend himself and grasping the blade of the stabbing weapon.

- The fatal stab wounds included stab wounds of left external jugular vein, thoracic aorta, left lung, liver and transverse colon. There was severe internal bleeding with a hemothorax bilaterally of 1,500 cc's, and hemoperitoneum of 1000 cc.

Diagnoses included:

- Multiple stab wounds of the head, neck, and body with:
- Avulsion of the lower portion of the nose
- Perforation of the left external jugular vein
- Perforation of the thoracic aorta, left lung, liver, and transverse colon
- Hemothorax bilaterally
- Hemoperitoneum of 1000 cc.
- Defense-type wounds of both hands
- Postoperative status – Thoracotomy, Drainage wounds
- Abrasions of both knees.

The conclusive opinion was that the deceased was a 42-year-old white male, who died of multiple stab wounds of the head, neck, and body. The manner of death was deemed homicide. Multiple photographs were obtained of the body, face, neck, and back. Multiple photographs were obtained of the stab wounds with rulers included for measurement.

Supplemental Police reports

On February 10, 1976, a supplemental report by Officers McKay and Gorny noted their interview with Mr. Kurutz, who had been in the garage the previous evening at about 9:20 p.m. after leaving night school. Mr. Kurutz claimed to have heard a "thumping" sound to his left, and observed two white males about 30 yards away. Subject 1 was about 30 years old, 6 feet, 190/200 pounds and wearing dark rimmed glasses, a Russian fur hat, and a black overcoat. Subject 2 was about 40/45 years old, 5 feet 9 or 10 inches, with a stocky build and thinning hair, wearing a gray overcoat. The subjects were walking leisurely and looked at him. He felt he could identify subjects.

On February 10, 1976, detectives Condemi and Amity went to Miller's home and interrogated him about the murder. Miller initially lied claiming that Goldblum took him home and was not aware of Wilhelm's death.

However, after he was told by the police that his story and that of Goldblum "were not consistent" he related that Wilhelm drove Miller and Goldblum to the top floor of the parking lot and that *"no sooner that they stopped the car when Goldblum struck the victim with a wrench. The victim opened the car's door and fell to the ground. At this, Goldblum got out of the car and began stabbing the victim with a shear type instrument.*

The victim kept calling for Miller to help him but Miller did not. After Goldblum stabbed the victim he through (sic) him over the railing and then he and Goldblum left through the stairway." Miller emphatically stated he did not know that Goldblum intended to kill or stab the victim and if he would have known, he would not have gone along.

Miller stated that he knew that the wrench and the stabbing shears were kept in Wilhelm's car under the front seat. Miller had a scratch on his nose, a small laceration on the second finger of the left hand and several scratches on the arms and wrist. Miller stated that he got the scratches playing with his cat. Miller was very nervous during the interview and then started to complain of chest pain, and then appeared to pass out. The detectives then called for an ambulance who took Miller to SouthSide Hospital's emergency room. The E. R. doctor told the detectives that he treated Miller *"for coronary, and also hypertension."*

On February 11, 1976, Detective Lenz searched a yellow Ambassador sedan. The interior was negative for blood results. The search produced several burnt matches and suspected tobacco. There was no other evidence of value noted.

On February 13, 1976, Officers Hennigan and Watson requested that Detective Cotter of the latent print section take photographs of the outer garments that Mr. Goldblum had allegedly worn on the night of the murder. His wife provided a black topcoat, navy blue blazer, pair of grey slacks, and multicolored tie. There was evidence that the slacks had been recently cleaned or not worn, since they were pressed. Photographs were obtained with attention to the inside pockets.

On March 2, 1976, Mr. Miller was questioned by Detectives Freeman and Cooper, Miller repeated his story that as soon as he and Goldblum went into Wilhelm's car Goldblum asked if he could use Miller's gloves, which the latter used to keep in the back seat of George Wilhelm's car.

Miller stated that "*as George went the car, I heard a thump and Zeke (Goldblum) hit him on the head with a wrench of some type. Then George fell and his nose was bleeding, up against ah, the car's steering wheel. Zeke came out and started to stab him and he was saying "This will shut you up, you faggot!'. "* He (Goldblum) *kept stabbing him and stabbing him. George kept screaming and hollering as he was going around the garage. 'Help me Clarence, help me! Please help me! Please help me' And I was so scared I couldn't – I could do nothing.*"

But then Miller added that he tried to help Wilhelm "*a couple of times but Zeke (Goldblum) pulled me away*" stating that Wilhelm was dragging himself and crawling all over the garage. Then Miller said that Goldblum must have hit Wilhelm as he backed him against the wall. Wilhelm started to fall over and, as he was falling Goldblum grabbed him by the belt buckle. Wilhelm's pants fell off, and he landed with a thump.

After that, Miller stated that he and Goldblum left the garage. Miller related that he took the top coat which he wore at the time of the assault, put it in a bag and discarded it in a city garbage truck. When asked why, Miller responded "*Wee I was – I don't know why I did it. I just threw it – and ah, I just did it, that's all.*" Miller claimed that he said nothing to Goldblum because he "*was frightened.*" Miller indicated that the grass shear used in the stabbing had only one blade (half of the grass shears), which Wilhelm had made, about two years before, and Miller and Wilhelm used to pull down signs of political opponents. Miller also stated that while in the process of leaving the garage, he saw a guy standing to the left of the elevator.

Miller also stated that Goldblum owed Wilhelm a lot of money, and Wilhelm was "*bugging him*" and that Goldblum had asked Wilhelm to put fire to a restaurant he owed.

When the detectives confronted Miller and asked why the dying Wilhelm would tell the police: "*Clarence Miller did this to me,*" Miller replied: "*That I don't know. The only thing I could figure is George figured that I- because I didn't help him, I just stood there and let, let, let Zeke stab him.*"

On April 2, 1976, Detectives Gorny and Freeman questioned Clarence Miller about the fraudulent land deal in which George Wilhelm paid money for getting land which was never acquired, and then Wilhelm tried unsuccessfully to have the moneys repaid. Miller claimed that Goldblum had participated in the land fraud, however he acknowledged that that the contact with Wilhelm was made only by him and an associate of his.

During his re-direct testimony of Cornelius Kelly (an acquaintance of Miller) by Mr. Dixon – the County District Attorney, Kelly was asked whether *"did anyone suggest to him that he should testify falsely."* He replied: *"Well let me think a second. Yeah. Clarence said once 'I'll tell you what to say.' I said 'You ain't tell me nothing to say, I'm going to say it the way it is.'"*

Crime Lab report

On February 26, 1976, the Confidential Report of Laboratory findings of the Pittsburgh and Allegheny County Crime Laboratory were released by Director C. McInerney. Hairs recovered from a hat from the Ambassador sedan were compared to Miller and Wilhelm, and could have come from Wilhelm. The rectal swabs of Wilhelm showed numerous spermatozoa heads. Red crusts on the grass shears were human blood group A, PGM type 2-1. The whole blood of George Wilhelm was group A, MN, PGM 2-1. The fingernail scrapings of Wilhelm were negative. Three hairs from the inside the gloves were collected, and one was of animal origin. The two remaining hairs were compared to samples from Wilhelm, Goldblum, and Miller. The hairs exhibited the same microscopic characteristics as Miller's and could have come from Miller. The hairs were different from Wilhelm and Goldblum. The whole blood of Goldblum was group A, MN, PGM 2-1. The tobacco found inside the fire exit on the 8th floor was pipe tobacco and appeared to be the same type as the blend found in the Ambassador. A small smear of Goldblum's clothing found blood on the right sleeve cuff of a yellow shirt. However, not enough material was present for further testing. The clothing of Miller was examined. No significant stains were noted on any of the articles.

Statement of Clarence Miller to the Police

On March 2, 1976, Detective Freeman and Cooper took the recorded statement of Clarence Miller. He had been arrested and kept in the County Jail, and charged with the murder of George Wilhelm. His attorney, Mr. Murovich was present. Miller stated that he would answer all questions without his attorney present. He stated that:

- Goldblum had told him that Wilhelm was shaking him down for some money, and he wanted to meet with George on Monday night (Feb. 9, 1976).
- Goldblum had called him Monday morning to set up the appointment, and Mr. Miller called George.
- Wilhelm picked him up and dropped him off at the McDonald's, where they met with Goldblum at about 8:45 p.m.
- Miller stated that he was under the impression that Goldblum was just going to beat up Wilhelm. He stated he did not know that Goldblum was going to stab George.
- Goldblum asked George to give him a ride to his car. As they got into Wilhelm's car, Goldblum asked Miller if he could use his gloves.
- On the 8th floor, as George went to stop the car, Goldblum hit him on the head with *"a wrench of some type."* Then George fell and his nose was bleeding, *"and musta hit his nose on the steering wheel."*
- Miller stated that Wilhelm fell out of the car, and Goldblum "Zeke", got out and started to stab him, saying, *"This will shut you up faggot."*
- Miller stated that Wilhelm was yelling for help, but that he was too scared to help him and couldn't do anything.
- Miller stated that Goldblum had Wilhelm backed up against the wall, and then as Wilhelm started to fall over, Goldblum grabbed his belt and he went over the edge and his pants fell off.
- Miller stated that he and Goldblum then walked down the stairs and ramp and walked out. Goldblum then returned to him his gloves and *"he (Miller) threw them away."*

- Miller stated that they walked to Goldblum's car and that Goldblum took off his overcoat and pants and put them in a garbage bag. Miller also stated that he took his overcoat and also put it in the bag which he threw into a garbage truck.
- Miller stated that Goldblum told him *"keep quiet about it. We'll have an alibi that we three left and George went his way, and I took you home...They'll believe me before they believe you because my father is a Jewish Rabbi and I'm a lawyer."*
- Miller stated that he asked Goldblum what he was going to do, and that Goldblum said *"I'm just going to put a Jewish curse on him...I'm going to beat the hell out of him."* He stated that Goldblum offered him *"fifty bucks for this."*

Testimony of Clarence Miller at Coroner's Inquest

At the Coroner's Inquest, Miller testified to similar events as to the police, except that he added a number of details, claiming again that Goldblum first hit Wilhelm on the head with a hard object, possibly a wrench, Wilhelm then fell out of the car and Goldblum started to stab him. Miller stated that he then went out, *"shook up"* and that Wilhelm then asked him for help saying *"Help me Clarence. Help me. Help me Clarence."* When Miller was asked why then he did not assist Wilhelm and he responded, *"I don't know why. I was scared."* Miller claimed that when Goldblum entered Wilhelm's car he was wearing gloves, but he then asked Miller for an additional pair of gloves, which Miller kept in Wilhelm's car.

When asked whether he had blood on his clothing, Miller answered: *"I don't know. No."*

Testimony of Clarence Miller at Goldblum trial

On August 20, 1977, Mr. Miller testified at trial that:

- Miller stated that he left Wilhelm at the McDonald's to meet Goldblum in an alley by Smithfield and Grant Street. When Goldblum arrived, Miller stated that he saw him putting on another pair of trousers over top of his other trousers.
- Miller stated that as they walked to the McDonald's, Goldblum told him *"He's going to beat the hell out of him."*

- Miller stated that they were sitting in a booth when Wilhelm asked Goldblum (Zeke) *"You got my damn money?"* Goldblum answered, *"Yeah I got your money. Don't you worry about it; I have your money for you."* This made Wilhelm happy.
- They talked about politics, and then Miller states that Goldblum said, *"How about you guys taking me up to the garage and getting my car? It's parked up in the garage."* They then left in Wilhelm's car, a blue Plymouth, with Wilhelm driving, Miller in the passenger seat, and Goldblum *"right in back of George."*
- Miller stated that Goldblum directed Wilhelm to keep driving until they got to the very top of the garage, 8th level floor. There were no other cars in that area that night.
- Miller stated that when the ignition turned off, he heard a thump, and saw Wilhelm lean forward and fall out of the car. He stated that Goldblum then began stabbing him. He claimed he had no advance notice that was going to happen.
- Miller stated that Wilhelm was screaming *"Help me Clarence, help me, help me Clarence"* but that he (Miller) just *"froze."* Miller stated that while stabbing George, Goldblum angrily screamed *"like he was crazy,"* *"This will shut you up faggot; this will shut you up faggot."*
- Miller stated that Wilhelm was *"leaning up against the car door, and Zeke was just stabbing him. Then George was on the ground, crawling sideways, dragging his back leg."*
- Miller claimed that Wilhelm *"crawled around the car, then to the far wall, then back to the right front side of the car,"* while Goldblum kept stabbing him. He stated that when Wilhelm got back to the wall by the car, *"he managed to pull himself up"* only *"partly"*. He was then struck by Zeke (Goldblum) around the chin or chest, and fell over backwards. Miller stated that he is not sure if Goldblum hit Wilhelm with his fists or a weapon, but thought it was a weapon that *"looked like a pipe wrench or something."*
- Miller stated that: *"As he (George) went backward, Zeke grabbed him by his waist trying to pull him up, and as he pulled, his (George) pants came down, and all of a sudden I heard a thump"* when Wilhelm body hit the lower floor.

- Miller stated that what Goldblum used to strike Wilhelm *"looked like a pipe wrench or something. I don't know if it was a wrench or not, it looked like it."*
- Miller stated that he tried to help Wilhelm who was about 2 feet from the rear of the car and *"got down and started to, or he (Wilhelm) started to reach my wrist and I pulled him, I pulled my hand away."* Miller claimed that he was scared and that's why he did not help Wilhelm better. When asked why he did not stop Goldblum, Miller said that he was *"scared and did not try to stop Goldblum "because I (he) never seen anybody do anything like that."* Miller said that he did not know beforehand that *"Goldblum was going to hit him (Wilhelm) with a wrench and stab him and throw him over the wall."*
- Miller acknowledged that he knew for some time that the sheers and wrench used in the attack, had been *"always in Mr. Wilhelm's car"* and were located *"right in back of the front seat, like in the back, in the front"*, Miller stated that in the in the past the shears had been used by him and Wilhelm *"to tear [campaign] signs down"* of political opponents. Miller said that George had modified the shears by discarding one blade of it, and leaving the other with handle intact, in order to make their work easier.
- He stated that after Wilhelm went over the wall, he and Goldblum walked down a couple of stairs, and then took the ramps down to the Liberty street level.
- Miller stated that while Goldblum was stabbing Wilhelm, that he saw someone standing by the elevator. *"Right then Zeke started to stab George right by the car…and he was   just looking straight at us."* He stated the man appeared large, and thought he recognized him as a friend of Tony Franz. He stated that the man was about 20-30 feet away, and that he had *"a good enough look."*
- Miller stated that he attempted to find this man, and asked about him, but was unable to find him, and had not seen him since then.
- Miller stated that after they exited the garage, as they were walking to Zeke's (Goldblum) car, Zeke said *"just handed me my gloves…and I (Miller) threw them away."* He claimed he

307

threw them down on the sidewalk beside the parking garage. He claimed that he kept his gloves in the back of Wilhelm's car to use for campaigning, and that was how Goldblum had them.

- Miller stated that he had known about the shears used that night, that *"they were always in Mr. Wilhelm's car...George and I used them to tear signs (campaign) down."* He claimed that Wilhelm had taken the other blade off to make it easier to knock signs down. Miller stated that tape was kept on the handle so that it could be wrapped around a pole to use.
- Miller stated that Wilhelm kept the shear in back of the front seat, as well as a hammer, a staple gun, and an old monkey wrench.
- Miller stated that when they returned to Zeke's (Goldblum's) car, that Goldblum opened the trunk, took off the pants he had on, and put them in a plastic garbage bag. He stated Goldblum also put his overcoat in the bag.
- Miller stated that he noticed blood on his own raincoat.
- Miller stated that as they were driving, Goldblum told him, *"Look, if anyone asks you what happened that night, you tell them that we met together at McDonald's restaurant downtown, you and I, we left there and George was still there...Stick with that story."*
- Miller claimed that he was scared, and Zeke (Goldblum) said, *"Just keep your mouth shut and don't tell anybody because it will be my word against yours."*
- Miller admitted that he had cheated, planned, and schemed against George Wilhelm during his lifetime. He denied any feeling of hatred or revenge against Wilhelm, and stated that they were pretty close.
- Miller stated that he had given Wilhelm's phone number and address to Goldblum in the past. He stated that Goldblum had never told him any reason why he could not set up a meeting with Wilhelm himself.
- Miller stated that he had lied to the police about wearing a topcoat the previous night of the murder, and had found blood on the topcoat and disposed of it in a garbage truck in his neighborhood.

- Miller stated that he had gotten blood on the topcoat by the pocket when Mr. Goldblum had handed him the bloody gloves, and he had gotten blood on his hands which he then wiped onto the topcoat.
- Miller stated that when he got home, he was shaking and when his wife asked what was wrong, he replied, *"I seen a man get killed."*
- Miller stated that he had not told the police there was blood on his pants, and that *"I don't know if they put that in their report, but they made a mistake."*
- Miller stated that the police collected the pants that he had been wearing that night, his shirt, and a blue winter jacket.
- Miller stated that the overcoat that Mr. Goldblum was wearing that night had a spot of blood around the belly by the buttonhole.
- Miller stated that the railing was about up to his waist high.
- Miller stated that when Goldblum handed him his gloves, nothing was said, and then he (Miller) threw the gloves along the street going up Seventh Avenue.
- Miller stated that on February 18th, he appeared at the Coroner's inquest under oath. At that time, he stated that he did not know where his overcoat was, and answered yes to the question, *"Did somebody take it from you?"* And then he said, *"I misplaced it somewhere."* Then, when the next question was asked, *"Nobody took it from you, you just mislaid it?"* he answered *"Yes."*
- On March 2nd, when Miller was interviewed by the police, he was asked why he threw the coat into the garbage truck. He replied *"I don't know why. I just did it."* He admitted at trial that he had lied that he did not know why he had thrown the coat away.
- Miller stated that the first time he told anyone that blood got onto his coat because it was on the gloves that Goldblum handed to him was sometime in July of 1977, to Detective Freeman at the Public Safety Building. He stated that had been a verbal statement that he decided to make after talking to his priest and his attorney.

- Miller stated that after George Wilhelm parked the car with him and Goldblum inside, *"a few minutes"* passed before Wilhelm was struck.
- Miller stated that he had been sitting turned a little bit toward Wilhelm, and was able to see Goldblum in the back seat.
- Miller stated that as soon as Wilhelm parked and turned off the ignition, without forewarning, *"All of a sudden I heard a thump, George fell forward, fell out of the car and Zeke (Goldblum) started to stab him."* Miller stated that previously Goldblum, who was sitting in the back of the car, had exited the car from driver side and proceeded to stab Wilhelm shouting to him, *"This will shut you up, faggot; this will shut you up, faggot."* Thereafter Miller elaborated and said that when Wilhelm fell forward and hit his head on the steering wheel, he started bleeding from his nose. Initially Miller said that he could not identify the stabbing weapon but thereafter described it as grass shears.
- Miller stated that as Goldblum was stabbing Wilhelm, Wilhelm was *"hollering"* crying: *"Help me, Clarence: Please, for God's sake, help me Clarence, help me."* Miller stated that he *"froze."*
- Miller stated that, *"Wilhelm was first leaning against the car door, like this (demonstrating) and Zeke (Goldblum) was just stabbing him"* and thereafter Wilhelm was *"crawling sideways"* towards the ramp, to the *"far wall from where he parked,"* while Goldblum continued to stab him. Then Wilhelm crawled back towards his car as he *"crawled from one side of the garage to the other, on the opposite side."* Then Wilhelm *"managed to get up, get himself up partly, and he got partway and Zeke hit him somewhere up around here (indicating) and he over and started to fall backward."*
- Miller stated that he is 5 feet 11 inches tall, and weighed about 210 pounds on that night.
- Miller stated that he and Wilhelm were close friends, and admitted that he had *"fleeced him"* and *"set him up to be beaten up for $50."* He stated that the lack of money was important to him, and that he was upset that he had never been paid the $50.

- He stated that the police had first told him that the last words spoken by Wilhelm were, *"Clarence Miller did this to me,"* on February 10th, and that's why he was being arrested for murder.
- He admitted that he had lied to the police when, after he had been informed of Wilhelm's dying declaration, he had stated that he had parted company with Goldblum and Wilhelm around 8:30 p.m."
- Miller then testified extensively how he and two of his associates (Fred Orlowsky and Ted Dedo) concocted a plan to defraud Wilhelm by claiming that they had the political influence to facilitate the sale of a public land to Wilhelm. Wilhelm gave them $20,000 as a first payment for the land and then the land acquisition did not materialize. Miller did not claim that Goldblum was involved directly in the fraud, but claimed that he went to him for advice and also shared with him some of the profits.
- Miller also claimed that Goldblum asked Wilhelm to burn down his restaurant, which Wilhelm did, but then declined to pay Wilhelm for the arson, because Goldblum claimed that he did not have available money.

Testimony of Charles Goldblum at trial

On August 20, 1977, Mr. Goldblum testified at trial that:

- He had not known George Wilhelm in 1974 and 1975 and while Miller mentioned his name to him beforehand, he did not meet Wilhelm until the day before the assault (Sunday, February 8, 1976). Wilhelm, Miller and Goldblum met at a McDonald's restaurant.
- Goldblum stated that he never showed Miller holes in the wall of his restaurant, as Miller claimed, which allegedly would have facilitated the arson.
- In December 1974 or January 1975, Miller mentioned the name of George Wilhelm to him, because Miller told him that he and another person by the name of Dedo, *"bilked"* and defrauded Wilhelm of $21,000 dollars, by promising to use political influence (which Miller did not have) to approve the purchase a piece of public land, in which Wilhelm was interested. Miller stated that he did not know what to do, as

311

Wilhelm asked for his money back and asked to meet Goldblum for advice. Miller was concerned because apparently he devised the fraud, and was concerned that the FBI may investigate him, as he had been previously investigated by the FBI for committing perjury in an affidavit. Goldblum met with him but advised him to seek the help of another lawyer, and told Miller that he had two options, either to return the money or to hire a good criminal attorney. Miller stated then that he would return the money to Wilhelm.

- Goldblum was not aware of what Miller did for a living, except that the latter told him of being very involved with the Republican Party.
- Goldblum stated that he did not have anything to do with the land fraud.
- Goldblum stated that Miller had told him that he saw another attorney who drafted for him a letter in the land fraud case
- Goldblum stated that on the day of the assault, February 9, 1976, about 9:00 p.m., he met with Mr. Miller in front of a bank outside of the office where he was employed, and thereafter went with him to a McDonald's restaurant where Wilhelm was waiting for them. At the restaurant, Goldblum introduced himself to Wilhelm as being Miller's attorney, and Wilhelm looked disturbed about it, probably because he saw bringing an attorney to the meeting with Miller as an unfriendly act. Goldblum stated that at the restaurant Miller did not follow his advice to repay the money to Wilhelm, declining to return the money, and putting the blame on another participant in the land fraud, who fraudulently had represented himself to Wilhelm as being Manella, a person connected politically to a U.S. Senator. Miller stated that he repeatedly tried unsuccessfully to telephone and contact Manella, who Wilhelm had met, in the belief that the impersonator was indeed Manella. (Goldblum had previously told Miller that if he was not prepared to make an arrangement for returning the money to Wilhelm, there was nothing that he (Goldblum) could do). Wilhelm then got upset but Miller pacified him by insisting that they are friends and that eventually he would reach Manella by phone, as the latter had Wilhelm's moneys for the land. The meeting lasted

about 5 to10 minutes, and was interrupted by Wilhelm who, realizing that the meeting is not going to be short, stated that he must go and move his car as it was parked illegally. As Wilhelm was going out of the restaurant, Goldblum took Miller aside, telling him that he did not follow his advice. Goldblum and Miller then accompanied Wilhelm to his car, which was illegally parked on the street. The car was parked a few minutes away and after reaching it, all three entered the car to continue their meeting, with Wilhelm being the driver, Miller in the front passenger seat and Goldblum in the back seat. Wilhelm drove his car to the 8th floor, the roof of the garage *"and just -- just before the -- the car was parked on the roof a –um—um Miller pops a surprise on both Wilhelm and myself (Goldblum) and that he can't pay Wilhelm immediately but is going to take me (Miller) – take me a few years,"* apparently in installments over the next few years. Then Wilhelm became very upset and he and Miller started a heated argument with Miller starting to yell while Wilhelm very angrily accused Miller that he has done something wrong with the intended acquisition of the land. (While in the car, Goldblum did not observe anything being placed on the back seat).

- The heated argument ignited a fight between Wilhelm and Miller and *"they were hitting each other and they were grappling in the front seat"* and Goldblum recalled that Wilhelm hit Miller in the face, at least one time. Then Wilhelm fell on the floor of the parking garage, and started to yell for help. Miller also exited the car at about the same time, and then Goldblum saw that Miller *"had what appeared to be a big knife"* with some blood on it. Goldblum stated that he did not see Miller stabbing Wilhelm in the car. (When Goldblum was shown the stabbing weapon,n he stated that he never held it in his hands). After exiting the car Miller went behind the car and *"ran around to where Wilhelm was lying, right by the driver's door.*

- As Wilhelm was yelling for help, Miller screamed, *"Shut up you faggot,"* while either stabbing or hitting him. Goldblum was in the car and could see Miller but not Wilhelm, as the latter was on the ground. Seeing that, Goldblum decided to get away, and when exiting the car, saw Wilhelm and Miller toward the rear of the car, *"grappling and Mr. Wilhelm getting away from him (Miller) again."* Then Miller put the victim down and sat on the victim, stabbing him 10 and possibly 20 times. Goldblum then stood there watching the stabbing. After the stabbing, *"Mr. Miller got to his feet and starts dragging Mr. Wilhelm to another (opposite) wall."* Goldblum recalled that he saw that Miller *"had one hand on his (Wilhelm's) collar and one on his pants while dragging him."* During this time, Wilhelm was *"twitching his arms and his head was twitching."* Then, Goldblum saw Miller placing Wilhelm, whose face was very bloody, on the ledge by the North side, reaching down and picking Wilhelm's legs up and quickly flipping them over the railings. Wilhelm fell and hit a lower floor with a thump. When he heard the thump Goldblum stated that he went back to the wall and saw Wilhelm and turned around and as he was walking away, he saw a man by the elevators (Mr. Kurutz) who had exited from an elevator, and apparently saw them. Goldblum stated that he was filled at the time with fear, disgust and shock. Goldblum walked then to Miller, stood next to him, and Miller turned to him and extended his hands which were gloved. (Apparently to convey that was not putting Goldblum in danger because he did not hold the stabbing weapon any more). Goldblum joined Miller and both looked over the fence and saw the non-moving body of George Wilhelm down on the roof of the passageway. Then Goldblum ran away.

- Goldblum stated that when he walked up to look where Wilhelm went over, he may have got a spot of blood in the shirt's cuff, from the railing on which Wilhelm was placed prior to his fall. Goldblum saw a lot of blood on the roof at the South wall and deliberately tried not to step on it. Goldblum testified that he saw blood stains on the front of Miller's clothing (both matching trousers and jacket of a grey, checkered overcoat gray checkered leisure suit, as well as on Miller's raincoat.

- As Goldblum was running desperately away from the scene, down 3-4 flights of stairs, Miller was *"chasing"* after him. When Goldblum reached his car which was parked nearby in the alley, Miller was there having entered uninvited, and proceed to sit on the front passenger side, very much against Goldblum's wishes. Goldblum told Miller to get out of his car, but Miller started begging him to help, claiming he could not take a bus home. Then Goldblum, who was afraid of Miller, agreed. Miller then stated "*You've got to help me*" and Goldblum's initial reaction was that he did not want to see him again. Miller then continued to say: "*No, you have to help me, you have to help me*"; "*Look you are a lawyer, they'll believe you*"; "*Neither one of us want to be placed up there, so let's just say that we both left him at the restaurant*"; "*Let's tell the police that we left him at the restaurant and that you took me home.*" Goldblum then relented and went along and agreed to lie to the police if questioned.

- After taking Miller to his home, Goldblum returned to his home. Miller called Goldblum in the early hours of morning asking him again, whether Goldblum will help him or not, saying, "*You won't hurt me? You're going to help me?*" Goldblum assented. After this conversation, at about 9:00 a.m. Goldblum went to his regular work. When Detectives Cooper and Longacre initially came to question him, Goldblum did not tell them the truth but the story concocted by Miller.

Note of Commutation Request by Charles Goldblum

In a Note of Commutation Request, Goldblum confessed that he "*planned the arson, made the preparations and hired Clarence Miller to set the fire.*" He stated that the reason for the arson were financial problems with his restaurant in which his parents invested more than $100,000. Goldblum recognized that he had wrongfully acted wrongfully, "*immaturely and impulsively*", but firmly denied that George Wilhelm had anything to do with the arson, that the arson was done by Miller, and that he (Goldblum) at the time of the arson, did not know even know Wilhelm.

Goldblum stated that in February of 1976, Clarence Miller told him about George Wilhelm, and disclosed to him, that in 1973 and 1974, he (Miller) defrauded Wilhelm of several thousand dollars, by pretending to sell Wilhelm land in North Carolina which was in fact owned by the Federal Government. At that time in February 1976, Goldblum did not know Wilhelm.

Goldblum stated that Miller had asked him to meet with him and Wilhelm, as he (Miller) would be prepared to *"make Wilhelm whole"* (*i.e.* to return the money).

However, at the meeting, Miller reneged on his promise, and, as a result, Miller and Wilhelm begun to argue and then fight. During the fight, Miller stabbed Wilhelm to death. Goldblum stated that before dying, Wilhelm told a policeman, *"Clarence, Clarence Miller did this to me."*

Goldblum claimed that the evidence of the trial pointed to Miller as being Wilhelm's attacker. He stated that initially he did not report the truth to the police incriminating Miller, because he was concerned over their previous involvement in the arson of Goldblum's restaurant.

Testimony of Dr. Joshua Perper at Goldblum's trial

On August 23, 1977, I was questioned at trial on Direct by District Attorney, Mr. Dixon. My testimony included that:

- I stated that I had performed the autopsy of George Wilhelm on February 10, 1976.
- I stated that there were wounds or incisions present, some of which were performed at the hospital, and other types of wounds which were clearly distinguishable.
- I stated that there were a total of 25 wounds located both on the front and back of the body. The location of each wound was stated and each wound described. This included a severe stab wound of the nose which almost completely amputated the lower part of the nose, and the segment which measured 2 x 1 ¼ inches.
- There was a stab wound present on the left side of the neck which measured 1" in length and slightly more in depth, which penetrated the muscles of the neck and one of the major superficial veins of the neck, which was the left external jugular vein.
- There was a deep stab wound which penetrated to a depth of 6 inches and perforated the sternum, the right 7th and 8th ribs, and perforated the liver close to the gallbladder.

- I stated that such a stab wound in a downward direction toward the liver would have had to have been a powerful blow.

- There was a deep wound in the space between the 6th and 7th ribs which penetrated the left lung. There was also a stab wound in the left upper quadrant of the abdomen which penetrated the muscles and just perforated the underlying intestines.

- There was a deep wound of the palm of the right hand called "defense wounds." There were also multiple incised wounds on the fingers of the left hand in a transverse manner along the fingers, also consistent with "defense wounds."

- I also demonstrated the wounds found on the back of the body, on the back of the head behind both ears, and those which ran obliquely across the blade of the left shoulder. There were multiple stab wounds in the lower part of the right back, in the left-lower back, and the mid-lower back, some in groups. These were indicated on a body diagram in the autopsy report.

- There was also an irregular bruising on the right side of the forehead caused by blunt force trauma, possibly due to a fall or blunt instrument. There were abrasions on both knees consistent with either a fall or crawling on hands and knees on a hard surface.

- I noted that one of the left lower back wounds penetrated 7 inches from the skin to the abdominal cavity and cut the aorta.

- I noted that an examination of the grass shears was consistent with the injuries that were produced on the body, and that there were stab wounds with a "back," with an incised end and blunt end which fit and corresponded in measurement with the back of the shears. Most of the wounds were consistent with that type of instrument.

- I noted that scrapings are routinely taken from underneath the fingernails. The scrapings from this case were sent to the Crime Laboratory. It was noted that the responsibility of the Coroner's Office is to take the specimens, preserve them, and transfer them for analysis.

- I explained the findings of photographs taken of the head showing the wounds to the nose, the laceration of the back of the head extending into the right ear, and the stab wounds of the back.
- I opined that the cause of death was due to severe internal bleeding due to stab wounds of the liver and aorta.
- The superficial wounds were not a significant contributory cause of death.
- On cross-examination, I noted that the abrasion of the head and knees were wounds that would not have bled.
- I opined that the blood spatter observed inside the car could have been caused by a penetrating injury that occurred inside of the car, and that a very sharp movement of the victim's head would have squirted the blood. It could also have been caused by flicking blood off the weapon itself.
- I noted photographs of the "defense wounds" of the left hand, although there were also defense wounds on the right hand which was not photographed.

Testimony of Detective Freeman at Goldblum trial

Also on August 23, 1977, Detective Freeman testified at Goldblum's trial. He stated that:

- The general area of the wall over which Mr. Wilhelm fell measured 3 feet 8 inches, and was 15 feet above the area where he landed.
- There were "drag marks" indicating that either the victim's feet or trousers were actually slid across the snow.
- He had the impression that somebody may have been crawling, but this was unclear due to the snow.
- There was a horizontal blood stain on the driver's side window on the inside window.
- He did not observe any blood on the steering wheel.
- He did not observe any blood on the back rest of the driver's seat or the driver's seat itself.
- There were no discernible fingermarks on the shears visible.
- There was no blood seen on the outside of the car itself.
- There was blood by the left rear corner of the car, and then going down to the south wall in a very heavy concentration,

and moving back to the north wall some on top of the concrete itself, and then a lot of blood down where he was found.

- There was a small line of blood droplets on the dashboard, each with a *"tail"* facing toward the passenger side, indicating that the blood came from the driver's side to the passenger side.
- There was no close up photograph of the dashboard taken.
- There was no blood visible on the wrench found in the car.
- There was clearly blood visible on the shears found on the 7th floor level.

Peter Marrone's testimony on Crime Lab's findings

On August 24, 1977, Peter Marrone testified at trial as the Chief Criminologist of the Allegheny County Crime Lab. He stated:

- A hat recovered from the car of Charles Goldblum contained hairs that could have come from George Wilhelm. They were different from the hair from Clarence Miller. (In subsequent testimony, it was revealed that this hat was actually found in the victim's (George Wilhelm's) vehicle, not Charles Goldblum's).
- He had examined the grass shears for blood stains. Some stains were on the blade, but *"most of the stains were on the taped portion of the handle."*
- The blood was human, type A, PGM 2-1. This was compatible with the whole blood of George Wilhelm.
- There was no evidence of significance in the fingernail scrapings obtained by the Coroner's Office. He stated that if the victim had imposed long scratches on the hands or arms of his assailant, that there could have been tissue or blood or hair, but not necessarily so.
- He had examined a pair of vinyl black gloves. The right hand glove in particular showed a dark brown stain inside the lining; the left hand glove had some staining but not to a great extent.
- The blood from the gloves was human, type A, PGM 2-1.
- Three hairs were recovered from inside the gloves. One was an animal. The other two were consistent with

Clarence Miller, and were different from Charles Goldblum, and different from George Wilhelm.

- He stated that the hair samples indicated that Miller had actually worn the gloves.

- He stated that it was possible for different people to wear and even to do heavy physical labor and leave no sample behind.

- He had examined some matches from the 8th floor exit to matches from an Ambassador automobile. Two of the matches were the same. There was also a comparison made of some pipe tobacco, which was also the same as that from the Ambassador.

- He examined clothing belonging to Charles Goldblum, including a yellow shirt, which had no stains or hairs on it. Another shirt, yellow and blue, had a very small reddish smear on the right cuff of blood. There was not enough of a sample for further analysis. Also examined were a black topcoat, a navy blue blazer, gray slacks, and a multicolored tie. No stains of significance were found.

- He examined clothing belonging to Clarence Miller including a pair of shoes, tee shirt, red blazer, red shirt, blue jacket, and plaid slacks. No stains of significance were found.

- He stated that there was no evidence of recent washing of the slacks belonging to Miller. It was noted that Miller had told Detectives Amity and Condemi that he had washed the blood off the cuffs of those pants. However, he stated that depending on what was used to wash them, it might not show.

- He stated that neither he nor anyone else from the Crime Lab had examined the crime scene.

- He stated that the blood type and PGM of Wilhelm and Goldblum were the same.

- He stated that the hat found on the front seat of Goldblum's car had hair fibers of the same characteristics of Wilhelm. (It was later reported by Mr. Dixon and verified by Officer Hill that the hat was found in the victim's car on the front seat and not in Mr. Goldblum's car as mistakenly repeated.)

- He had examined the wrench found at the scene at the garage, and stated there were no traces of blood or hair on the wrench.
- He stated that normally speaking in the performance of his duties, he is not generally called to all homicide scenes to make an investigation. He stated that the lab has a service agency respond, and that the city itself has its own mobile unit crew. He stated that the city's mobile crew assists the investigating officers in collecting evidence and photographs of the scene. Then the lab performs tests and makes analysis of the reports, rather than travel to crime scenes.
- He stated that you wouldn't necessarily find hair on an instrument such as the wrench striking someone on the back of the head. He stated that it was unlikely to find residue of skin if the victim were struck on the forehead or head.
- He stated that slacks from Mr. Goldblum's home were picked up February 10th, and submitted to the lab on February 13th. He had no knowledge of where they had been stored in the interval.

Testimony at trial of Officer Edward Hill

On August 25, 1977, Officer Edward Hill of the Mobile Crime Unit testified at trial, stating that:

- The Crime Unit is a technical service for the detective division for obtaining photographs, fingerprints, and collecting evidence and transporting it to the crime lab.
- Officer Hill stated that a half of a shear was found at the 7th floor. The victim's car was on the 8th floor. A wrench was found inside the car on the front seat. The handle of the wrench was found on the ground near the wall. Photographs were obtained of all evidence that was collected.
- The victim's car, a Plymouth, was towed to the Public Safety building and examined after being allowed to dry out. Blood scrapings were obtained from the dashboard. Blood and hair were also obtained from the left front and rear doors. The back seat was vacuumed for fibers or

hair. No other photographs were taken of the inside of the car besides those taken initially at the crime scene.

- No attempt was made to obtain fingerprints from inside the car due to severe cold and damp and a high degree of humidity.

Sworn Affidavit by Mr. Peter Dixon

On June 17, 1988, attorney Peter Dixon made a sworn statement that he was the trial prosecutor in the case of Commonwealth of Pennsylvania v. Charles J. "Zeke" Goldblum and the companion case of Commonwealth of Pennsylvania v. Clarence Miller. He stated that he had recently been exposed to new information concerning the case against Mr. Goldblum which was not available to him at the time of trial.

He stated that that new information caused him to go back and carefully review and study the trial transcript in this matter. Based on this review, he came *"to the very firm conclusion that Charles Goldblum had nothing to do with the murder of George Wilhelm other than being a frightened witness to that murder and an accessory after the fact."* He also stated that *"it is very unlikely that Charles Goldblum participated in the land fraud perpetrated against George Wilhelm, or that George Wilhelm participated in the arson of Mr. Goldblum's restaurant."*

Peter Dixon concluded his affidavit stating: *"Despite my best efforts in trying these cases, a miscarriage of justice has occurred."*

Letters of Judge Donald Ziegler to the Clemency Board

Judge Donald Ziegler wrote no less than three (3) consecutive letters to the Board of Clemency, pleading for the release of Charles Goldblum, because the crime was committed by Clarence Miller, as the victim clearly asserted in his dying declaration.

Letter 1 - On January 5, 1989, U.S. District Judge Donald Ziegler, the Judge that had presided over the case of the Commonwealth v. Charles Goldblum wrote a letter to the Board of Pardons. He supported the application for clemency, and stated that substantial leniency should be granted in this case, and Mr. Goldblum should be released from confinement within the foreseeable future. He noted Mr. Goldblum's education and lack of any previous criminal involvement, a stable and supportive family, and Mr. Goldblum's exemplary record while confined. He stated that *"I have been troubled for years by the dying declaration of the victim, 'Clarence Miller did this to me.' It is a moral and legal precept that a person is presumed to speak the truth when he is faced with death. The victim knew that he was dying and he never mentioned the name of Charles Goldblum. In short, the conviction was based on the testimony of Miller, and the jury's apparent dislike for Mr. Goldblum. In my opinion, Mr. Miller's testimony was suspect and quite frankly, if I was the fact finder, I would have rejected as unpersuasive much of the testimony of this individual."* Considering these factors, *"I recommend that the request be granted and urge that Mr. Goldblum be released from prison without undue delay."*

Letter 2 - On January 14, 1994, U.S. District Judge Donald Ziegler wrote another letter to the Pennsylvania Board of Pardons. He stated that Charles Goldblum had served over 17 years of confinement, and no citizen should be confined for a greater period of time for acts which, while criminal, amount to stupidity. *"Charles Goldblum does not constitute a threat to this or any other community, and I am confident that he has the intelligence and ability to become a productive citizen."*

Judge Ziegler stated that Goldblum had only witnessed and did not participate in Wilhelm's homicidal stabbing by Miller. Judge Ziegler emphasized *"Mere presence at the scene of a crime does not constitute evidence of complicity in a homicide."*

Judge Ziegler stated that Goldblum's involvement in the arson of his restaurant was the product of financial desperation and a fear of embarrassing his parents and family.

The Judge concluded by stating that Charles Goldblum is *"a man with potential who deserves a break at this point of his life. Seventeen years of confinement is sufficient to repay the people of this state for crimes for which he was convicted."*

In additional letters to Pennsylvania Board of Clemency, Judge Ziegler reiterated his pleas to release Goldblum from prison, because the stabbing homicide was perpetrated by Miller and Goldblum was only a passive observer, and the conviction was based on jury believing the suspect testimony of Miller and their dislike of Goldblum. The dates of these additional letters are January 5, 1989, January 14, 1994, and December 14, 1998.

Evaluation report of Dr. Cyril Wecht

On September 1, 1994, Dr. Cyril Wecht, a well-known forensic pathologist, wrote to the Pennsylvania Board of Pardons regarding: Commutation Petition of Charles Goldblum. He had reviewed the autopsy report by the Coroner's Office on February 10, 1976, and numerous police and other investigative reports, statements, interrogatories, and various court documents.

Dr. Wecht concluded: *"It is my professional opinion, based upon a reasonable degree of medical certainty, that Mr. Goldblum was not the individual who inflicted the fatal stab wounds on Mr. George Wilhelm."*

This determination was based on the following findings evaluated by Dr. Wecht:

- The nature, extent, and direction of the various stab wounds.
- The blood spatters found on the dashboard of the car had a left to right direction, indicating that the individual sitting in the front passenger seat would have been the person who inflicted the fatal wounds.
- Mr. Miller admitted to being in the front passenger seat and to changing his clothing following the event and destroying the clothing he was wearing during the stabbing.
- There was no blood found on the clothing that Mr. Miller stated Mr. Goldblum was wearing.
- The victim's unambiguous dying declaration that, *"Clarence. Clarence Miller did this to me."*

Sworn affidavit by Dr. Cyril Wecht

On February 7, 1996, in a sworn affidavit, Dr. Wecht stated that no pre-trial inquiries were made of the Coroner's Office concerning the significance of available forensic evidence by defense counsel, and thus, he was not called upon to review the evidence or offer an opinion at trial. Also, he stated that, Dr. Perper, the prosecutor of George Wilhelm's autopsy was not asked during his court testimony by the prosecutor to give his expert opinion concerning the likelihood of Mr. Goldblum's role. Dr. Wecht stated that the presence of blood spatters on the dashboard of Mr. Wilhelm's car established that the stabbing began while he was in the car, by the individual in front of or immediately to the right side of him, Clarence Miller.

Given the number and severity of the stab wounds, *"it is unimaginable to me that Mr. Wilhelm's assailant would not have gotten a significant amount of blood on his clothes. Yet, Mr. Wilhelm's blood was not found on the clothes seized from Mr. Goldblum."* Mr. Miller admitted that he had attempted to dispose of his own clothes which were stained with blood. Additionally, *"Mr. Miller testified that Mr. Goldblum wore his gloves while committing the murder. The only person that has been linked to the gloves through scientific evidence is Miller himself."* Finally, Dr. Wecht considered the dying declaration of the victim, and the *"great weight that the law puts upon such statements as a strong presumption that someone about to die will truthfully identify his killer."*

Affidavit of John Balshy, Crimes Investigator

On March 15, 1996, John Balshy submitted an affidavit. He stated that:

- He is a private investigator who specializes in criminal investigations, police procedures, evidence, and forensics.
- He found errors and oversights inconsistent with sound forensic and homicide procedures including;
- Not all of the evidence collected at the crime scene was analyzed by the crime lab, and critical photographs were not taken.
- The vehicle was impounded by the police, but no photographs were taken of its interior.
- The splatters on the dashboard were scraped without first being photographed.
- The scraped blood was removed from the surface without being photographed using a measurement scale to indicate the length and width of the blood pattern in relation to the surface on which it was found.
- An attempt to type the scraped blood removed from the dashboard was not made until two hours before Peter Marrone of the Crime Lab was to testify at the Goldblum's trial, making blood typing impossible.
- Fingernail scrapings taken from the victim were not thoroughly analyzed.

- He stated that if the evidence had been preserved properly, if a photograph with a scale present had been taken of the blood spatters, and if the blood spatters had been precisely measured for size, length, and width, a forensic criminologist could have determined the angle of impact of the blood, which could have illustrated to a fair degree of precision where the victim and the assailant were positioned at the time of the assault, and how the spattering of blood on the dashboard occurred.
- There is no evidence that the Police attempted to gather as much evidence as possible to determine which of the two defendants was the assailant who wielded the grass shears.
- That the Police, after learning that Miller had discarded his clothing, did not further investigate who the assailant was.
- That the fingernail scrapings were read as *"negative"* and did not describe the composition or ingredients of the scrapings.
- That Goldblum's counsel, H. David Rothman, did not conduct a private investigation of the crime scene.
- That a private investigation would have assisted the defense and raised serious doubts as to the Commonwealth's theory of the case.

Affidavit by Dr. Michael Baden and Dr. Barbara Wolf

On November 25, 1996, Dr. Michael Baden and Dr. Barbara Wolf, both experienced forensic pathologists, submitted an affidavit based on the autopsy report and forensic evidence in the murder of Mr. Wilhelm.They stated that:

- Based on the autopsy report, autopsy photographs, police reports, crime lab reports, transcripts from trial, and Chrysler Motor Corp. specifications of the 1966 Plymouth Fury (victim's car), they opined to a reasonable degree of medical certainty that Mr. Goldblum was not the individual who inflicted the fatal stab wounds to Mr. Wilhelm.
- The positions of the passengers in the car, the crime scene evidence, and the autopsy report are not consistent with the testimony of Mr. Miller.
- Blood spatters on the dashboard indicate that the stabbing occurred in the car, and is not consistent with the testimony of Mr. Miller that no stabbing occurred in the car.

- The left to right direction of the blood spatter on the dashboard is consistent with Mr. Wilhelm being stabbed by a person sitting to his right in the front passenger seat - the uncontested position of Clarence Miller.
- The lack of blood on Mr. Goldblum's clothing, and the admission of Mr. Miller that he disposed of his clothes which were stained with blood from Mr. Wilhelm.
- The black vinyl gloves recovered from the garage with blood stains were linked through forensic evidence only to Mr. Miller by hairs taken from inside the gloves.
- The dying declaration of the victim identifying Clarence Miller as his murderer is supported by the forensic evidence.

Report of Dr. Henry Lee, criminologist

On January 17, 1997, Dr. Henry Lee, Director of the Forensic Research Training Center, issued a report after reviewing the autopsy report, autopsy photographs, portions of transcripts of the trials of Charles Goldblum and Clarence Miller, the deposition of Pittsburgh Police commander Ronald Freeman, the affidavit of Dr. Cyril Wecht, the affidavit of Dr. Barbara Wolf and Dr. Michael Baden, and the letter from Isabel Storch, Assistant City Solicitor of Pittsburgh. His report included the following statements of fact:

- A summary of the death scene and body findings: the fact the Mr. Wilhelm, the victim of a homicide, drove his car shortly prior to his death to a parking garage, with the front passenger being Mr. Miller and the back passenger Mr. Goldblum.
- That the autopsy report and photographs indicated that Mr. Wilhelm had been inflicted with approximately 25 stab wounds/injuries.
- That according to the testimony of Detective Freeman, the following blood stain patterns were observed at scene:
- Blood smears were found on the interior of the driver side window.
- Blood spatters on the dashboard with a left to right direction.
- Bloodstains on the outside of the driver door.
- Bloodstains on the ground at the left rear of the car, and bloodstains on the walls.

- An examination by the Allegheny County Forensic Science Laboratory examination of Mr. Goldblum's clothing showed a marked lack of blood stains except for a small indistinguishable stain on the left cuff.
- A wrench found on the front seat inside the vehicle had no blood-like materials on it.
- Handprint type of impressions were observed on the "packed snow" surface at the crime scene.
- According to Mr. Freeman, the investigation file of this case was missing.
- According to Attorney Storch, the crime scene photographs were also missing.
- According to U.S. District Court Judge Donald Ziegler, he stated that the dying declaration of Mr. Wilhelm indicated that Clarence Miller did this to him.

Dr. Lee concluded:

- Without the crime scene reports and crime scene photographs and crime scene video tapes available, a reconstruction of the crime is almost impossible.
- Based on the limited information available, a partial reconstruction was made by Dr. Lee which indicated that there are many scientific facts indicating that Mr. Goldblum was not the individual who committed this crime, including:

  1. The blood spatter of the dashboard was consistent with a medium velocity cast-off pattern, from left to right.
  2. The location of the spatters was inconsistent with Mr. Wilhelm being stabbed by a person in the back seat of the vehicle.
  3. The number of stab wounds and locations of those wounds strongly indicate that there was a struggle between the victim and perpetrator.
  4. The amount of blood lost (by the victim) further supports that there should have been a significant amount of blood on the assailant's clothes.

5. Mr. Goldblum's clothing revealed a marked lack of blood. Mr. Miller admitted that he disposed of his clothes which had become stained with Mr. Wilhelm's blood.
6. The absence of a laceration from a blunt force injury, indicate that a stabbing occurred in the car. This is inconsistent with Mr. Miller's testimony that no stabbing occurred in the car.
7. The only person to whom a pair of bloody black vinyl gloves recovered from the parking garage was linked through forensic evidence was Mr. Miller.
8. Examination of the wrench found no trace of blood, bone, tissue, or hair. This scientific fact is clearly inconsistent with testimony by Mr. Miller that Mr. Goldblum clubbed Mr. Wilhelm on the back of the head with a wrench.
9. There were no fingerprints or any body fluid from Mr. Goldblum on the knife or wrench. These facts further support that there is no physical evidence to link Mr. Goldblum to this crime.
10. The dying declaration of the victim identified Clarence Miller as his murderer before he died.

Based on all the above facts, Dr. Lee opined that to a reasonable degree of forensic certainty, Mr. Goldblum was not the individual who inflicted the fatal stab wounds to Mr. Wilhelm.

Letters of Judge Donald Ziegler to Clemency Board
On December 14, 1998, U.S. District Judge Donald Ziegler wrote to the Lieutenant Governor's Office, Board of Pardons, with respect to clemency for Charles Goldblum. He had received a copy of the affidavit executed by Peter Dixon, the prosecutor in the Goldblum case. Mr. Dixon concluded that *"Charles Goldblum had nothing to do with the murder of George Wilhelm other than being a frightened witness to that murder and accessory after the fact,"* based on new information presented to him.

Judge Ziegler noted that Mr. Goldblum had been confined for over 20 years, and his *" uneasiness with the verdict of the jury has been expressed to the Board of Parole and a former Governor on several occasions."* He felt that clemency should be granted at this time due to: the length of incarceration, the affidavit of the prosecutor, the dying declaration of George Wilhelm, the questionable credibility of Clarence Miller, written requests of the trial judge, and Charles Goldblum's exemplary prison record. Judge Ziegler had previously submitted two such letters.

Blood spatter pattern report by Herbert MacDonnell, Dir. Laboratory of Forensic Sciences

On December 13, 2000, Herbert Leon McDonnell, Director of the Laboratory of Forensic Science, a well-recognized blood spots expert, released his forensic report. He had reviewed the testimony of Ronald Freeman regarding his description of apparent bloodstains on the dashboard within the vehicle in this case. He stated:

- The description was sufficiently detailed for him to able to form a qualified opinion regarding the blood stains on the dashboard.
- There were a *"line of droplets"*, *"not a lot of blood"*, and *"discerned droplets and they started on the -towards the driver's side was the largest spot, and then they descended into smaller circles."*
- Each circle had a *"tail"* and the *"tail"* was facing toward the passenger side.
- Based on the description of the above findings the forensic scientist with known expertise in analysis of blood stains patterns, concluded:
- The description by Detective Freeman of blood spots arrayed in a line and not randomly was an accurate classical portrayal of cast-off bloodstain pattern, with the droplets' tails pointing towards the passenger's side which were ejected from left to right (from the driver side to the passenger side) and Detective Freeman recognized them as such in his testimony.
- The source of the cast-off blood spots with the above-oriented tails was some type of object such as a finger, a small club, a knife or a screw driver. The object would have to have been close to the dashboard when it was swung as the blood spatter could not have originated from such an object if it had been swung very far away from the dashboard, such as in the back seat area.

- The December 18, 2000 transcript of Toby Wolson describing repeatedly the pattern of blood spots as "*low force*" is incorrect both in term (the correct term is "*low velocity impact*") and in essence as "*low velocity*" impact could not likely have produced the bloodstain pattern that was described by Mr. Freeman. Low velocity impact describes an "*impact spatter*" which occurs during a beating or simply clapping the hands together when they are wet with blood, has a random distribution of spatter, and not a line of bloodstains as described by detective Freeman.
- It is almost a certainty that the stain pattern described by Detective Freeman did not result from an impact to "*a source of blood*"

Transcript of interview of Dr. Cyril Wecht by attorney Villanova
On November 22, 2012, Dr. Wecht was interviewed by attorney James Villanova, and James Ramsey, the lead investigator for Zeke Goldblum. Dr. Wecht stated that:

- He was never contacted by the district attorney's office, the defense attorney, or anyone else, and was not involved in the case, as Dr. Perper performed the autopsy and testified at trial.
- He states that in January 1996, he was contacted by the attorney representing Charles (Zeke) Goldblum about records at the Coroner's office pertaining to the case, and it was then for the first time, that it was brought to his attention that the records were no longer there, they had disappeared. He stated that in his experience that was very rare.
- He stated that the files are ordinarily kept at the Coroner's office and that there was no explanation at all as to what happened. He stated that he believed it should have been pursued in a more serious nature to find out who was the most likely person responsible.
- He stated he could not recall an entire file missing, and certainly not a case of a controversial nature that was being pursued by attorneys and which required a revisiting of files to wind up missing. He recalled that the

same file was missing from the District Attorney's office, and the Pittsburgh Police. He had never heard of any other file being missing from three separate places like that.

- He stated that the missing files included photographs of the blood spatter, and more importantly, statements that were made and obtained in the original investigation. Things which, with regard to Miller, allowed him to totally walk away and, to a very great extent, dump everything on Goldblum.

- He stated that *"it's just impossible with repeated stab wounds, especially instrumentality of that size producing very substantial wounds,"* that someone would not have blood come back on them. He notes that there was no blood on Zeke Goldblum's clothes, and that Miller admitted that there was blood on his clothes, and that he changed out of his clothes. Also, the blood spatters *"definitely move from left to right,"* so it fits with Miller sitting to the right of Wilhelm, as he's stabbing him, left to right.

- He stated that the blood spatters were more consistent with the movement of the shears in and out of Wilhelm's body, than aortic spurting from the wound itself.

- He stated that it was inexplicable that the defense attorney, Mr. Rothman, though he had not contacted the Coroner's office to further question Dr. Perper or himself, would not have consulted with other criminologists, blood spatter experts or forensic pathologists.

- He noted that the trial became an even bigger cost of labor, much bigger, with the son of a very distinguished Rabbi and an attorney on trial, than if it had been Clarence Miller on trial. *"There's no question that anybody, if you don't recognize, then you are being deliberately choosing to ignore the realities of this case...now I've got myself a big case, this is something special."*

- He stated that the photographs of the blood spatter on the dashboard, which were suddenly missing at the time of trial, would absolutely have been of assistance to anyone to show that those blood spatters could not have occurred from a person in the back seat.

- He stated that the defense attorney not raising the question at trial regarding the whereabouts of the photos, was *"totally, totally, totally incomprehensible and unacceptable, and from the standpoint of a criminal defense attorney, unforgivable. It is gross, gross malpractice; there is no other way to say it, gross incompetence."* *(Note:* Wecht was wrong on this *issue.* Rothman had no idea that additional photos were taken. As far as Rothman knew, there was only one photo taken of the interior of the car. It was a wide shot, and not a close-up of the dashboard.)

- He stated that this case *"was truly unique..."* in which the trial judge, a very distinguished judge who went on to become the Chief Judge of the local Federal Court, wrote a letter saying that he doesn't believe that Goldblum was the murderer. And that Peter Dixon, a veteran trial attorney and assistant DA who tried the case, had written a letter. He stated that *"I must truly say that this is the greatest travesty of justice that I have ever experienced not only in cases in which I have been involved, but cases I have followed, cases I am aware of..."*

- He further added that it was astounding that there had been no post-conviction hearing, and that the sentence was life without parole, and that the Pennsylvania Supreme Court had not heard the case, given the gross incompetence of the defense attorney.

Answers to Medico-legal questions

Based on the materials reviewed and to the best of my medical knowledge within a reasonable degree of medical certainty, I am replying to the following medico-legal questions, posed to me by attorney James Villanova:

1. Do you recall being assigned to carry out the autopsy of George Wilhelm in relation to his February 9ᵗʰ, 1976 homicide, in furtherance of your duties as the Chief Forensic Pathologist of Allegheny County?

The answer is affirmative, and the review of the performed autopsy report and my testimony transcript has refreshed my memory as to the details of the case.

2. Miller testified that Goldblum initiated the assault by striking Wilhelm in the back of the head with a wrench. An abrasion was found on the right forehead of the victim. Considering that Goldblum allegedly attacked Wilhelm from the rear seat, is this not an incongruous location for the blunt force abrasion? Generally speaking, what would be the most likely location for a blow to land on a victim's head if a blunt instrument was being swung from directly behind in an enclosed space, such as a vehicle?

The most likely location of a blunt force injury on the head of a driver, assaulted by a rear seat occupant with a blunt force object, would be on the victim's back of the head or side of the head. An attack on a driver sitting in a front seat by an attacker sitting behind the victim in a rear seat, would be extremely unlikely to produce only a single blunt force injury, a minor abrasion (scratch) on the right forehead of the victim. In the case of Mr. Wilhelm, an attack from the back would have required at least one single contusion or abrasion on the back of the head, and no such injury was observed. Furthermore it is highly unlikely and there is no good reason why a back seat assailant would hit the forehead area of the driver rather the exposed back of the latter's head.

Furthermore, in the police report, Miller claimed that Goldblum hit George Wilhelm in the head with the wrench *"as soon as the ignition was turned off."* At trial, he claimed that *"several minutes passed"* before Zeke hit George.

Furthermore, as I testified at the trial on Mr. George Wilhelm's autopsy, the victim had multiple stabbing and cutting wounds, and only a minor bruise of the forehead, consistent with contusion/abrasion with no disruption of skin (laceration) which could not have resulted in significant bleeding within the car.

However, he had a small stab wound of the forehead which in view of the drop-off blood pattern in the car, and Goldblum's testimony that after Miller exited the car, he was holding bloodied shears, are an indication that Wilhelm started to be stabbed by Miller while he was still in the car, because of the line of drop-off blood stains was horizontal and from left to right.

3. When a blunt force instrument, such as a wrench or a bat, is used to strike a victim in the head, how common is it for that instrument to have no blood, hair or skin tissue on it?

When an individual is struck on his head with a significant force with a blunt force instrument, such as a wrench or a bat, is very common to observe on the weapon, blood and/or hair of the victim or fragments of crushed tissue.

4. According to Freeman's cross-examination by Rothman, Freeman noticed a line of horizontal blood inside the driver's side window, about halfway up the window (pages 1236-1238 of the trial transcript). What sort of weapon would most likely produce a horizontal line of blood? A blade? A blunt instrument? A wound gushing blood?

The pattern of blood spattering described by detective Freeman is a "Cast-off Pattern", a bloodstain pattern resulting from blood drops projected or thrown onto a surface by a bloody object in motion. Other names used are Spatter Family (linear cast-off), Spatter (projection mechanism cast-off) and Spatter Groups (swing cast-offs)

Cast-off blood spattering is typically linear and therefore can indicate the directionality of the moving object causing them, *i.e.* vertical, horizontal or oblique, and at the end of the trajectory there is a "tail pattern" of smaller blood spots. So, for example, if an assailant is swinging a bloody weapon from side to side, horizontally, he will create a horizontal, linear pattern of blood drops, and if the "tail" (of smaller drops) is on the right this would indicate that the moving bloody object that created the drop-off pattern, moved horizontally from left to right.

From the drop-off blood pattern, one cannot deduce what was the moving object, except through circumstantial evidence. In Mr. Wilhelm's death case, most likely the drop-off blood pattern was from the bloodied shears, as also indicated by Goldblum's testimony, that as soon as Miller exited from the car, he was holding bloodied shears. The fact that eventually Miller confessed to have actively participated in the attack on George Wilhelm by holding him down, supports the veracity of Goldblum's observation, and is consistent with the drop-off pattern of blood inside the car.

In Mr. Wilhelm's case, the pattern of blood spot present in the car was in a line of horizontal blood spots with "tails" oriented to the right, clearly indicating a pattern of cast-off blood spots, flung from the left to right, either from a fling of the weapon, the victim's or assailant's hand or from an injury of the victim's body. However, in my opinion and in the opinion of the renowned blood expert (Mr. McDonnell), with which I agree, the cast-off blood pattern was very close to the front of the vehicle, and could not have originated from an assailant seated in the back of a car. Furthermore, drop-off blood stains are, as noted above, produced by a moving or swinging object or weapon and not by a wound gushing blood.

5. According to Freeman's testimony at trial, he noted "discernible droplets" of blood, which "...descended into smaller circles..." in "...what is called "a tail" and the "tail" was "facing toward the passenger side of the automobile and that indicated that the blood came from left to right... or traveled from the driver's side of the automobile to the passenger's side of the automobile." (Pages 1218-1219 of the trial transcript). Based on your past experience, what is the most likely cause of such a blood pattern? A blade being flicked? Blood spurting from a wound? Is it likely that such a blood pattern could be caused by a blunt force blow?

(See also answer to question number 4, above). The very small amount of blood present and its pattern is consistent with cast-off drops from a sharp wound caused by a cutting weapon, and not by a significant blunt force trauma that would cause bruising and not a cast-off blood pattern, as long as the skin and underlying tissues were not lacerated. In this case, no blunt force lacerations of skin of the head were seen. The pattern of the blood spots was that of blood cast off from the flicking weapon, and not from blood spurting from the wound originating from an artery. As no blood or hairs were found on the wrench, it is very unlikely that the cast off originated from it, unless the weapon was wiped.

6. Can you draw any conclusions as to who the most likely assailant was, based on this tailing blood spatter pattern and its location?

The most likely source of the blood would be from an assailant using a sharp weapon seated in the front passenger seat because if the right front passenger struck the driver to the left, then the bleeding in the impact area will smudge the weapon with blood and when the bloody weapon is flung backward and horizontally, it would create a drop-off pattern from left to right.

7. Miller testified that Goldblum initiated the assault with a single strike of a monkey wrench to the back of the head, and then stabbed Wilhelm to death outside of the car. If this is true, would you expect to see the blood spatter described by Detective Freeman "inside" of the vehicle?

The answer is negative (See answers above to question number 4, 5 and 6). Furthermore, the pattern of cast-off blood on the dashboard could not have originated from a back assailant located significantly away way from the dashboard.

8. On page 5 of his March 2nd, 1976 interview with Detective Freeman, Miller stated "that Wilhelm fell forward after Zeke (Goldblum) struck him and hit his nose on the steering wheel of the car, causing it to bleed." If an individual were to forcefully strike their nose on the steering wheel of a car, thus causing it to bleed, would the steering wheel reasonably be expected to have blood on it?

An impact on the back of the head propelling a victim to fall forward, striking his nose against the steering wheel would have resulted in substantial nasal bleeding, and such bleeding was not observed on or around the steering wheel.

9. Freeman testified at trial that he observed no blood on the vehicle's steering wheel (page 1238 of the trial transcript). In your opinion, does this observation cast doubt on the validity of Miller's recollection of the assault? If not, could you please explain why?

Freeman did not see any significant amount of bleeding on the steering wheel and therefore this negative finding clearly casts a doubt on the veracity and validity of Miller's story. See answer to question no. 8, above.

10. According to Miller's testimony, Wilhelm fell from the vehicle after being struck with a monkey wrench, and Goldblum began to stab him as he leaned against the driver's side door, before sliding to the ground (trial transcript page 675, Miller-direct). If, while leaning against the driver's side door of the vehicle, Wilhelm was repeatedly stabbed with the 7-inch blade of the murder weapon, would you reasonably expect blood to be present on the driver's side door?

The answer is affirmative. If Wilhelm would have been stabbed while leaning against the driver's door, one would have expected to see at least some blood smudged, smeared or cast-off on the door.

11. During Detective Freeman's cross-examination, he testified that no blood was observed on the outside of the car (trial transcript page 1201, Freeman-direct, and pages 1242-1243, Freeman-cross). Does the absence of blood on the outside of the driver's side door conflict with Miller's contention that Wilhelm was stabbed repeatedly while leaning against the door? Would it be reasonable to say that Detective Freeman's testimony casts doubt on the factual validity of Miller's version of the assault? If not, please explain why?

As noted above, the absence of any blood on the driver's side door while Wilhelm was stabbed repeatedly while leaning against the door, conflicts with Miller's version of the assault that Wilhelm was stabbed repeatedly while leaning against the door, and therefore Detective Freeman's testimony invalidates Miller's story. Most likely, Miller concocted this story in order to exculpate himself and to place the murder far away from his front passenger seat. However, Miller's version of the attacks was eventually totally invalidated by his confession after the trial that he was physically involved in the attack and stabbing death of George Wilhelm.

12. During this murder, both of the primary suspects were located in an isolated space (the vehicle where the assault occurred), with the suspects in two distinct positions (Goldblum in back behind the victim driver and Miller in front

right passenger seat). In similar cases, can you recall if it was standard practice by the prosecuting attorney to ask who you thought committed the assault during your testimony at trial as the pathologist?

Prosecuting attorneys do not commonly ask me (or any forensic pathologist for this matter) who specifically committed the murder, although it may happen. However, they may ask whether, in view of the forensic evidence, an assailant located in a particular position or place might have physically committed the criminal act or were more likely to commit it.

13. Were there ever any circumstances that caused you to testify at trial as to who a likely assailant was after your autopsy examinations? If so, what were they?

The answer is affirmative: both in term of confirming a specific assailant or excluding a specific innocent person. For example such cases which I worked on included:

In confirming a specific assailant:
- Matching an irregular fingernail mark on the neck of a strangled victim to a partially broken finger nail of the assailant.
- Matching, like in a puzzle, a skin fragment found at the scene of murder, to a lacerated wound on the suspect's thumb.
- In excluding a specific accused as being the murderer:
- By proving that a father accused of homicide for assaulting his baby child who had only minor injuries (alleged to have been from a fall) and a severe concussion, was innocent. My examination and evaluation of the case substantiated that the child died of myocarditis and sickle cell anemia, which were missed by the initial forensic pathologist who performed the autopsy. The initial pathologist acknowledged his mistake.
- By showing that an 11 year-old young girl accused of assaulting and killing a baby brought in her home for babysitting was innocent and the baby had prior old abuse injuries and healing injuries which could not have been developed during the babysitting stay, and that

some bruises on the body, claimed to be acute were not so, and did not result in blood staining of the child's clothing.

14. Is it common practice, generally speaking, for prosecuting attorneys to ask you general questions on the phenotype of the likely assailant (*i.e.* tall or short? Physically powerful or average in build? Left or right-handedness?)

It is common practice for prosecuting attorneys to ask me the height and weight of the victim, and less common to ask me the size and weight of an assailant, unless during a hypothetical, addressing whether the phenotype was reflective of the capability or lack thereof for the defendant to carry out a homicide. Left or right handedness of an assailant was asked from me very rarely.

15. If it was uncommon for you to testify as to the identity, location, or phenotype of the assailant at trial, did you ever advise the police or prosecuting attorneys on these matters before trial, during the investigation? If so, how common was this practice?

It was uncommon for me to testify as to the identity or phenotype of an assailant at trial. I may be asked hypothetically whether an assailant of a certain body build might have committed the criminal assault, or whether an assailant by virtue of medical conditions or drug intoxication could have committed the criminal assault. I may be asked for the likely location of a defendant during a criminal assault or whether the age of injuries were consistent with a defendant's alibi.

On the other hand, police, prosecutors and criminal investigators very often discussed with me before trial matters relating to the identity, location or phenotype of a specific assailant.

16. Did either Dixon or Freeman ask you specifically who (front passenger or rear passenger) would have most likely inflicted the wounds inside the car?

This is a very, very old case, and I do not have any recollections about specific discussions in the above case either with Detective Freeman or Mr. Dixon, the prosecuting attorney.

17. If so, do you remember advising them whether the more likely assailant was sitting in the back or the front of the vehicle?

See answer no. 16 above.

18. If so, can you recall what reason they may have had for not asking you this question in front of a jury during the trial itself?

Obviously, I do not direct my examination or cross examination in criminal trials, and I do not speculate what was the reason of the parties for asking or not asking specific questions. In this case, I do not recall what the reason for Detecting Freeman or the prosecution for not asking the above question. However, in many cases I pondered why not either the prosecution or defense asked better probing questions. Clearly, in this case, both the police investigation and the prosecution's preparation and questioning were wanting, as they resulted in the wrongful conviction of Goldblum for murder instead of Miller, the belatedly confessed murderer who was named by the victim as being the assailant.

The detectives failed to ask Miller salient questions, for example, how it was possible for Goldblum to retrieve the murder weapons from below the front seat when he was seated in the back seat of the car for the first time and was not aware of the location of the weapons, did not attempt to verify Miller's gratuitous claim that the murder happened as a result of a monetary conflict between Goldblum and Wilhelm, because of money owed to Wilhelm. The police investigators' shortcomings were implicitly recognized (after the trial) in the sworn affidavit by Mr. Dixon, the prosecuting attorney at trial who characterized Goldblum's conviction as a *"Miscarriage of Justice."* Judge Ziegler, the sitting judge at the trial in his three letters to the Board of Clemency also asserted that Goldblum did not commit the murder but was only a passive observer, and that the jury wrongfully opted to convict Goldblum in spite of the victim's death declaration that Clarence Miller had attacked him, based on Miller's testimony. At the time of the trial, Judge Ziegler considered Miller's testimony highly *"suspect"* and non-credible, and clearly stated that if he would have been the trier of fact and not the jury, he would not have considered it. In retrospect, Judge Ziegler proved to be right in his assessment that Miller's testimony was suspect and not credible in claiming innocence in George Wilhelm's murder and accusing Charles Goldblum of having perpetrated it, as ultimately, Miller confessed that he was directly and physical involved in the assault on Wilhelm, though, true to form, he still pushed blame onto Goldblum and claimed he was involved as well. A claim disputed by the available evidence.

19. Based on your experience with similar cases you have dealt with in the past, namely, a violent and prolonged struggle in an enclosed space, how common is it for an assailant to escape such an assault with no defensive wounds?

In my experience as a forensic pathologist, I found that it is very uncommon in cases of a violent and relatively prolonged struggle in an enclosed space, when the assailant and the victim are close to each other, for an assailant to escape such an assault with no defensive wounds of his own, when grappling with and/or stabbing a victim.

20. When Clarence Miller and Charles Goldblum were arrested, it was noted that Miller had a number of scratches on his arms, hands, and face (Feb. 10th, 1976, Supp. Report by Condemy & Amity, page 4, para. 4). Such scratches are consistent with defensive wounds resulting from a struggle. Goldblum had no such wounds. Based on your past experience, is it rationally sound that Goldblum committed a violent and prolonged assault without receiving any defensive wounds? Is it rationally sound that Miller, if he was an innocent bystander as he claims, received such wounds?

In my opinion, the multiple scratches on Miller's hands, arms and face, in addition to a finger laceration, were highly consistent with defense wounds resulting from a fight or physical assault, and the investigators and prosecutors failed in their duty to confirm them, document them photographically, and ensure their evaluation by a forensic pathologist.

In view of the victim's (Wilhelm) dying declaration that very clearly designated Clarence Miller as the only stabbing assailant, coupled with fact that Miller eventually confessed to his direct physical involvement in the killing, makes the injuries present on Miller very likely to have been defense wounds. Miller's claim that those injuries were inflicted on him by a playful cat was very suspicious because playful cats may cause scratches (abrasions) but not also actual lacerations (tears of the skin), like the laceration present on Miller.

The lack of similar injuries on Mr. Goldblum (as well as his clothing that were not stained with blood, except in a minor spot of blood on a shirt cuff) is consistent with him not being the homicidal assailant of Wilhelm, but only a passive observer.

21. Based on the defensive wounds, who was the more likely assailant in the vehicle on February 9th, 1976?

Based on the presence of defense wounds on Mr. Miller and their absence on Mr. Goldblum, the more likely assailant in the vehicle on February 9, 1976 was Mr. Miller. This is certainly reinforced by both the death declaration of Wilhelm designating Miller as his assailant by his full name without mentioning at all Goldblum, and by Miller's belated confession that he homicidally assaulted Wilhelm.

22. What quantity and type of blood release occurs when the jugular vein has been stabbed? (A slow leak? Spurts?) Please give amount and rate.

It takes about 5 minutes to die from a cut of external jugular vein, 2 minutes from a cut of internal jugular vein and about one minute if both are cut. The fairly rapid blood loss from the jugular veins is due to their relative large size and the reflux of blood flowing back the other way because the valves in the jugular veins don't prevent the reflux of blood. The flow of blood is continuous and not in spurts. The total loss of a pound of blood from such injury is fatal. Lacerated or cut veins do not spurt like arteries, but result in a continuous flow leak, depending on the size of the involved vein. The loss of a pound of blood from a major vein such as the external jugular artery is fatal, unless timely stopped. Obviously, additional internal bleeding wounds may further accelerate the death. In this case, Mr. George Wilhelm had stab wounds injuries of aorta, lung, and liver with significant bleeding, both within chest and abdomen.

23. Having read relevant reports and testimony to the injuries suffered by the victim, would it be reasonable to say that the victim would have bled profusely during the assault?

The answer is affirmative, as also confirmed by the blood at the murder scene and by autopsy findings showing marked internal bleeding.

24. In dealing with similar cases in the past where a violent assault occurred in an enclosed space, did you find that the assailant's clothing usually ended up bloodied?

The answer is affirmative. In stabbing homicides, particularly but not exclusively in enclosed spaces, in which the assailant and victim are close to each other, like in the case of Wilhelm's stabbing, the clothing of the assailant would be blood-stained or smudged.

25. Having read the extent and violence of the injuries suffered by Mr. Wilhelm, would it be reasonable to say that an assailant in an enclosed space, such as the vehicle where the initial assault occurred, would have been covered in a significant amount of blood?

The answer is affirmative, especially in this case in which Mr. Wilhelm had multiple stab wounds which bled not only internally but externally, leaving substantial trails of blood at the scene.

26. The clothes Goldblum wore the evening of Wilhelm's murder were identified by Clarence Miller, Goldblum's wife and by Richard Kurutz (the eye witness from the parking garage who saw both men at the scene). They independently gave statements to the police as to what Goldblum was wearing that evening, and it was stipulated at trial that the clothes recovered by the police, were in fact, the clothes he wore the evening of the murder. They were one black topcoat, one navy blue blazer, a yellow dress shirt, one pair of grey slacks, one multi-colored tie. Considering the bloody nature of the assault, can you reasonably account for the absence of blood on Goldblum's clothing, in light of Miller's accusation that he was the assailant?

The virtual absence of blood spots on Goldblum's clothing, except for a spot of blood on his shirt that was so minimal that it could not have been further serologically analyzed, is definitely inconsistent with Miller's accusation that Goldblum was the assailant, and consistent with Goldblum not being involved in a criminal assault of Mr. Wilhelm. Furthermore, Mr. Goldblum did not try to get rid of and dispose of his clothing worn during the attack. On the other hand, Mr. Miller precipitously and expeditiously disposed of and washed some of the clothing he wore at the time of the assault.

Miller's above actions (especially in view of his belated confession that he was physically involved in the stabbing of Wilhelm), raise a very strong presumption that he did so because his clothing was extensively stained with Wilhelm's blood, and perhaps some of his own from the defense wounds Miller had.

Miller's belated acknowledgment that he was physically involved in the stabbing of Mr. Wilhelm implicitly substantiates that his clothing was significantly smeared with blood. His lying about the disposal of his clothing during the attack and his attempt to submit to the police other clothing than the one he was wearing at the time, make this determination even more substantial.

On the other hand, during Dr. Peter Marrone's (the Crime Lab director) direct examination at trial by ADA F. Peter Dixon, he clearly stated that he observed only a small blood smear on Goldblum's right sleeve, about one inch up from the cuff (trial transcript, Marrone direct, pages 1798-1800.) This was the only bit of blood found on Mr. Goldblum's clothes.

27. Considering the nature of the assault, the victim's wounds, and the amount of bleeding, one would expect this one small blood smear to be consistent with what you would expect to find on the assailant's clothing?

Considering the nature of the assault, the victim's wounds and the resulting amount of bleeding, one would expect significant blood staining on the assailant's clothing and not just the small blood smear on Goldblum's right shirt sleeve, above one inch from the cuff, which was even insufficient for laboratory testing. (See answer #26 above).

28. In light of Clarence Miller's ultimate admission that he disposed of his topcoat early the next morning after the murder

since it was stained with blood, does this not cast suspicion on him and raise doubt as to the validity of his testimony that Charles Goldblum committed the assault?

Definitely so. Clarence Miller's ultimate admission that he disposed of his topcoat on the night of the murder since it was stained in blood and subsequently washed his trousers, coupled with the dying declaration of Wilhelm that only Miller assaulted him without mentioning Goldblum at all, made when Wilhelm was clearly lucid (as he complained about pain and ask what was his condition), should have cast heavy suspicion at trial that indeed Miller was the killer and not Goldblum, who did not discard his clothing worn at the time of the assault and had only a small blood spot on a cuff of his shirt.

In retrospect, the ultimate admission of Miller definitively determines that his accusations against Goldblum were false, and Miller's claims to have been an innocent bystander trying to help the victim were clear, unadulterated and brazen perjury. Furthermore, Miller not only initially lied to the police that his clothing was not bloody, but compounded the lie. He gave the police the clothes he wore on the night of the murder, but they had been thoroughly washed by then.

Miller's ultimate admission of his involvement verifies the assumption that should have been raised at the trial that Miller's prompt disposal and discarding of his clothing at the time of the assault indicated that they were substantially or extensively stained with the blood, considering the multiple stab wounds sustained by Wilhelm, his extensive and severe external bleeding and the proximity of the assailant to the victim.

Viewed in retrospect, the above findings coupled with Miller's belated confession of being physically involved with the murder of George Wilhelm, do not only cast suspicion on him and the validity of his testimony that Charles Goldblum committed the assault, but totally demolish the foundation of Miller's testimony and makes it clear it was perjury.

Unfortunately, at the trial, the jury was swayed by the perjured testimony of Miller and by its antipathy for Goldblum in voting for Goldblum's conviction. It should be noted that a number of years after the trial, Judge Ziegler, who was the sitting judge at the trial, wrote no less than three consecutive letters to the Pennsylvania

Board on behalf of Charles Goldblum in which he emphatically stated among other reasons for releasing him from prison:

- *"Although the jury chose to believe Clarence Miller, and convict Mr. Goldblum of murder, I have been troubled for years by the dying declaration of the victim, 'Clarence – Clarence Miller did this to me.'"*
- *"The victim knew that he was dying, and he never mentioned the name of Charles Goldblum."*
- Judge Ziegler chose to *"emphasize that the victim's dying declaration namely, 'Clarence. Clarence Miller did this to me,' is the most unique dying declaration that I have encountered..."*
- *"In my opinion, Mr. Miller's testimony was suspect and frankly, if I was the fact finder (and the Jury) I would have rejected as unpersuasive much of the testimony of this individual."*
- *"In short, the murder conviction was based on the testimony of Miller and the jury's apparent dislike for Mr. Goldblum."*

29. According to the prosecuting attorney at the time of the Wilhelm murder trial, the assault on George Wilhelm was planned by Charles Goldblum. According to the trial testimony, the grass shears used in the assault was from the floor of the victim's vehicle (transcript page 691, Miller- direct), the gloves Goldblum allegedly used during the assault belonged to Miller and were found in the rear of the victim's car (transcript page 691, Miller- direct), and the assault occurred in a well-lit area (trial transcript pages 1188-1189, Freeman- direct) near the elevator bank in a public garage, which was attached to Gimbel's, a department store open for evening shopping at the time of the assault. Based on your experience with thousands of prior homicides, are these the hallmarks of a planned, calculated assault?

No. The assault on Wilhelm is clearly not consistent with a planned, calculated attack because it occurred in a public garage, during shopping hours, when the victim's cries for help could be heard by the public, the victim may be promptly found and the assailant observed. As a matter of fact, this was actually what happened; Wilhelm's cries for help were heard by a garage worker (John Regan), who went to help him, and Miller and Goldblum were seen at the scene by another witness (Richard Kurutz).

Miller's confession after the trial that he physically participated in the stabbing attack on Mr. Wilhelm, makes ludicrous his trial testimony that his gloves, which had some hair of his inside (and no hairs of Goldblum), were given by him to Goldblum shortly before the attack. In view of the belated confession of Miller that he physically participated in the stabbing attack against Wilhelm, it is very likely that he was wearing his gloves. It would be absurd to conceive that when Miller carried out the assault, he would give his gloves to Goldblum, instead of protecting his own hands.

30. Out of the thousands of cases you worked throughout your career, can you recall, generally, how many times photographic evidence was not available at trial due to it being misplaced? If you cannot, would it be fair to say that it is so rare you cannot recall any instances specifically?

I do not remember the number of times, but it rarely happened, and I do not remember any specific case.

31. Is it standard operating procedure for the on-scene Crime Lab technicians or forensic examiners to photograph all blood stains and spattering at the scene of the crime?

The answer is affirmative. Police investigators and detectives, and the forensic examiners at a murder scene mark routinely the location and presence of blood spots at a murder scene and document them by both descriptions and photographs. Failure to do so is clear professional negligence.

32. If there were blood stains or spatters present at the scene that were not photographed, would you consider this an inadequate cataloguing of the physical evidence?

The failure to photograph blood stains or spatter found at the scene of a homicide constitute a clearly inadequate cataloguing of physical evidence.

33. In your opinion, is it harmful to a defendant's case to not have access to photographic crime scene evidence at the time of trial?

Clearly, yes. Lack of access to photographic scene evidence may result in misinterpretation of the blood-spattering findings and may substantially or fatally undermine the chance of a credible defense, and cause or contribute to a miscarriage of justice.

34. Would you classify the losing of key photographic evidence in a capital murder case to be sloppy or unprofessional work by the prosecuting body whose task it was to maintain critical evidence?

Unexplained loss of key photographic evidence in a capital murder case is clear evidence of sloppy, unprofessional or negligent work by the legal custodian of such critical evidence.

35. Throughout your career, were you ever involved in a murder case in which, absent photographic evidence, interpretations or analysis of blood spatter evidence was given based on written or verbal description?

Yes, but very rarely.

36. Do you recall working with Dr. Cyril Wecht during your time at the Allegheny County Coroner's Office?

Yes. I closely worked with Dr. Wecht between 1972-1980 years. I was the Chief Forensic Pathologist and he was the elected Coroner of Allegheny County.

37. In your opinion, was Dr. Wecht a qualified, reliable and trustworthy professional during your common work at Allegheny County Coroner's Office?

In all cases whether criminal or civil in which I worked with Dr. Wecht during my tenure as Chief Forensic Pathologist (1972 -1980) when he was the Coroner, I found him to be a qualified, reliable, and trustworthy professional.

38. Would you agree with Dr. Wecht's assessments as to the relevance of the blood evidence both found in the vehicle and the absence of blood on Charles Goldblum's clothes, found

on pages 11-13 of Dr. Wecht's November 22nd, 2012 interview? If not, please explain why?

My independent review on the relevance of blood evidence found in the vehicle and the absence of blood on the clothes of Charles Goldblum is congruent and consistent with above noted Dr. Wecht's statements, findings and opinions.

39. In light of the case materials provided and the affidavits and letters of F. Peter Dixon, Judge Donald Ziegler, and Dr. Cyril Wecht, would you feel comfortable agreeing with their assessment that Charles Goldblum was likely innocent of the stabbing death of George Wilhelm? If not, why?

The answer is affirmative. I do agree with F. Peter Dixon's, Judge Donald Ziegler's, and Dr. Cyril Wecht's assessments and statements included in their affidavits and letters, that Charles Goldblum was likely innocent of the stabbing death of George Wilhelm. As a matter of fact, I do not ever recall a case in which both the prosecution and the sitting judge disclosed belatedly after the trial, in public documents, that the prosecution and the conviction of a homicide defendant by a jury was wrong. Mr. Dixon, who was the prosecutor at the time of Goldblum's trial, explicitly stated in his sworn affidavit that the jury's conviction of Goldblum in Wilhelm homicidal death was: *"a miscarriage of justice."*

40. In your time working with law enforcement, how many times have entire investigative files turned up missing?

Very rarely, if ever. It is not impossible, because if, for example, a law enforcement official legitimately takes an entire investigative file out of his office, this file may subsequently be lost or stolen. However, during my years as a forensic pathologist, I do not recall any such particular case whether explainable or not. Misplaced or missing files or documents are usually retrieved.

42. Throughout your career working on murder investigations, how many times have files from the Coroner's office, the Mobile Crime Unit and the Police department turned up missing on the same case?

Never, to my recollection, was I aware of a case in which files of a homicide were simultaneously missing from the files of the Coroner's Office, the Mobile Crime Unit, and the Police Department.

Discussion of evidence

After reviewing the above summarized documentation and evidence, it is my professional opinion, within a reasonable degree of medical certainty, that the stabbing murder of George Wilhelm was not committed by Charles Goldblum but by Miller alone for the following reasons:

Physical evidence exculpatory of Goldblum and inculpatory of Miller: Miller's testimony at trial was inconsistent with physical evidence, because of the following findings:

1. Blood spattering in the victim's car inconsistent with Miller's testimony at trial that the assault was initiated by Goldblum hitting Miller with a blunt object and subsequently stabbed him outside the car, while Miller helplessly observed the stabbing. The relatively minor injury to Wilhelm's forehead is also inconsistent with a significant blunt force injury from a rear seat assailant or with dropped-off cast blood pattern. Furthermore, Miller changed repeatedly his statement about the wrench in the police report. Miller stated that he knew that George kept the wrench and shear in the car under the front seat. He specifically mentioned: the grass shears were used several times, prior to the attack, by him and Wilhelm for putting up political signs, and *"it was right in the back of the front seat, like in the back in the front."* At the trial, he initially said he wasn't sure if it was a wrench in Goldblum's hand, and then later said, it was the same wrench that George kept in the car. Miller never explained how it came that the murder weapons used (shears and wrench), whose location under the car's front seat he knew, could have come into Goldblum's hands, who was for the first time in Wilhelm's car. Before Goldblum's trial, the investigators should have asked Miller this obviously important question.

2. Goldblum was for the first time in Wilhelm's car, and obviously did not know the location of the shears and wrench and could not see them because they were under in the front sitting area of the car.

3. It would be absurd to believe that when he carried out the assault, Miller would give his gloves to Goldblum, instead of concealing his own hands.

4. Miller stated that Goldblum repeatedly stabbed Wilhelm while the latter was positioned against the car door. Why was there no blood smearing at all on the outside of the driver's door or anywhere else on the exterior?

5. Miller's statement that he gave Goldblum his own gloves to wear before the assault, is clearly a lie, as the gloves contained hair from Miller and not from Goldblum, and in view of Miller's belated post-trial confession that he was indeed physically involved in the stabbing of Wilhelm. It would be absurd to conceive that when he carried out the homicidal assault, Miller would give his gloves to Goldblum, instead of protecting his own hands.

6. Goldblum had a minimal amount blood on one cuff of his shirt, which was inconsistent with a close-by assailant stabbing a victim who bled profusely, especially from a cut of the jugular vein, known to cause massive bleeding. On the other hand, Mr. Miller, who confessed after the trial that he was physically involved with the stabbing of Wilhelm, hurried to destroy his clothing because they were bloody, as he clearly admitted to the police.

7. The presence of wounds on Miller's face, hand, and wrist, which very well could have been defense wounds (especially considering his belated confession of involvement) and which unfortunately were never photographed and assessed by a forensic pathologist.

8. Miller's claim that Goldblum stabbed Wilhelm repeatedly who was leaning against the car driver's door is non-credible, as the car's door didn't have even a minimal smudge of blood.

9. Furthermore, Miller claimed that Goldblum repeatedly stabbed Wilhelm as he was crawling away, dragging his leg on the ground. But there was no blood trail around the

car to the far wall, although the victim bled profusely from multiple stab wounds. There was only a small amount to the rear of the car, then a much larger amount by the wall over which Wilhelm fell to the level below. Most likely the wall was where Wilhelm was additionally stabbed by Miller.

10. Miller contended that what precipitated the murder was the fact that Goldblum owed Wilhelm money, but according to Goldblum. The opposite was true, and the fateful meeting on the day of murder and the murder of Wilhelm that followed were because of money owed to Wilhelm by Miller, who had defrauded him in an phony land deal. The police never questioned relatives, close associates or friends of Wilhelm to determine the actual truth. This was a crucial failure, because in accepting Miller's testimony that Goldblum had been the attacker (now evident to have been perjurious because of Miller's confession of his involvement in stabbing Wilhelm), the jury implicitly accepted Miller's testimony of Goldblum's alleged motivation for the murder, which was equally perjurious.

11. Miller lied repeatedly to the police investigators regarding his clothing he wore at the time of the assault, and unreasonably denied that his gloves were not worn by him during the assault.

12. Miller very likely lied in claiming that Goldblum was involved in a fraudulent land scheme, when he and an associate defrauded Wilhelm, and then refused to return the money. Miller acknowledged that they were the only ones who spoke with and contacted Wilhelm, and then refused to return the money given to them by Wilhelm. Wilhelm was obviously very upset with Miller because of that. There was no reason for Wilhelm to be upset with Goldblum as Miller claimed. There is no evidence at all implicating Goldblum in the fraudulent scheme except for Miller's statement that he shared some of the profit with Goldblum. Furthermore, Goldblum testified that he never saw Wilhelm prior to the day of the attack. Mr. Dixon, the prosecutor in the case, in his signed affidavit after the

trial, specifically stated: *"I have also concluded that it is very unlikely that Charles Goldblum participated in the land fraud perpetrated against George Wilhelm or that George Wilhelm participated in the arson of Mr. Goldblum's restaurant."*

After his arrest, Clarence Miller underwent a psychiatric examination and was diagnosed as having *"a personality disorder"*. It is well known that people with personality disorders have little concern for truth and no reluctance for lying and some are inventive pathological liars. Miller definitely fits the profile of a pathological liar as documented by the following findings:

a. Miller acknowledged that he defrauded, prior to the trial at least two people, Charles Goldblum and George Wilhelm, and a Federal Agency, and he was being investigated by the FBI. Miller admitted to police investigators that "he had cheated, planned, and schemed against George Wilhelm during his lifetime."

b. On the day of the assault, Miller lied to Wilhelm that the money would be returned to him by Manella, a fictitious person impersonated by one of Miller's co-conspirators in the fraudulent land deal. On the day of the murder, Miller lied and told Wilhelm that he tried repeatedly to telephone Manella and was unsuccessful in contacting him, and that thereafter he will re-pay the owed money in 2-3 years. Wilhelm was very upset at Miller. Miller reversed the roles and falsely claimed that the debt was due to Wilhelm.

Furthermore, before belatedly confessing to his involvement in the murder of George Wilhelm, both during the police investigation before Goldblum's trial and in his trial testimony, Clarence Miller constructed a web of lies, apparently based on three cardinal principles: primarily, that he will assign his own criminal actions to others, he will alter crucial evidence or make it unavailable, and either claim to have a poor memory of the events or that he did not know why he would do some actions which might have incriminated him. In addition to the lies noted above, there many more lies, some which are listed below:

1. Miller lied that Wilhelm did the arson for Goldblum, when in fact he, Miller, carried out the arson of Goldblum's restaurant. (Goldblum clearly stated that he did not know Wilhelm at the time of the arson and met him for the first time the day before the murder).
2. Miller lied that Goldblum shared in the money from the land fraud on Wilhelm, when in fact Miller inadvertently acknowledged that the fraud was perpetrated by him and two of his associates, without Goldblum's participation.
3. Miller lied in his statement that the meeting between Miller, Wilhelm and Goldblum, was scheduled because Wilhelm demanded money owed from Goldblum when in fact the meeting was done because of Wilhelm's demands that Miller re-pay the money for the fraudulent land deal.
4. Miller most likely lied when he stated that Goldblum asked him for his gloves and was wearing them while attacking Wilhelm: a claim which became ludicrous in view of Miller's confession that the indeed was physically involved in the stabbing death of Mr. Wilhelm.
5. In view of Miller's belated confession that he physically participated in stabbing Wilhelm to death, it is clear that he perjured himself during his sworn testimony at trial when he swore he had only been a frightened, passive observer, that he responded to the victim's cries for help and even tried somehow to save him.
6. Miller further lied when he stated that his trousers happened to be blood-stained *"from (him) trying to help the victim."*
7. Miller claimed that he saw Goldblum taking out the shears and the wrench from under the front seat: How this could happen?

8. Miller was in the front passenger seat and did not claim that he turned back his head to see Goldblum. It was the first time that Goldblum had been in Wilhelm's car, and he did not know where the shears and wrench were stored. If those objects were under the front seat, they were unlikely to be detected from the back seat, and furthermore Miller never said he told Goldblum where to find them.

9. In view of Miller's confession, and his blood-soiled clothing, it is most likely that Miller lied when he claimed that his scratches and finger laceration had been caused by a playful cat. Cats may scratch but do not cause skin laceration unless they bite, and most cats don't have rabies, so they don't bite their owners

10. Miller lied when he stated that he believed that Wilhelm and Goldblum were lovers, when in fact Goldblum met Wilhelm personally for the first time at their meeting the day before the homicide on February 8, 1976.

11. Miller stated initially that he saw Goldblum hitting Wilhelm but was unaware of the nature of the hitting object. Why could that be when Miller previously testified seeing Goldblum retrieving the wrench and shears from underneath the front seat? Clearly it was much easier for a front occupant to retrieve those objects.

12. Miller's statement that Wilhelm was hit by Goldblum and fell forward against the steering and hurt his nose, that it started to bleed, is also very likely a lie. How could blow impacts to the nose cause rather copious bleeding, and yet no blood spots or smears were seen on the steering wheel or in its vicinity.

13. In view of Miller's belated confession that he was physically involved in the stabbing of Wilhelm, it is clear that Miller lied when he responded to a question during the investigation: "Why would Wilhelm the victim, solely designate in his dying declaration only Miller, by his full name - *Clarence Miller*- as being the assaulter," Miller's answer was clearly a lie, when he stated: *"That I don't know. The only thing I could figure is George figured that I - because I didn't help him, I just stood there and let, let,*

let Zeke (Goldblum) stab him" The truth was that Miller knew very well why Wilhelm designated him as the attacker; Miller confessed later that indeed he had assaulted Wilhelm and therefore Wilhelm's dying declaration was true when it designated him as the murderer.

14. Miller obviously lied by claiming ignorance when he was asked by the Police why he discarded his topcoat he wore at the time, throwing it in a in a garbage truck following the homicidal attack on Wilhelm. He disingenuously answered: *"Well I was – I don't know why I did it. I just threw it – and ah, I just did it, that's all."*

15. In view of the belated confession of Clarence Miller that he *was involved in the stabbing of* Mr. Wilhelm, it is crystal-clear that Miller lied repeatedly to investigators and to the examining psychiatrist and then perjured himself in court stating that he was only a passive observer and that Goldblum committed the assault. He embellished his lies by stating that he did not intervene because he *"had never seen anybody do anything like that before"* and *"was scared."* He further lied, stating in court testimony that he tried to help the victim and that after the murder, piously claiming he *"had difficulty sleeping (because) I seen a man getting killed, Sir."*

16. Miller attempted to suborn a trial witness, Cornelius Kelly (an acquaintance of Miller) to commit perjury. As noted above, when Kelly was asked during the re-direct examination by Mr. Dixon – the Assistant County District Attorney- whether *"did anyone suggest to him that he should testify falsely."* He replied: *" Well, let me think a second. Yeah. Clarence said once "I'll tell you what to say." I said "You ain't tell me nothing to say, I'm going to say it the way it is."*

17. Uncontested declaration or statements. The death declaration of Mr. Wilhelm to the emergency medical team that he had been attacked by Miller, mentioning twice his name: *"Clarence...Clarence Miller did this to me,"* without mentioning at all Goldblum's name as an attacker. The first time after being found following the

stabbing, Wilhelm stated just *"Clarence did it"* and when asked to repeat, Wilhelm repeated that Clarence Miller had done it. It was clear that at the time of his death declaration's statement Wilhelm was lucid, as subsequently before dying he complained of pain and inquired about his medical condition.

18. The belated confession of Miller while imprisoned, that in fact he was physically involved in stabbing Wilhelm, although he claimed that Goldblum participated in the assault, although that had been only one stabbing weapon (then grass half shears shears) that was used in the attack, and Miller did not claim that he passed the weapon to Goldblum, or that Goldblum passed the stabbing weapon to him.

19. Well-reasoned reports by recognized national and international forensic experts: Dr. Cyril Wecht and Dr. Michael Baden, forensic pathologists, Dr. Henry Lee – a criminalist ,and Mr. Herbert McDonnell – an authority in the field of blood splatter interpretation, documented that the physical evidence point to Miller as the assailant and not to Goldblum. The findings observed independently by the forensic experts are consistent with my findings and conclusions as outlined in this report.

20. Failures of the investigating and/or prosecuting authorities including:

21. Failure to evaluate thoroughly the reliability of Miller's statements, and ask him critical questions, e.g. Miller acknowledged knowing that the grass shears and wrench were under front seats of Wilhelm's car but was never asked how come that they ended, as Miller claimed, in the hands of Goldblum, a rear seat passenger.

22. Failure to verify the truth of Miller's statement that Goldblum committed the murder at the fateful meeting on the evening of the murder and that Goldblum's motivation for murder was money owed by Goldblum to Wilhelm, which Goldblum was unwilling to repay. Miller was in fact the one that owed money to Wilhelm for the fraudulent land deal and was unwilling to repay him. The police failed to question relatives or friends of Wilhelm to verify

what the reason for the meeting was, and who owed money to whom at the time.

23. Failure to document photographically blood spatter patterns at the murder scene.

24. An unusual and inexplicable occurrence of disappearance after the trial of important documentary evidence off all three investigative custodian agencies: Coroner's Office, the Police Department, and the Mobile Crime Unit's Office.

25. Failure of the initial Defense attorney at trial to secure expert forensic opinion in the evaluation of forensic evidence.

26. Years later a sworn affidavit by Mr. Dixon, the prosecuting attorney at Goldblum's trial, stated that he was convinced, based on additional evidence which he had access after the trial, that Goldblum was innocent of the murder, was not involved in the land fraud and that his conviction was in truth *"a miscarriage of justice."*

27. Judge Donald Ziegler, who was the sitting judge (and became subsequently a Federal judge) in Goldblum's trial, wrote letters on Goldblum's behalf to the Clemency Board in January 1989, January 1994, and December 1998. In his letters Judge Ziegler clearly stated that he intervened in Goldblum's case because:

28. *"Although the jury chose to believe Clarence Miller, and convict Mr. Goldblum of murder, I have been troubled for years by the dying declaration of the victim: "Clarence – Clarence Miller did that to me."* The judge added: *"It is a moral and legal precept that a person is presumed to speak the truth when he is faced with death. The victim (George Wilhelm) knew he was dying and he never mentioned the name of Charles Goldblum."*

Furthermore, Judge Ziegler:

- Characterized the death declaration of George Wilhelm as being *"the most unique dying declaration that he encountered"* during his career.

- Unambiguously stated: *"In short, the murder conviction was based on the testimony of Miller and the jury's apparent dislike of Mr. Goldblum."*

- Stated: *"In my opinion, Mr. Miller's testimony was suspect and quite frankly, if I was the fact finder (and not the jury), I would have rejected as unpersuasive much of the testimony of this individual."*

- Stated that both the evidence in the case as well as an affidavit received from Mr. Dixon, the prosecutor at the trial, clearly indicated that Mr. Goldblum did not commit the murder. In his December 14, 1998 letter to the Board of Pardons, Judge Ziegler literally quoted the statement in Dixon's affidavit: *"Charles Goldblum had nothing to do with the murder of George Wilhelm, other than being a frightened witness and an accessory after the fact."* Judge Ziegler added that the *"mere presence at the scene does not constitute evidence of complicity in a homicide and there may be merit to the version of homicide as stated by Mr. Goldblum."*

In fact, the Judge's letters proved correct in retrospect, labeling Miller's testimony as "suspect" and non-credible in the view of Miller's belated confession that he indeed was involved in the stabbing of George Wilhelm. The occurrence of such public post-trial admission by both the prosecutor and the trial judge is rather unheard of, and is great testimony to their conscience and moral integrity. The clear implication of the documents submitted by Mr. Dixon and Judge Ziegler, the prosecution and conviction of Goldblum for error were a grave mistake, for which they felt bad, and I am sure if they would have been able to go back in time, they would undoubtedly correct it.

Conclusion:
After reviewing the voluminous documentation listed at the beginning of my report, it is my professional opinion within a reasonable degree of medical certainty that Mr. Goldblum did not commit the stabbing assault of Mr. George Wilhelm, that Clarence Miller who was named by the victim in a dying declaration, indeed

carried out the homicidal attack on George Wilhelm, who ultimately confessed that he was involved in the murder, and that indeed Mr. Goldblum had been a passive observer during the homicide and that conviction of homicide, based on the perjured testimony of Clarence Miller. Goldblum's trial and conviction for the stabbing murder of George Wilhelm were as frankly characterized in Mr. Peter Dixon's, the prosecuting attorney in Goldblum's trial, a clear "miscarriage of justice"

As discussed in detail in my report above, a confluence of all the forensic findings in the case unequivocally support this conclusion, some of the most salient including:

- The death declaration of the victim, Mr. George Wilhelm, who was clearly lucid and asserted twice that Clarence Miller was the assailant.

- Miller's significant and recurrent pattern of lying both to police investigators and during his trial testimony.

- Ultimately, the belated admission of Clarence Miller that he indeed was physically involved in the stabbing death of Mr. Wilhelm, uncovered that Miller's trial testimony in which he claimed being a frightened passive observer of the homicide and even tried to assist the victim, was very clearly perjury.

- The testimony of Charles Goldblum fit the forensic evidence and was consistent with a fight between Miller and Wilhelm in the car, with the scratches on Miller, which could very well have been inflicted during the fight, the laceration on Miller's finger, which could well have been a cut from his own weapon during the attack (a common defense wound seen on the hand of attackers with a sharp edge weapon). Although Goldblum did not see Miller stabbing Wilhelm in the car, he saw him immediately after exiting from the car holding a bloody knife, consistent with the stabbing occurring in the car and accordingly consistent with the drop off pattern of blood splatter on the car's dashboard from the bloodied stabbing weapon.

- The forensic evidence exculpatory for Charles Goldblum.

- Reports of three eminent forensic scientists that are independently consistent with the findings and conclusions of this report that the evidence pointed to Miller as having been the homicidal attacker of George Wilhelm, and not Charles Goldblum.

- The multiple failures of police investigators including: vigorously questioning Miller and verifying some of his crucial statements, including the ones blaming Goldblum for the stabbing of Wilhelm because of allegations that Goldblum owed money to Wilhelm and was unwilling to pay. In fact, the converse was true, and Miller was the one who owed money to Wilhelm. This issue could have been easily resolved and the truth determined, if friends or relatives of Goldblum had been questioned whether they know who owed money to Wilhelm. This never happened. Another failure was to press Miller about how Goldblum, who was for the first time in Wilhelm's car on the night of the murder, could have known that the shears and wrench were concealed under the car's front seat.

- Unexplained loss of significant entire case files, including blood stains photographs by all three custodial agencies of records (The Police, Mobile Crime Unit's Office and the Coroner's Office) is another significant and unprofessional failure.

- Judge Ziegler's letters to the Board of Pardons that Mr. Goldblum should not have been convicted, because of the clear dying declaration of the victim naming Miller as his assailant, and that Goldblum's conviction by the jury had been based on Miller's testimony, (now proven to be perjurious), and which the judge considered at the time of the trial to be suspect and non-credible, and which the judge would not have accepted if he would have been the trier of fact and not the jury.

- The affidavit of Peter Dixon, the prosecuting attorney in Goldblum's trial who, after reviewing additional evidence, unequivocally concluded that Mr. Goldblum was in fact not guilty of homicide, and had not been involved in the fraudulent land deal, and that Goldblum's conviction for murder in the death of George Wilhelm, was in fact: *"a miscarriage of justice."*

Joshua A. Perper M.D., LL. B., M.Sc. May, 2013

Post-conviction Proceedings (1976 to 2015)

Almost immediately after he was convicted of murdering George Wilhelm and being sentenced to life in prison, Zeke Goldblum began appealing the verdict. An extensive timeline of legal actions regarding his pursuit of justice appears at the end of this chapter.

The following text is taken from the Continuation Sheet of Zeke's 2009 Petition for Commutation. It briefly chronicles the progression of legal actions taken over the years, as well as a glimpse of what he has done during the decades he has spent in prison.

Appeals and Subsequent Events

At Miller's trial, which began 9 months after my trial concluded, Miller's attorney tried to have his statements to the police suppressed. The basis for his application for suppression was that Miller had been involved in an accident as a child from which he suffered brain damage. An expert psychologist and an expert psychiatrist testified to Miler's brain damage and resulting memory impairment. The attempt to suppress Miller's statements were unsuccessful, and he too was convicted of first-degree murder.

When my attorneys discovered this new evidence of Miller's mental condition, they filed Petition with the Supreme Court of Pennsylvania for a remand to the trial court for a hearing to determine whether or not I was entitled to a new trial based on after-discovered evidence. This request was denied.

After Miller's direct appeal was turned down, he filed a Petition under the Post Conviction Hearing Act, claiming that his lawyer was ineffective for not raising an insanity defense. Miller stated his position:

That the statements I gave to the police and signed that I saw Charles Goldblum stabb (sic) George Wilhelm are not true because at that point I blacked out and remember nothing. I wasn't even aware of my own existence let alone anything that happened to George Wilhelm.

We petitioned for remand again, and it was granted. Miller withdrew this petition on the advice of his attorney and the District

Attorney's Office. The District Attorney has never offered any explanation of what part they played in this and why they were advising Miller at this point.

At the hearing, the expert witnesses testified that Miller had a mental defect resulting from an accident as a child. They explained that Miller had an impaired memory that filled in memory lapses with "confabulation," the medical term for unconscious lying. According to the experts, Miller's test results showed a significant memory deficit.

The hearing went well, and my lawyers felt we would be granted a new trial. Unfortunately, they were wrong. We then retained a new lawyer who filed Post Conviction and Habeus Corpus Petitions. These too were unsuccessful.

In 1996, I filed a second Post Conviction Petition which questioned the manner in which the police investigation was conducted, destruction of evidence, and the failure of my trial lawyer to investigate the blood spatter evidence. One of our crime-scene experts told us that if the police had conducted a complete and objective investigation, the assailant could have been identified beyond question. This was not done, and no good explanation has been given.

Judge O'Brien turned down my petition without an evidentiary hearing. This decision was reversed on appeal and remanded for a hearing.

Judge O'Brien retired, and the case was assigned to Judge McDaniel, who took an unusual step. She only allowed my trial attorney, Dr. Wecht, and Toby Wolson, an expert for the Commonwealth, to testify. She did not allow Dr. Lee, Dr. Baden, Dr. Wolf, Dr. McDonnell, or Mr. Balshy to testify. She also did not allow members of the Board of Pardons who had interviewed Clarence Miller to testify. We found out through a deposition that Miller had confessed his participation in Wilhelm's murder to Mr. Gigliotti and Attorney General Fisher, who were members of the Board of Pardons when I last applied.

Judge McDaniel stated that the remand order mandated excluding my witnesses even though there was no such limitation in the language of the remand order. The only limitation in the order was that the hearing was to cover only the claim of ineffective assistance of counsel. Neither she nor the Superior Court cited any prior case-authority to support her ruling.

In nearly all cases involving a claim of actual innocence, a petitioner is allowed to make a full record. I have never been given that opportunity. Because of this, there have been conclusions that are fundamentally wrong. Because we were not allowed to call our experts, the courts wrongly decided that no conclusion could be drawn from blood spatter unless there is a picture of the blood spatter. Toby Wolson, the Commonwealth's expert, testified to this. However, according to Dr. McDonnell, Dr. Lee, and Dr. Wecht, this is absolutely wrong.

Conclusions based on the clear description of the blood spatter contained in Detective Freeman's testimony are appropriate. While we filed affidavits with the Court, we were not allowed to call these witnesses to dispute Mr. Wolson. Ultimately, his opinion became the key reason the courts turned down my petitions. They decided that I could not prove anything as a result of the description of the blood spatter contained in Detective Freeman's testimony based on the testimony of Mr. Wolson alone. This has resulted in rewarding the police and prosecutors for their improper conduct.

At the very least, the investigation was substandard if no pictures of the dashboard blood spatter were taken, whether as result of neglect or oversight. However, it is equally plausible that a picture of the blood spatter was in fact taken, and then at some point discarded in order to impede my ability to prove my innocence.

(Added 2016) In his April 24, 2008 deposition with my attorneys, Detective Freeman admitted that he saw the photos showing the blood spatter on the dashboard, but said he could not remember where or when. He also said that he believed Dixon had the photos, but he didn't use them at trial. During a 2011 interview with Jim Ramsey, Sgt. Modispatcher recalled looking at the case-file as recently as a few days prior to the start of the trial and seeing dashboard photos of the blood spatter from Wilhelm's car. Furthermore, Detective Crisanti who photographed the scene, testified at a deposition and has since given a separate statement that the blood spatter would have been photographed before it was scraped off the dashboard during the evidence-gathering, as this was standard procedure for all homicides.

The petition in state court was unsuccessful. We then filed a successive petition for Habeus Corpus. While the Third Circuit permitted us to proceed, ultimately we were unsuccessful. One judge in the Third Circuit dissented, because I had never been allowed to fully present my case.

When we requested the police records, the City informed us that they were missing. My case was one of the most notable of the 1970s. The record was voluminous, and there were three separate copies in the archives. That such a large and significant police file, kept in triplicate, would turn up missing, is hard to fathom.

We subsequently also asked for the separate file that is kept in the Mobil Crime Unit. Again, we were told that this record was also missing. We also asked for the file from the Police Photo Lab. Here too the file had disappeared.

In December of 1995, our crime scene expert, Mr. John Balshy, went to the Coroner's Office to examine their files. At that time, the entire file was in the Coroner's Office, but Mr. Balshy was not allowed to see part of the file, which in itself was not legal. After Dr. Wecht took office as the Coroner in January of 1996, my attorney was notified that both copies of the file were now also missing. It was common knowledge that Dr. Wecht had written a letter to the Board of Pardons in support of my 1993 application for commutation. Someone did not want the record to be in the Coroner's Office when Dr. Wecht's term began.

In a letter dated November 1, 2004, Dr. Wecht wrote:

On average, the Allegheny County Coroner's Office generates approximately 7,000 files each year on cases. Since the time I returned to the office in 1996, I would estimate that nearly 65,000 case files have been generated without any others having been reported missing.

I do not believe for one moment that the missing files were happenstance.... Quite simply, both files were stolen from this office for purposes known only to the thief, but most likely to prevent my administration or any other person or agency from scrutinizing any misconduct, of which had most likely occurred in these cases. The odds of this scenario being accidental are infinitesimal.

Dr. Wecht asked the County Police to investigate the missing Coroner records. Their investigation led to no charges being filed. We later learned that the County Police, after investigating for a full week, did not have a case file. According to Detective Elizabeth Hoover, a memorandum known as a "blue special" was submitted to her supervisor. The County Police claim to have purged this memorandum a few years after completing the investigation of the Coroner's Office.

We retained an expert to determine whether or not the missing records could be considered random events. Dr. Stephen Fienberg, a Professor of Statistics and Social Science at Carnegie Mellon University, conducted an analysis of the first four missing records. We had not as yet learned that the Allegheny County Police "blue special" memorandum had also been purged within a few years after the investigation was terminated.

Dr. Fienberg stated:

...If the probability is 1/10, the upper bound on the probability that all 4 files are missing is 0.0001. If the probability is on the order of 1/100, an upper bound on the probability of losing all 4 files totally at random is 0.00000001.

I therefore conclude that finding 4 missing files at random is an extremely rare event. The alternative to assuming that we have observed such a rare event is to conclude that there is a connection among the files being lost, i.e. that they were not lost at random.

All the files concerning this case have turned up missing from several different archive locations. This is not just a coincidence. In all likelihood, these files were intentionally destroyed. While I cannot state who specifically took the files from their archives, it can certainly be presumed that only police or other governmental workers had access to these records. I have never been given my day in court on this issue.

The District Attorney has always opposed our requests for discovery and information. They also were able to convince the Courts to limit our scope of inquiry. It is logical to ask why they have always opposed complete disclosure, unless someone in their office or the Police Department has something to hide.

I do not claim a massive conspiracy against me, and I have no proof that anyone in particular has done anything. However, the following facts and circumstances cannot be disputed:

a. My case is clearly one where the police had to determine whether Miller or I was the assailant. Therefore, caution and care were called for.

b. The police cannot produce pictures of the blood spatter on the dashboard. According to Detective Freeman's 2008 deposition and Modispatcher's 2011 interview, these photographs were definitely made and seen, however, they came up missing at the time of my trial. As noted above, Crisanti, the police photographer, stated that it is standard procedure to always photograph evidence before it is removed.

c. The police did not type the blood found on the dashboard, but offered no explanation why not.

d. Shortly after his arrest, Miller flunked a polygraph test.

e. Miller had scratches on his face, wrist, and arms, as well as a laceration on a finger.

f. The dying declaration of the victim expressly named Miller. The police and prosecutors claimed this means that Miller set up the victim. This interpretation of the dying declaration is not credible and raises legitimate questions.

g. The police lost all three copies of the file for an important homicide.

h. The police Mobile Crime Unit file is missing.

i. The police photo lab records are missing.

j. The Coroner's file, intact in December 1995, turned up missing a month later, when Dr. Cyril Wecht took office. It was well known that Dr. Wecht had expressed his doubts about the proper outcome of my case before this disappearance of files.

k. The prosecutors, by their own admission, presented testimony that they themselves did not believe to be true. Both F. Peter Dixon, the trial prosecutor, and James Gilmore, who represented the District Attorney at my last commutation hearing stated that they did not believe Wilhelm had anything to do with the burning of my restaurant.

l. Aside from the testimony of Clarence Miller and the hearsay testimony of William Hill, there was no evidence linking me to the land fraud. The police had evidence that I received no proceeds from the fraud. When Miller's home was searched, copies of the deeds were found. When my home was searched, no evidence was found.

m . In early 1995, an article about my case was published in the Pittsburgh Post-Gazette. When the reporter, Mike Bucsko, question how my files were lost, he was threatened by Police Commander Ronald Freeman. Commander Freeman told Mr. Bucsko that if he mentioned the missing police records in the article that Mr. Bucsko would not get information from him again.

n. In late 1995, another reporter from the Post-Gazette, Tim Meenes, spent a day at the State Correctional Institution at Pittsburgh, where Miller, whose nickname was Boomer, was housed. When Meenes asked Boomer what he was in for, he replied, "I killed a man." When asked why, Miller replied, "For asking too many questions! Crime pays! I love it here."

o. A false charge was filed against me and later dismissed on motion of the Commonwealth. The witness, Ronald O'Shea, who originally testified at the preliminary hearing for the Commonwealth, admitted that the charge was false and that he had been given the idea and information by Detective Ronald Freeman.

p. Detective Freeman helped raise funds for Miller's bail. Detective Freemen approached the pastor of Miller's church and asked him to raise funds from the members of the congregation to post the bond on Miller's bail. Why would a homicide detectives help someone he has arrested to get released on bail? Police detectives we consulted with have never heard of a police officer doing this. It is, at a minimum unusual, and more likely, highly questionable conduct.

Question 9. Why do you believe your request for pardon or commutation should be granted?

Highly respected experts have reviewed my case and concluded that I did not kill George Wilhelm. The trial prosecutor, F. Peter Dixon, and my trial judge, the Honorable Donald. F. Ziegler, believe I am innocent. It is a rare case where both the prosecutor and the trial judge have openly called for clemency.

The most important reason for this Board to act favorably is the overwhelming proof of my innocence. However, there are two additional reasons that flow from my claim of innocence. First, there was a concerted effort to put all the case records beyond my reach in order to hide something. Second, the courts have not been fair to me. With no explanation, I have been denied the opportunity to present my claims. The courts consistently refused to look into the missing files, the questionable police investigation, and acts of misconduct.

That Miller flunked a polygraph was kept from my defense until after trial. The fact that Miller had brain damage was kept from my defense until after trial. In his 1980 PCRA petition, Miller recanted his statements implicating me in Wilhelm's murder. Years later, Miller admitted to a reporter that he killed someone. Miller admitted to members of the Board of Pardons that he participated in the assault and lied about it in his testimony. One of the police detectives was involved in a trumped-up charge against me. All of the files and records have disappeared.

None of the above led to meaningful inquiry.

I have not been dealt with fairly.

As mentioned above, the Commonwealth unfairly kept out Dedo's testimony. The combination of the dismissal of charges and his subsequent refusal to talk to my lawyers gives valid cause to question what happened.

As mentioned above, Mr. Dixon admits that this was wrong on his part. In light of the facts the prosecution was aware of, their interpretation of the dying declaration defies reason.

Please keep in mind that the land fraud was the true motive for the killing.

As mentioned above, the prosecutors never believed that George Wilhelm had anything to do with the arson. If I had no part in the land fraud, and Wilhelm had no part in the arson, it logically follows that I had no reason to kill George Wilhelm.

I know that the Board of Pardons does not want new trials and that my claims are not what the Board of Pardons usually deals with. However, these facts support my claim that I was never dealt with fairly.

I have maintained a good prison record and have not become bitter, as many have. I have done what I can do to be productive. This has not always been easy.

I have served more than 32 years, a substantial penalty for my crimes. No one can argue that I have gotten off lightly. I will be 60 years old in April 2009.

Question 20: Specifically, why do you need a pardon or commutation?

I am arthritic, have three compressed discs, and stenosis in my spine. Since my last application, I have had back surgery, and my arthritis has worsened. I am approved for light duty only. It has become more difficult to take care of myself.

While it is too late for me to have a career or children, I hope to spend my last years with my family. My parents are nearing the end of their lives and desperately want me freed while they are still alive. For more than 20 years, they visited me regularly. My mother still comes to see me as often as she can, but it is difficult for her. She has had knee and hip replacements and major surgeries on her neck and back. She also has a pacemaker and defibrillator. I admire how hard she works to remain self-sufficient. My father has been moved to a nursing home. If not released, I will never see him again. My mother is torn between wanting to visit me and being with my father.

(Added 2016) My father has since passed away during my incarceration and my mother is 93 years-old and nearing the end of her life, and desperately wants me freed while she is still alive.

My parents and siblings have spent a considerable amount of time and money to prove my innocence and secure my release. They have looked after all my needs. My family has never let me down. They spent a huge amount of their time and savings for attorneys and investigators.

My parents visited me every week when I was housed at SCI Huntingdon and they still resided in Pittsburgh. That amounted to a whole day and driving nearly 300 miles every week. When they moved to Baltimore, they still came twice a month. They have never let me down.

All my nieces and nephews have been told about me and have come to visit me. I admire my brothers and sisters for their courage in handling this situation.

As I stated above, I have been incarcerated for more than 32 years. In light of all that has happened in my case, I respectfully ask this Board to allow me to live out the rest of my life with my family.

Question 21: How have you contributed to the community and what efforts have you made to rehabilitate and improve yourself?

Since 1976, I have maintained a good record. I worked in the Dental Clinic, Correctional Industries, and the Electric Shop at SCI Huntingdon. I worked in the Library and the Activities Department while at SCI Somerset. I work in the Library at SCI Mahanoy, where I have been housed since 1997.

I was active in the Jewish Congregation, Lifers, and Jaycees at SCI Huntingdon. I chaired several Committees for the Lifers and helped establish the greeting card project. I chaired a project in cooperation with the Salvation Army to assemble food baskets for needy families before Thanksgiving. It was a great success. I served as Treasurer, Vice-President, President, and Chairman of the Board of the Jaycees.

I was awarded the highest honor bestowed by the U.S. Jaycees, known as the Ambassador. This award requires the recommendation of Jaycee officers at local, state, and national levels. Few Jaycees, institution or otherwise, are given this award. I was Shamos of the Jewish Congregation for several years and coordinated the Torah Dedication Service. The service received positive news coverage in the local papers and the Department of Correction newsletter.

At SCI Somerset, I was the Secretary of the inmate betterment organization, known as SOAR. I helped draft the constitution and by-laws when the organization was formed.

At SCI Mahanoy, I worked on the Job Fair Committee of the Resident Benefit Organization, known as RBO. I also served one year as vice-president.

I have been a Laubach tutor for many years. I have informally tutored several other prisoners preparing to take the GED.

I trained and served as a peer facilitator. I have worked in the Long Distance Dads program under the Chaplin's Office for the past five years, which has been very rewarding for me. I was facilitator for the Citizenship Program, until it was phased out.

I took some college courses while at SCI Huntingdon to stimulate my mind. I keep myself occupied with reading and staying abreast of events.

I have written some poetry. Some years ago, the Pennsylvania Prison Society published a pamphlet of poems that I wrote. I also won a second place in the PEN contest.

I have worked to not become isolated while in prison.

Timeline of Legal Actions (1976 - 2015)

The chain of legal proceedings that followed the murder of George Wilhelm did not end with the convictions of Charles Goldblum and Clarence Miller.

Numerous petitions have been filed over the decades in the case of Commonwealth of Pennsylvania v. Charles J. Goldblum as Zeke has pursued justice through the judicial system. Proceedings have cost a huge amount of money for legal fees and associated costs to pursue these claims, as well as a significant expense to the state to respond to them.

The following timeline tracks the primary legal actions that have occurred involving the Pennsylvania Courts. It does not include any actions involving the Pennsylvania Department of Corrections. In addition to chronicling of the intricate chain of post-conviction legal arguments Goldblum has pursued, this timeline offers insights on the evolution of the investigation and prosecution.

1976
1. Feb 9 - George Wilhelm murdered
2. Feb 10 - Clarence Miller and Charles Goldblum arrested and charged
3. Feb 11 - Miller and Goldblum arraigned
4. Feb 18 - Coroner's inquest
5. Feb 19 - Miller and Goldblum indicted.
6. Feb 19 - Application for bail pursuant to Rule 4004
7. Mar 4 - Order - Court refuses pre-trial bail
8. Mar 5 - Order - doctor permitted to visit defendant at jail
9. Apr 5 - Application for discovery and preliminary pretrial conference, Application invoking privilege, Application for evidentiary hearing on applicant's application invoking privileges
10. Apr 6 - Reply to Application invoking privileges, Application for Examination, Order - Supreme Court setting bail
11. Apr 7 - Order - Bond is accepted upon condition said security is posted and guaranteed by a surety company approved by the Court
12. Apr 29 - Order - Rule to show cause issued upon the Commonwealth, Order - Rule to show cause issued upon

PGH National Bank, Order - Court personnel to refrain from making judicial statements, Application for exercise of the Court's supervisory power, Order - Rule to show cause issued upon Earl Cavanaugh, Esq.
13. May 17 - Supplemental Application for Discovery
14. Jun 7 - Order - Rule to show cause issued on 5/17/76 pursuant to supplemental application for discovery is discharged and dismissed Order - Rule to show cause dated 4/5/76 is discharged and dismissed, Application for postponement
15. Jun 11 - Order re: defendant's bail
16. Jun 24 - Application for permission to depart the jurisdiction
17. July 9 - Application for pretrial conference
18. Sep 9 - Supplemental application for discovery is filed
19. Sep 29 - Application for continuance is denied
20. Nov 22 - Application to revoke bail, Order - Warden of Jail to permit doctor visitation
21. Dec 1 - Order to permit psychologist to examine defendant

1977

1. Feb 15 - Commonwealth petition to extend time for commencement of trial
2. Order – trial scheduled to begin on or before expiration of 120 days to the final order from the Supreme Court in re: Commonwealth v. Clarence Miller
3. Apr 6 - Order allowing jail visitation
4. May 13 - Application to include charges of accessory after the fact to murder and voluntary manslaughter charges.Application to suppress testimony of Clarence Miller
5. May 25 - Order scheduling trial
6. Jun 23 - Application for postponement. Application for continuance
7. Aug 18 - *Voir Dire.* Goldblum's trial begins
8. Aug 30 - Guilty verdict, verdict slip, transportation order
9. Sep 6 – Application filed in arrest of judgement/new trial. Application denied
10. Sep 7 - Order scheduling argument, transportation order

11. Sep 14 - Order – post-trial motions denied
12. Oct 3 - Life sentence imposed, Certification of defendant's indigence, Order - public defender appointed
13. Oct 24 -- Notice of appeal

1978

1. Mar 7 – Opinion
2. Dec 12 – Petition filed for the procurement of records in *Forma Pauperis,* Motion for leave to Goldblum and proceed in *Forma Pauperis*

1979

1. Jan 30 – Petition denied
2. Mar 7 - Order- Forma Pauperis and Record are granted
3. Jun 22 - Motion filed in Pennsylvania Supreme Court for Production
4. Jul 12 – Supreme Court transfer jurisdiction to Superior Court

1980

1. May 23 – Superior Court denies motion and reconfirms life-sentence
2. Jun 5 – Application for re-argument filed
3. Jun 20 – Petition for allowance of Appeal filed in PA Supreme
4. Aug 11 – Application for re-argument denied
5. Sep 23 – PA Supreme Court grants petition for allowance of appeal
6. Oct 13 – Supreme Court grants petition for Allowance of Appeal
7. Dec 5 – Brief is filed on Goldblum's behalf

1981

1. Jan 19 – Supreme Court grants remand to Superior Court for evidentiary hearing on after-discovered facts
2. Apr 27 – Motion for Production

1982

1. Jan 11 - Motion to Compel
2. Jan 18 - Transportation order
3. Apr 12 - Commonwealth's brief in opposition to after-discovered evidence claim advanced at evidentiary hearing
4. Apr 27 - Motion for new trial

5. May 3 - Order - New trial denied
6. May 10 - Opinion on Remand
7. May 14 – Supplemental brief is filed
8. July 2 - Supreme Court reverses Superior Court's reversal of conspiracy charge
9. **Dec 9 – Application for re-argument denied**

1986

1. Mar 7 - Petition filed under Post-Conviction Hearing Act
2. Jun 11 - Commonwealth's answer to Post-Conviction Petition
3. Jun 23 - Order - PCRA is denied
4. Jul 23 - Notice of Appeal
5. Sep 11 - Stipulation
6. **Nov 18 - Opinion on stipulation**

1987

1. Aug 17 – Brief filed in Superior Court
2. **Sep 11 - Order of Court - briefs and application for re-argument made part of the record**

1988

1. Feb 2 - Superior Court Judgment Order affirming opinion below
2. Mar 3 – Petition filed for allowance of appeal filed in Pennsylvania Supreme Court
3. **Jun 27 – Petition denied**

1989

1. July 14 – Petition filed for writ of Habeus Corpus filed

1990

2. May 10 – Oral arguments heard
3. Oct 31 – Petition denied
4. **Nov 29 - Petition filed for application of probable cause**

1991

1. Jul 9 – Brief filed on trial claims
2. **Nov 26 – Circuit Court affirms judgment of Superior Court**

1995

1. Sep 28 - Petition filed to request information from the Allegheny County Crime Lab
2. Oct 2 - Petition filed to request information from the Allegheny County Coroner's Office

3. Oct 6 - Commonwealth's motion to vacate hearing and reassign case and/or dismiss discovery petition

1996

1. Jan 12 - Motion filed for post conviction collateral relief
2. Jan 16 - Amended post conviction Relief Act petition
3. Praecipe for appearance
4. Petitioner's motion for discovery
5. Jan 23 - Order - DA ordered to respond to PCRA
6. Feb 8 - Order of 1/23/96 is withdrawn
7. Affidavit of Cyril H. Wecht
8. Feb 15 - Commonwealth's answer in opposition to discover motion and request for immediate hearing on the discover motion and order of 2/8/96
9. Mar 18 - Affidavit of John Balshy
10. Apr 9 - Petitioner Charles J. Goldblum's response to the Commonwealth's opposition to discover motion
11. Apr 19 - Petitioner Charles J. Goldblum's revised response to the Commonwealth's opposition to discover motion
12. Jul 9 - Copies of police reports and supplemental reports in the possession of the DA
13. Nov 12 - Commonwealth's answer to amended post-conviction petition (Second Petition)
14. Dec 2 - Affidavit of Michael M. Baden, M.D. and Barbara C. Wolf, M.D.
15. Dec 10 - Commonwealth's answer in opposition to Baden/Wolfe affidavits
16. Dec 12 - Notice of Intention to dismiss pursuant to Pa. R. Crim. P. 1507
17. Dec 16 - Motion to strike
18. Dec 18 - Commonwealth's answer in opposition to motion to strike motion for extension of time to respond to a proposed PCRA dismissal
19. Deposition transcripts of Salvatore S. Crisanti, Joseph G. Stotlemyer, Ralph Pampena, Herbert Buettner, Joseph E. Modispatcher, Anthony Condemi, and Edward Fagan
20. Dec 19 - Order for extension of time is granted
21. Dec 20 - Commonwealth's answer in opposition to motion for extension of time

1997

1. Jan 6 - Motion to strike deposition transcripts
2. Jan 10 - Motion for extension of time within which to respond to Commonwealth's motion to strike deposition transcripts
3. Jan 15 - Petitioner's motion for leave to amend petition under post-conviction Relief Act
4. Petitioner's response to notice of intention to dismiss pursuant to Pa. Crim. P. 1507
5. Feb 14 - Order of Court dismissing PCRA Petition
6. Mar 5 - Motion for reconsideration of order
7. Mar 14 - Notice of Appeal
8. Mar 20 - Superior Court amended application and allowed *pro se* brief
9. Mar 25 - Memorandum re: statement of reasons pursuant to Pa. R.A. 1925 (a)
10. Jun 26 - Superior Court Order - withdrawal of counsel is granted

1998

1. Feb 19 - Stipulation pursuant to Pa. R.A.P. 1926
2. Nov 4 – Motion filed for Oral Argument
3. Nov 17 – Motion denied by Superior Court

1999

1. Jan 7 - Motion filed to examine Coroner's records
2. Jan 11 - Commonwealth's motion to vacate hearing and dismiss "Motion to Examine Coroner's Records" for lack of jurisdiction
3. Jan 13 - Order - Motion to examine Coroner's records is denied
4. Aug 13 - Superior Court judgment order and opinion

2000

1. Jan 26 - Motion for videotaped deposition of H. David Rothman
2. Motion for videotaped deposition of Clarence Miller
3. Jan 31 - Commonwealth's answer in opposition to motion for videotaped depositions of Rothman and Miller
4. Feb 14 - Petitioner's memorandum of law in support of motions for videotaped depositions of Rothman and Miller

5. Feb 15 - Order - Motion for videotaped depositions of Rothman and Miller denied June 26 PCRA hearing brief
6. Petition for leave to amend PCRA petition
7. July 25 - Transportation order
8. Aug 1 - Commonwealth answer in opposition to petition for leave to amend PCRA petition
9. Aug 9 - Petitioner's response to Commonwealth's answer in opposition to petition for leave to amend PCRA petition
10. Aug 17 - Transportation Order
11. Sept 28 - Motion regarding presentation of rebuttal expert
12. Oct 17 - Commonwealth answer in opposition to petition for leave to amend PCRA Petition Caption
13. Oct 25 - Transportation Order
14. Nov 21 - Motion for continuance
15. Commonwealth's answer in opposition to motion for continuance
16. Nov 29 - Order - court finds H. David Rothman, Esq. not ineffective for failing to call Dr. Cyril Wecht as defense witness
17. Dec 21 - Petition is dismissed

2001

1. Jan 19 - Notice of Appeal is filed
2. Jan 29 - Brief filed on behalf of petitioner
3. May 3 - Order - Appellant to file a Concise Statement of Matters on Appeal
4. May 17 - Petition for extension of time to file brief in support of statement of matters on appeal
5. Petitioner's concise statement of matters to be complained of on appeal
6. May 18 - Order - defendant to file a brief by 6/1/01
7. June 1 - Petition for extension of time to file brief in support of concise statement of matters on appeal
8. Order of Court - Brief due by 6/20/01
9. Jun 19 - Brief in support of petitioner's concise statement of matters to be complained of on appeal

2002

1. Jan 29 – Brief filed in Superior Court
2. Nov 25 - Petitioner filed petition for allowance of appeal to Commonwealth Supreme Court

2003

1. May 20 - Supreme Court denied petition
2. Aug 14 - Petition for writ of Certiorari filed to Supreme Court of United States

2004

1. Jan 12 - Supreme Court denied the petition
2. Feb 26 - Motion filed for order District Court to consider second application
3. Mar 4 - Commonwealth files memorandum in opposition
4. Mar 29 - Third Circuit Court grants petitioner's motion
5. Apr 2 - Petition for writ of habeas corpus filed in US District Court
6. July 8 - Commonwealth files answer
7. Oct 12 - Motions filed for evidentiary hearing and for Commonwealth to produce critical records
8. Oct 14 - Motions denied
9. Oct 19 - Motion filed for answer to motion on evidentiary hearing, Motion denied
10. Oct 20 - Appellant filed motion for leave of court to serve respondents
11. Oct 29 - Commonwealth responded
12. Nov 1 - Appellant filed motion for leave to file reply brief
13. Nov 15 - Motion denied

2005

1. Feb 3 - Motion for leave denied
2. Apr 28 - Motion filed for reconsideration of denial
3. May 3 - Commonwealth files response
4. May 11 - Motion for reconsideration is denied
5. May 27 - Objections to denial filed
6. May 31 - Appellant files reply to Commonwealth's response
7. Oct 28 - Court issues report and recommendation
8. Nov 25 - Appellant files objections
9. Dec 13 - District Court dismisses petition

2006

1. Jan 6 - Appellant files notice of appeal
2. Feb 9 - Appellant files a petition for Certificate of Appealability
3. Feb 15 - Commonwealth files response

4. Feb 27 - Appellant files a reply to response
5. Nov 6 - Third Circuit Court grants Certificate of Appealability
6. Nov 30 - Third Circuit Court denies relief

2013

1. Jul 1 - Appellant files third petition for post-conviction relief

2014

2. Apr 7 - After several extensions, appellant files completed response petition
3. Apr 14 - Court dismisses petition
4. May 13 - Notice of appeal is filed
5. June 3 - Concise statement is filed
6. Aug 19 - Court denies petition

2015

1. Feb 23 – Brief filed in PA Superior Court
2. Aug 3 - Board of Pardons denies Application for Extradition to Israel
3. Nov 30 - Petition for Allowance of Appeal in Pennsylvania Supreme Court

Continuing proceedings will be posted at **www.freezeke.com**

The Public Record

As a sensational story, the murder of George Wilhelm, its investigation, and the subsequent prosecution of Charles Goldblum and Clarence Miller were the subject of continuing and extensive media coverage.

It is informative to follow the evolution of coverage on this case. Consider the several critical roles newspaper coverage played; in creating public perception of the case; in chronicling the progress and proceedings of the investigation; in following the process of the prosecution and defense; and eventually in shaping of jury options of the defendants.

This section of *Willful Blindness* presents a selection of 12 articles that covered the case, starting with the arson of the Fifth Avenue Inn on November 30, 1975.

The articles appeared in the Pittsburgh Press (PP) and the Pittsburgh Post-Gazette (PG), and are presented with the permission of the papers.

The complete archive of 117 articles reporting on the case is available at www.freezeke.com on the page **The Public Record**.

1. PP Dec 1, 1975 – Another Major Fire
2. PP Feb 10, 1976 – Man Killed in Downtown Stabbing
3. PG Feb 19, 1976 – 2 Suspects Ordered Held In Garage Stab Slaying
4. PG Aug 22, 1977 - Goldblum Stabbed Ross Man With Shears, Miller Tells Jury
5. PP Aug 24, 1977 – Victim Named Miller As Slayer, Cop Says
6. PG Aug 26, 1977 – Goldblum Denies Plot With Miller
7. PG Aug 27, 1977 – Bystander to Slaying – Goldblum
8. PG Aug 31, 1977 – Goldblum Guilty, Gets Life Term
9. PG Sep 7, 1977 – Goldblum Seeking Conviction Reversal
10. PG May 24,1980 – Court Reverses Goldblum Conspiracy Conviction
11. PG Feb 5, 1995 – Judge haunted by dying man's last statement
12. PG Nov 22,1998 – Murder conviction might be reversed

Pittsburgh Press – December 1, 1975

—Press Photo by Ross A. Colonza

ANOTHER MAJOR FIRE hit the city last night, this time a four-alarm blaze which struck the Fifth Avenue Inn Restaurant, formerly Goldstein's, Uptown. No injuries were reported for the fire which broke out at 6:25 and took more than three hours to bring under control. Cause of the fire was not determined. This was the third large city fire in four days — the first claiming five lives in Allentown on Thanksgiving Day and the second causing evacuation of a North Side family Saturday night. Damages were estimated at $225,000.

Pittsburgh Press – February 10, 1976

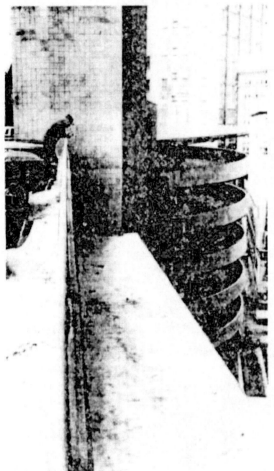

Man Killed In Downtown Stabbing

Homicide detectives were investigating three deaths today, including one victim who was stabbed repeatedly with 13-inch grass shears and tossed from the eighth floor of a Downtown parking garage.

Two others were found shot to death in a parked car in the Hill District. The coroner's office ruled it a double homicide.

Police said George R. Wilhelm, 43, of 52 Gailey Ave., Ross Twp., was stabbed last night and pushed from the eighth floor of the Smithfield-Liberty Parking Garage at Smithfield Street and Liberty Avenue.

He landed on a seventh floor ledge and walkway.

Wilhelm died about 12:15 a.m. in Mercy Hospital, about 2½ hours after he was attacked and robbed. His car was found on the eighth floor.

Jack Brennan, general manager for Stanwix Parking Inc., which owns the garage, said Wilhelm drove into the garage about 9 last night and went to the top floor although there were "many open spaces" on each parking level.

After he was stabbed, he apparently walked to the side where he fell or was pushed over the railing onto the ledge and walkway that leads to the Duquesne Club and Gimbels Department Store.

His calls for help were heard by a club employe, who notified police.

At the request of the family, homicide detectives were withholding the victim's personal background.

Charles Lenz, acting head of the homicide squad, said there was "a possibility" a warrant would be issued today for a suspect in the case.

The other victims, found in a parked car in the 800 block of Herron Avenue, were identified by authorities as Harrison McCoy, 50, of 1835 Cliff St., Hill District, and Rachel A. Fulmore, 31, of 3111 Cordell Place, Arlington Heights.

—Press Photo by Edwin Morgan

STAB VICTIM George R. Wilhelm, 43, of Ross Twp. toppled over railing onto this ledge at Smithfield-Liberty Parking Garage last night after being robbed on the garage's eighth floor. He died later in Mercy Hospital of wounds inflicted with grass shears.

386

Pittsburgh Post-Gazette – February 19. 1976

Charles Goldblum, left, and Clarence Miller arrive for hearing.

2 Suspects Ordered Held In Garage Stab-Slaying

By GABRIEL HETON
Post-Gazette Staff Writer

A codefendant in the slaying of a Ross Township man in a downtown parking garage charged from the witness stand at a coroner's hearing yesterday that the other suspect, a 38-year-old lawyer, actually killed the victim.

Clarence Miller, 38, of 351 Glenarm Ave., Brookline, testified that he stabbed Charles (Zeke) Goldblum of 834 Glen Lytle Road, Greenfield, repeatedly stab with a pair of grass shears on the night of Feb. 9 on the eighth floor of the garage.

But Miller's testimony contradicted the dying declaration of the victim, as presented yesterday by a city police officer, that Miller stabbed Wilhelm.

On advice from his attorney, Goldblum did not testify.

Despite t h e conflicting testimony, Stanley M. Stein, coroner's solicitor, held both men for the grand jury.

Miller, called to the stand by Asst. Dist. Atty. Edward Petru, testified he saw Goldblum hit Wilhelm over the head with what appeared to be a wrench in the Smithfield-Liberty Parking Garage. Then, Miller said, Goldblum began to stab Wilhelm.

Miller told Stein he met Goldblum that night in the lawyer's car parked in an alley near Wood Street. He said they both walked to a McDonald's restaurant at 608 Wood St. where they met Wilhelm to discuss business until about 8:45 p.m.

Miller said Goldblum asked Wilhelm to drive him to the parking garage over-

looking Liberty Avenue where Goldblum said, he had parked his car.

Once on the darkened eighth floor, Miller said. "Zeke hit him on the head and Back George fell out of the car and Zeke started to stab him."

He said Wilhelm kept wheeling around, screaming, "Clarence!" "Clarence, help me!" as Goldblum stabbed him, with Wilhelm's own shears that he had kept on the rear seat of his car.

Then, he said, Wilhelm backed himself against a concrete wall about three feet from high and fell over.

As Wilhelm fell, Miller said, Goldblum grabbed him by the belt buckle, pulling Wilhelm's trousers below his hips before Goldblum lost his grasp.

Under cross-examination by Louis Kwall, one of Goldblum's attorneys, Miller said he was too frightened to stop Goldblum.

"Do you know how many times Mr. Goldblum stabbed him?" Kwall asked.

"I'm no sadist," Miller replied. "I didn't stand there and count when somebody's stabbing somebody."

While no pathology report was introduced into evidence, Dr. Cyril Wecht, county coroner, said Wilhelm was stabbed nine times in the face and about the trunk of the body.

Officer Thomas Popicki testified he w a s among the first officers at the scene. He said he was kneeling by Wilhelm, comforting h i m a n d saying, "Take it easy. Take it easy."

Then, Wilhelm muttered the name, "Clarence," Popicki said.

"I said, 'What?' and he said 'Clar-

ence—Clarence Miller—he did this to me,'" Popicki testified.

"His clothes were rumpled, and his pants were halfway down," the officer added. "His nose was just hanging there — there was blood everywhere."

As Wilhelm was being taken away in a litter Popicki said he heard him say, "I'm going to die. I know I am going to die."

Wilhelm died at Mercy Hospital 2½ hours later from loss of blood, according to a coroner's report.

Miller's attorney, Vincent C. Murovich Jr., carefully guided Miller's testimony often objecting to Kwall's cross-examination into Miller's background with Wilhelm and Goldblum.

Petru also interrupted Miller frequently when it appeared Kwall's questioning might lead Miller into giving details of the motive for the slaying.

Miller was allowed to testify, however, that he met both men about two years ago during a Republican party rally and that Miller had since become "very close" friends with Wilhelm.

He said he and Wilhelm often worked together for the party by hanging campaign signs. He said Wilhelm made the theory about five years a g o to cut weeds growing around campaign signs. Miller said they also used the shears to pry opponents' campaign posters from poles while erecting their own.

During the meeting at McDonald's, Miller said it was, "Wilhelm's pressing for tax paper" money or else he claimed Goldblum owed him Miller denied he

knew anything about the debt except that Wilhelm apparently had performed some service for Goldblum.

He also testified Goldblum shouted to Wilhelm as he struck him. "This will shut you up, you faggot."

After the assault, Miller said, Goldblum drove him home, warning him not

to discuss it. Miller said Goldblum pointed out he is the son of a prominent Jewish rabbi, and police would believe Goldblum before t h e y would believe Miller, the codefendant testified.

Goldblum is the son of Rabbi Moshe V. Goldblum of the 6400 block of Beacon Avenue, Squirrel Hill.

Pittsburgh Post-Gazette – August 22, 1977

Goldblum Stabbed Ross Man
With Shears, Miller Tells Jury

By JOYCE GEMPERLEIN
Post-Gazette Staff Writer

Clarence Miller shifts his lower jaw soundlessly when he is not testifying against his former buddy, lawyer Charles (Zeke) Goldblum.

However, on Saturday in an otherwise deserted, quiet county Courthouse, Miller did a lot of talking and did not mince words in accusing Goldblum, 21, of the ferocious stabbing death of a Ross Township man in the Smithfield-Liberty Parking Garage, Downtown.

The pace of the murder-arson-fraud trial quickened during the marathon, 9:30 a.m. to 10 p.m. weekend session when Miller, who is the prosecution's star witness against Goldblum and also is charged with first-degree murder, said:

• He (Miller) set up his good friend, George Wilhelm, 42, on Feb. 9, 1976, for a beating in exchange for $50 and only tried one time to help him when Goldblum stabbed the victim 29 times with one blade of a pair of grass shears.

• Even though, in the summer of 1974, he (Miller) and a friend hatched a weird, ill-fated and sometimes comical plot to defraud Wilhelm in a North Carolina land deal, the two remained amicable and traveled about Allegheny County putting up and tearing down political posters.

• He, himself, never took an active part in Wilhelm's murder on the top floor of the garage on Feb. 9, 1976, instead, Goldblum slew the victim because Wilhelm kept nagging the lawyer for money.

• He noticed a shadowy figure — a stocky man with a crewcut — standing near an elevator during the murder. The man, whom he recognized as a friend of a friend, has not been found by Miller or police.

• Goldblum told him (Miller) to forget about the murder. "They'll (police) take my word before yours because you're a crumb-bum and I'm a lawyer and my dad's a rabbi."

Miller's direct examination consumed about half of the nine-hour court session Saturday. Much of the remaining time was eaten up by a cross-examination by defense attorney H. David Rothman.

One salient point surfacing in the questioning was that Miller, although stoutly contending he was sure about what happened that night, said he cannot remember much of at least three statements he made to officers at various times between Feb. 10, 1976, and April.

When he first was arrested, he told police he and Goldblum met with Wilhelm at a Downtown McDonald's and left him there — alive. He told Rothman on Saturday that he was too frightened of Goldblum to tell the truth and that he pushed a bloodied raincoat into a garbage truck.

However, Miller said he was shaking so badly when he got home to Brookline after the murder that his wife asked him what was the matter.

"I told her I just seen a man get killed," Miller said, adding that he did not elaborate nor did his wife question him further.

Miller testified that Goldblum's motivation for the killing was to "stop George from bugging him about money." Miller has said he, Goldblum and two other men faked the victim of money two years before and but the plot was discovered and repayment promised.

Miller, who is 42 years old and semi-illiterate, has frequently mentioned that he and his coterie of friends were attracted to each other by a love for "politics."

He said he is proud to know many lawyers and judges, but was too upset to think of calling one when he was arrested.

Rothman is expected to continue his cross-examination today in the trial.

Criminal Division Judge Donald Ziegler, who is presiding at the case before a jury of eight men and four women, has kept his promise of conducting night sessions.

Since 4 p.m. Thursday, more than 22 hours of testimony have been offered by only 10 witnesses. The sessions begin at 9:30 a.m. and, with 3½ hours reserved for dining, continue until 10 p.m.

The judge may even conduct the trial next Sunday, if necessary.

Ziegler's purpose is to compact the testimony into as few days as possible because the jury is being lodged, at the county's expense, in a Downtown hotel.

They have been told not to read, watch television, listen to radio reports about the trial.

Asst. Dist. Atty. Peter Dixon is requesting the death penalty for Goldblum, of Greenfield, whose family and friends have been constant spectators at the trial.

Of the 10 witnesses so far, only one has been a law enforcement agent. Details of the arrests and murder—from police and a coroner's representative—are expected later this week.

Rothman contends that his client did not participate in the land fraud and arson—"if indeed it was arson"—and especially the murder. Rothman says the plots are figments of Miller's imagination and especially will stress Wilhelm's dying declaration: "Clarence Miller did this to me."

On Saturday, Dixon led Miller in describing how Wilhelm was struck in the back of the head with a wrench by Goldblum, fell out of the car and was chased around the deck of the garage by the accused.

After "Zeke" kept sticking him and sticking him" with the blade, Miller said, the victim began to fall backwards onto a railing. Then, Goldblum grabbed Wilhelm's belt but was unable to stop him from falling to a landing below. He died 2½ hours later.

In other testimony late Friday and Saturday:

• Miller said Goldblum, on Nov. 30, 1975, enlisted his and that of Thaddeus Dedolo in setting a fire at Goldblum's 5th Avenue Inn, Uptown, but they refused.

He stated that Goldblum showed them how easy it would be to pour a flammable liquid through holes drilled into second-floor walls. Failing to persuade them, Goldblum said he would "get the faggot to do it."

The next day, Miller said, the defendant remarked that "I did a pretty good job" and said Wilhelm, to whom the term "faggot" had referred, helped him in exchange for a promise of $1,500 and some of the money swindled at the earlier land deal.

• Diane Sheets, a waitress at the inn, said Goldblum seemed to be a good proprietor and initiated improvements before the fire.

• The restaurant's manager, Edith Wilson, testified that Goldblum was conscientious about the eatery, that there were cans of a chafing-dish heating fluid—leftover from the previous owner's catering service—in the basement, and that the sprinkler system was working before the fire.

Mrs. Wilson said Miller had been in the shop that day and many times before and "I never liked him—I thought 'Here comes Clarence again.'" When she left the restaurant after 5 p.m., Goldblum remained, she said, to do some paperwork.

She said he did not try to hurry her out of the building even though they had quarreled about the placement of Christmas decorations—Goldblum objected to a manager, saying it was against his religion.

The restaurant manager said Goldblum called her after she arrived home for "a casual talk" but, in the middle of the conversation, an operator interrupted with an emergency call informing Mrs. Wilson of the fire.

She said Goldblum appeared to be upset about the loss of his business.

ART BUCHWALD looks at the world a little differently than most . . . see his column today on Page 1 of the Post-Gazette's Daily Magazine.

"Hardened wax affected my hearing for 35 years!"

Pittsburgh Press – August 24, 1977

Victim Named Miller As Slayer, Cop Says

By DOUG HARBRECHT

A city police officer, Thomas Pobicki, today repeated the last words of George Wilhelm, a murder victim he found on the ramp of a Downtown parking garage.

"Wilhelm just said, 'Clarence,' it kind of stunned me," said Pobicki. "I thought he was trying to tell me his name."

"Then he said, 'Clarence Miller did this to me.'"

Pobicki gave his account of the death scene at the Criminal Court trial of Charles "Zeke" Goldblum, 28, an attorney who Miller claims wielded the grass shears that inflicted more than 20 wounds on the victim.

As Wilhelm was placed on a stretcher, Pobicki testified he heard the victim say, "I'm going to die, I know I'm going to die."

His testimony followed that of a fellow police officer who told of an offer of $2,000 from Goldblum to kill Miller, the defendant's onetime friend and now the chief witness against him.

Detective John Mook, an undercover operative at the time, testified last night that he posed as a "hit" man and Goldblum asked for Miller's elimination last Nov. 19, more than nine months after the Wilhelm murder.

"I'm an attorney, and I want to get back to practicing law," Mook quoted Goldblum as saying. At the time, Goldblum was out on bond awaiting trial in the death of Wilhelm, 42, a disabled truck driver who was a friend of Miller and was due a $40,000 disability settlement.

Goldblum, 28, is charged with slashing Wilhelm more than 20 times with the blade from a pair of grass shears Feb. 9, 1976 in the Smithfield-Liberty parking garage Downtown.

Miller, as he did in previous preliminary hearings, accused Goldblum of masterminding a plot to swindle Wilhelm by playing on his dreams of owning North Carolina land where he could mine stones and precious gems.

The 40-year-old Miller also accused Goldblum in testimony of telling him about the "job" he did on Goldblum's Fifth Avenue Inn, Uptown, which burned Nov. 30, 1975.

Miller testified that Goldblum needed the insurance money to pay debts, some of which involved the land swin-

(Continued on Page A-4, Column 4)

County Misused Aid For Poor, Suit Charges

Continued next page

389

Slay Victim's Last Words
Blamed Miller, Cop Testifies

(Continued from Page A-1)

die when Wilhelm discovered he had been duped.

Monk testified his meeting with Goldblum was arranged by Andrew Kistner Bey, who a police informant told detectives had been approached by Goldblum to make the hit.

But on cross-examination by defense attorney H. David Rothman, Monk recalled that as Goldblum was leaving him, he said:

"Watch yourself. He's (Miller) no slouch. I saw Clarence Miller kill a man."

In his opening to the jury of eight men and four women in the courtroom of Common Pleas Judge Donald Ziegler, Rothman said he would try to show that Miller stabbed Wilhelm, then tried to blame the slaying the land fraud, and "any arson" on Goldblum.

Ziegler allowed Monk to testify as a prosecution witness, even though the alleged solicitation to commit murder occurred nine months after the parking

Dems Sue

garage slaying.

Under state case law, evidence that a defendant had threatened to kill a chief prosecution witness is admissible as evidence on grounds it tends to show consciousness of guilt.

Goldblum will be tried later on the solicitation to commit murder charges, along with an additional charge that he tried to hire another hit man to kill

Illinois Governor
Vetoes Laetrile OK

SPRINGFIELD, Ill. (UPI) — Gov. James R. Thompson, citing lack of medical knowledge and saying he fears black market dealings, today vetoed a measure which would have allowed terminal cancer patients to take the controversial substance Laetrile.

"Laetrile has never been shown to be effective against cancer in any reputable clinical study. . . . I cannot justify its use without becoming a hidden partner in deception," Thompson said in the veto message signed in Chicago.

four men, including three city homicide detectives, while he was in the County Jail. His bond was revoked by Ziegler after he was arrested on the first charge.

The prosecution's closest thing to eyewitness testimony came yesterday from Richard Kurutz, 29, a Braddock steelworker who was going to technical school Downtown at nights.

Kurutz said he heard a thud as he stepped off the elevator on the eighth floor of the garage to go to his car the night of the murder.

He looked to his left and saw two men peering over the railing near the spot where Wilhelm was discovered wounded on the roof of a connecting ramp.

Kurutz said he could not see the faces of the men in the dark at about 30 yards, but one of them—a tall one in dark rimmed glasses—stepped back and saw him.

The two men then walked off slowly, Kurutz testified. He said he drove home, thinking nothing of what he saw until a report of the murder on the 11 o'clock news. He said he contacted homicide detectives the next day.

Pittsburgh Post-Gazette – August 26, 1977

Goldblum Denies Plot With Miller

By JOYCE GEMPERLEIN
Post-Gazette Staff Writer

Charles (Zeke) Goldblum testified yesterday that he neither was a chum nor a partner in crime of Clarence Miller, a prosecution witness who has said just the opposite regarding a two-year scheme of fraud, arson and murder.

Goldblum, a Greenfield lawyer, began testifying in his own defense at 3 p.m. yesterday after the prosecution had presented more than 55 hours of testimony. Today Goldblum is expectd to deny Miller's accusations that he furiously stabbed George Wilhelm, 42, of Ross Township, in the Smithfield-Liberty Parking Garage, Downtown, on Feb. 9, 1976.

Yesteray, a calm and neatly attired Goldblum was guided by defense attorney H. David Rothman in saying he was innocent of bilking Wilhelm in a $20,000 land fraud and setting fire to an Uptown restaurant.

Asst. Dist. Atty. Peter Dixon contends those crimes motivated Goldblum to kill Wilhelm, supposedly the paid arsonist and the victim of the North Carolina land fraud.

Goldblum's navy-blue suit was tight across his broad shoulders and back as he leaned toward the microphone to address the jury. His thick brown hair and side burns were neat as was a burgundy print tie and light blue button-down shirt.

Goldblum is a solidly built man, but has a jailhouse pallor because he was rearrested earlier this year and charged with conspiring to murder Miller.

In three hours of testimony yesterday, Goldblum denied

• Associating socially and in business dealings with Miller who said that the two were such good friends from 1972 until the murder that they even took frequent jaunts to houses of prostitution in West Virginia. Goldblum denied ever making those visits.

CHARLES GOLDBLUM

• Asking Miller and another man to help set a fire on Nov. 30, 1975, at Goldblum's business, the Fifth Avenue Inn, Uptown.

• Soliciting Wilhelm to pour a flammable liquid through the restaurants' walls to accelerate the blaze.

• Setting the fire himself in order to receive insurance money in excess of $200,000.

• Having anything to do with a 1974 plot to bilk Wilhelm in a North Carolina land deal. Goldblum said Miller mentioned the problem to him and he gave him advice but only as an attorney concerned about federal charges that Miller might be in line for.

• Knowing George Wilhelm at all

(Continued on Page 4, Column 1)

United Technologies

Goldblum Denies Scheme, Friendship With Miller

(Continued from Page 1)

until the day before the homicide, when he said they met at a Downtown restaurant to talk about politics.

▶ Engineering the drawing up of a fake deed in October of 1974 that persuaded Wilhelm that he was the owner of the North Carolina land.

Goldblum said that on Oct. 10, 1974, when Miller claimed the conspirators met in a Downtown bar, he was at a tax seminar in Reston, Va. He said the seminar was arranged and paid for by his employer, Arthur Young & Co., a certified public accounting firm.

For the first half hour of his testimony, the defendant answered the question: "Who is Charles Goldblum," the young man who has been the silent subject of the jury's scrutiny since last Thursday.

His head tilted and speaking loudly and firmly Goldblum said:

He was born April 9, 1949, to Moshe and Evelyn Goldblum of Squirrel Hill. His father is a rabbi at Beth Shalom Temple in Squirrel Hill.

He married six years ago but last fall became separated from his special education teacher wife, Rosalie. In 1971, he graduated from Washington and Jefferson College with a bachelor's degree in history and three years later from Duquesne University law school.

Summers, he taught Hebrew School, worked at religious camps and was a cantor for Jewish high holidays. He is one of five children.

In August, 1974, he was hired at Arthur Young in the Koppers Building, Downtown.

"Technically, I have never practiced law. I never tried a case."

He worked as a clerk and researcher for Clerk of Courts Robert Peirce when he was a senior at Duquesne. Until his arrest, he also taught accounting classes at the University of Pittsburgh.

He said he was too busy with work and school to have known Clarence Miller as well as Miller claims.

He said Miller nagged him now and then when they would happen to be on a street about getting into politics.

Goldblum went into great detail yesterday about the purchase of the Fifth Avenue Inn property and business. He explained that the property was owned by his father and mother with a $100,000 mortgage, but that he himself leased the business from them.

Goldblum said he was at the restaurant the day of the fire but only heard of it on television as he was dining with a Squirrel Hill cousin.

Criminal Divison Judge Donald Ziegler told the jury early yesterday that the case, which he earlier estimated would take two weeks, was progressing rapidly. He told the jurors they may begin deliberating on the first degree murder, land fraud, and arson charges as early as Sunday.

Dixon will ask the jury to find Goldblum guilty of the premeditated murder of Wilhelm, and, if they return that verdict, will request that they sentence Goldblum to death.

Miller also is charged with first degree murder and reportedly has made no deals with prosecutors for his upcoming September trial.

Pittsburgh Post-Gazette 27, 1977

Bystander to Slaying—Goldblum

By JOYCE GEMPERLEIN
Post-Gazette Staff Writer

Lawyer Charles Goldblum testified in his own defense yesterday that he was an innocent bystander to a parking garage murder in February, 1976, but driven to "exercise poor judgment" in hiring a hitman 10 months later.

Goldblum, 28, said he was duped by Clarence Miller, 40, into believing that they had a lawyer-client relationship in February. And for that, he found himself watching helplessly as Miller fought with, stabbed and then dumped George Wilhelm's body over the ledge of the Smithfield-Liberty Parking Garage.

In dramatic, day-long testimony, Goldblum admitted outright that he tried to hire someone to kill Miller because "of everything that had happened to me and everything that I had lost. I wanted him killed because he has been lying about me."

Miller was the prosecution's star witness against Goldblum in testimony last week. He said Goldblum stabbed Wilhelm while he (Miller) stood by.

For the first time since taking the witness stand at his own murder-fraud-arson trial, Goldblum lost his smooth and rapid-fire delivery. When his attorney, H. David Rothman, asked him why he did not aid the victim, Goldblum momentarily lowered his voice, rocked in his chair, stammered and said he was ashamed.

Later, he said he even cried.

Late yesterday afternoon Asst. Dist. Atty. Peter Dixon began his cross-examination which focused on Goldblum's admission that he had tried to have Miller killed before the current trial.

The solicitation to murder Miller, who also is charged with the homicide, was virtually the only thing in the prosecution's case to which the defend-

ant admitted. His story of the murder has run exactly contrary to that of the prosecution's main witnesses.

Rothman asked the defendant why he decided to have Miller killed.

Goldblum said that it was because of Miller's statements that he had been jailed, lost his job, his wife and his prestige.

He said he had stopped taking medication that a psychiatrist had given him to fight depression.

"I've been quite fed up so I exercised poor judgment and agreed to a meeting with a man who would do the job."

That man turned out to be an undercover police officer, John Mook. Mook bickered with Goldblum at that November meeting and $2,000 was determined to be the going rate.

The defendant said a man he had met before he was released from jail on bond first suggested to him that the killing could be arranged.

When Dixon asked him why he wanted to go through with the killing, Goldblum said "Everytime the law would point its finger at Mr. Miller, he put a hand on my shoulder and dragged me in too."

Dixon asked him if he told Mook how he wanted the killing done. Goldblum responded that they had not specifically made those arrangements.

He said that in retrospect the plan seemed absurd, but "I suppose I wanted it to be something logical. I guess I wanted to know they (the hitmen) would do it right."

Goldblum stressed that he only decided to take that course of action against Miller because he was angry, frustrated and "I guess very mixed up."

He said he now is relieved that the plan did not get off the ground and was glad to see Miller, alive, at the trial.

Goldblum, however, did deny several

pieces of testimony given by Mook earlier.

Mook made a reference to having asked Goldblum whether he wanted more than Miller's arms and legs broken, and, if so, he would have to pay a higher price.

Goldblum said he told Mook he wanted a professional job but the arm-and-leg descriptions were "strictly embellishments" by the detective.

Earlier yesterday Goldblum related the events of Feb. 9, 1976, when Wilhelm, 42, of Ross Township, was stabbed 25 times.

Goldblum said he did meet Wilhelm for the first time on Feb. 8 and then again the next day because he was trying to give Miller moral support and free legal advice.

Goldblum said Miller sought his help in breaking the news to Wilhelm that he had been bilked of more than $20,000 in a 1974 North Carolina land deal.

Goldblum testified that Miller promised him he would take his advice and tell Wilhelm about the fraud. How-

(Continued on Page 5, Column 3)

Fox Will Buy Claber Chain For $3 Million

Fox Industries, franchiser of Foodland Markets, announced yesterday it will purchase the eight-store Claber chain from Fisher Industries of Cleveland for more than $3 million.

Richard H. Schaefer, president of Fox Industries, said the acquisition will enable the firm, primarily a food distributor but also a supplier of health and beauty aids, to expand its nonfood

Pittsburgh Post-Gazette – August 31, 1977

Pittsburgh Post-Gazette

Humid

First Newspaper West of the Alleghenies

FINAL EDITION

192nd Year

WEDNESDAY, AUGUST 31, 1977

15 CENTS

Goldblum Guilty, Gets Life Term

Continued next page

Victim's Dad Didn't Want Execution

By JOYCE GEMPERLEIN
Post-Gazette Staff Writer

It was as though lawyer Charles (Zeke) Goldblum had not heard yesterday's sweeping verdict: guilty of fraud, arson and—most crucially—guilty of first-degree murder.

He swallowed almost imperceptibly, moved his feet — first planted apart as he sat beside defense attorney H. David Rothman — and waited for the next decision: whether he would be sentenced to death or life in prison for the February, 1976, stabbing of George Wilhelm, 42.

One-half hour later he had the answer: life in prison.

And the jury's 10-minute sentencing decision may have been sealed by a message from the victim's father, Walter Wilhelm.

"Extend mercy" to Goldblum, he asked the jury through Asst. Dist. Atty. Peter Dixon.

Dixon told the eight men and four women jurors that he had spoken with the elder Wilhelm and "although his son was shown no mercy," he is inclined to request it for Goldblum and his parents.

"And I feel," Dixon continued, "that in this long, difficult and tragic case, it is fitting to have this splendid breath of fresh air, this extension of humanity in a situation where easily a contrary feeling could exist.

"And I would join with the Wilhelm family in that recommendation... in spite of it all (my recommendation is) to find for life imprisonment and spare the life of Charles Goldblum."

Ten minutes later, the decision was in and the jury was dismissed after its grueling 11½ days in court. The reasons for their guilty-on-all-counts verdict probably will remain a mystery to outsiders because Criminal Division Judge Donald Ziegler advised them not to discuss the case with newsmen.

Goldblum, the son of a Squirrel Hill rabbi and a 1974 graduate of Duquesne University Law School, was handcuffed and sent to the County Jail.

However, Ziegler immediately ordered him taken to the hospital at

CHARLES (ZEKE) GOLDBLUM

Western Penitentiary, where he will await the filing, within seven days, of post trial motions.

The transfer from the County Jail to the Northside prison was ordered because Goldblum has remarked that he would commit suicide. He made the statement again yesterday.

Although the jury made the ultimate decision on the life term, it still is up to the judge to determine the sentences on the arson, fraud and solicitation to commit arson convictions.

All are felonies. The maximum sentence for arson is 10 to 20 years, for fraud 3½ to 7 years, and for the solicitation, 5 to 10.

Ziegler could impose consecutive or concurrent terms on those charges or

(Continued on Page 2, Column 1)

Goldblum Found Guilty, Faces Life Sentence

(Continued from Page 1)

he could suspend the sentencing altogether by virtue of the life term.

Dixon said parole for Goldblum "is a dim prospect" in light of the additional convictions and, thus, cannot be calculated with accuracy.

The jury began deliberations on the four charges at 4:05 Monday night and continued until 10:15 p.m. They resumed yesterday morning at 9:15 a.m. and, when they were served lunch in the jury room at 1:30 p.m. yesterday, announced a verdict had been reached.

Their 6½-hour decision took less time than Dixon's and Rothman's final arguments on Monday.

Goldblum, formerly of 4246 Glen Lytle Road, Greenfield, was convicted of

• Conspiring with others in the 1974, $20,000 bilking of Wilhelm, who thought the men could use political muscle to help him buy a gem-laden plot of government land in Clay County, N.C.

• Asking other persons in November, 1975, to burn down his business, the 5th Avenue Inn Restaurant, Uptown.

• Committing arson on Nov. 25, 1975, by pouring Sterno, a flammable heating liquid, through holes in the walls to obtain some $200,000 in insurance money.

• Killing Wilhelm, a disabled truck driver, on the top floor of the Smithfield-Liberty Parking Garage, Downtown, on Feb. 9, 1976.

Wilhelm was stabbed 25 times in the face and upper body with a blade from a pair of grass shears. He either was tossed or fell from the garage's railing to the roof of a passageway several floors below. He died some two hours later, but not before he told an officer, "Clarence Miller did this to me."

Miller's Trial Nears

Miller, 40, formerly of Brookline, also is charged with first-degree, or premeditated, murder in Wilhelm's slaying. He was the prosecution's chief witness at Goldblum's trial, but will be tried himself on Tuesday.

Miller's attorneys said their client has passed two polygraph tests, which asked the question "Did you stab George Wilhelm?"

The lie detector test results, while not admissible in court, were considerations in detectives' and prosecutors' investigation and pursuit of the case.

Dixon said no deals have been made with Miller, who testified that he stood by helplessly while Goldblum wielded the blade.

Goldblum, who said he and Miller were friends only when Miller needed free legal advice, testified that the killing happened just the other way around.

The lawyer described Miller as a lunatic who hacked away at the victim — Miller's best friend — relentlessly that night between 9:15 and 9:23 while he was frozen in shock.

Dixon said at a brief press conference yesterday afternoon that he could not comment on Miller's upcoming trial, but said the evidence shows him

to be deeply involved in the brutal incident and schemes which preceded it.

Wilhelm, of Ross Township, was described repeatedly in court as a "good and honest man," who perhaps was gullible but in no way a contributor to his own death.

The victim's father and two brothers were constant spectators in court — until yesterday when the verdict was handed down.

The Goldblum family, too, was everpresent in the front row of Ziegler's courtroom. His father, Rabbi Moshe Goldblum, who heads the Beth Shalom Congregation on Beacon Street in Squirrel Hill, was not in the courtroom when the verdict was read.

In court and in the hallways during the daytime and night sessions, the Goldblums rallied around the defendant and appeared to be a warm, tightly knit family, most often gracious in spite of their own trial.

His mother, Evelyn, at first did not cry or even show emotion when the verdict was read. One of Goldblum's younger sisters sobbed.

Throughout the trial, the judge, attorneys and court observers remarked that the jury was exceptionally alert — a cut above the normal panel.

Judge Compliments Jury

Ziegler complimented them for their diligence and endurance, partly because they — and four alternates — have spent each night of the trial lodged in the William Penn Hotel, Downtown.

Dixon said he never had seen a jury that took its duty so seriously.

The prosecutor said although he could not guess the precise mechanics of the jury's collective mind, he felt Goldblum's own testimony contributed to his conviction.

Part of Rothman's contention regarding the murder charge was that Goldblum was involved only to the extent of being an observer and a lawyer who was misinformed about the boundaries of "attorney-client confidentiality" ethics.

Goldblum contended he did not report witnessing the murder because he thought it violated those rules of privileged information.

Perhaps one of the most damaging days of testimony for Goldblum was last Tuesday, when he admitted to the jury that last November while he was out of jail on bond from the murder arrest, he "exercised poor judgment" and tried to hire someone to kill Miller.

The man he eventually contacted was John Mook, an undercover city policeman.

Goldblum was charged with solicitation to commit murder and will be tried later.

The jury did not learn, however, of additional complaints that have been filed against Goldblum last Jan. 4 he was charged with trying to buy death for three city detectives and a County police informant who told officers about the plot to kill Miller.

Goldblum additionally is accused of offering a County Jail inmate $10,000 to eliminate Lt. Ralph Pampena, head

of the city homicide squad; city homicide detective Ronald B. Freeman and police officer Mook; and Andy Kisner Bey, the informant.

He will be tried on those charges later.

Yesterday's fraud, arson and solicitation to commit arson convictions are felonies. The judge could impose consecutive, or concurrent sentences for those or, he could suspend sentencing by virtue of the life term.

Goldblum, dressed in business suits and pasty-complexioned throughout the trial, seemed dazed as the procedure yesterday wound to a close. His lack of physical reaction was surprising to many observers because of a statement he made in court on Monday.

He told Ziegler he felt "he was out of the woods on the homicide charges" and could not conceive a jury finding him guilty of any charges in the death.

Goldblum was born April 9, 1949, and was married to Rosalie Lehman in 1971. He and his wife separated last fall in the midst of his arrests. In 1971, he graduated from Washington and Jefferson College with a concentration in history, and three years later and with good grades he graduated from Duquesne's law school.

He described himself as being attentive to his Jewish faith and upbringing and a regular teacher at religious camps. He served as a cantor at various synagogues. He is one of five children.

In August, 1974, he was hired by the accounting department of Arthur Young & Co. in the Koppers Building, Downtown. He never has tried a case as a lawyer and said "technically, I have never practiced law."

During the summer of 1974, he worked as a clerk-researcher for former Clerk of Courts Robert Peirce. He was a part-time accounting teacher at the University of Pittsburgh.

Under state law, first-degree murder verdicts must be given to the jury for sentencing, a procedure normally left up to the judge.

Flood Victim's Body Found

Special to the Post-Gazette

JOHNSTOWN, Pa.—The body of a young girl, believed to be the latest Johnstown flood victim, was recovered from the Conemaugh River last evening several miles below this Cambria County city.

The county coroner's office, which is running tests to determine the identity of the child, described as between 8 and 12 years old, believes she may be one of two children still missing from the Tanneryville area.

Her body was found by a cleanup crew that was dredging along the river in West Taylor Township at about 5 p.m.

If identified as a flood victim, she would bring to 76 the numbers of flood victims recovered to date. Seven males and five females are still missing.

Pittsburgh Post-Gazette – September 7, 1977

Goldblum Seeking Conviction Reversal

By JOYCE GEMPERLEIN
Post-Gazette Staff Writer

H. David Rothman, attorney for convicted murderer Charles Goldblum, yesterday filed a 21-point application asking that his client's murder, arson and fraud convictions be reversed or that he be given another trial.

The post-trial motions, a routine procedure in Criminal Court, involve procedures used during Greenfield lawyer Goldblum's marathon trial that ended last Tuesday afternoon with a first-degree verdict and life imprisonment.

In the four-page document, Rothman charges that the court (Criminal Division Judge Donald Ziegler) erred in, among other things:

▶ Not suppressing the testimony of Clarence Miller, 40, the prosecution's star witness who also is charged with the fatal stabbing in a Downtown garage of George Wilhelm, 42, of Ross Township.

▶ Failing to approve private prosecution of Miller for perjury.

▶ Failing to suppress Goldblum's statements to police the day of his arrest on Feb. 10, 1976.

▶ Allowing prospective jurors to be questioned about the death penalty. "The facts of this case did not warrant an inquiry into the death penalty under the guidelines propounded by the legislature," the application stated.

▶ Permitting the testimony of William Hill, president of the Fraternal Association of Steel Haulers, because they were "hearsay statements of the deceased ... allegedly indicating that the accused was an attorney involved in the victim's purchase of land in North Carolina."

▶ Failing to receive the total of evidence that could be gleaned from William Ronald Held, a youth who testified he saw Miller with "brown stains on his clothes" and carrying something glistening on the evening of the murder.

▶ Refusing to give immunity to Thaddeus Dedo, a local real estate salesman who is charged with conspiracy in the land fraud.

▶ Admitting the rebuttal testimony of Raynelle Williams, who testified she was the reformed madam of a Hill District house of prostitution and had known Miller, Goldblum and Fred Orlosky, also charged in the land fraud, for several years.

Rothman's petition, which is scheduled to be argued before Ziegler next week, also charges that errors were made when the judge gave legal instructions to the jury of eight men and four women.

Among the items, Rothman noted failures in giving detailed instructions to the panel involving the solicitation to murder Miller, the significance of a dying declaration, the credibility of Miller if they determined he was a perjurer, and the absence of testimony from a police informant.

Rothman also stated that the judge should have allowed him to make references to the jury concerning police entrapment, voluntary manslaughter and hindering apprehension—even though Goldblum asked that those aspects be omitted from the judge's charge.

Asst. Dist. Atty. F. Peter Dixon said yesterday that trial dates for Goldblum on five charges of conspiracy to murder Miller, two homicide detectives and a police informant were scheduled for next week.

However, Ziegler said he will consider on Monday whether the alleged solicitation to murder Miller should be severed from the latter solicitations and whether each should be postponed because of extensive publicity surrounding the case.

Ziegler said he also will determine on Monday whether Orlosky's and Dedo's charges should be dismissed—as their attorneys are expected to argue—because they lack merit or violate the state's speedy trial rule.

Ziegler said he will meet today with Miller's attorney concerning Miller's murder trial.

Pittsburgh Post-Gazette – May 24, 1980

Court Reverses Goldblum Conspiracy Conviction

By HUGH CHRISTENSEN
Post-Gazette Staff Writer

The state Superior Court has reversed the 1977 conviction of lawyer Charles J. "Zeke" Goldblum for conspiring to defraud a man by selling him land belonging to the federal government.

The appellate court directed a new trial for Goldblum on the charge that he conspired with Clarence Miller, 2451 Glenarm Ave., Brookline, and another man to defraud George Wilhelm, Ross Township, by selling him land in North Carolina which actually was federal property.

Left untouched by the ruling announced yesterday was Goldblum's conviction and life sentence for killing Wilhelm in February 1976. Goldblum, formerly of 4246 Glen Lytle Road, Greenfield, is serving a life sentence in the state correctional institution at Huntington.

A Common Pleas Court jury convicted Goldblum of murder, conspiracy to defraud, arson and solicitation to commit arson. Only the conspiracy conviction was reversed.

The court said Goldblum's attorney, an assistant public defender, erred by not asking trial Judge Donald E. Ziegler to dismiss the indictment for conspiracy. The indictment was defective because it failed to allege that the conspiracy had occurred in Allegheny County, Superior Court said.

According to Miller's testimony at Goldblum's trial, the two men defrauded Wilhelm of $10,000 in the land swindle, but Goldblum later promised Wilhelm he would get his money back.

On Nov. 28, 1975, the Fifth Avenue Inn, 1002 Fifth Ave., Uptown, which Goldblum owned, was destroyed by fire. Goldblum was convicted of arson and solicitation to commit arson in connection with the fire.

Miller testified that Wilhelm was the actual arsonist, and that he began demanding payment from Goldblum for the arson and for the land fraud.

Those demands led to Wilhelm's murder by Miller atop a Downtown parking garage Feb. 9, 1976, at Goldblum's instigation, the jury concluded.

Pittsburgh Post-Gazette February 5, 1995
Continued next page

INSIGHT

Judge haunted by dying man's last statement

Judge Donald E. Ziegler

Ziegler writes pardons board to gain clemency for man guilty in 1977

By Mike Bucsko
Post-Gazette Staff Writer

For nearly 20 years, seven words have played over and over in the conscience of Judge Donald E. Ziegler: "Clarence, Clarence Miller did this to me."

Those were the words a Ross man uttered to a Pittsburgh police officer in February 1976 as he lay on a bridge between a Downtown parking garage and the former Gimbels department store. He was bleeding to death from more than two dozen stab wounds.

Despite the so-called "dying declaration" of George Wilhelm, Clarence Miller became the key witness in the successful first-degree murder prosecution of another man, Charles J. "Zeke" Goldblum.

Ziegler, now the chief federal judge in Pittsburgh, presided over Goldblum's 1977 trial in Allegheny County Common Pleas Court. With Wilhelm's words still on his mind, the judge took the unusual step last year of writing letters to the state Board of Pardons and to former Gov. Robert P. Casey in support of Goldblum's bid for clemency.

"I could sit here for the rest of my life and do nothing," Ziegler said. "On the other hand, this is the one case in 21 years [as a judge] which seriously troubles my conscience about the result.

"When a person is about to meet his maker, he is presumed to speak the truth. Why didn't Wilhelm say, 'Clarence and Zeke did this to me?' Why would you say on your death bed, 'Clarence, Clarence Miller did this to me' unless it was true?"

Miller blames the murder on Goldblum. Goldblum, who also was convicted of arson and an attempt to hire a man to kill Miller, blames the stabbing on Miller.

Ziegler said he also was troubled by the numerous contradictions in Miller's testimony in the jury trial and in statements to police.

"Miller, quite frankly, was a terrible witness, in my mind unbelievable," Ziegler said.

Goldblum, 45, formerly of Greenfield, and

John Beale/Post-Gazette photos

Evelyn and Rabbi Moshe Goldblum of Dover, Del., with a photograph of their son, Charles, who has been imprisoned in a state prison near Somerset, Somerset County, for the past 17 years.

398

Goldblum, 45, formerly of Greenfield, and Miller, 58, formerly of Brookline, were convicted of first-degree murder in separate trials in 1977 and 1978. Both received life sentences. Both had applications for clemency hearings turned down by the state Board of Pardons in the past few months.

Goldblum's case went before the board Oct. 26, in the midst of a gubernatorial election in which a major issue was the commutation of the life prison term of convicted murderer Reginald McFadden, who is accused of raping and killing a woman in New York three months after his release.

Forensic pathologist Dr. Cyril H. Wecht, who was Allegheny County coroner at the time of the killing, also wrote to the pardons board on Goldblum's behalf.

Wecht has questioned several pieces of evidence used by prosecutors at Goldblum's trial. Wilhelm's autopsy was performed by former coroner Dr. Joshua A. Perper, Wecht's deputy at the time.

"Following my evaluation and analysis of all the materials, it is my professional

SEE **CLEMENCY**, PAGE B-8

During an interview at State Correctional Institution at Pittsburgh, Clarence Miller says he didn't kill George Wilhelm. He is serving a life sentence for the 1976 killing.

Continued next page

399

Haunted by death statement, judge pleads for clemency

CLEMENCY FROM PAGE B-1

> *"I'm guilty
> of accessory
> after the fact.
> I'm guilty
> of hindering
> apprehension.
> I'm not guilty
> of murder."*
>
> Charles I. "Zeke" Goldblum

A friendship gone bad

The quest for clemency

Pittsburgh Post-Gazette – November 22, 1998

Murder conviction might be reversed

By Mike Bucsko
Post-Gazette Staff Writer

Piece by piece, attorneys for Charles Goldblum have compiled a sizable array of evidence over the past few years to challenge the former Greenfield man's 1977 murder conviction.

Among the evidence are opinions of several forensic experts, including Allegheny County Coroner Dr. Cyril H. Wecht, who has written letters and submitted an affidavit in support of Goldblum's case.

Goldblum has for years had the support of the judge who presided at his trial, Donald E. Ziegler, who wrote the state Board of Pardons in 1994 in Goldblum's unsuccessful bid for clemency. Ziegler, a former Allegheny County Common Pleas judge, is now the chief judge in U.S. District Court in Pittsburgh.

Now the man who prosecuted the sensational murder trial of the rabbi's son has joined the chorus in favor of Goldblum's attempt to have his conviction reversed.

F. Peter Dixon, a former assistant district attorney who no longer practices law, has submitted an affidavit to Goldblum's attorneys in which he said he had "come to the

SEE **GOLDBLUM**, PAGE C-6

Continued next page

401

Evidence mounts to clear convicted murderer

GOLDBLUM FROM PAGE C-1

CPSIA information can be obtained
at www.ICGtesting.com
Printed in the USA
FFOW03n0850011116
28828FF